This is funny!
What does this mean?
I don't get it.

My brother has been the biggest fan of my comics my whole life. He started reading them in elementary school and continued all the way through junior high and high school. Even now that I'm a published comic artist, he still reads my stories! He's been a big help too—sometimes his input turns out to be the best advice I receive! So, a big congrats to my brother on getting hitched. Congratulations, you did it!!

Also, my current weight has ballooned to...75 kilograms!! (Nooo!!) I blame it on the holidays!

–Mitsutoshi Shimabukuro, 2009

Mitsutoshi Shimabukuro made his debut in **Weekly Shonen Jump** in 1996. He is best known for **Seikimatsu Leader Den Takeshi!** for which he won the 46th Shogakukan Manga Award for children's manga in 2001. His current series, **Toriko**, began serialization in Japan in 2008.

TORIKO VOL. 3
SHONEN JUMP Manga Edition

STORY AND ART BY **MITSUTOSHI SHIMABUKURO**

Translation/Christine Dashiell
Adaptation/Hope Donovan
Touch-Up Art & Lettering/Jim Keefe
Design/Sam Elzway
Editor/Alexis Kirsch

Published by VIZ Media, LLC
P.O. Box 77010
San Francisco, CA 94107

10 9 8 7 6 5 4 3 2 1
First printing, December 2010

THE WORLD'S
MOST POPULAR MANGA

www.viz.com

www.shonenjump.com

TORIKO

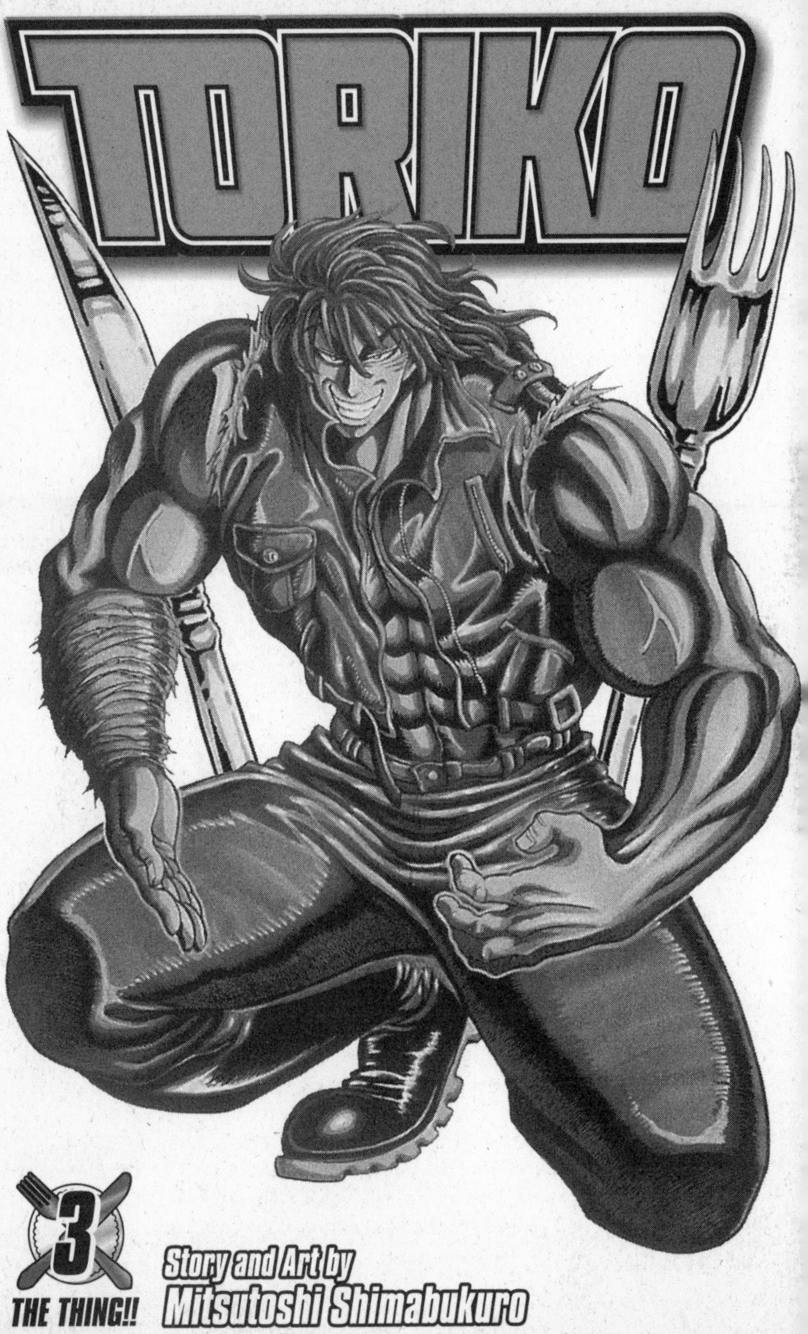

3

THE THING!!

Story and Art by
Mitsutoshi Shimabukuro

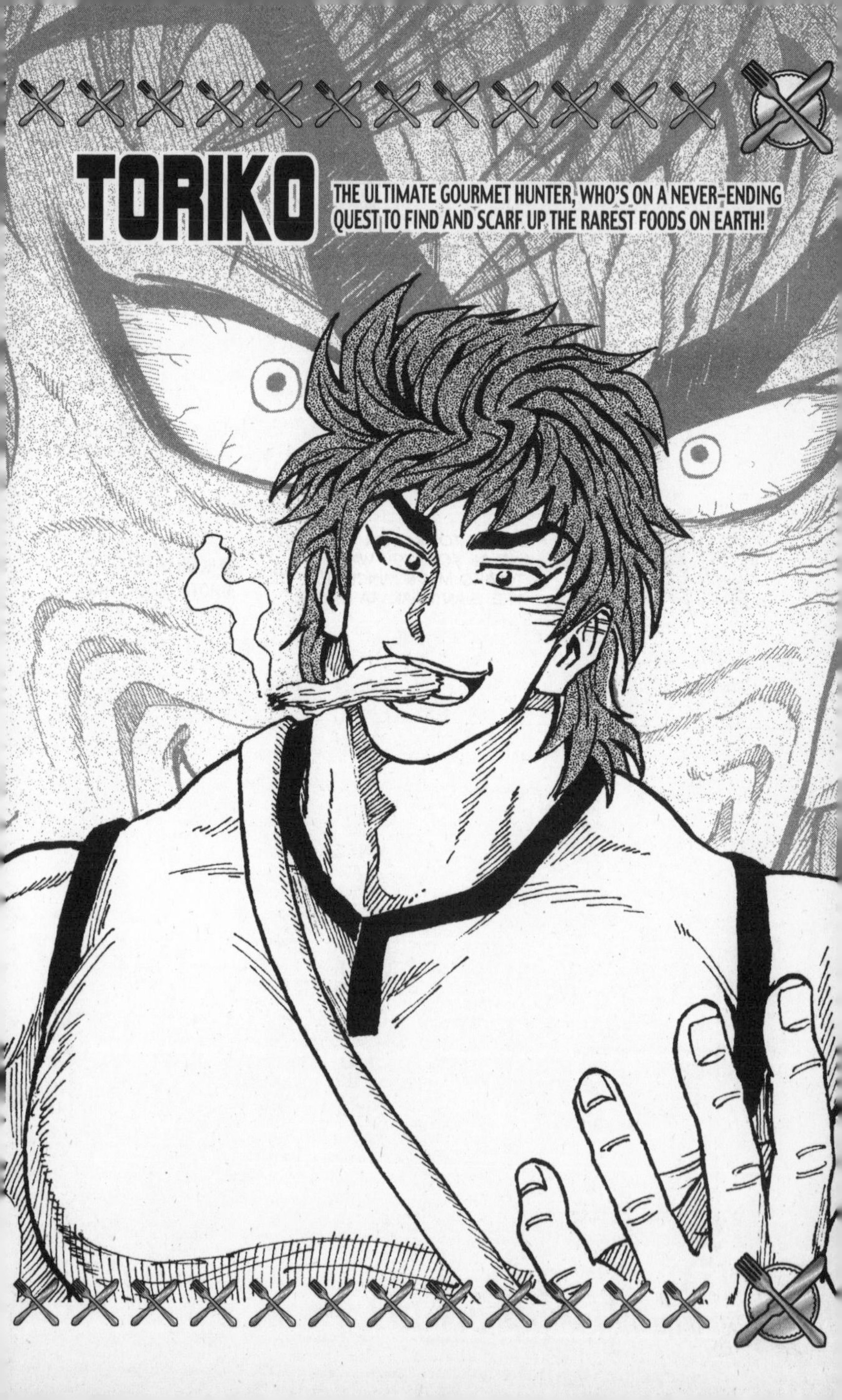
TORIKO
THE ULTIMATE GOURMET HUNTER, WHO'S ON A NEVER-ENDING QUEST TO FIND AND SCARF UP THE RAREST FOODS ON EARTH!

WHAT'S FOR DINNER

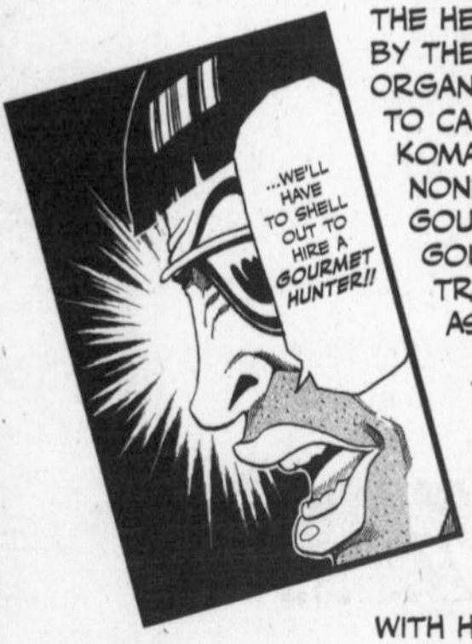
...WE'LL HAVE TO SHELL OUT TO HIRE A *GOURMET HUNTER!!*

IT'S THE AGE OF GOURMET! KOMATSU, THE HEAD CHEF AT THE HOTEL OWNED BY THE *IGO* (INTERNATIONAL GOURMET ORGANIZATION), WAS ORDERED BY HIS BOSS TO CAPTURE A GARARA GATOR! TO HELP KOMATSU IN THIS TASK, THE *IGO* HIRED NONE OTHER THAN THE LEGENDARY GOURMET HUNTER, TORIKO--A CHARISMATIC GOURMET HUNTER WHOSE IMPRESSIVE TRACK RECORD HAS EARNED HIM A TITLE AS ONE OF THE FOUR KINGS!!

WHEN KOMATSU LEARNED THAT TORIKO'S DREAM IS TO DESIGN THE BEST FULL-COURSE MEAL OF HIS LIFE, HE WAS SO MOVED THAT HE DECIDED TO JOIN TORIKO ON THE HUNT.

AND AS KOMATSU WATCHED, TORIKO MADE MINCEMEAT OF THE GIANT GARARA GATOR WITH HIS BARE HANDS!!

THEIR NEXT JOB WAS TO ACQUIRE THE RAINBOW FRUIT. BY USING HIS DEMONIC AURA TO INTIMIDATE THE SILVERBACK TROLL KONG GUARDING THE FRUIT, TORIKO WAS ABLE TO ACCOMPLISH HIS MISSION. UPON TASTING IT, TORIKO DECLARED THE DREAM-LIKE DELICIOUSNESS OF THE RAINBOW FRUIT WORTHY OF THE POSITION OF DESSERT COURSE FOR HIS FULL-COURSE MEAL!

● KOMATSU
A HOTEL CHEF WHO ADMIRES TORIKO.

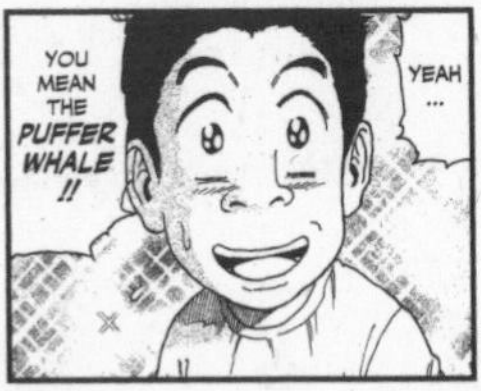
YEAH ...
YOU MEAN THE *PUFFER WHALE !!*

● UUMEN UMEDA
IGO BUREAU CHIEF

● COCO
A FORETUNE-TELLER/ GOURMET HUNTER AND ANOTHER ONE OF THE FOUR KINGS.

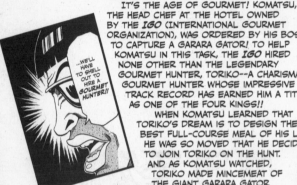

NOT LONG AFTER, TORIKO TRAVELLED TO EAT THE POISONOUS PUFFER WHALE! BRINGING ALONG COCO, A FORTUNETELLER/GOURMET HUNTER SCHOOLED IN THE ART OF PUFFER WHALE PREPARATION, TORIKO HEADED TO CAVERN LAGOON, WHERE DANGER CRAWLS AROUND EVERY TWIST AND TURN! THERE, KOMATSU LOST ONE OF HIS NINE LIVES, TORIKO DEFEATED A LEGENDARY DEVIL PYTHON, AND THE CREW SUCCESSFULLY CAPTURED PUFFER WHALES!

BUT WHILE THEY CAREFULLY EXTRACT THE WHALES' POISON SACKS, A MYSTERIOUS THREAT APPROACHES...

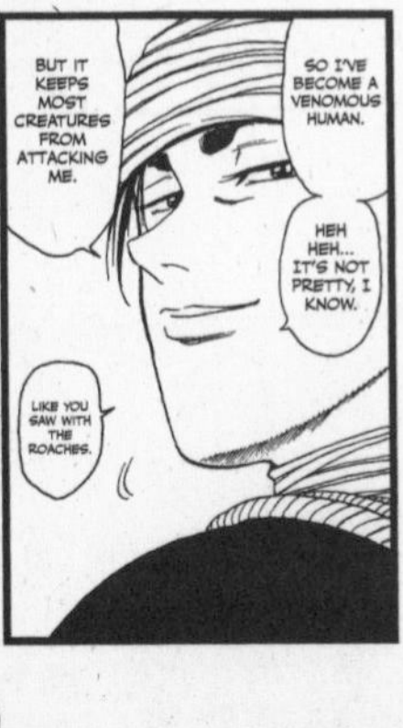
SO I'VE BECOME A VENOMOUS HUMAN.
BUT IT KEEPS MOST CREATURES FROM ATTACKING ME.
HEH HEH... IT'S NOT PRETTY, I KNOW.
LIKE YOU SAW WITH THE ROACHES.

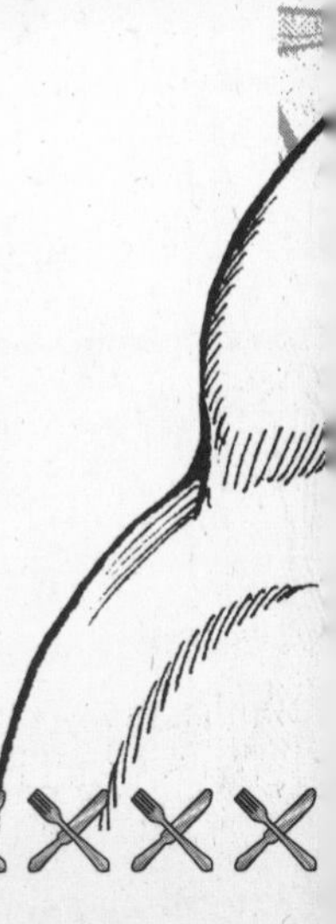

Contents

TORIKO

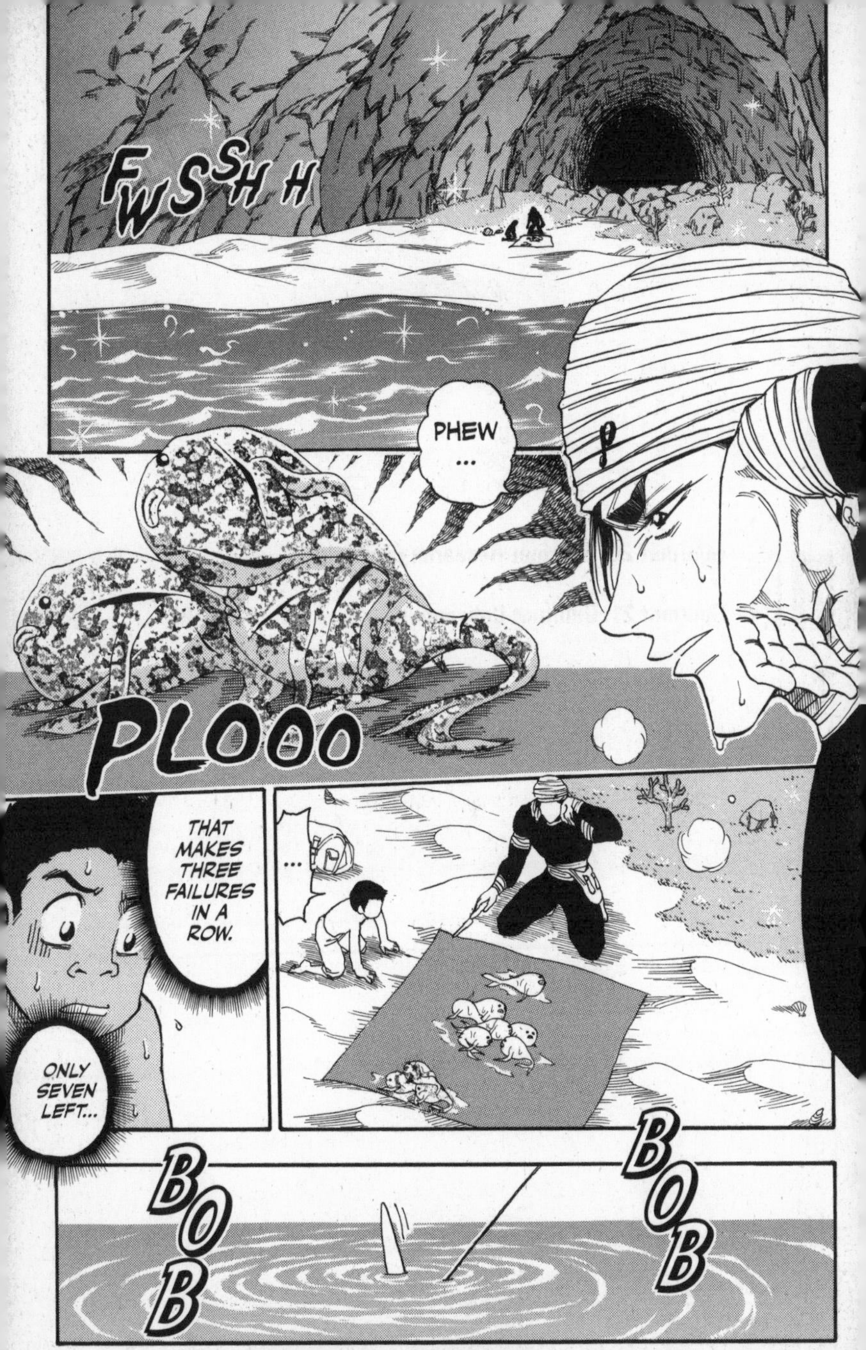
FWSSHH
PHEW ...
PLOOO
...
THAT MAKES THREE FAILURES IN A ROW.
ONLY SEVEN LEFT...
BOB
BOB

GOURMET 17: A TASTE OF POISON!!

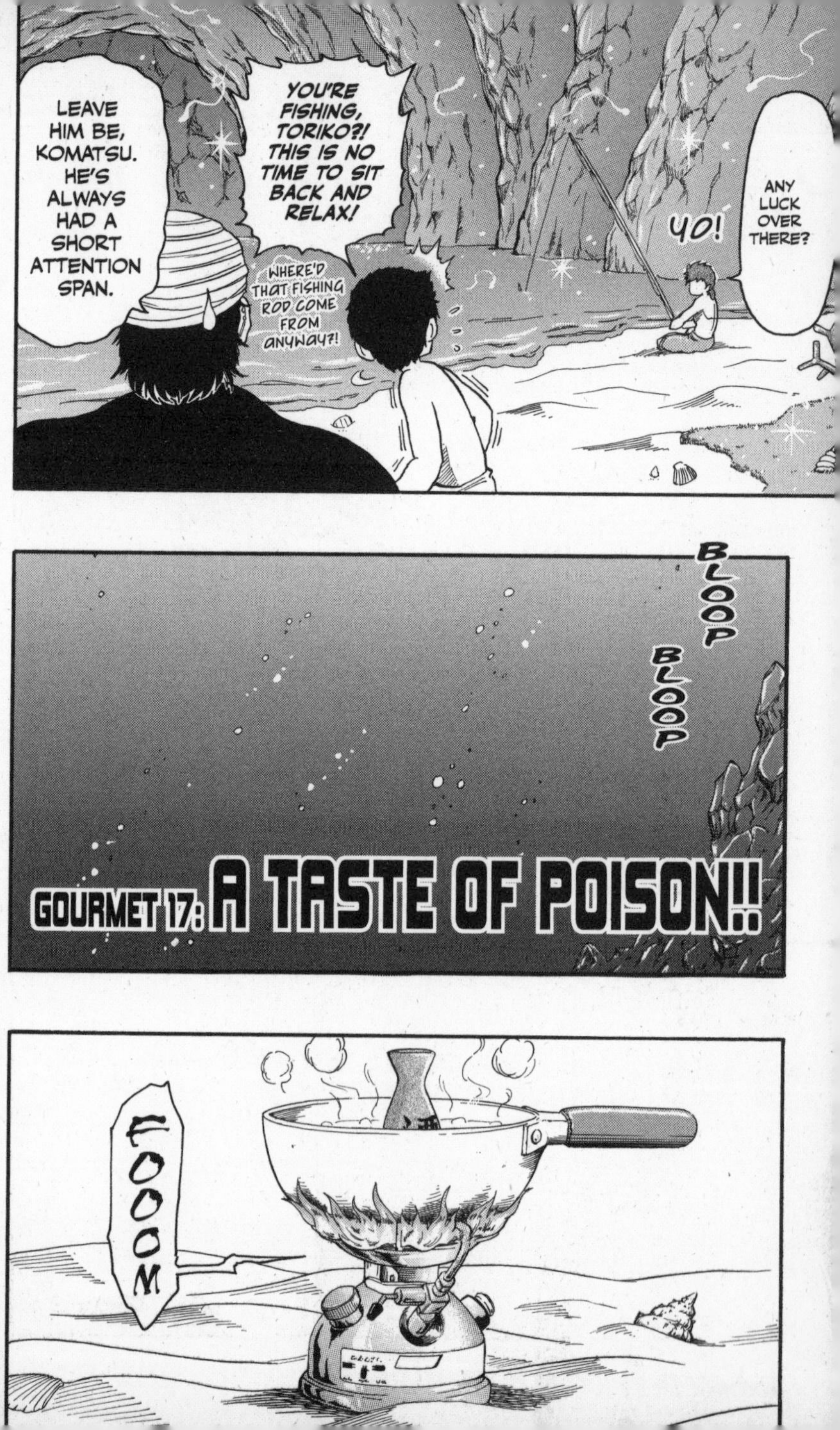
ANY LUCK OVER THERE?
YO!
YOU'RE FISHING, TORIKO?! THIS IS NO TIME TO SIT BACK AND RELAX!
WHERE'D THAT FISHING ROD COME FROM anyway?!
LEAVE HIM BE, KOMATSU. HE'S ALWAYS HAD A SHORT ATTENTION SPAN.
BLOOP
BLOOP
GOURMET 17: A TASTE OF POISON!!
FOOOOM

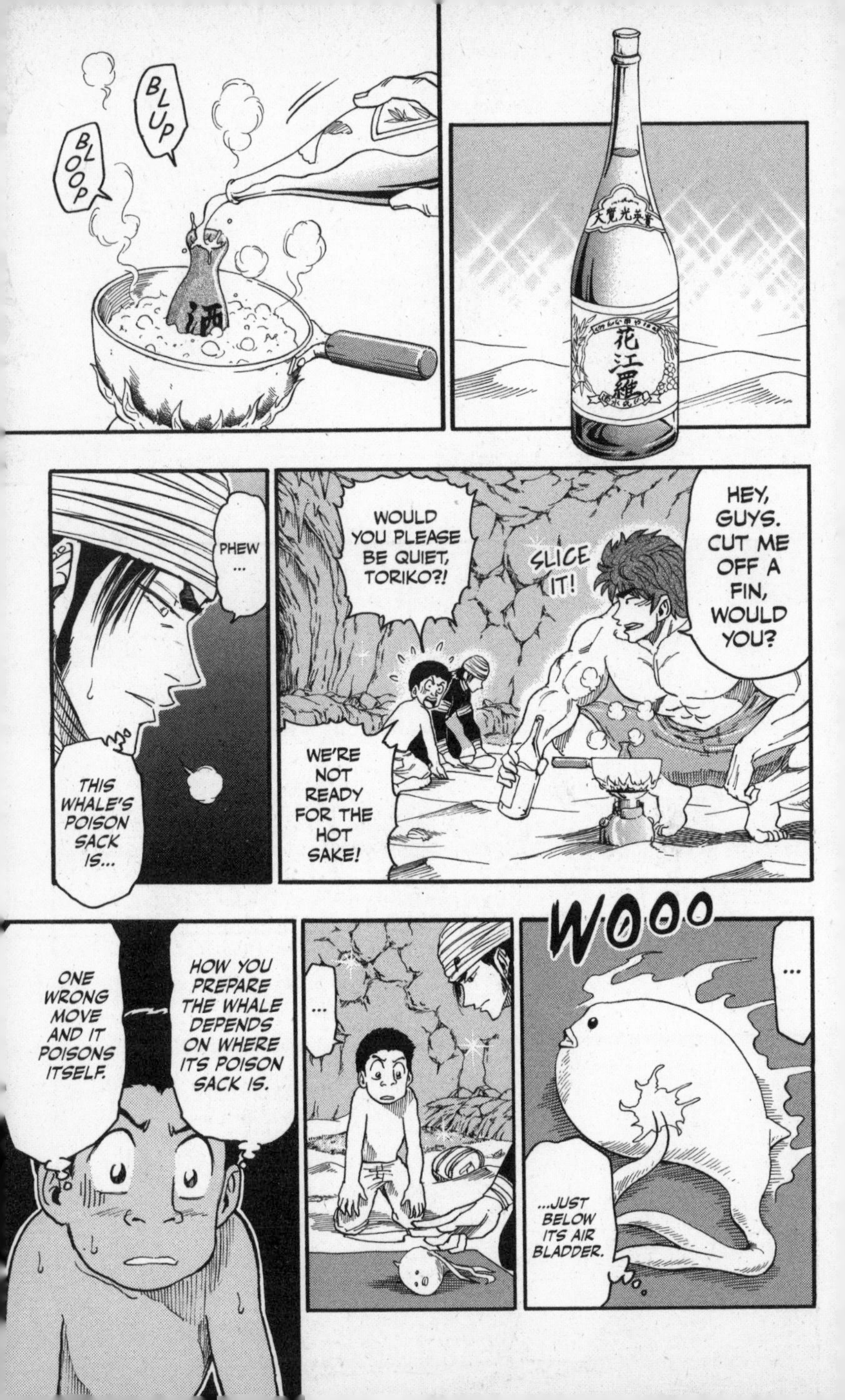
花江羅
BLUP
BLOOP
酒
HEY, GUYS. CUT ME OFF A FIN, WOULD YOU?
SLICE IT!
WOULD YOU PLEASE BE QUIET, TORIKO?!
WE'RE NOT READY FOR THE HOT SAKE!
PHEW...
THIS WHALE'S POISON SACK IS...
WOOO
...
...JUST BELOW ITS AIR BLADDER.
...
HOW YOU PREPARE THE WHALE DEPENDS ON WHERE ITS POISON SACK IS.
ONE WRONG MOVE AND IT POISONS ITSELF.

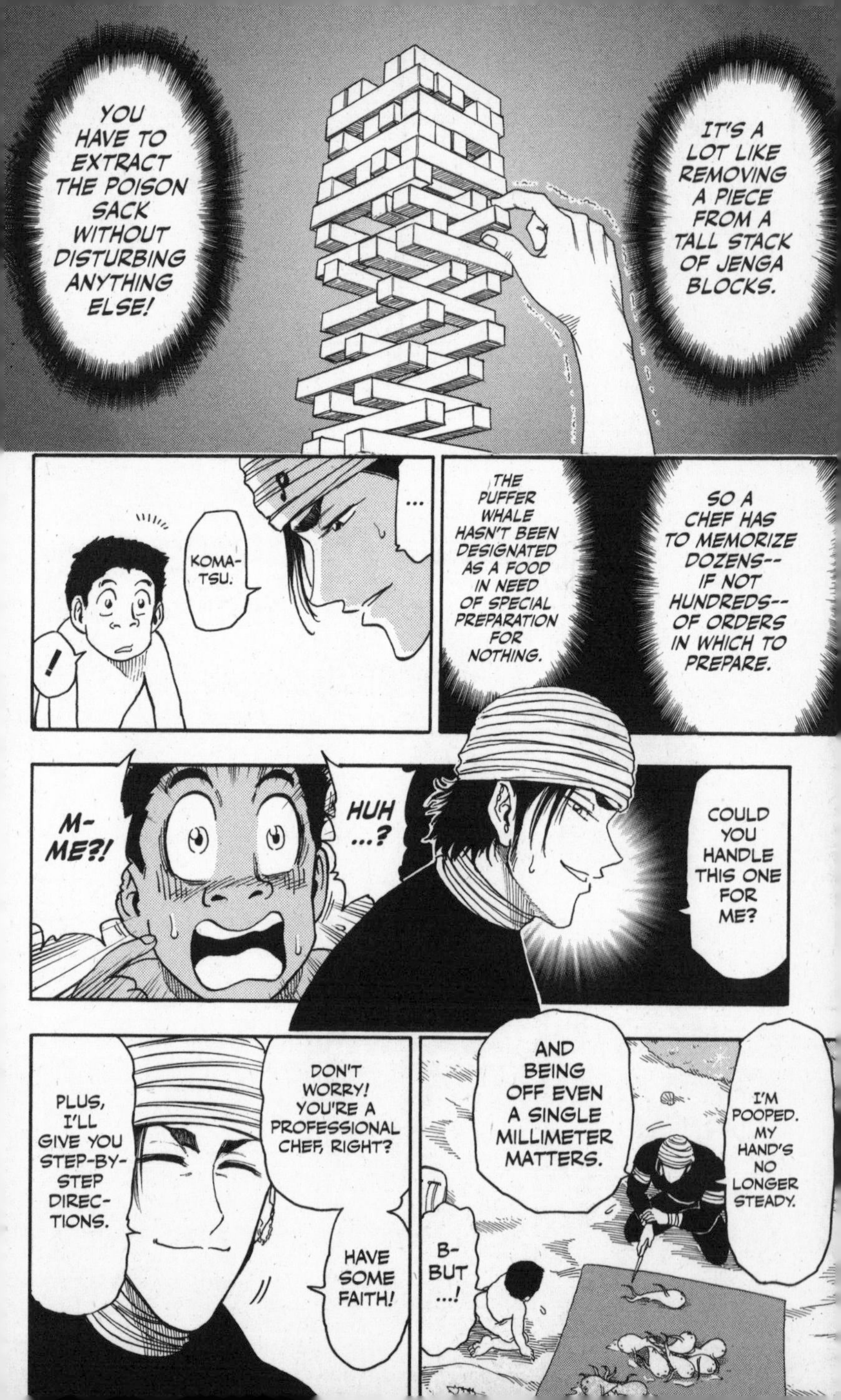
IT'S A LOT LIKE REMOVING A PIECE FROM A TALL STACK OF JENGA BLOCKS.
YOU HAVE TO EXTRACT THE POISON SACK WITHOUT DISTURBING ANYTHING ELSE!
SO A CHEF HAS TO MEMORIZE DOZENS-- IF NOT HUNDREDS-- OF ORDERS IN WHICH TO PREPARE.
THE PUFFER WHALE HASN'T BEEN DESIGNATED AS A FOOD IN NEED OF SPECIAL PREPARATION FOR NOTHING.
...
KOMA-TSU.
!
COULD YOU HANDLE THIS ONE FOR ME?
HUH ...?
M- ME?!
I'M POOPED. MY HAND'S NO LONGER STEADY.
AND BEING OFF EVEN A SINGLE MILLIMETER MATTERS.
B- BUT ...!
DON'T WORRY! YOU'RE A PROFESSIONAL CHEF, RIGHT?
HAVE SOME FAITH!
PLUS, I'LL GIVE YOU STEP-BY-STEP DIREC-TIONS.

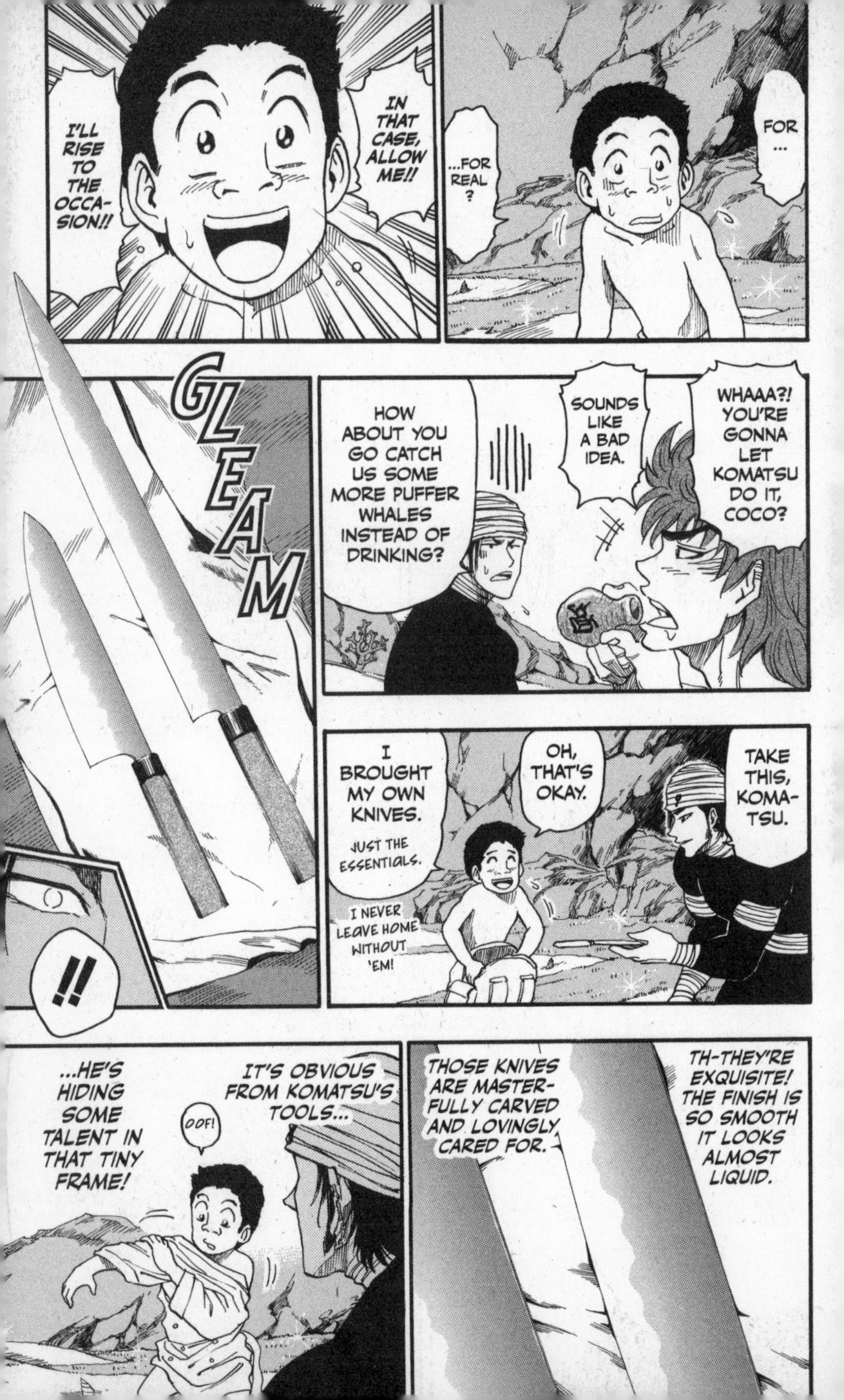
FOR...
...FOR REAL?
IN THAT CASE, ALLOW ME!!
I'LL RISE TO THE OCCASION!!
WHAAA?! YOU'RE GONNA LET KOMATSU DO IT, COCO?
SOUNDS LIKE A BAD IDEA.
HOW ABOUT YOU GO CATCH US SOME MORE PUFFER WHALES INSTEAD OF DRINKING?
TAKE THIS, KOMATSU.
OH, THAT'S OKAY.
I BROUGHT MY OWN KNIVES.
JUST THE ESSENTIALS.
I NEVER LEAVE HOME WITHOUT 'EM!
GLEAM
!!
TH-THEY'RE EXQUISITE! THE FINISH IS SO SMOOTH IT LOOKS ALMOST LIQUID.
THOSE KNIVES ARE MASTERFULLY CARVED AND LOVINGLY CARED FOR.
IT'S OBVIOUS FROM KOMATSU'S TOOLS...
...HE'S HIDING SOME TALENT IN THAT TINY FRAME!
OOF!

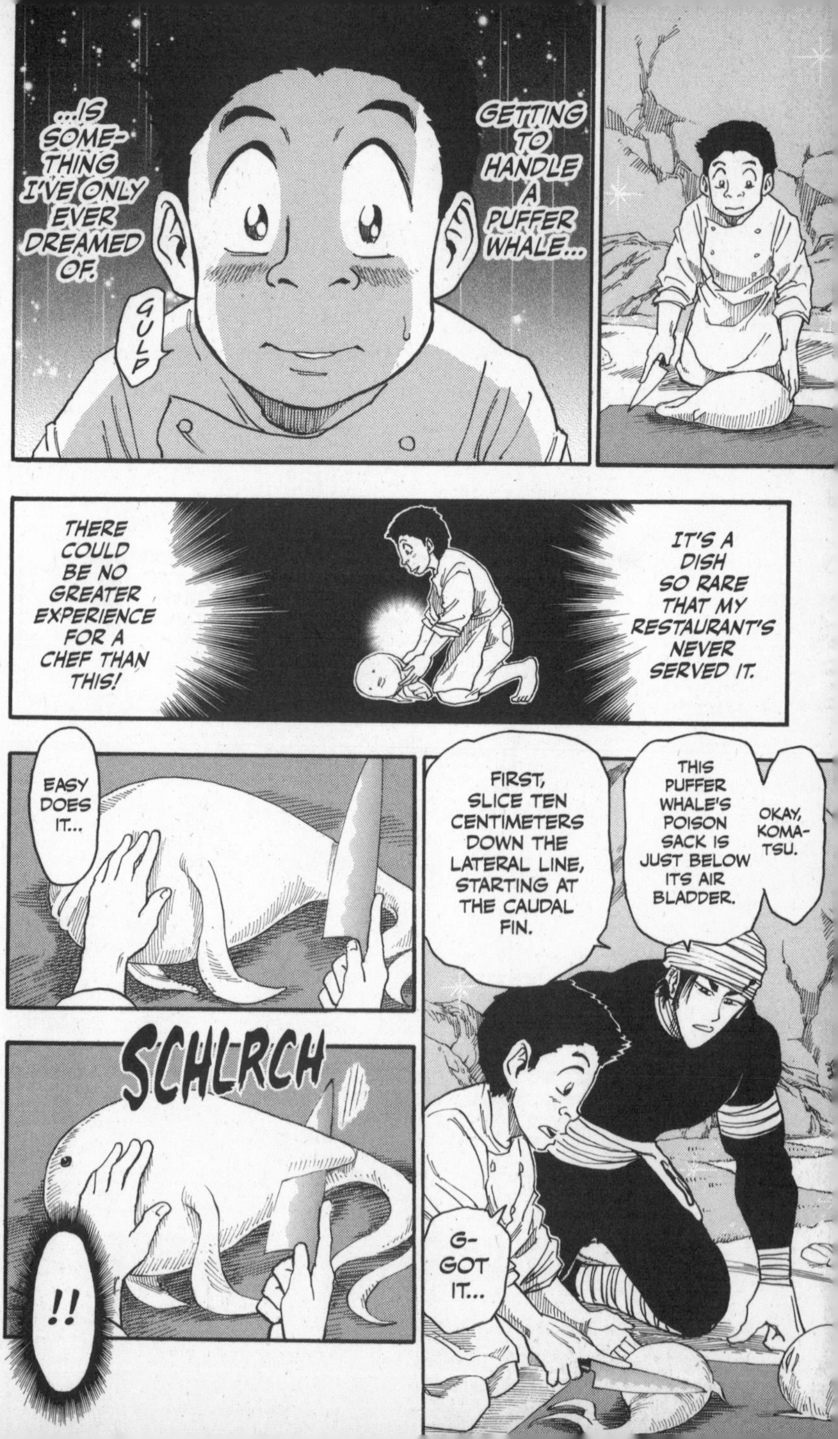
GETTING TO HANDLE A PUFFER WHALE...
...IS SOME-THING I'VE ONLY EVER DREAMED OF.
GULP
IT'S A DISH SO RARE THAT MY RESTAURANT'S NEVER SERVED IT.
THERE COULD BE NO GREATER EXPERIENCE FOR A CHEF THAN THIS!
OKAY, KOMA-TSU.
THIS PUFFER WHALE'S POISON SACK IS JUST BELOW ITS AIR BLADDER.
FIRST, SLICE TEN CENTIMETERS DOWN THE LATERAL LINE, STARTING AT THE CAUDAL FIN.
G-GOT IT...
EASY DOES IT...
SCHLRCH
!!

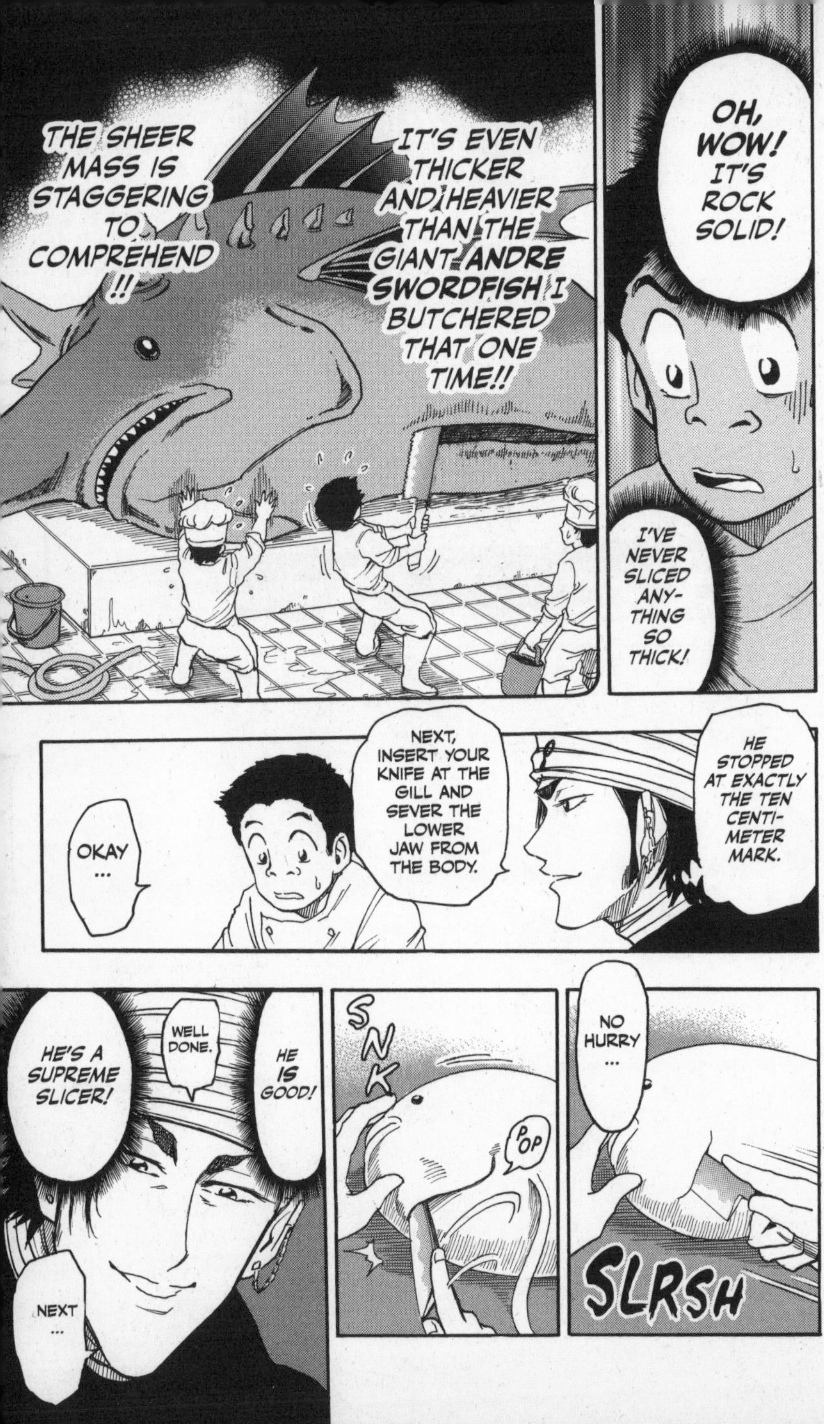
OH, WOW! IT'S ROCK SOLID!
I'VE NEVER SLICED ANYTHING SO THICK!
IT'S EVEN THICKER AND HEAVIER THAN THE GIANT ANDRE SWORDFISH I BUTCHERED THAT ONE TIME!!
THE SHEER MASS IS STAGGERING TO COMPREHEND!!
HE STOPPED AT EXACTLY THE TEN CENTIMETER MARK.
NEXT, INSERT YOUR KNIFE AT THE GILL AND SEVER THE LOWER JAW FROM THE BODY.
OKAY ...
NO HURRY ...
SLRSH
SNK
POP
HE IS GOOD!
WELL DONE.
HE'S A SUPREME SLICER!
NEXT ...

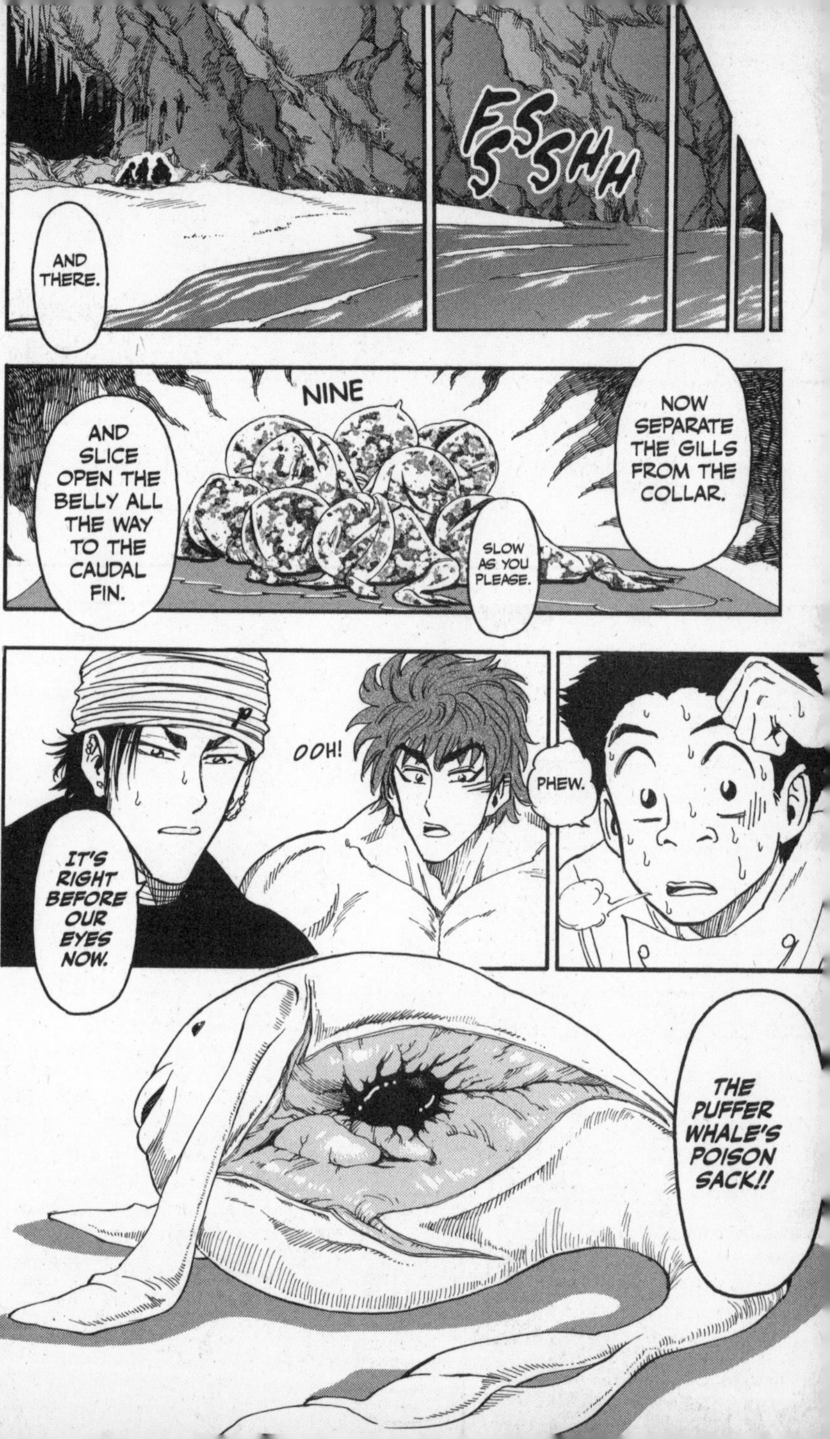
FSSHH
AND THERE.
NOW SEPARATE THE GILLS FROM THE COLLAR.
NINE
SLOW AS YOU PLEASE.
AND SLICE OPEN THE BELLY ALL THE WAY TO THE CAUDAL FIN.
PHEW.
OOH!
IT'S RIGHT BEFORE OUR EYES NOW.
THE PUFFER WHALE'S POISON SACK!!

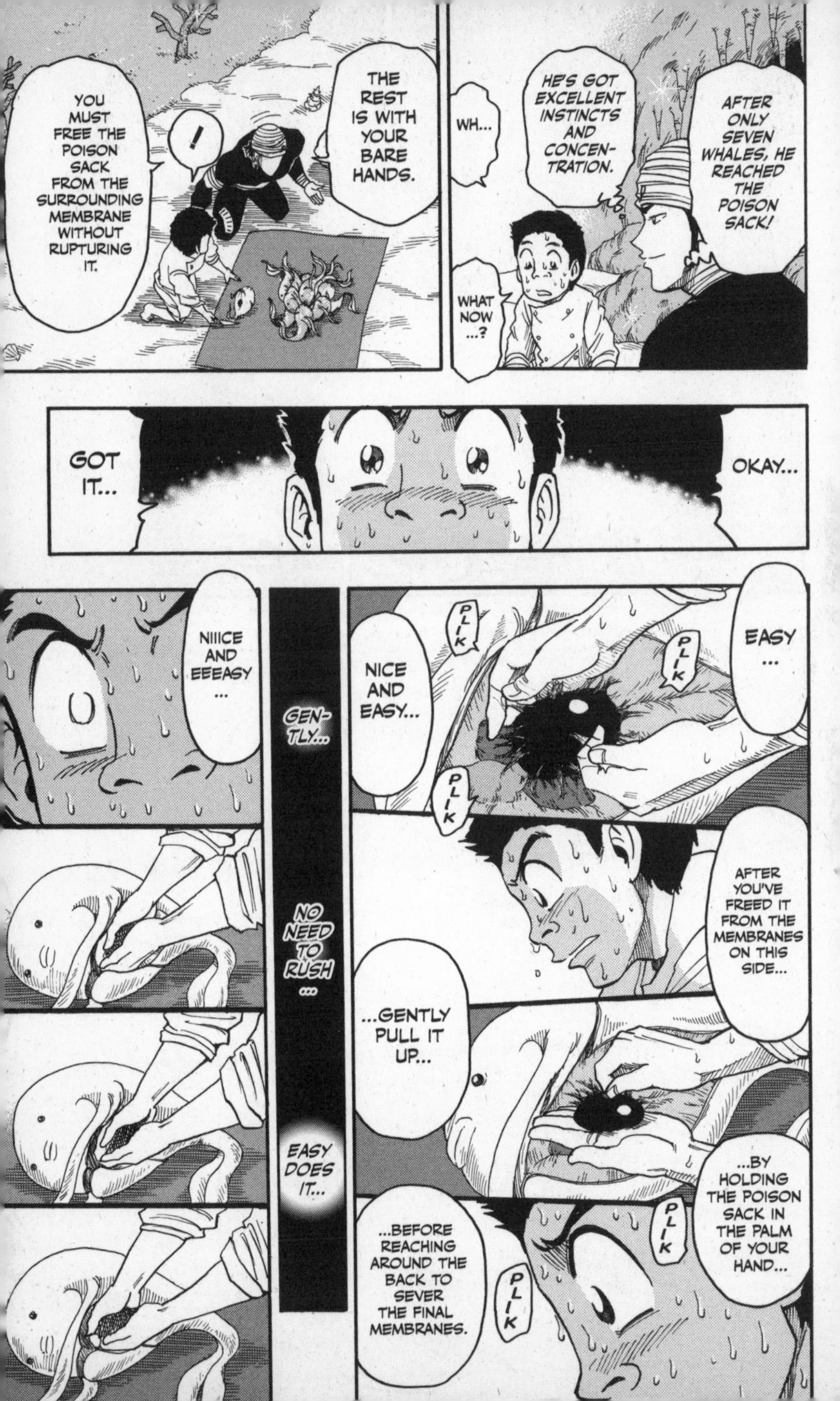
AFTER ONLY SEVEN WHALES, HE REACHED THE POISON SACK!
HE'S GOT EXCELLENT INSTINCTS AND CONCEN-TRATION.
WH...
WHAT NOW ...?
THE REST IS WITH YOUR BARE HANDS.
!
YOU MUST FREE THE POISON SACK FROM THE SURROUNDING MEMBRANE WITHOUT RUPTURING IT.
OKAY...
GOT IT...
EASY ...
PLIK
PLIK
NICE AND EASY...
PLIK
GEN-TLY...
NIIICE AND EEEASY ...
AFTER YOU'VE FREED IT FROM THE MEMBRANES ON THIS SIDE...
...GENTLY PULL IT UP...
...BY HOLDING THE POISON SACK IN THE PALM OF YOUR HAND...
PLIK
...BEFORE REACHING AROUND THE BACK TO SEVER THE FINAL MEMBRANES.
PLIK
NO NEED TO RUSH ...
EASY DOES IT...

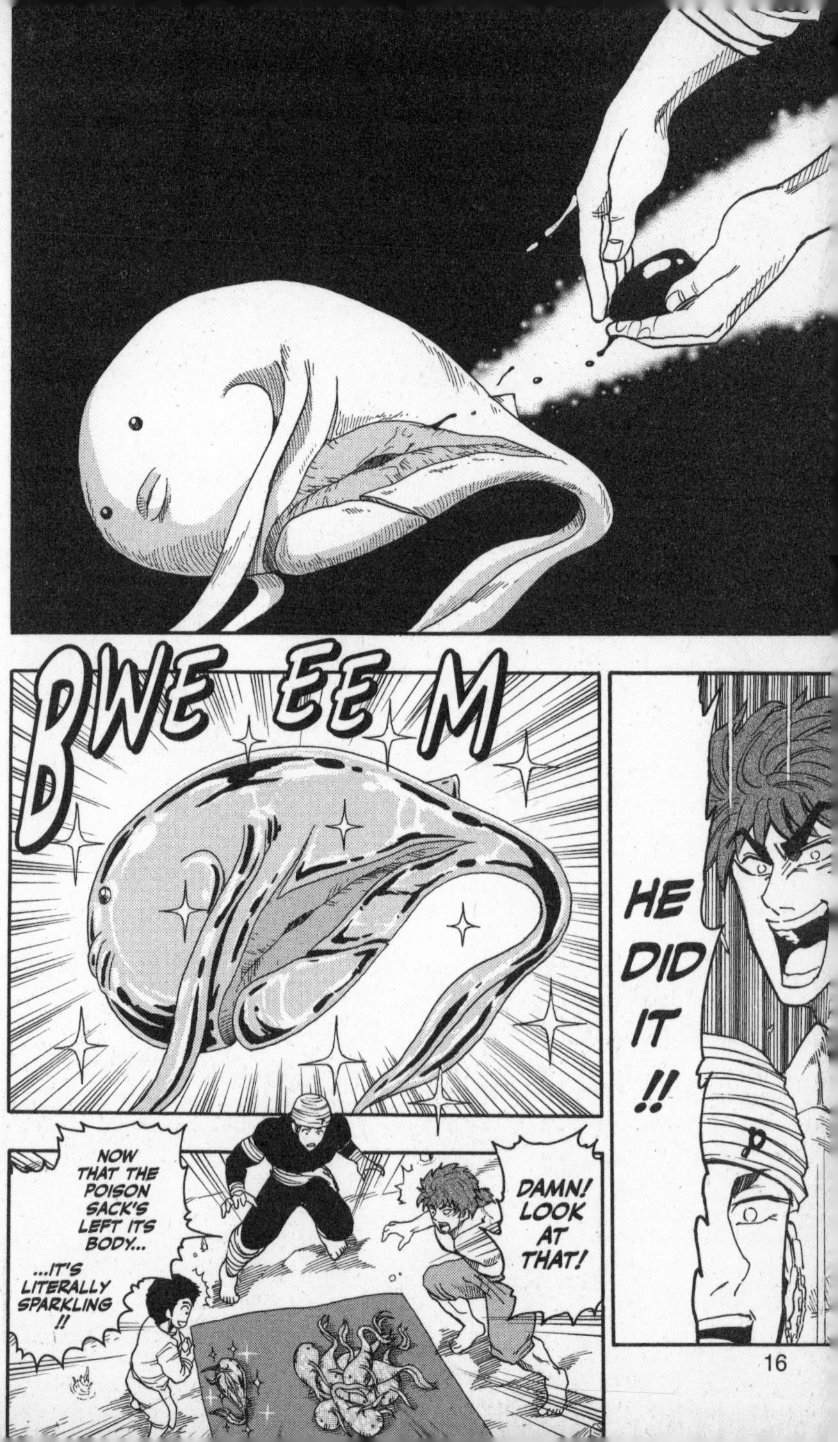

HE DID IT !!
BWEEEM
DAMN! LOOK AT THAT!
NOW THAT THE POISON SACK'S LEFT ITS BODY...
...IT'S LITERALLY SPARKLING !!

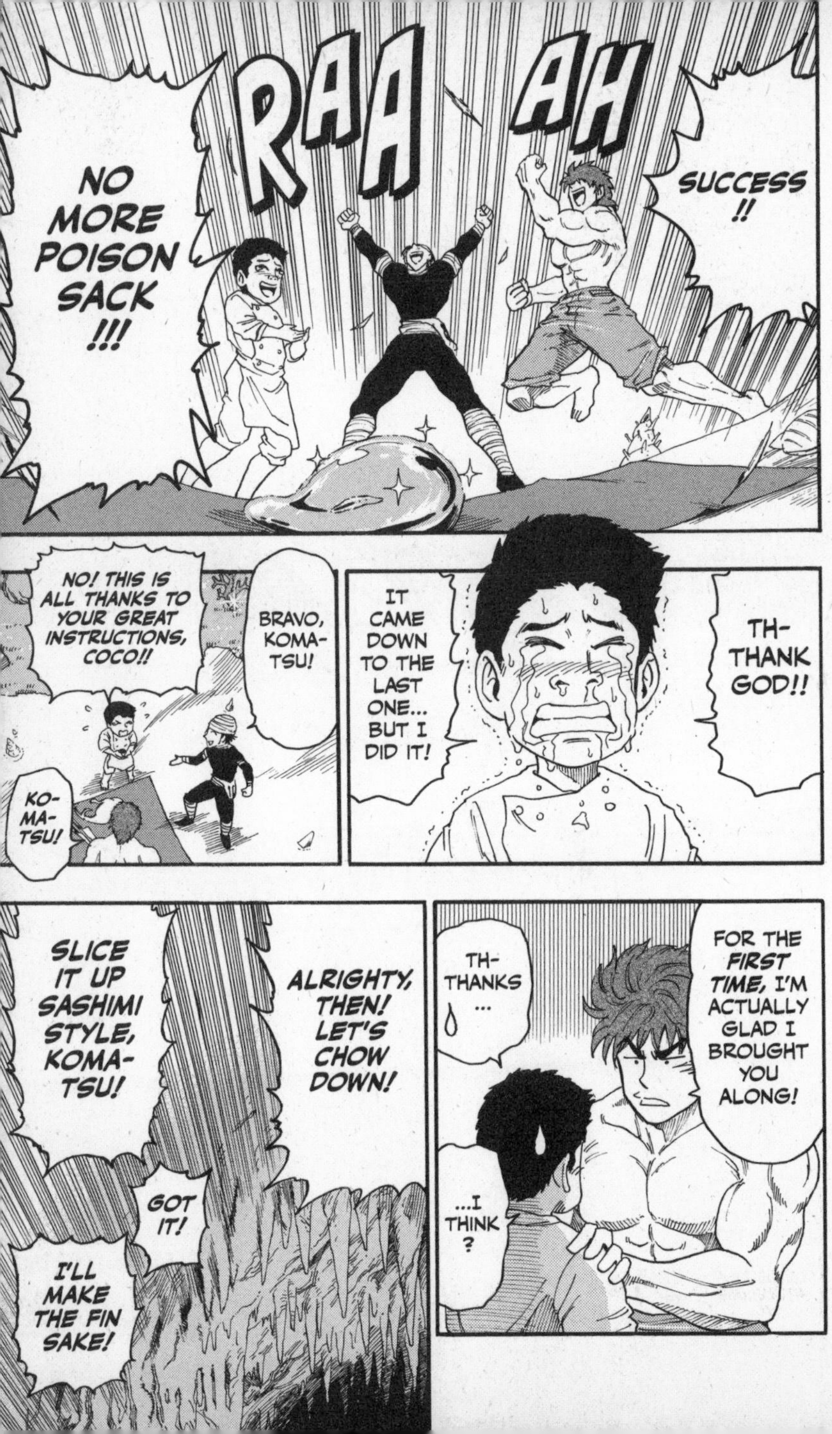
SUCCESS !!
RAA AH
NO MORE POISON SACK !!!
TH- THANK GOD!!
IT CAME DOWN TO THE LAST ONE... BUT I DID IT!
BRAVO, KOMA- TSU!
NO! THIS IS ALL THANKS TO YOUR GREAT INSTRUCTIONS, COCO!!
KO- MA- TSU!
FOR THE FIRST TIME, I'M ACTUALLY GLAD I BROUGHT YOU ALONG!
TH- THANKS ...
...I THINK ?
ALRIGHTY, THEN! LET'S CHOW DOWN!
SLICE IT UP SASHIMI STYLE, KOMA- TSU!
GOT IT!
I'LL MAKE THE FIN SAKE!

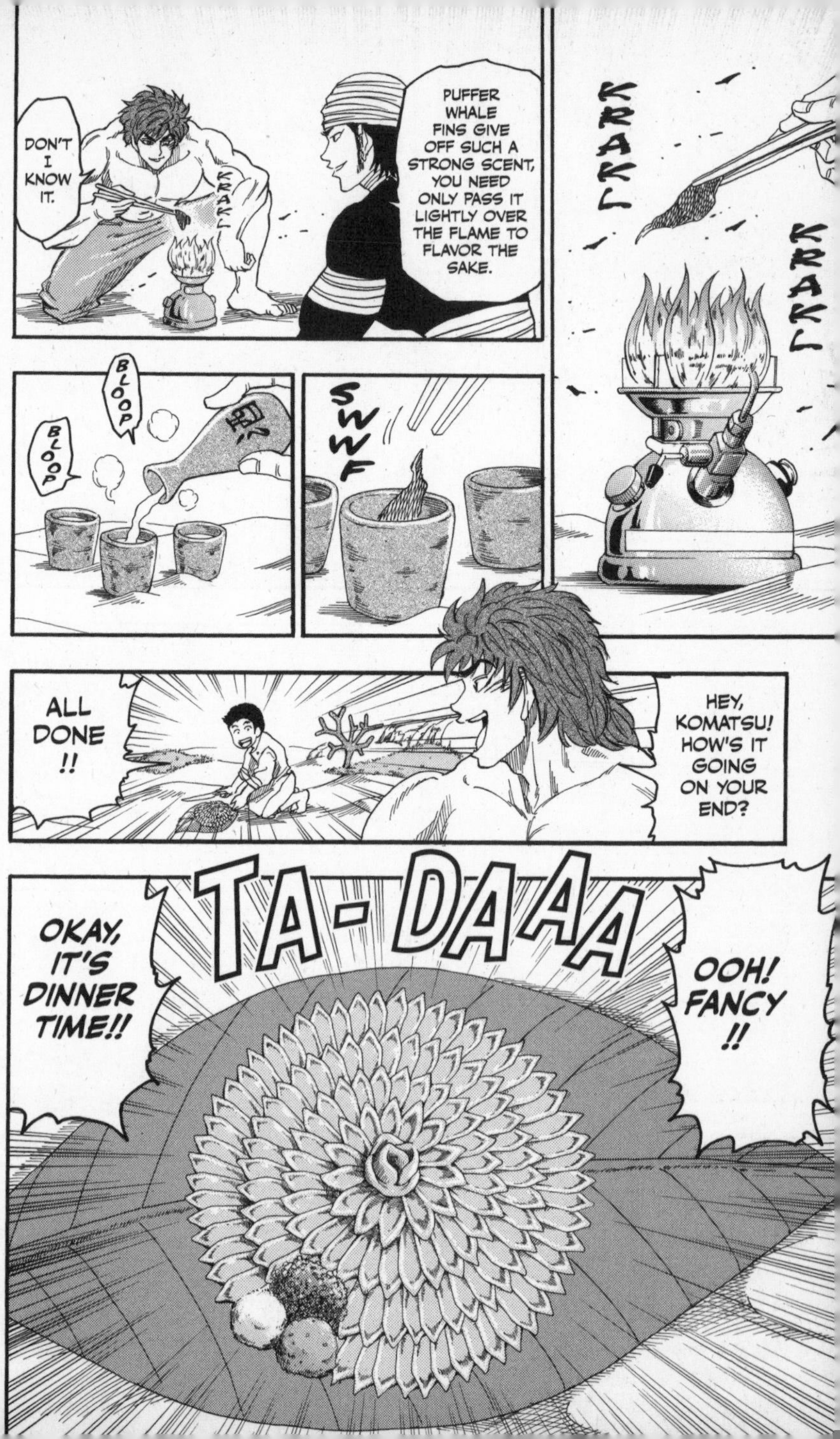
KRAKL
KRAKL
PUFFER WHALE FINS GIVE OFF SUCH A STRONG SCENT, YOU NEED ONLY PASS IT LIGHTLY OVER THE FLAME TO FLAVOR THE SAKE.
KRAKL
DON'T I KNOW IT.
SWWF
BLOOP
BLOOP
HEY, KOMATSU! HOW'S IT GOING ON YOUR END?
ALL DONE !!
TA-DAAA
OOH! FANCY !!
OKAY, IT'S DINNER TIME!!

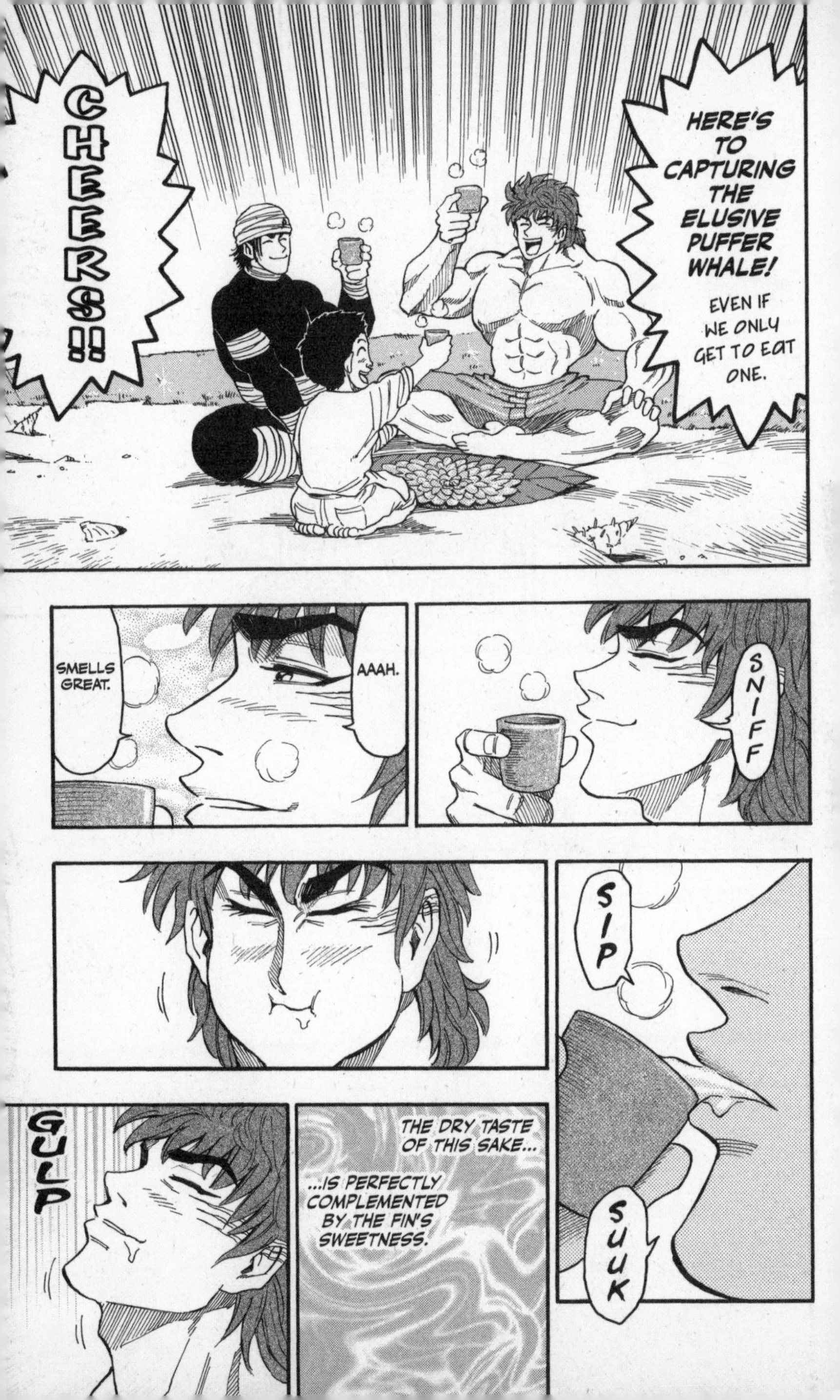
HERE'S TO CAPTURING THE ELUSIVE PUFFER WHALE!
EVEN IF WE ONLY GET TO EAT ONE.
CHEERS!!
SNIFF
AAAH.
SMELLS GREAT.
SIP
SUUK
THE DRY TASTE OF THIS SAKE...
...IS PERFECTLY COMPLEMENTED BY THE FIN'S SWEETNESS.
GULP

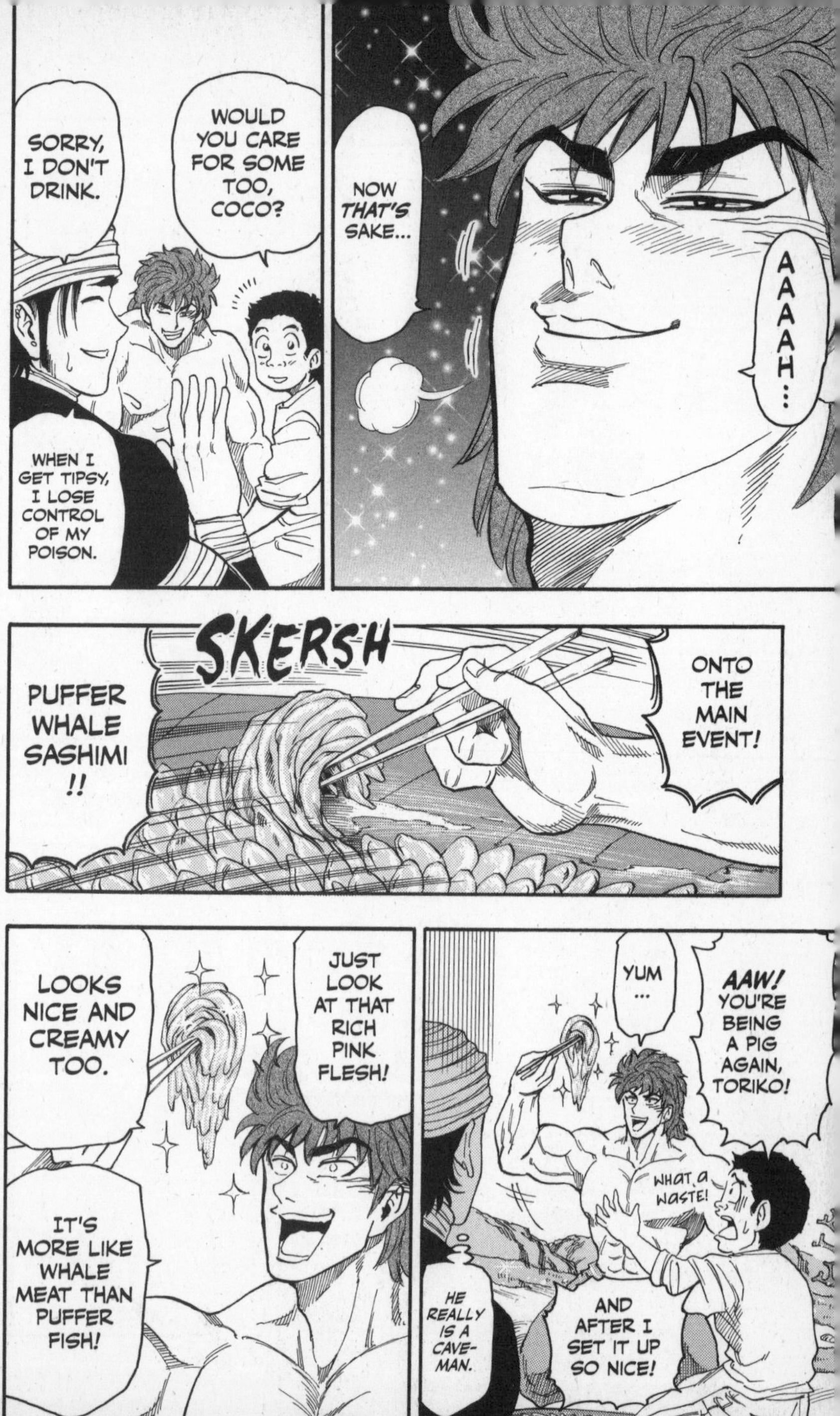
AAAAH...
NOW *THAT'S* SAKE...
WOULD YOU CARE FOR SOME TOO, COCO?
SORRY, I DON'T DRINK.
WHEN I GET TIPSY, I LOSE CONTROL OF MY POISON.
SKERSH
ONTO THE MAIN EVENT!
PUFFER WHALE SASHIMI !!
AAW! YOU'RE BEING A PIG AGAIN, TORIKO!
YUM ...
WHAT A WASTE!
AND AFTER I SET IT UP SO NICE!
HE REALLY IS A CAVE-MAN.
JUST LOOK AT THAT RICH PINK FLESH!
LOOKS NICE AND CREAMY TOO.
IT'S MORE LIKE WHALE MEAT THAN PUFFER FISH!

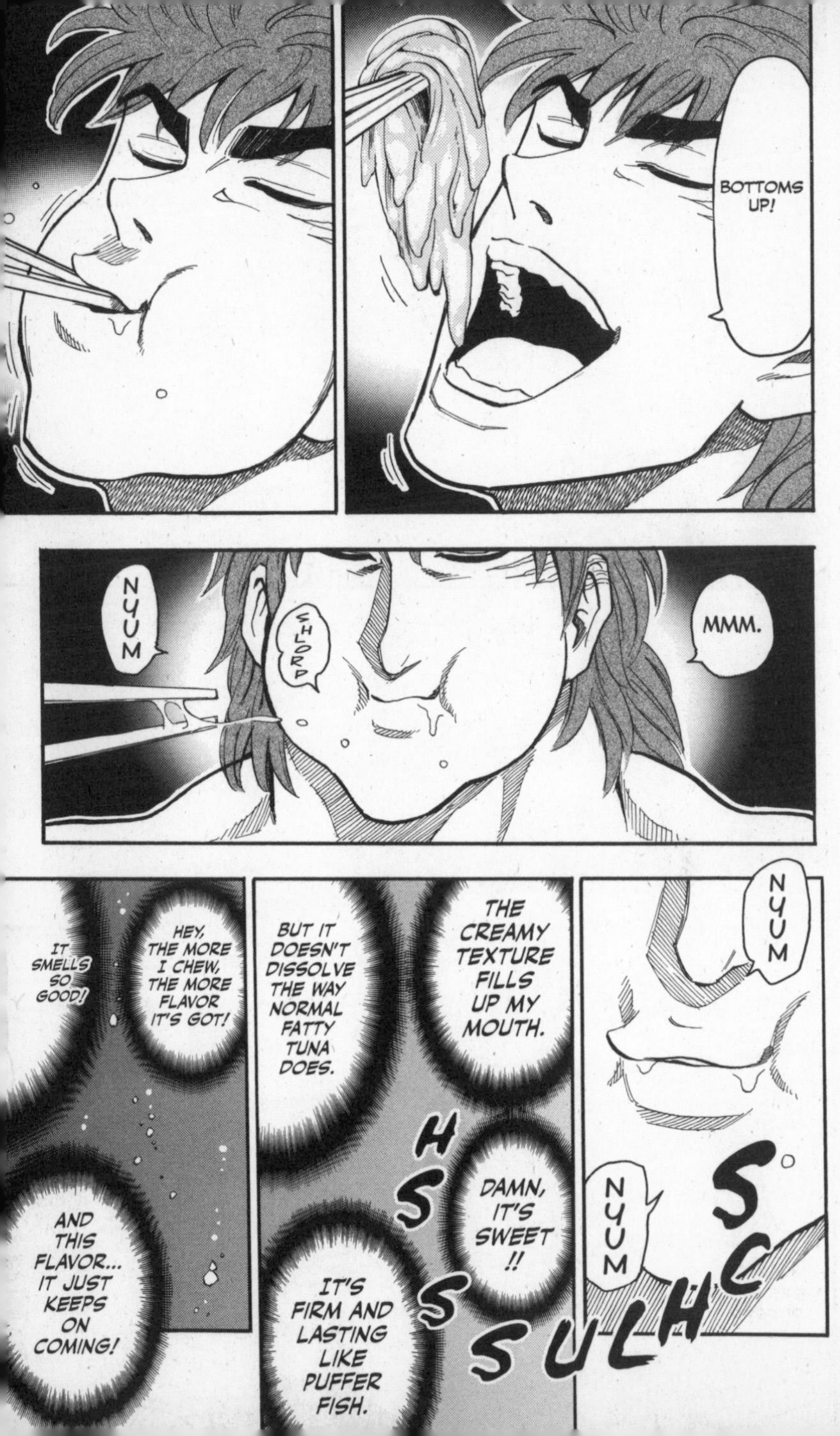
BOTTOMS UP!
MMM.
SHLORP
NYUM
NYUM
NYUM
SCHLUSSSH
THE CREAMY TEXTURE FILLS UP MY MOUTH.
BUT IT DOESN'T DISSOLVE THE WAY NORMAL FATTY TUNA DOES.
DAMN, IT'S SWEET!!
IT'S FIRM AND LASTING LIKE PUFFER FISH.
HEY, THE MORE I CHEW, THE MORE FLAVOR IT'S GOT!
IT SMELLS SO GOOD!
AND THIS FLAVOR... IT JUST KEEPS ON COMING!

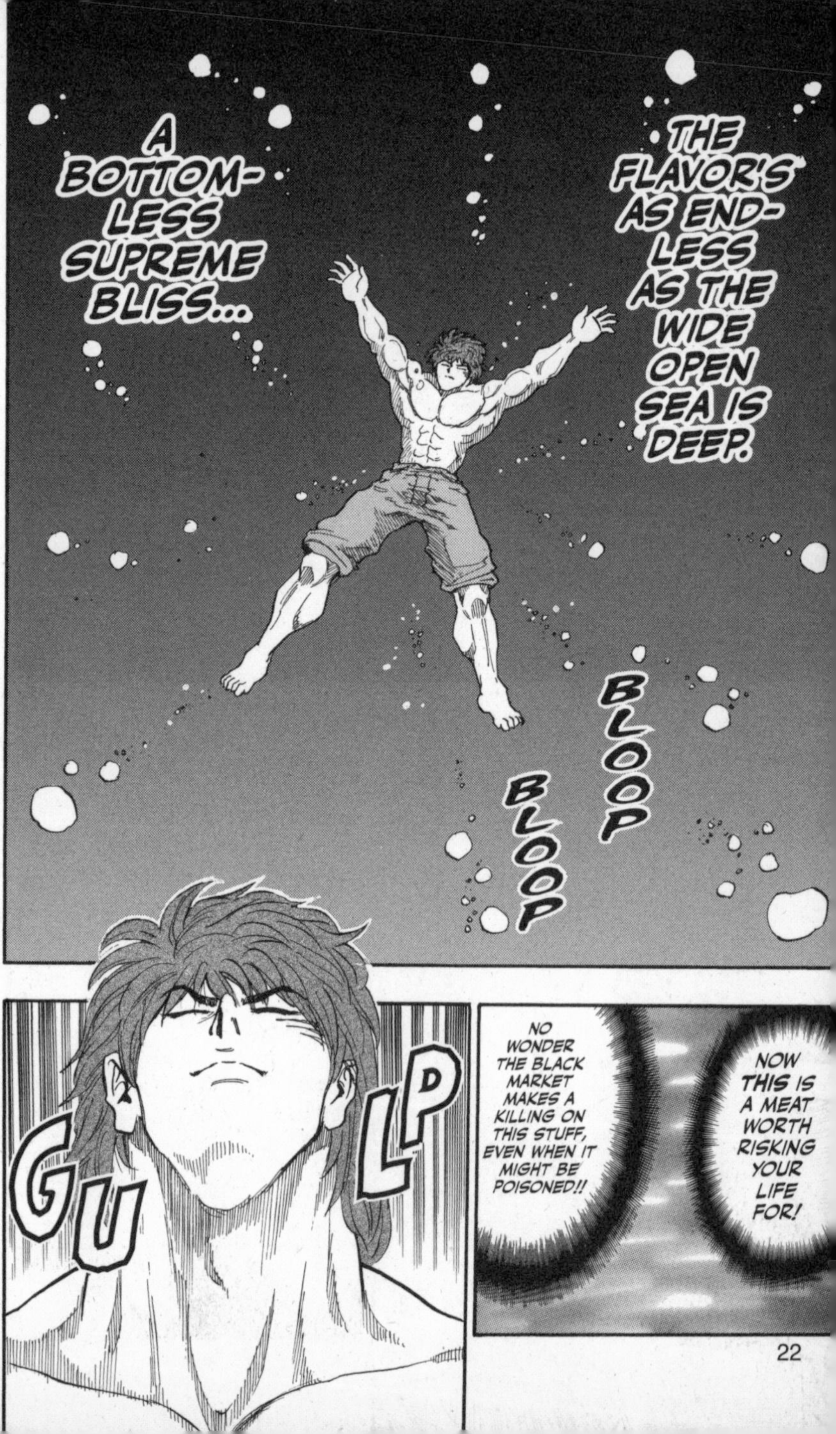
THE FLAVOR'S AS ENDLESS AS THE WIDE OPEN SEA IS DEEP.
A BOTTOMLESS SUPREME BLISS...
BLOOP
BLOOP
NOW THIS IS A MEAT WORTH RISKING YOUR LIFE FOR!
NO WONDER THE BLACK MARKET MAKES A KILLING ON THIS STUFF, EVEN WHEN IT MIGHT BE POISONED!!
GULP

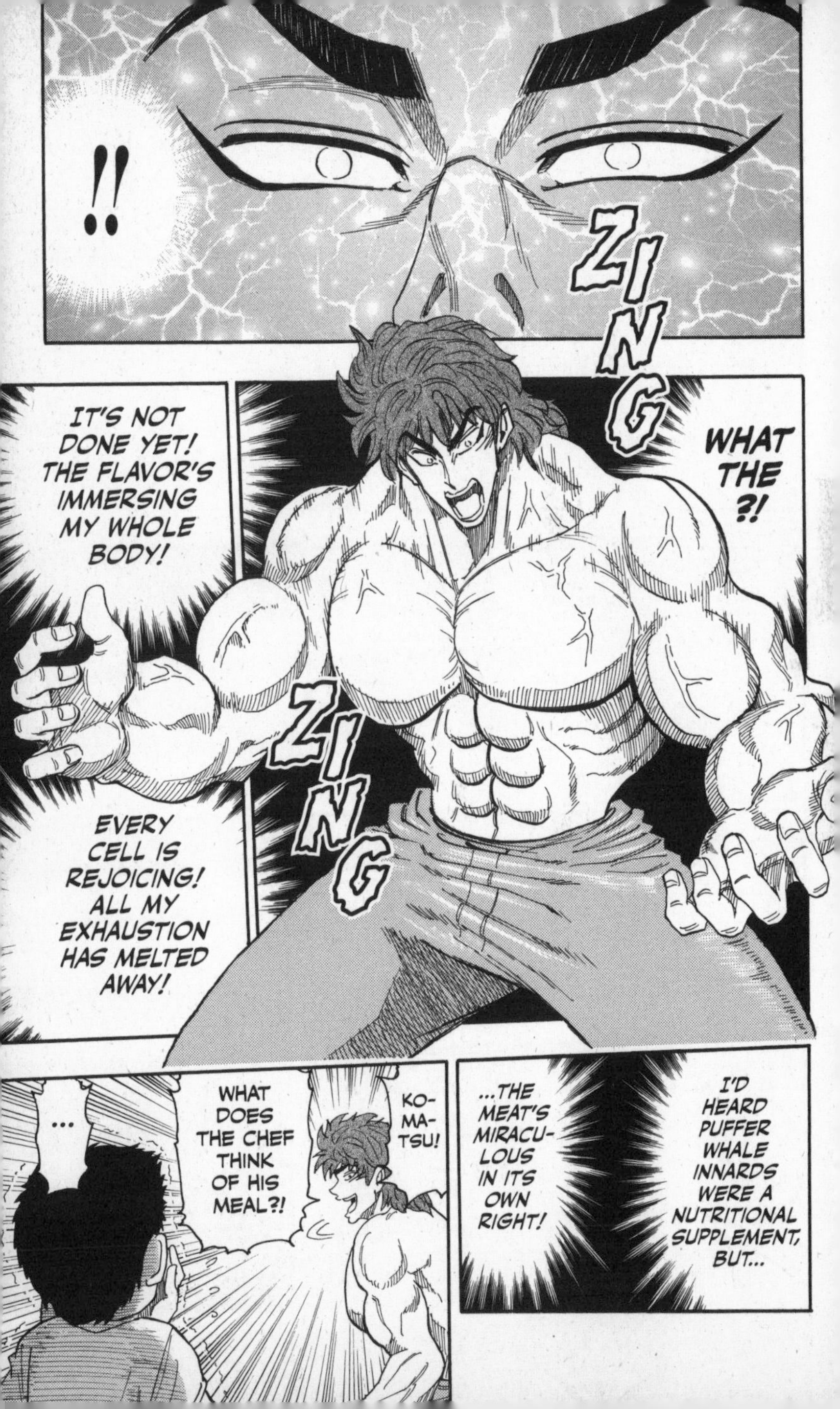
!!
ZING
WHAT THE?!
ZING
IT'S NOT DONE YET! THE FLAVOR'S IMMERSING MY WHOLE BODY!
EVERY CELL IS REJOICING! ALL MY EXHAUSTION HAS MELTED AWAY!
I'D HEARD PUFFER WHALE INNARDS WERE A NUTRITIONAL SUPPLEMENT, BUT...
...THE MEAT'S MIRACULOUS IN ITS OWN RIGHT!
KOMATSU!
WHAT DOES THE CHEF THINK OF HIS MEAL?!
...

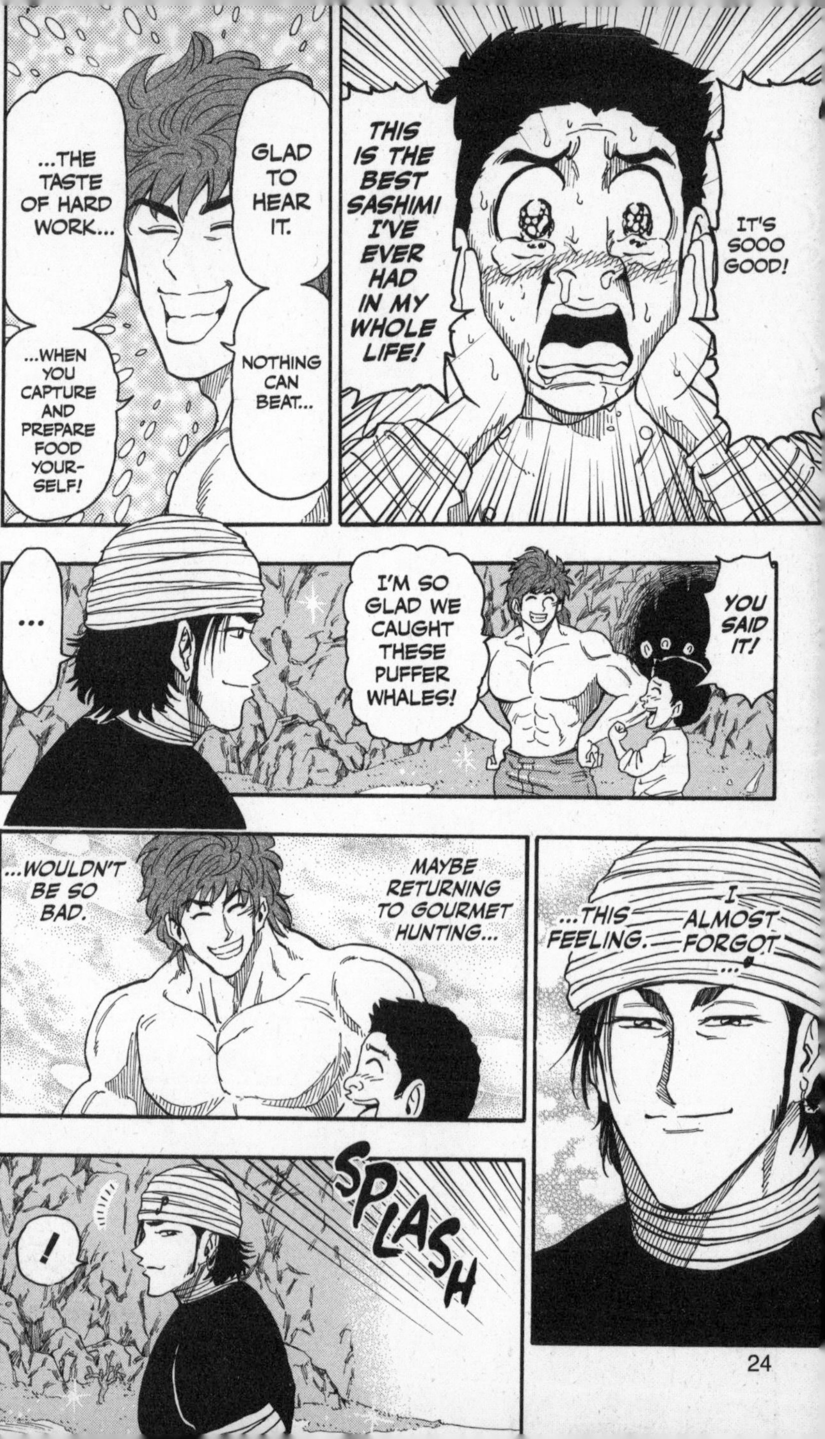
IT'S SOOO GOOD!
THIS IS THE BEST SASHIMI I'VE EVER HAD IN MY WHOLE LIFE!
GLAD TO HEAR IT.
NOTHING CAN BEAT...
...THE TASTE OF HARD WORK...
...WHEN YOU CAPTURE AND PREPARE FOOD YOURSELF!
I'M SO GLAD WE CAUGHT THESE PUFFER WHALES!
YOU SAID IT!
...
I ALMOST FORGOT...
...THIS FEELING.
MAYBE RETURNING TO GOURMET HUNTING...
...WOULDN'T BE SO BAD.
SPLASH
!

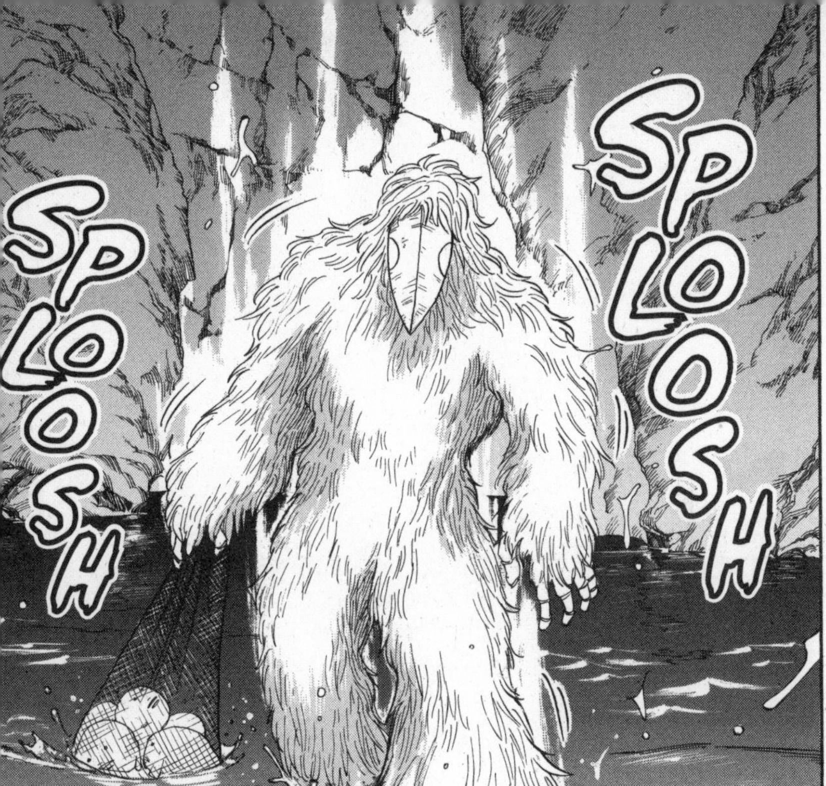
SPLOOSH
SPLOOSH
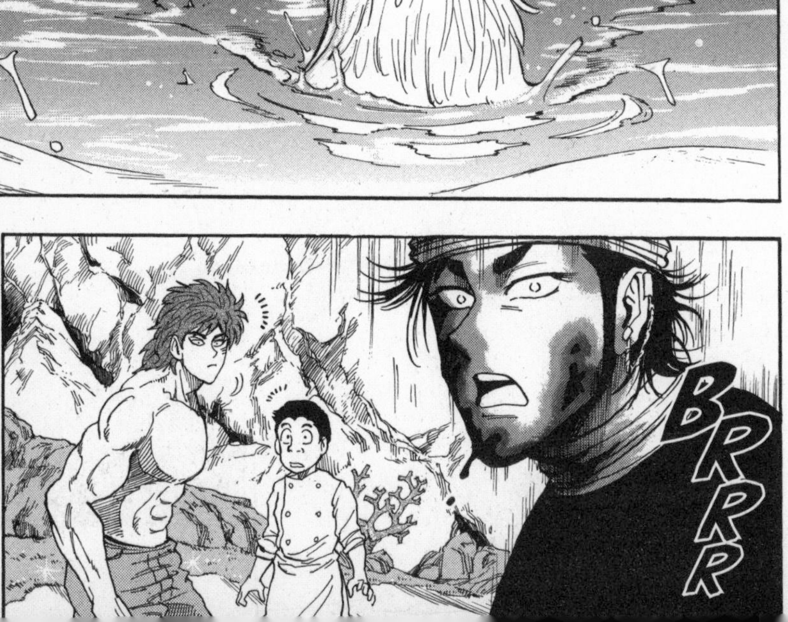
BRRRR

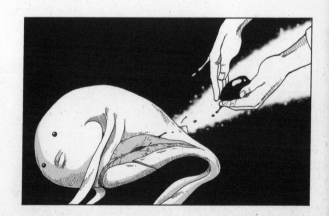

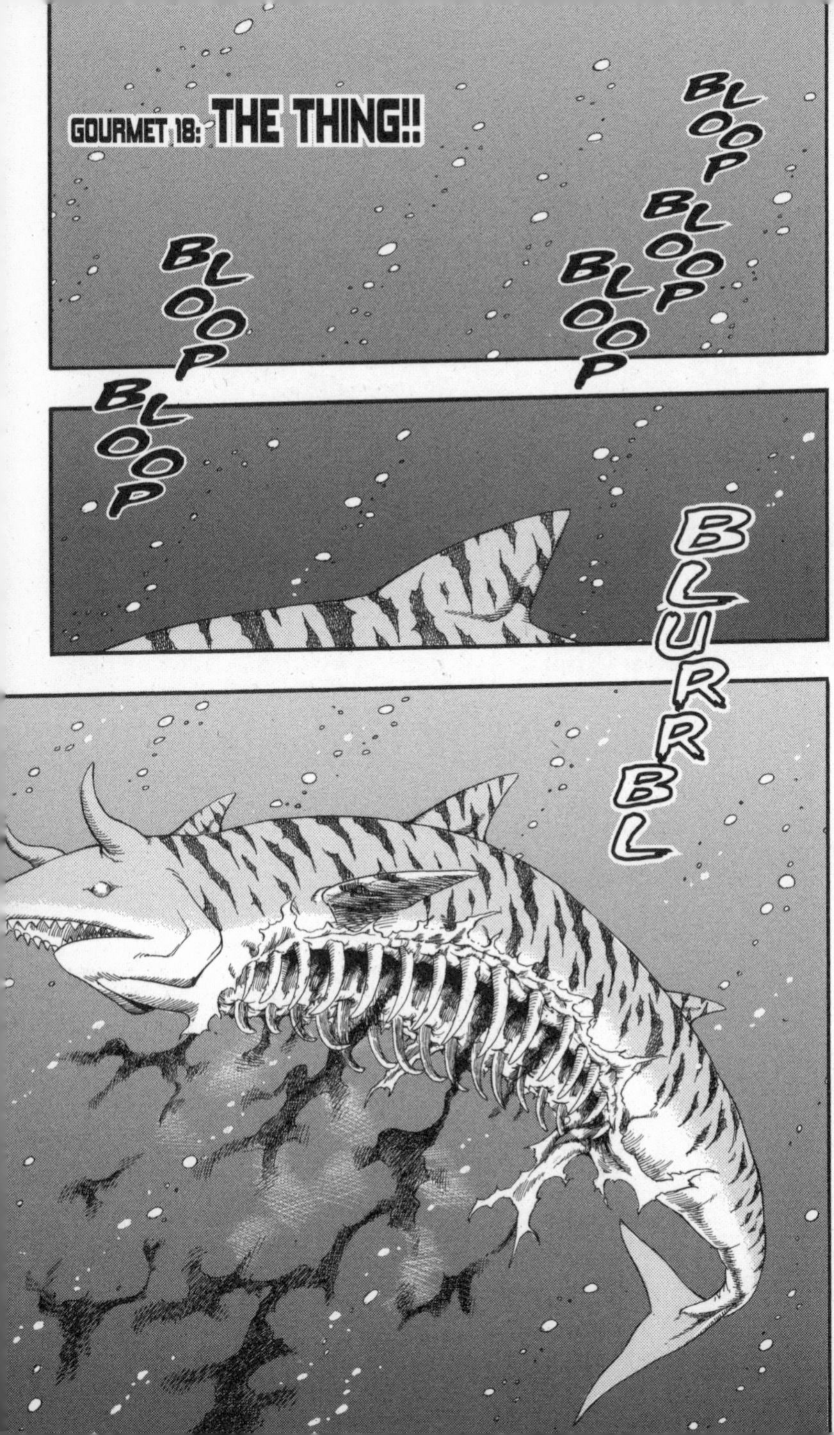
GOURMET 18: THE THING!!
BLOOP
BLOOP
BLOOP
BLOOP
BLOOP
BLURRBL

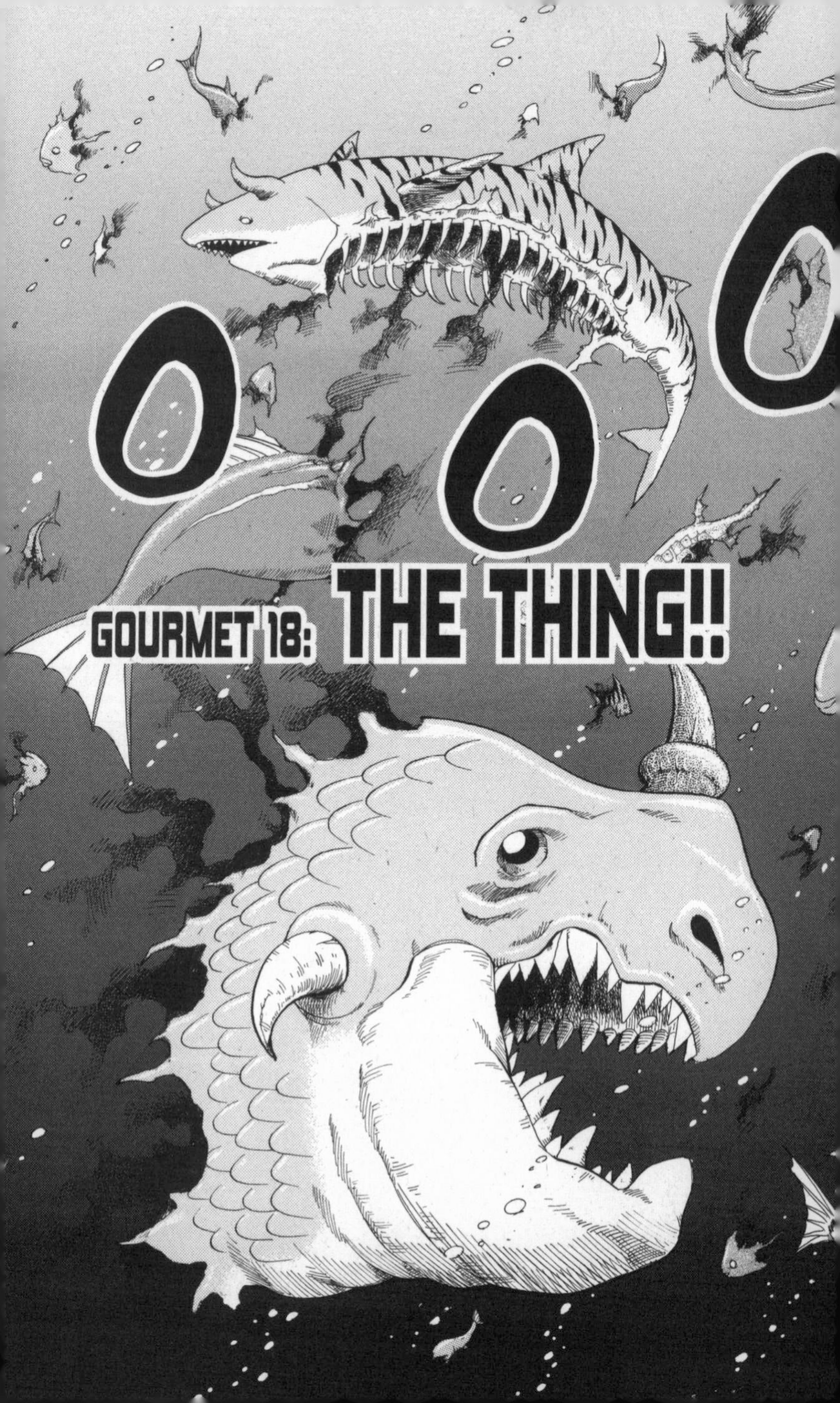
GOURMET 18: THE THING!!

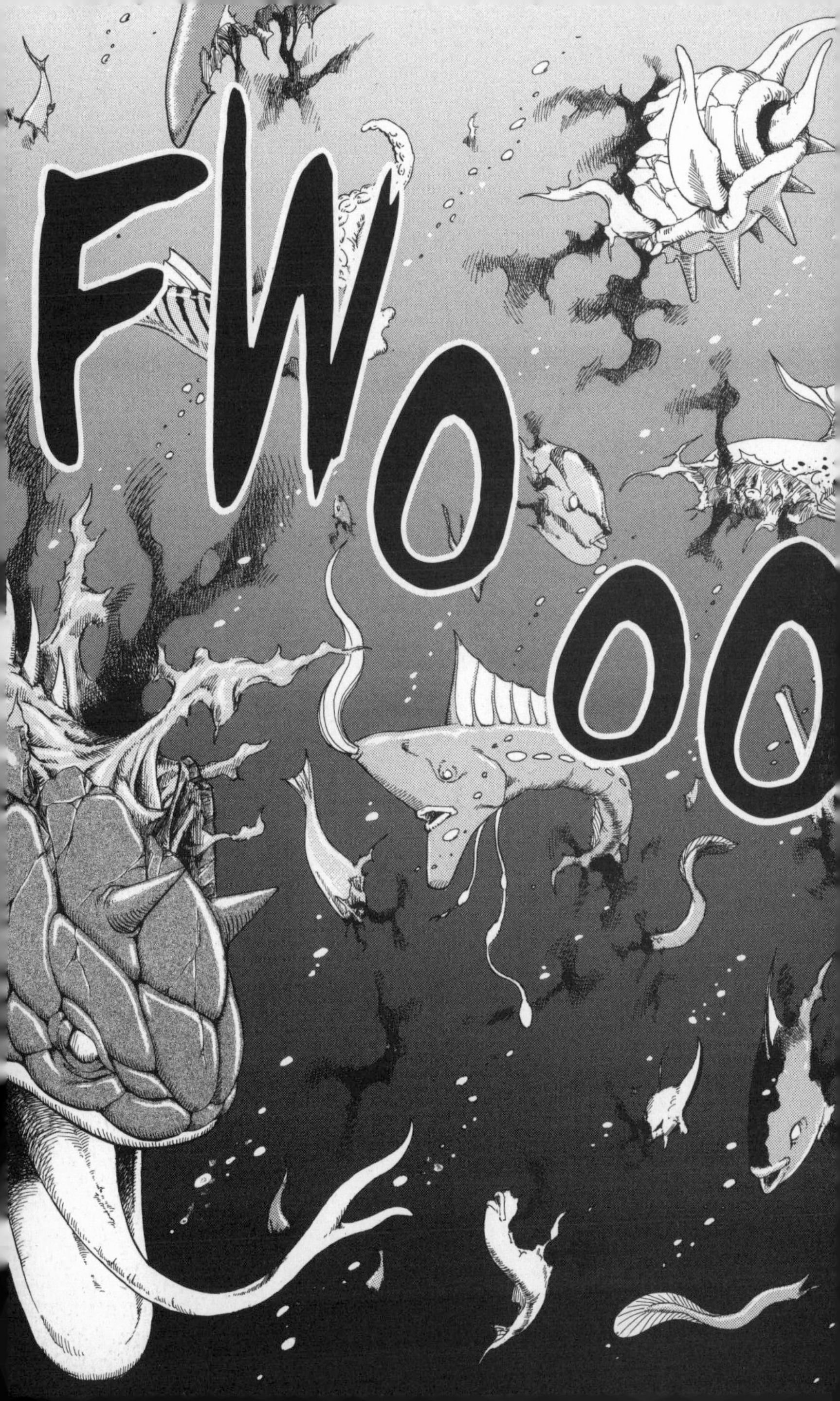
FWOOOO

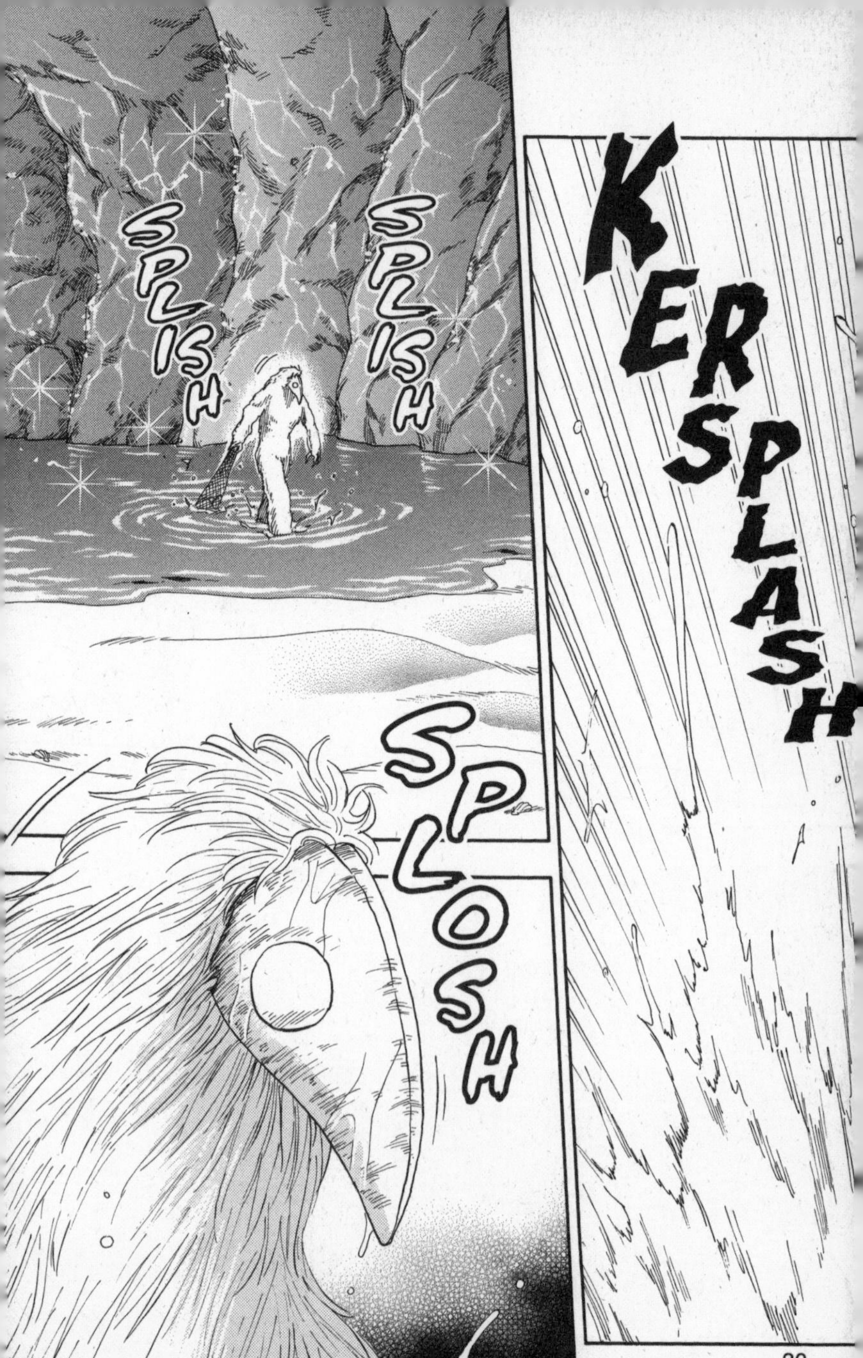
KERSPLASH
SPLISH
SPLISH
SPLOSH

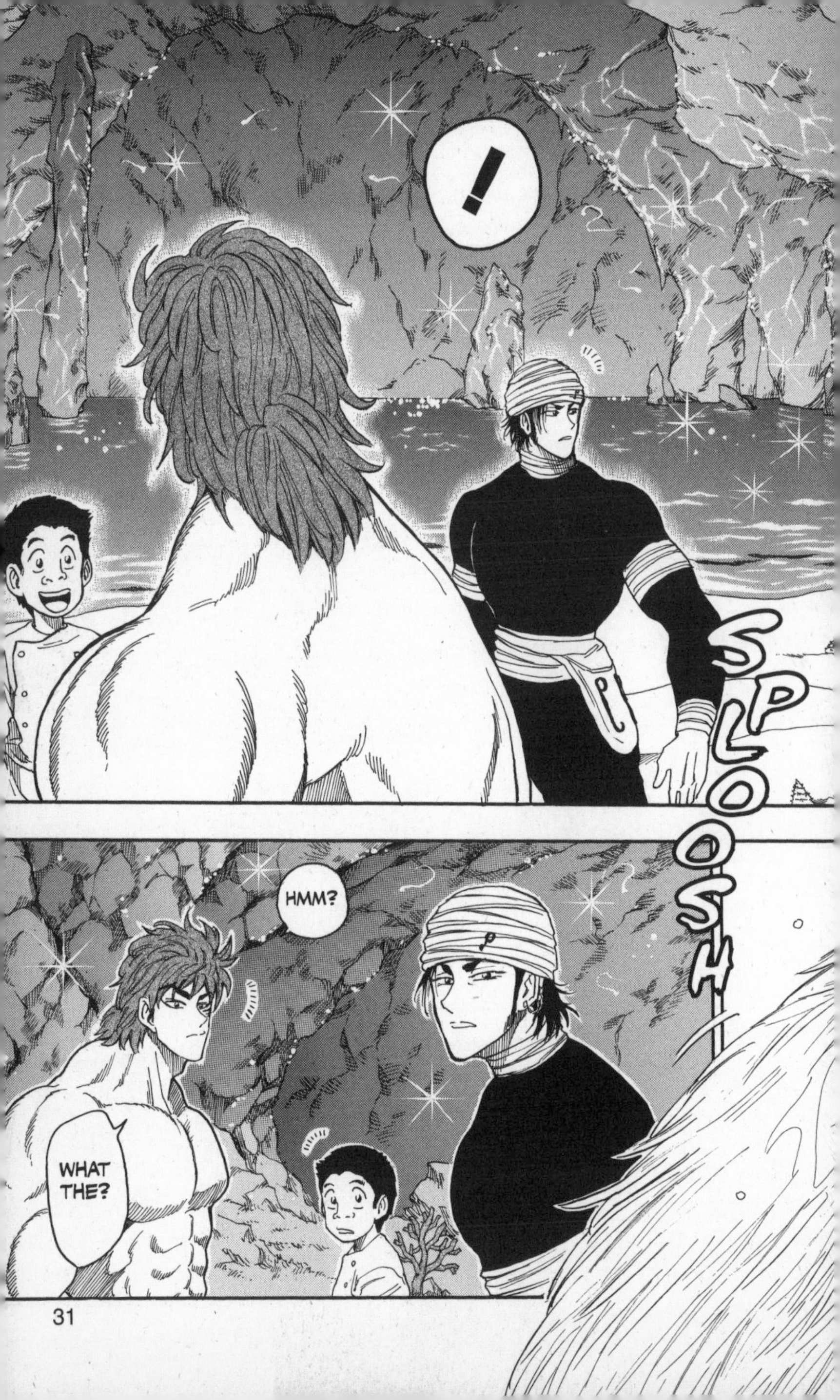
!
SPLOOSH
HMM?
WHAT THE?

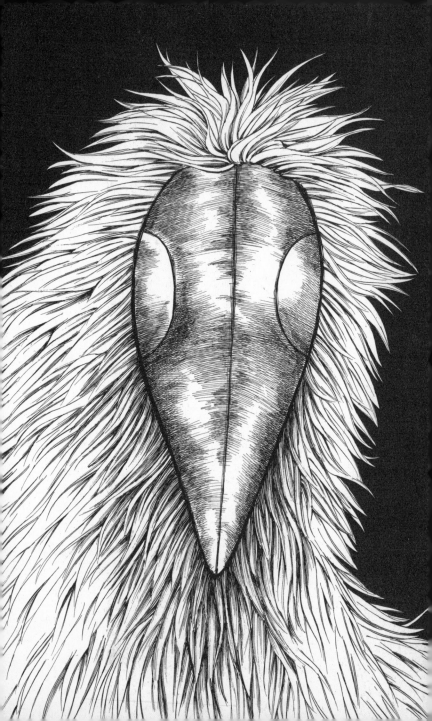

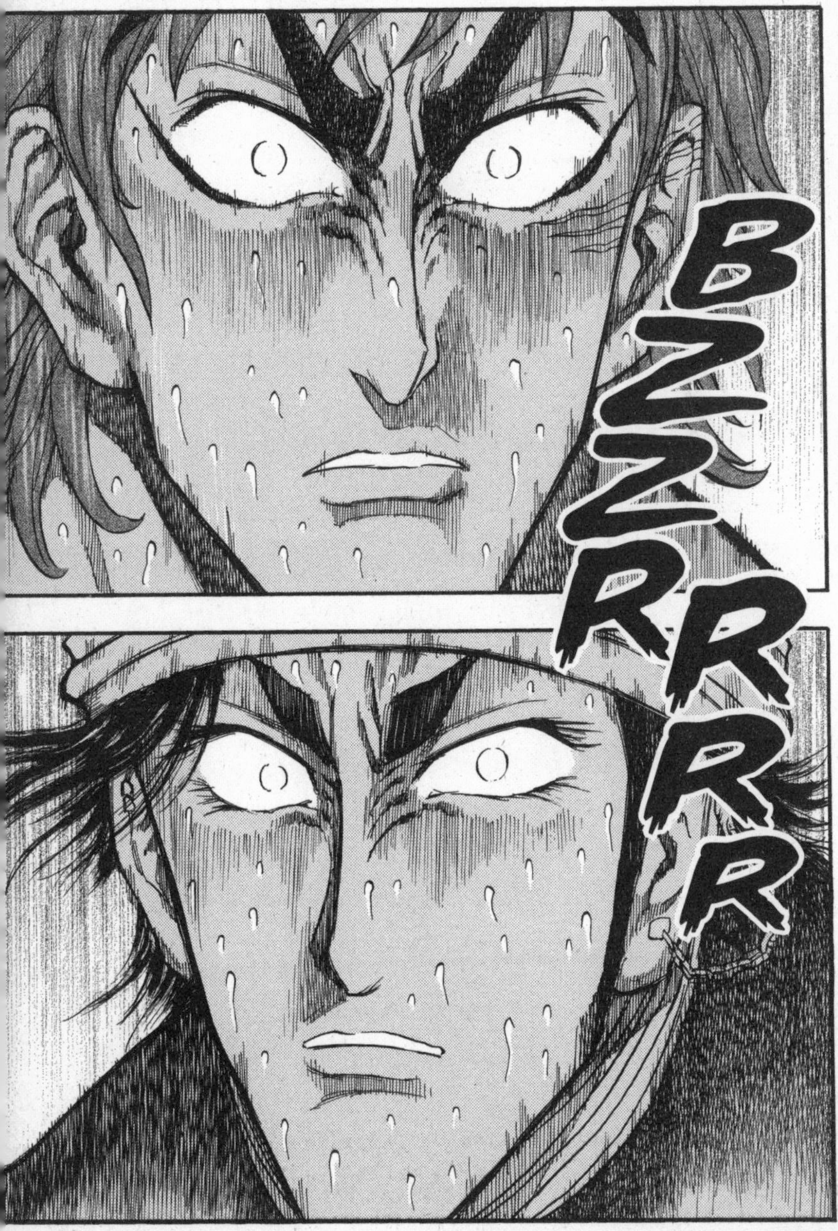
BZZRRRR

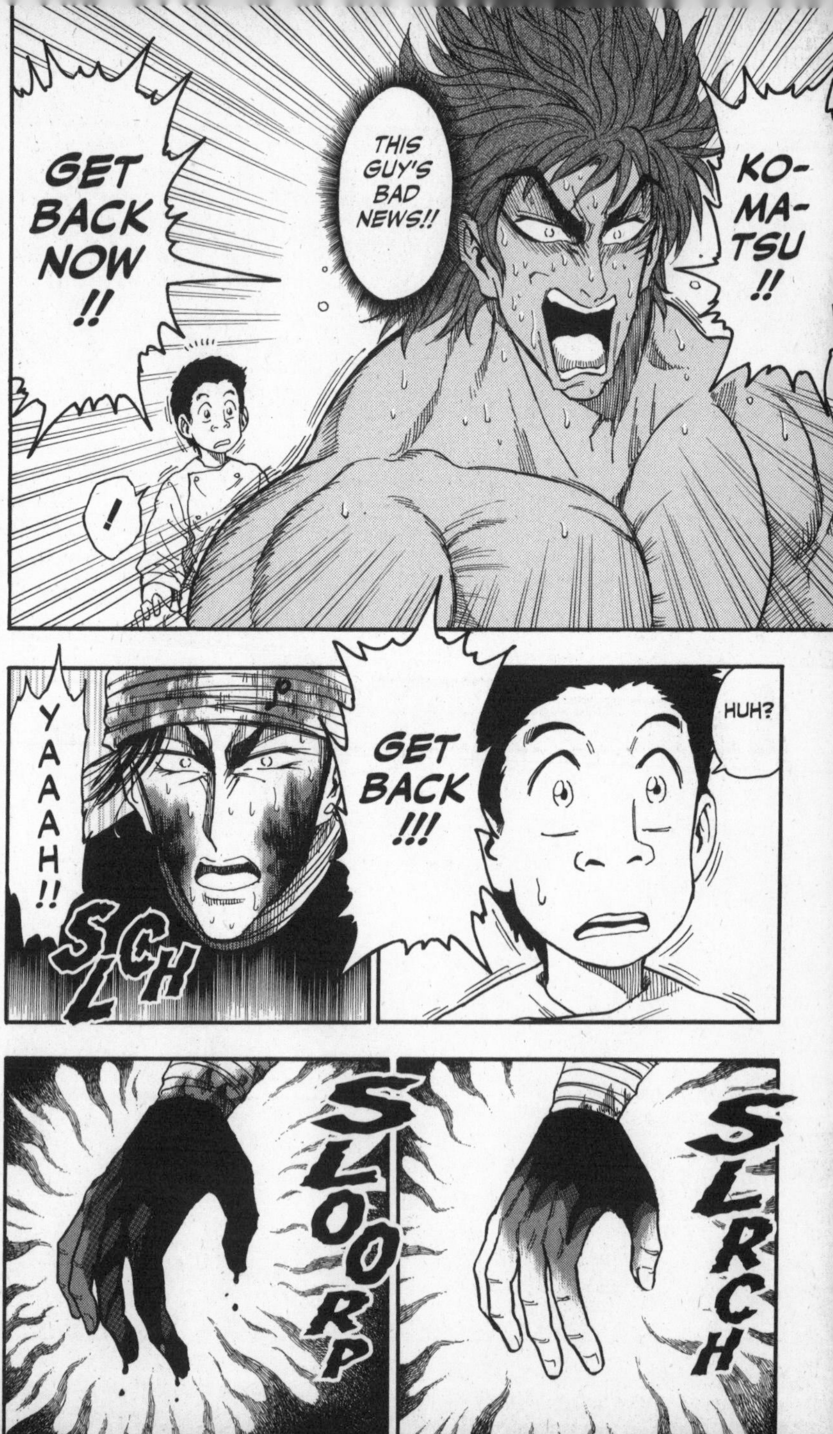
KO-MA-TSU!!
THIS GUY'S BAD NEWS!!
GET BACK NOW!!
!
HUH?
GET BACK!!!
YAAAAH!!
SCHLL
SLRCH
SLOORP

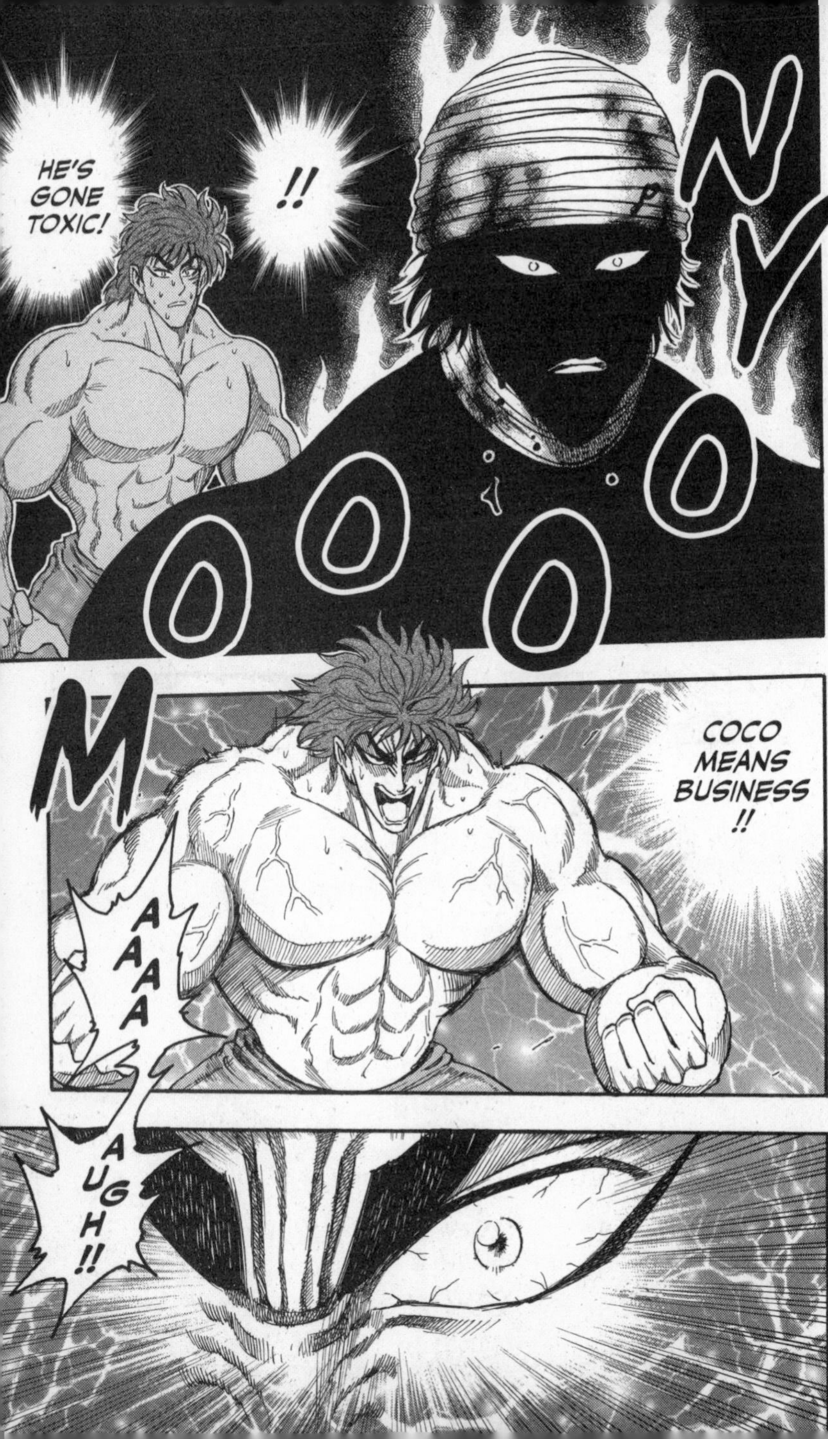
!!
HE'S GONE TOXIC!
NYOOOOM
COCO MEANS BUSINESS!!
AAAA
AUGH!!

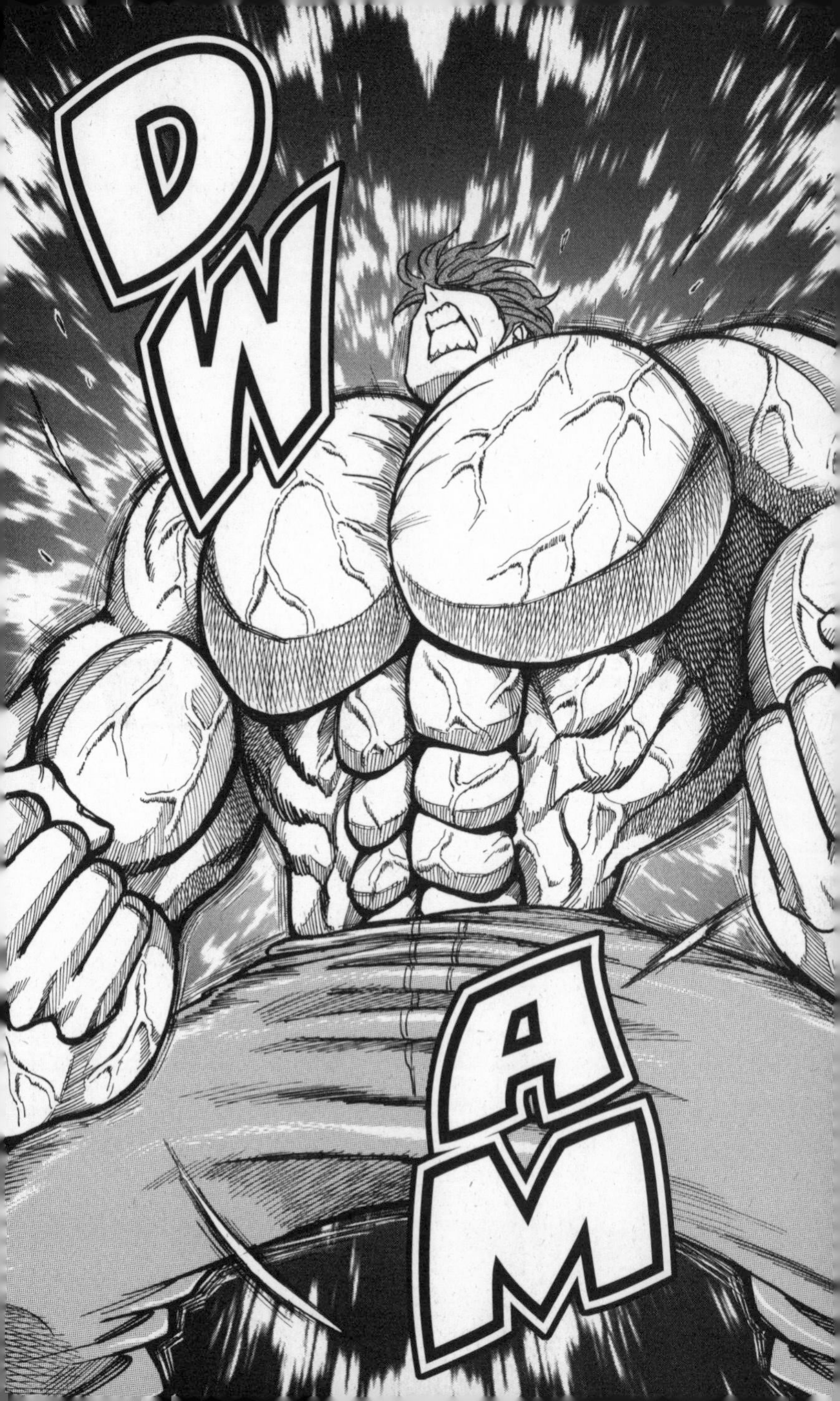
DWAM

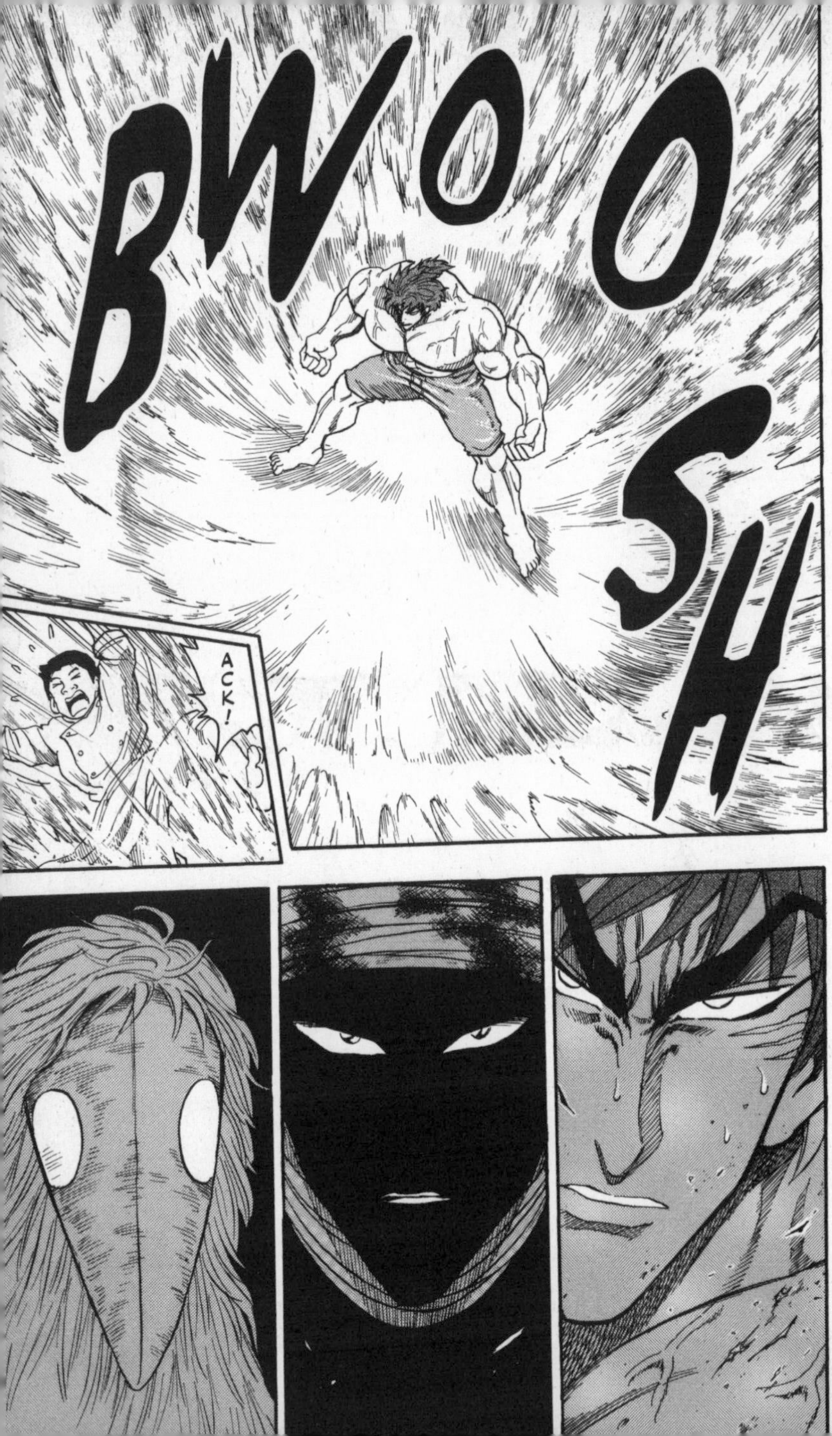
BWOOSH
ACK!

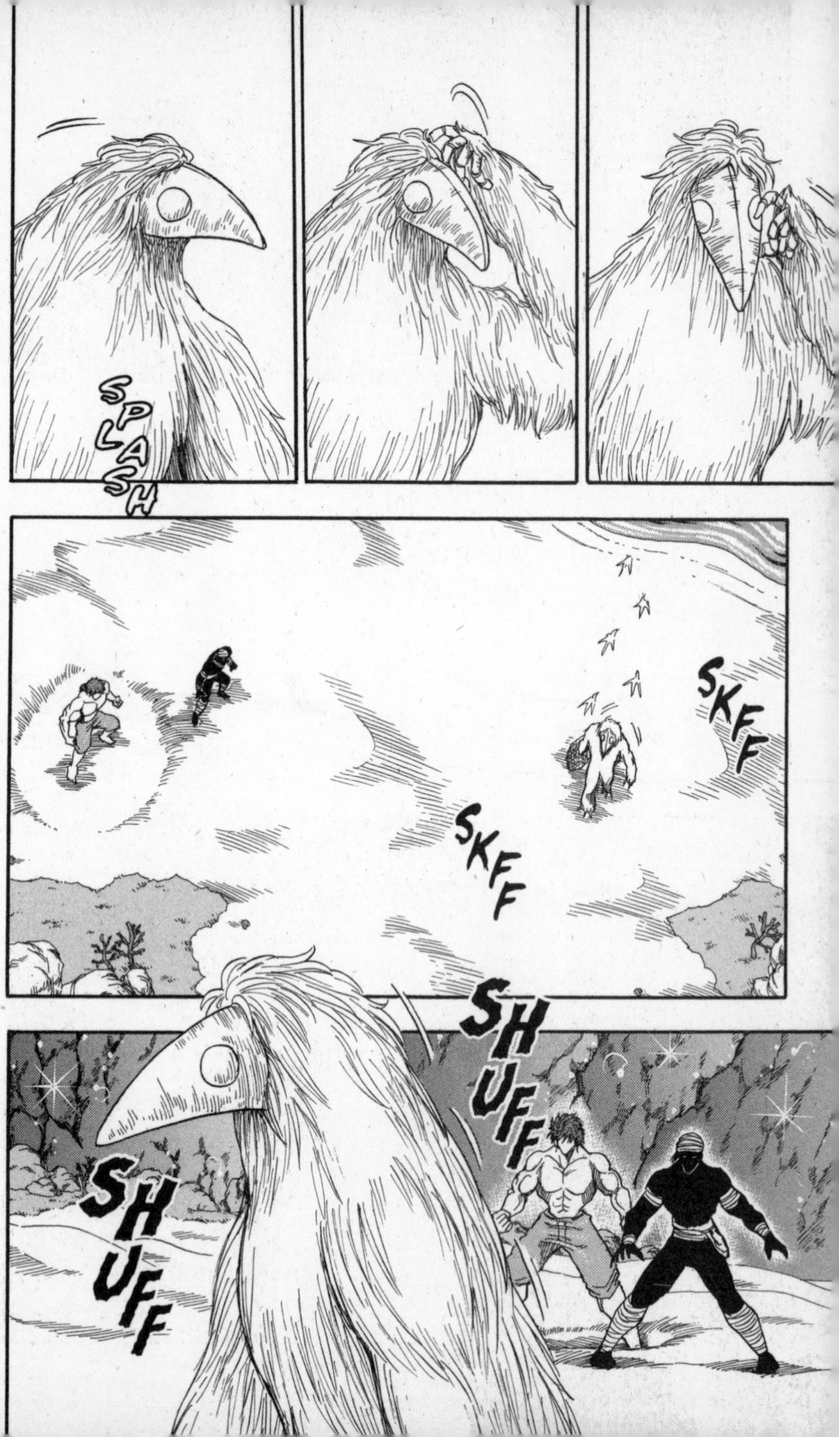
SPLASH
SKFF
SKFF
SHUFF
SHUFF

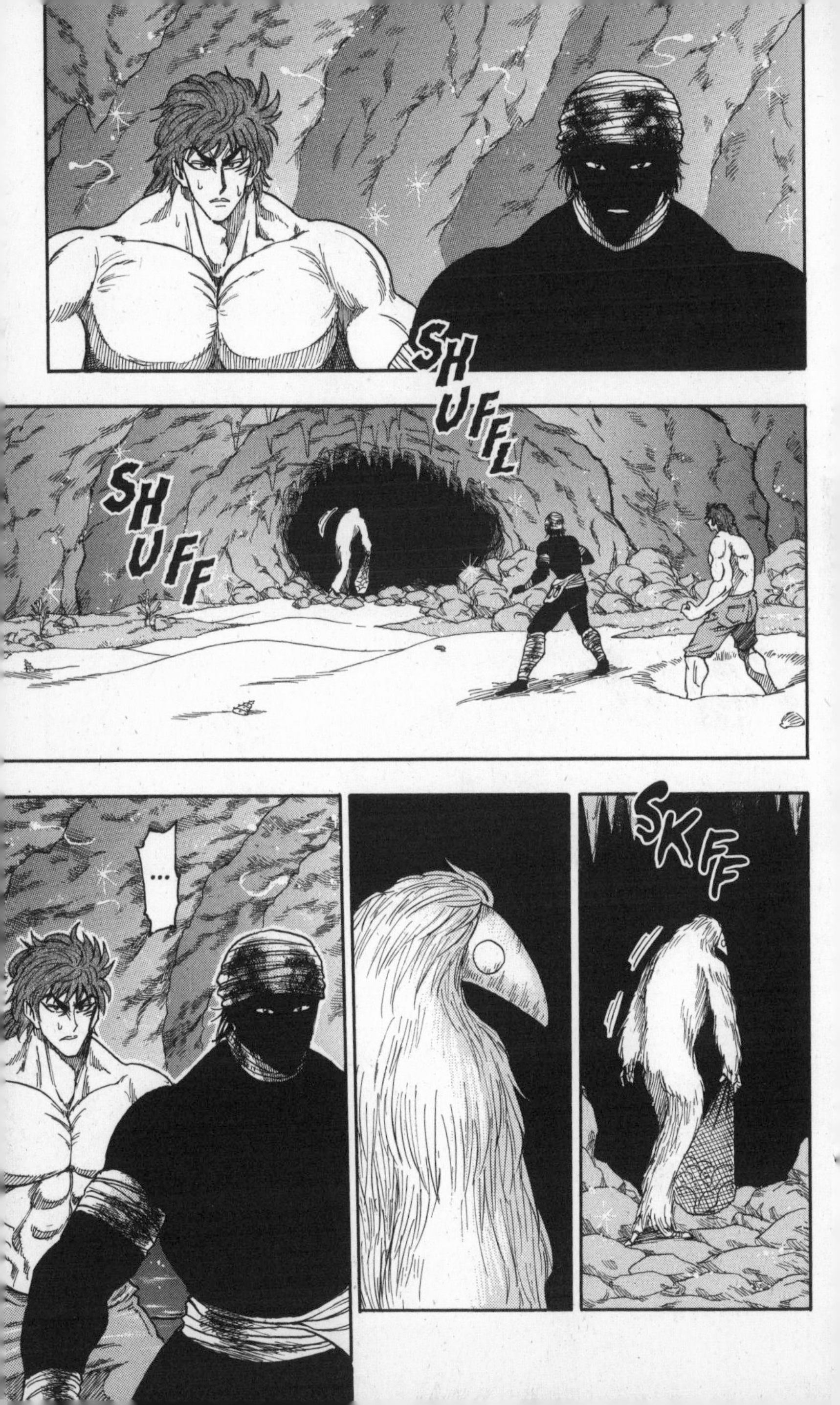
SHUFFL
SHUFF
...
SKFF

SSST

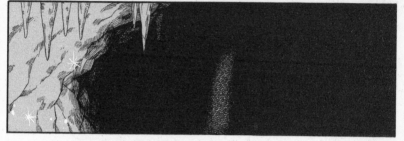

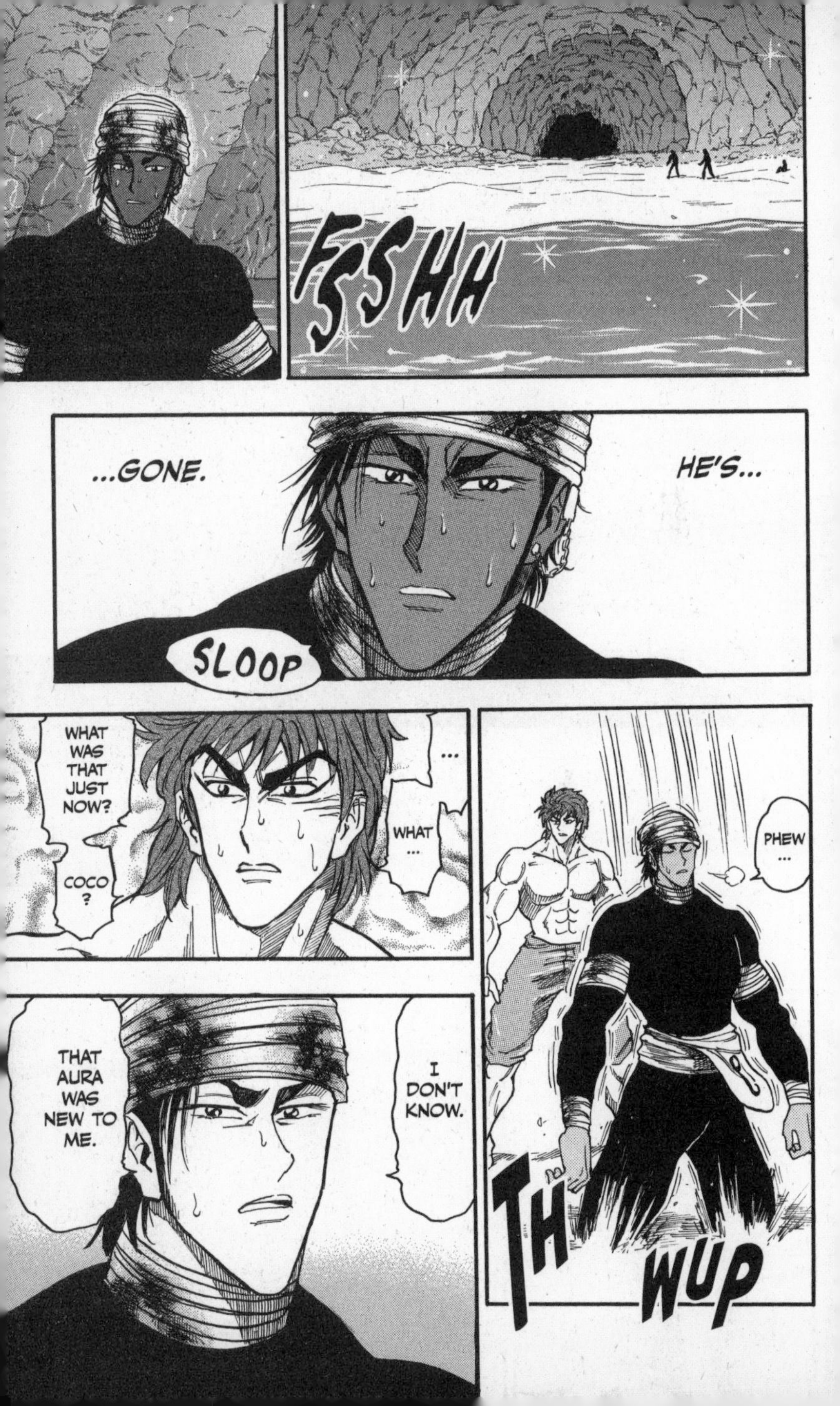
FSSHH
HE'S...
...GONE.
SLOOP
PHEW ...
THWUP
...
WHAT ...
WHAT WAS THAT JUST NOW?
COCO?
I DON'T KNOW.
THAT AURA WAS NEW TO ME.

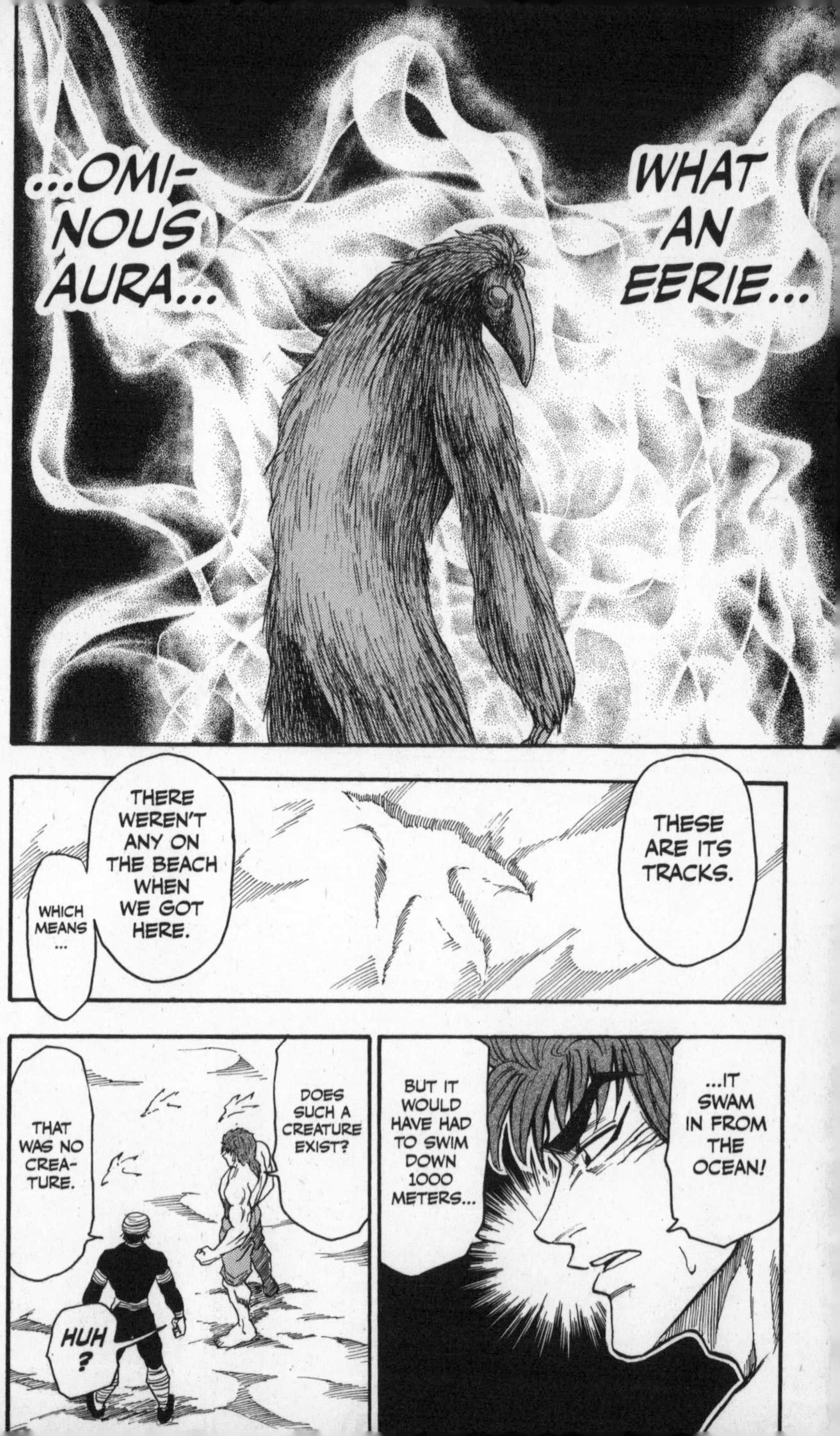
WHAT AN EERIE...
...OMI-NOUS AURA...
THESE ARE ITS TRACKS.
THERE WEREN'T ANY ON THE BEACH WHEN WE GOT HERE.
WHICH MEANS ...
...IT SWAM IN FROM THE OCEAN!
BUT IT WOULD HAVE HAD TO SWIM DOWN 1000 METERS...
DOES SUCH A CREATURE EXIST?
THAT WAS NO CREA-TURE.
HUH?

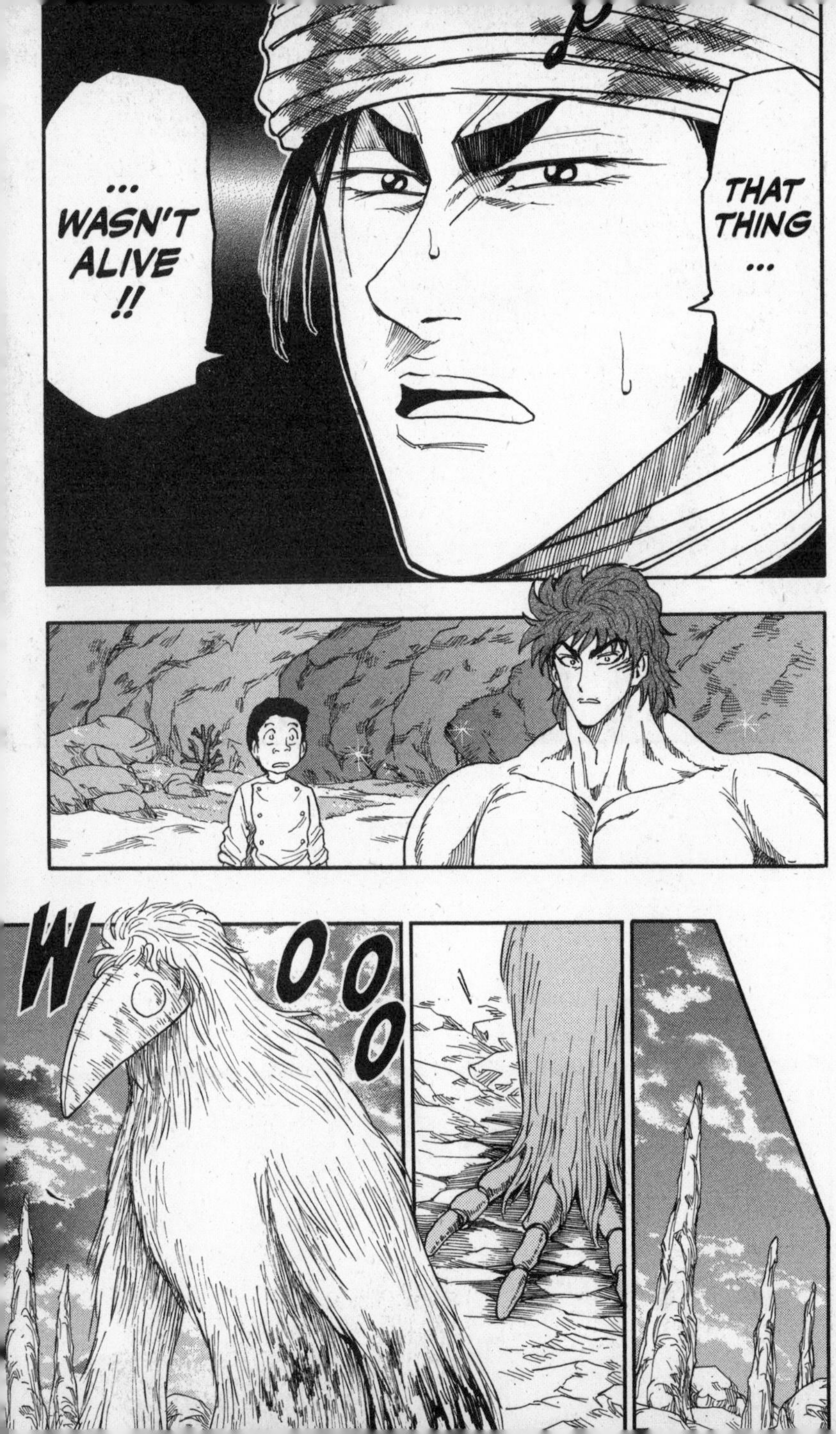
THAT THING ...
... WASN'T ALIVE !!
WOOO

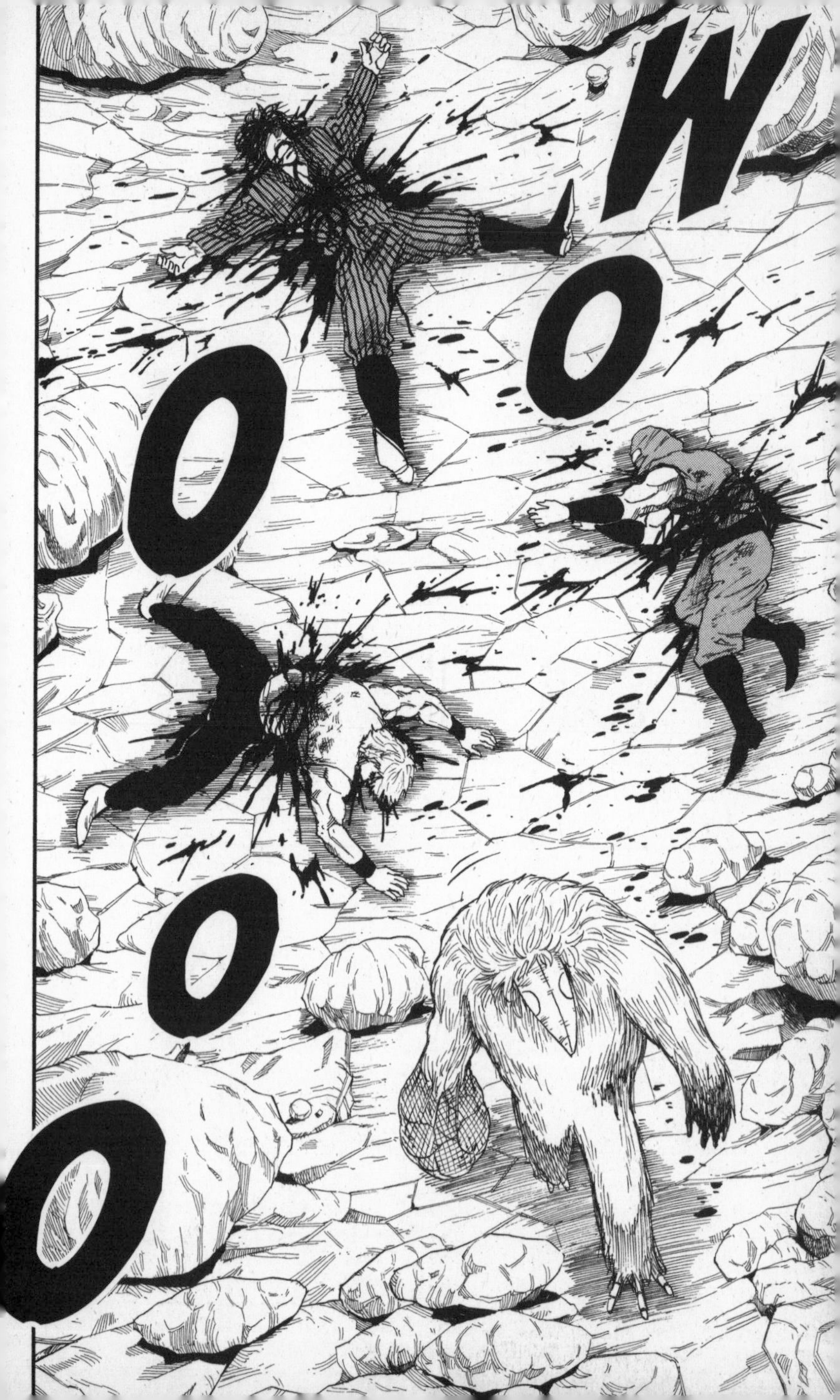
WOOOO

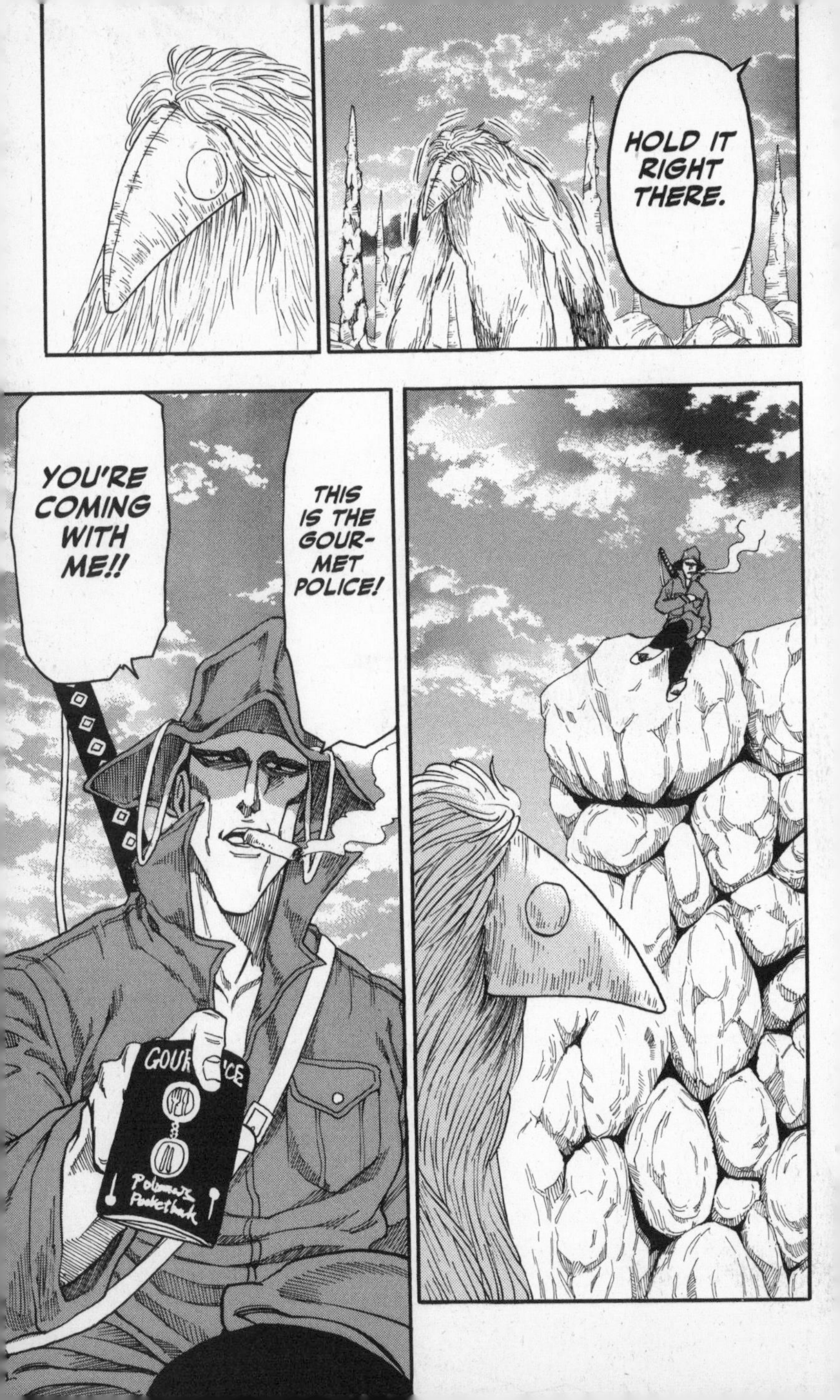
HOLD IT RIGHT THERE.
THIS IS THE GOUR-MET POLICE!
YOU'RE COMING WITH ME!!

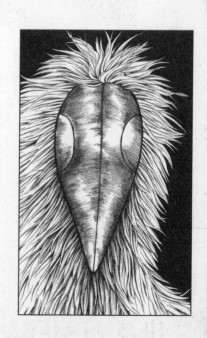

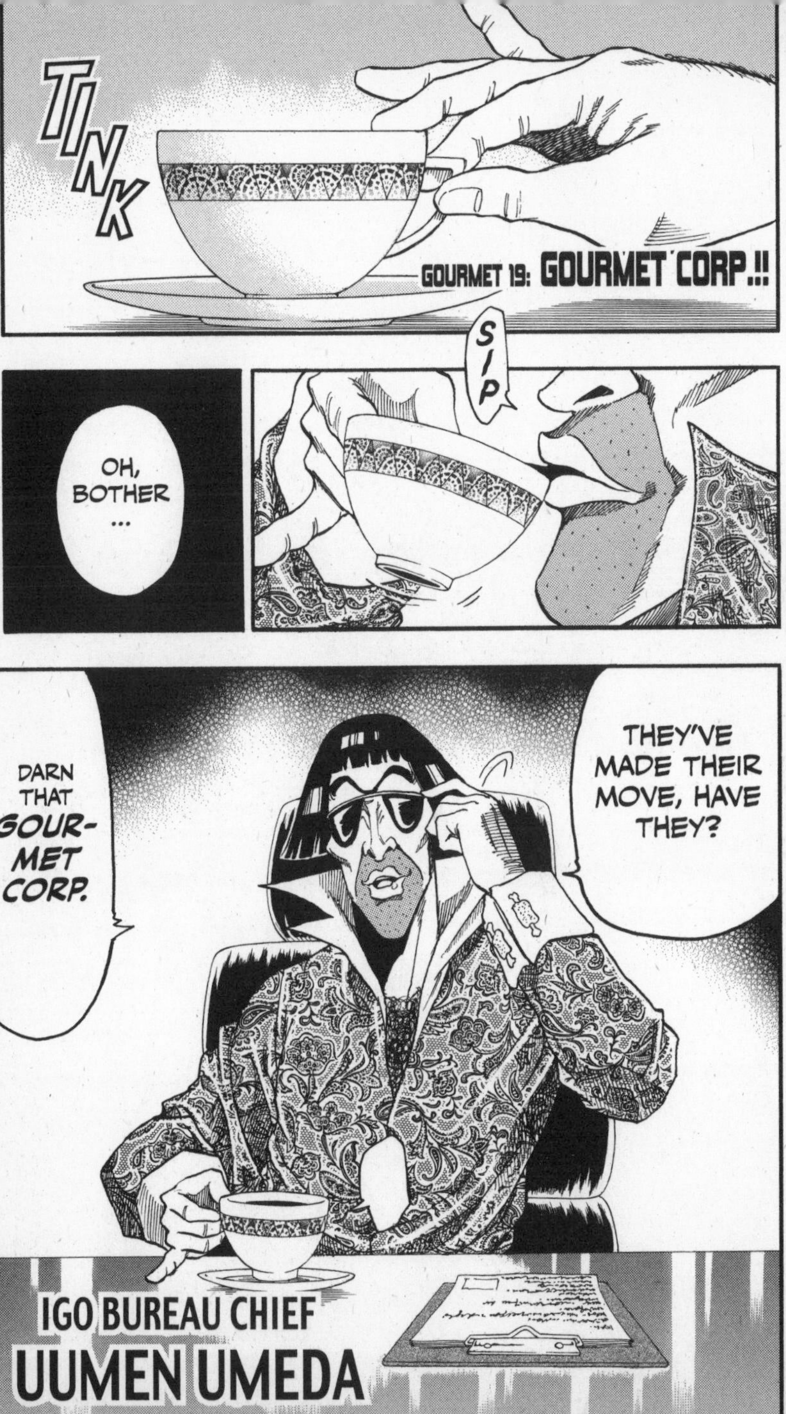
TINK
GOURMET 19: GOURMET CORP.!!
SIP
OH, BOTHER ...
THEY'VE MADE THEIR MOVE, HAVE THEY?
DARN THAT GOUR-MET CORP.
IGO BUREAU CHIEF
UUMEN UMEDA

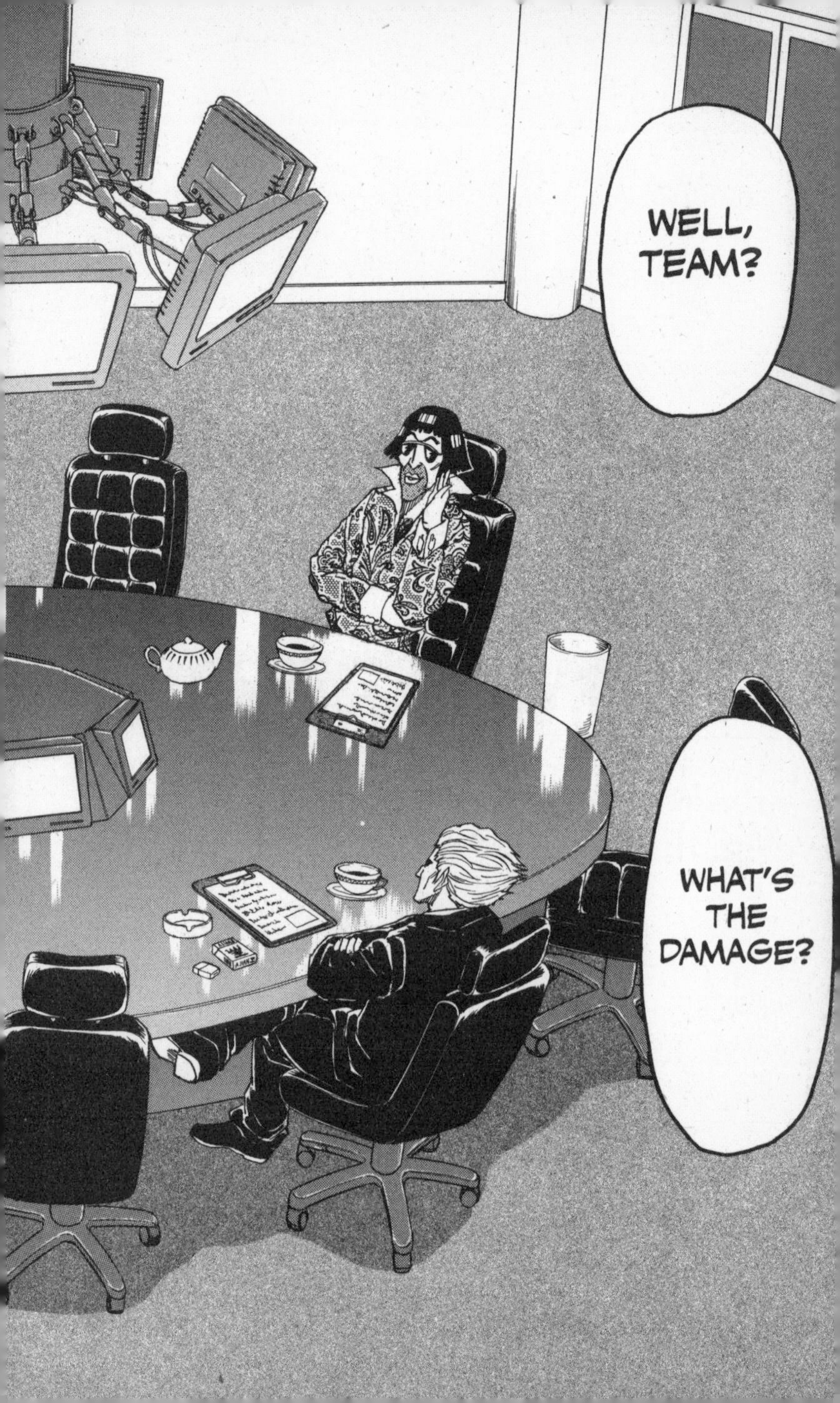
WELL, TEAM?
WHAT'S THE DAMAGE?

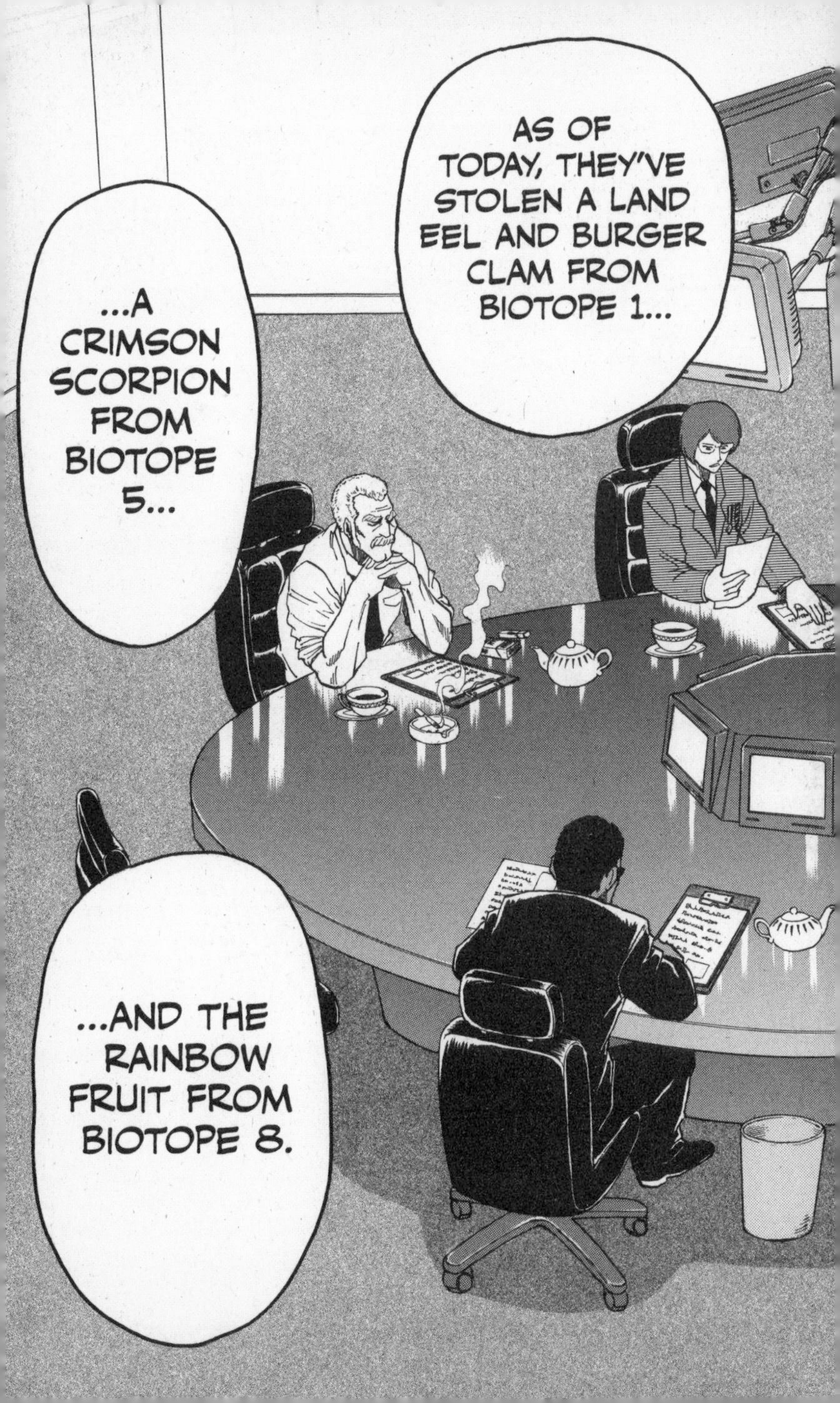
AS OF TODAY, THEY'VE STOLEN A LAND EEL AND BURGER CLAM FROM BIOTOPE 1...
...A CRIMSON SCORPION FROM BIOTOPE 5...
...AND THE RAINBOW FRUIT FROM BIOTOPE 8.

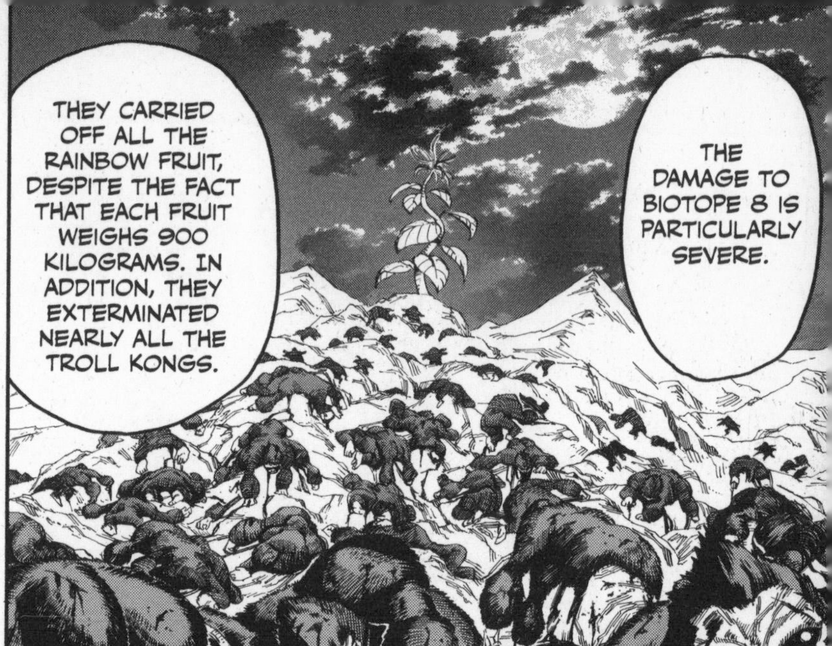
THE DAMAGE TO BIOTOPE 8 IS PARTICULARLY SEVERE.
THEY CARRIED OFF ALL THE RAINBOW FRUIT, DESPITE THE FACT THAT EACH FRUIT WEIGHS 900 KILOGRAMS. IN ADDITION, THEY EXTERMINATED NEARLY ALL THE TROLL KONGS.
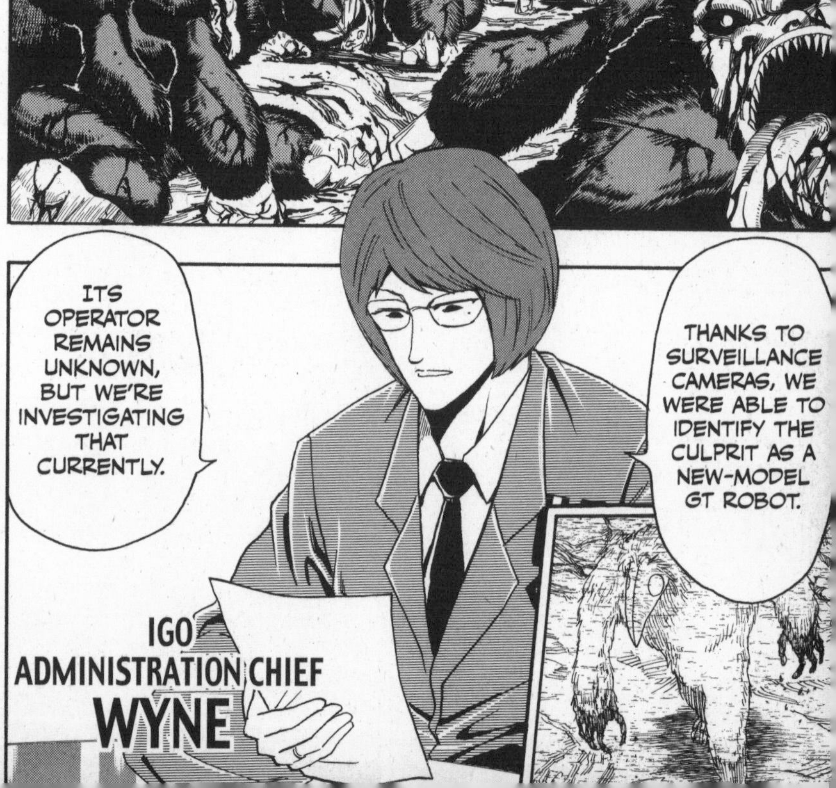
THANKS TO SURVEILLANCE CAMERAS, WE WERE ABLE TO IDENTIFY THE CULPRIT AS A NEW-MODEL GT ROBOT.
ITS OPERATOR REMAINS UNKNOWN, BUT WE'RE INVESTIGATING THAT CURRENTLY.
IGO ADMINISTRATION CHIEF WYNE

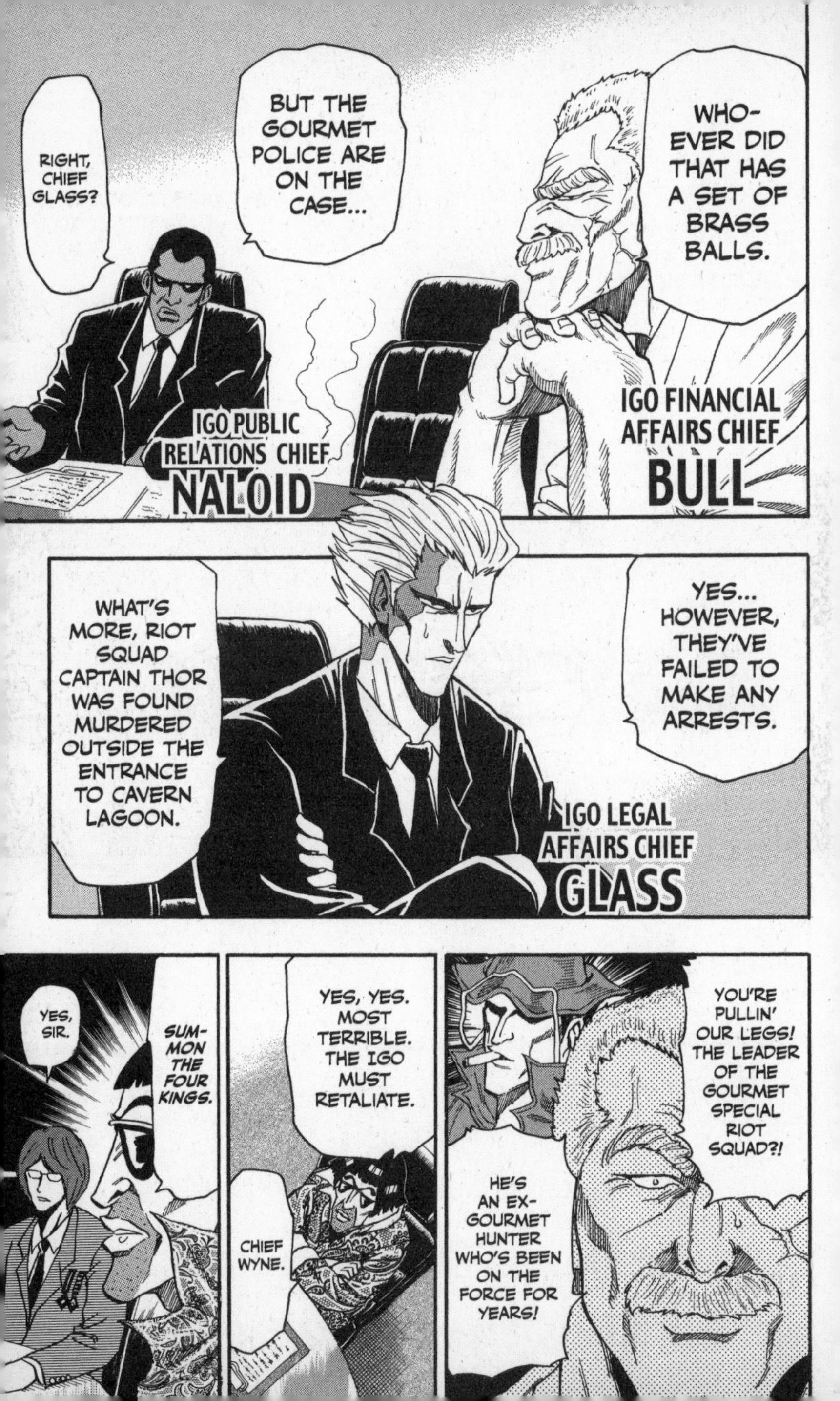
WHO-EVER DID THAT HAS A SET OF BRASS BALLS.
IGO FINANCIAL AFFAIRS CHIEF
BULL
BUT THE GOURMET POLICE ARE ON THE CASE...
RIGHT, CHIEF GLASS?
IGO PUBLIC RELATIONS CHIEF
NALOID
YES... HOWEVER, THEY'VE FAILED TO MAKE ANY ARRESTS.
WHAT'S MORE, RIOT SQUAD CAPTAIN THOR WAS FOUND MURDERED OUTSIDE THE ENTRANCE TO CAVERN LAGOON.
IGO LEGAL AFFAIRS CHIEF
GLASS
YOU'RE PULLIN' OUR LEGS! THE LEADER OF THE GOURMET SPECIAL RIOT SQUAD?!
HE'S AN EX-GOURMET HUNTER WHO'S BEEN ON THE FORCE FOR YEARS!
YES, YES. MOST TERRIBLE. THE IGO MUST RETALIATE.
CHIEF WYNE.
SUM-MON THE FOUR KINGS.
YES, SIR.

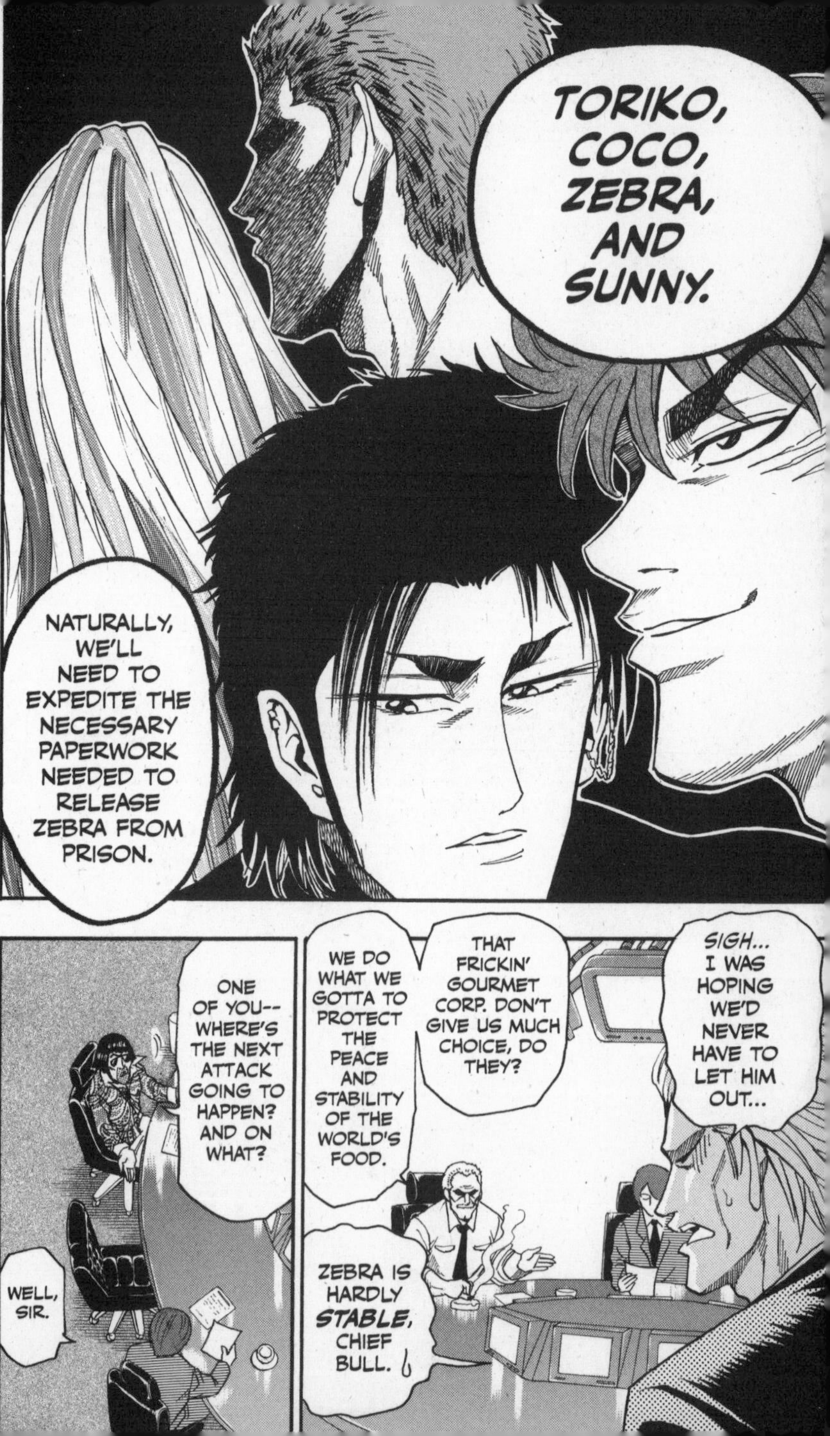
TORIKO, COCO, ZEBRA, AND SUNNY.
NATURALLY, WE'LL NEED TO EXPEDITE THE NECESSARY PAPERWORK NEEDED TO RELEASE ZEBRA FROM PRISON.
SIGH... I WAS HOPING WE'D NEVER HAVE TO LET HIM OUT...
THAT FRICKIN' GOURMET CORP. DON'T GIVE US MUCH CHOICE, DO THEY?
WE DO WHAT WE GOTTA TO PROTECT THE PEACE AND STABILITY OF THE WORLD'S FOOD.
ZEBRA IS HARDLY *STABLE*, CHIEF BULL.
ONE OF YOU-- WHERE'S THE NEXT ATTACK GOING TO HAPPEN? AND ON WHAT?
WELL, SIR.

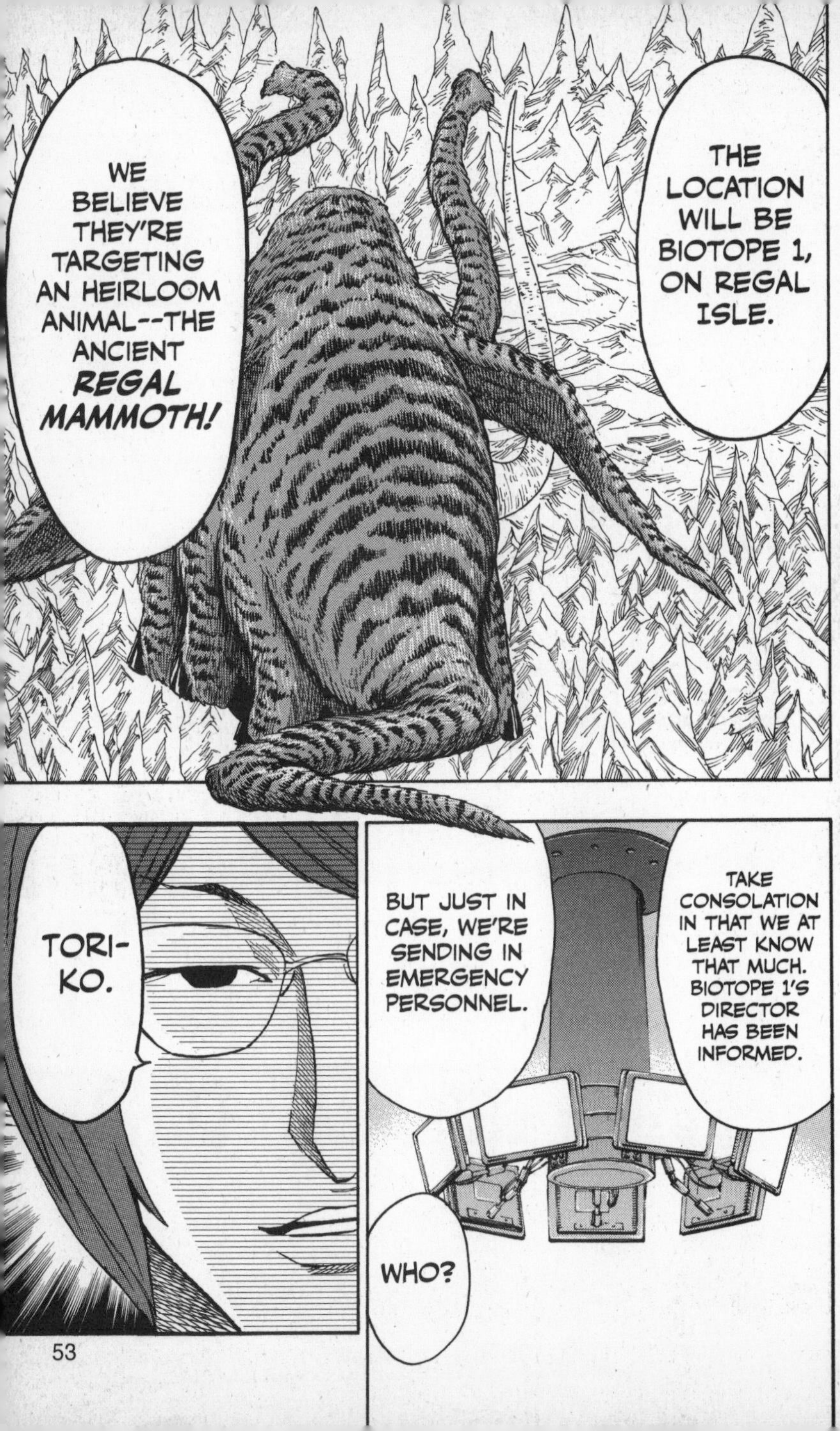
THE LOCATION WILL BE BIOTOPE 1, ON REGAL ISLE.
WE BELIEVE THEY'RE TARGETING AN HEIRLOOM ANIMAL--THE ANCIENT ***REGAL MAMMOTH!***
TAKE CONSOLATION IN THAT WE AT LEAST KNOW THAT MUCH. BIOTOPE 1'S DIRECTOR HAS BEEN INFORMED.
BUT JUST IN CASE, WE'RE SENDING IN EMERGENCY PERSONNEL.
WHO?
TORI-KO.

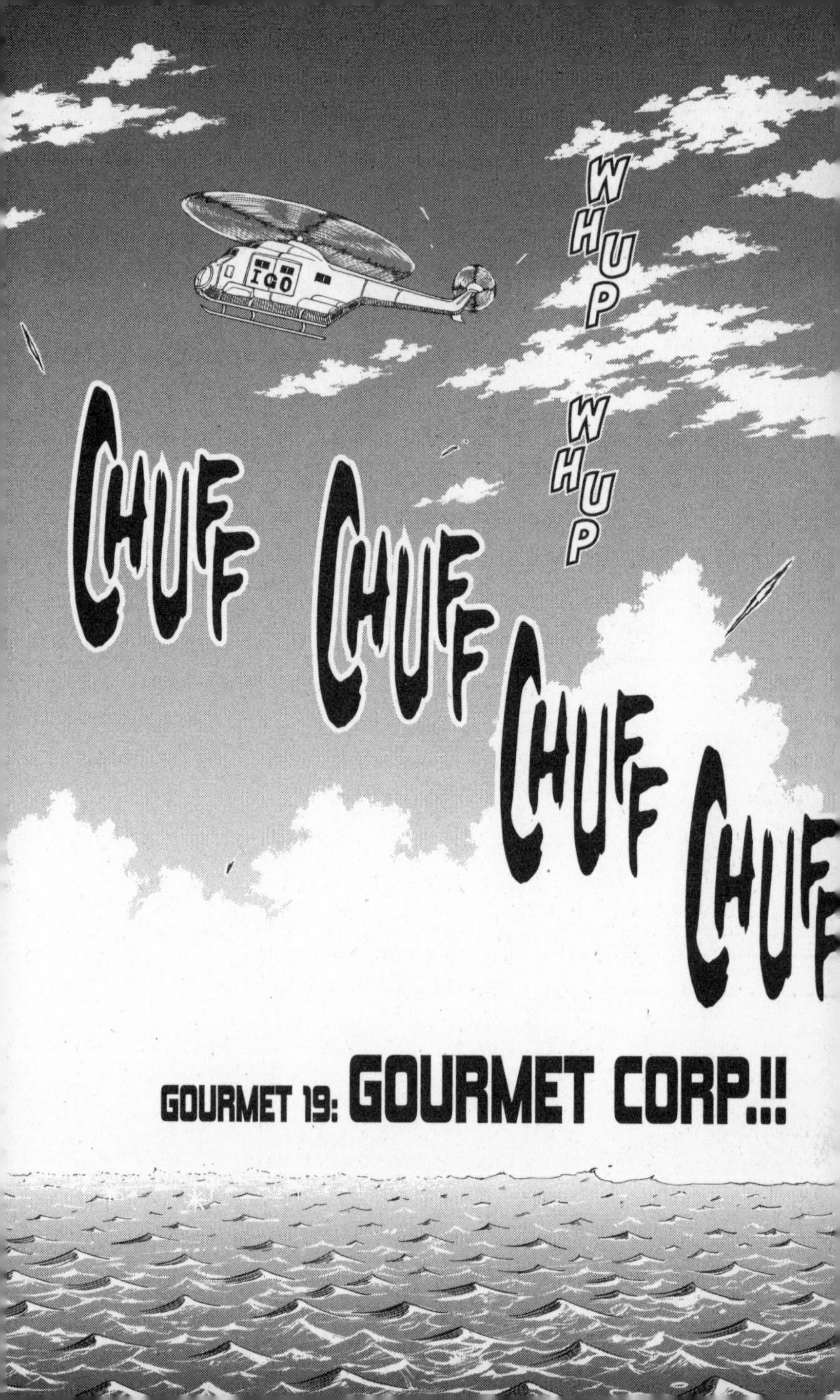
IGO
WHUP WHUP
CHUFF CHUFF CHUFF CHUFF
GOURMET 19: GOURMET CORP.!!

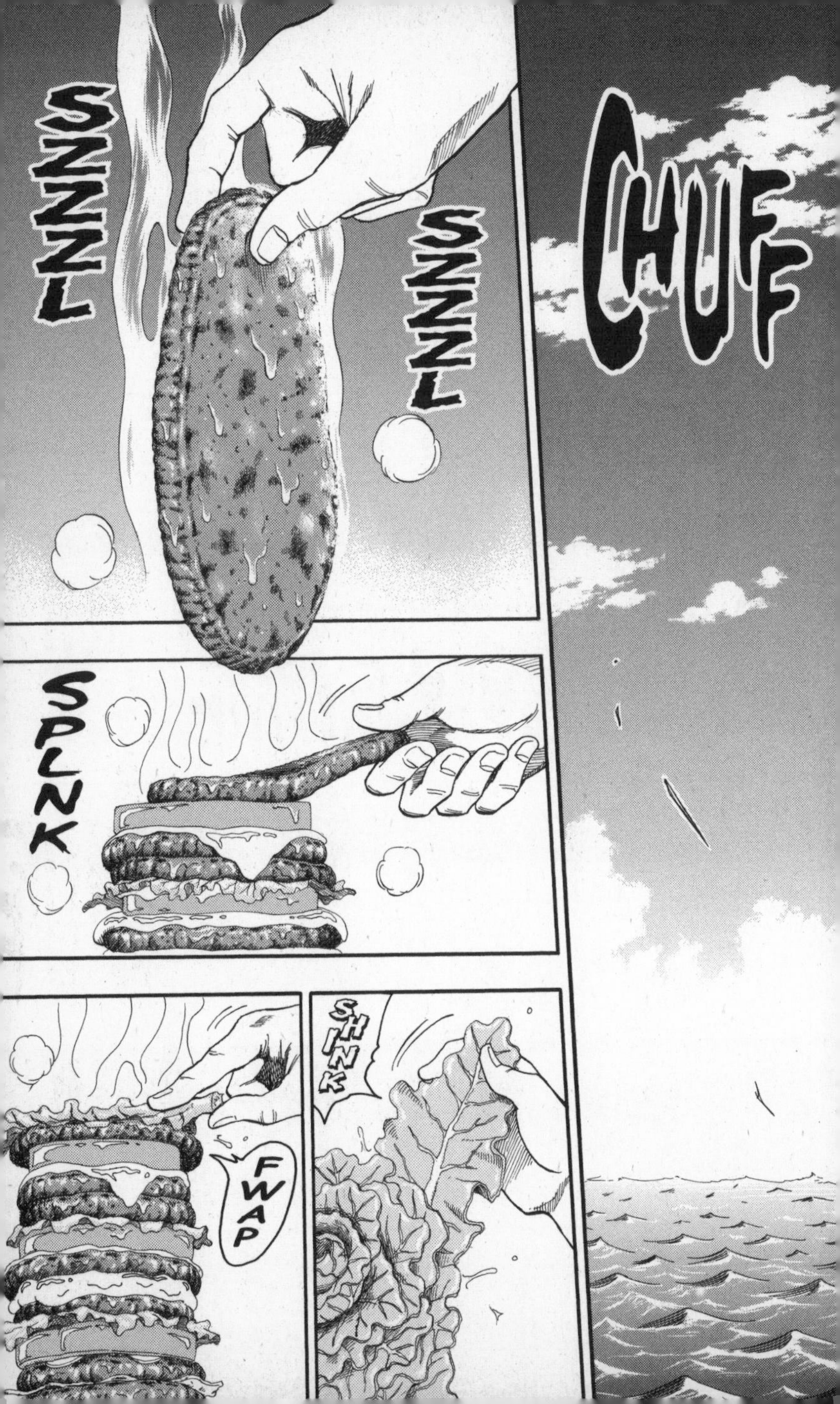
CHUF
SNZZL
SNZZL
SPLNK
SHINK
FWAP

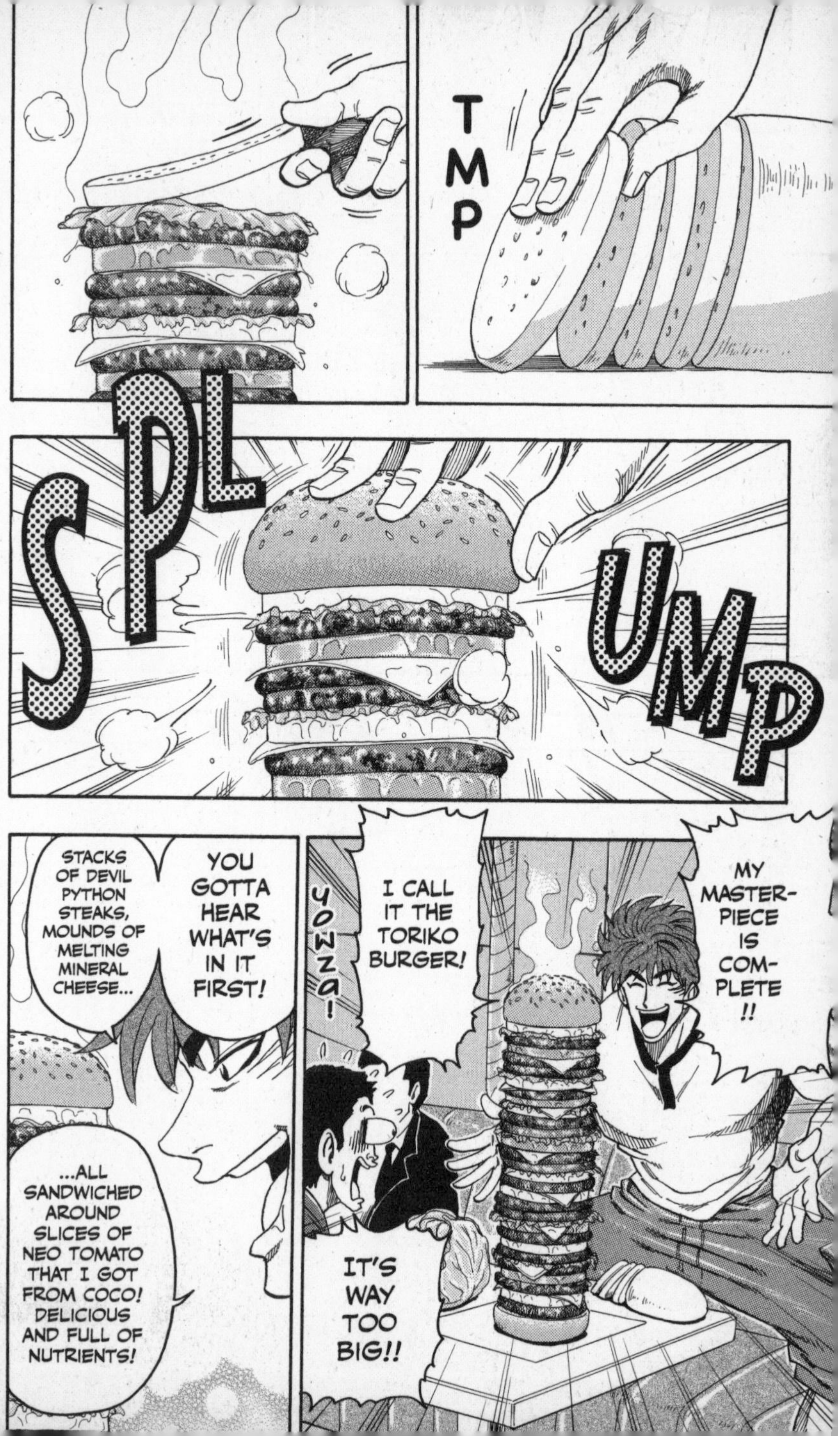
TMP
SPLUMP
MY MASTER-PIECE IS COM-PLETE!!
I CALL IT THE TORIKO BURGER!
YOWZA!
IT'S WAY TOO BIG!!
YOU GOTTA HEAR WHAT'S IN IT FIRST!
STACKS OF DEVIL PYTHON STEAKS, MOUNDS OF MELTING MINERAL CHEESE...
...ALL SANDWICHED AROUND SLICES OF NEO TOMATO THAT I GOT FROM COCO! DELICIOUS AND FULL OF NUTRIENTS!

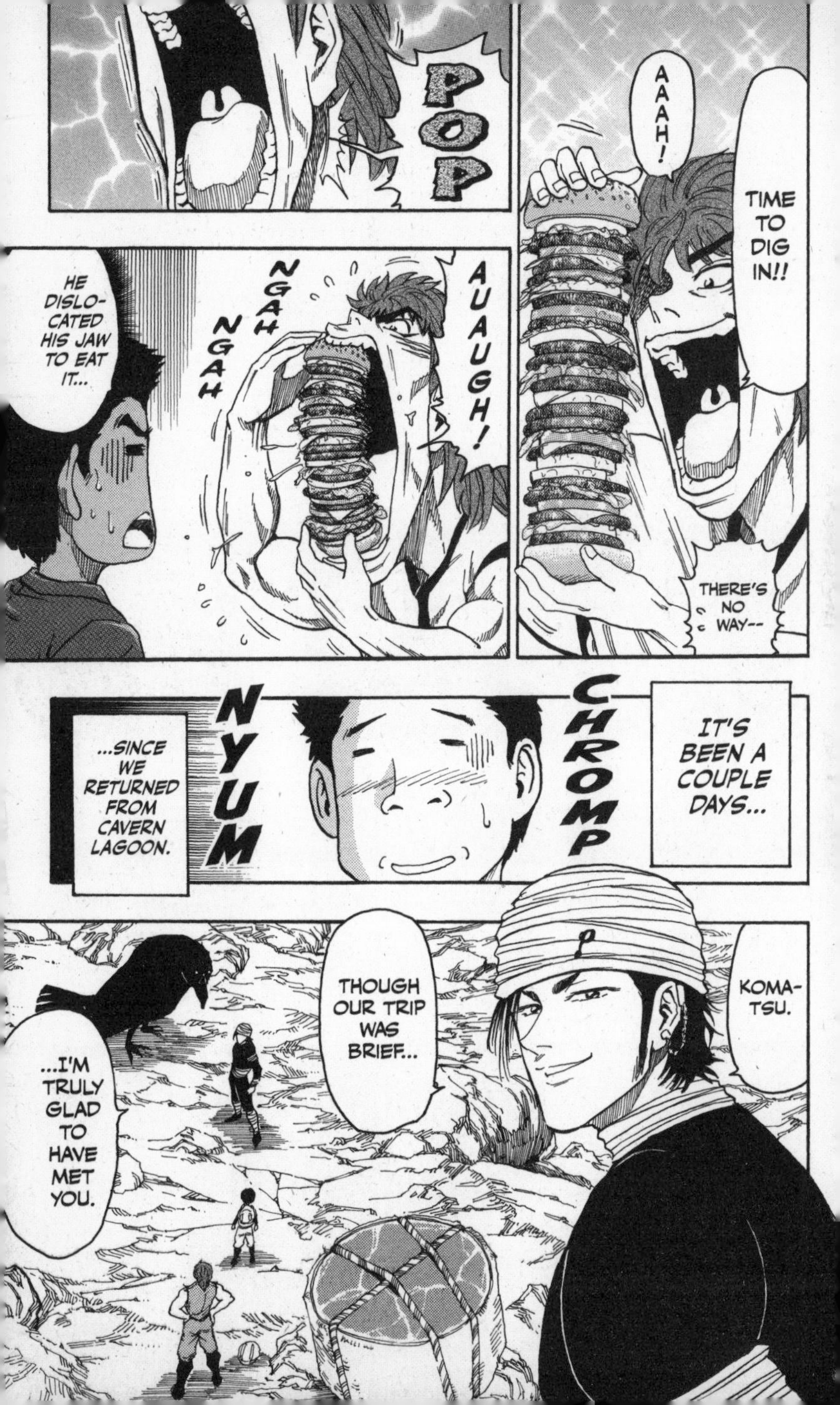
AAAH!
TIME TO DIG IN!!
THERE'S NO WAY--
POP
AUAUGH!
NGAH NGAH NGAH
HE DISLOCATED HIS JAW TO EAT IT...
IT'S BEEN A COUPLE DAYS...
CHROMP
NYUM
...SINCE WE RETURNED FROM CAVERN LAGOON.
KOMATSU.
THOUGH OUR TRIP WAS BRIEF...
...I'M TRULY GLAD TO HAVE MET YOU.

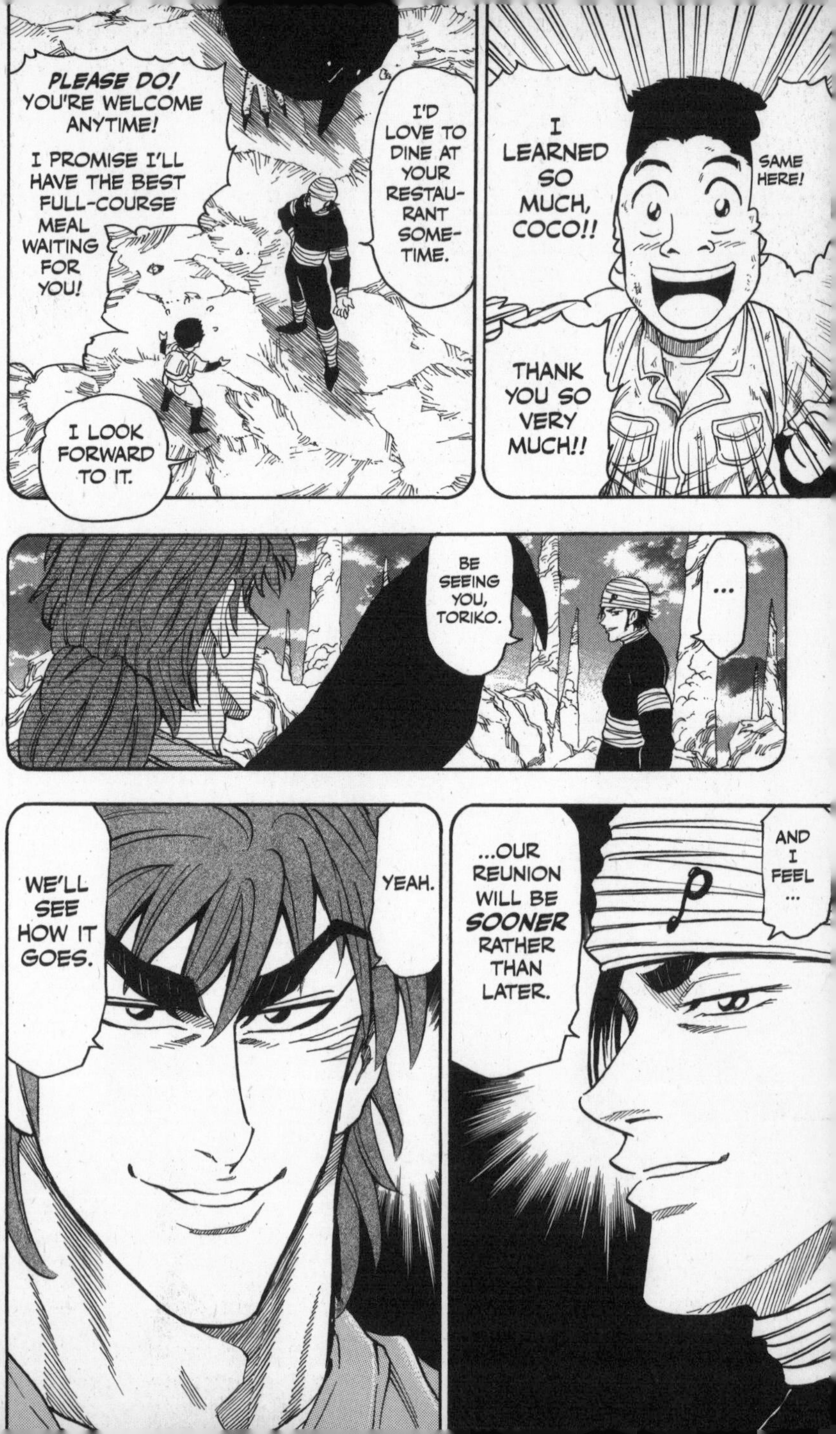
I LEARNED SO MUCH, COCO!!
SAME HERE!
THANK YOU SO VERY MUCH!!
I'D LOVE TO DINE AT YOUR RESTAURANT SOMETIME.
PLEASE DO! YOU'RE WELCOME ANYTIME!
I PROMISE I'LL HAVE THE BEST FULL-COURSE MEAL WAITING FOR YOU!
I LOOK FORWARD TO IT.
...
BE SEEING YOU, TORIKO.
AND I FEEL...
...OUR REUNION WILL BE SOONER RATHER THAN LATER.
YEAH.
WE'LL SEE HOW IT GOES.

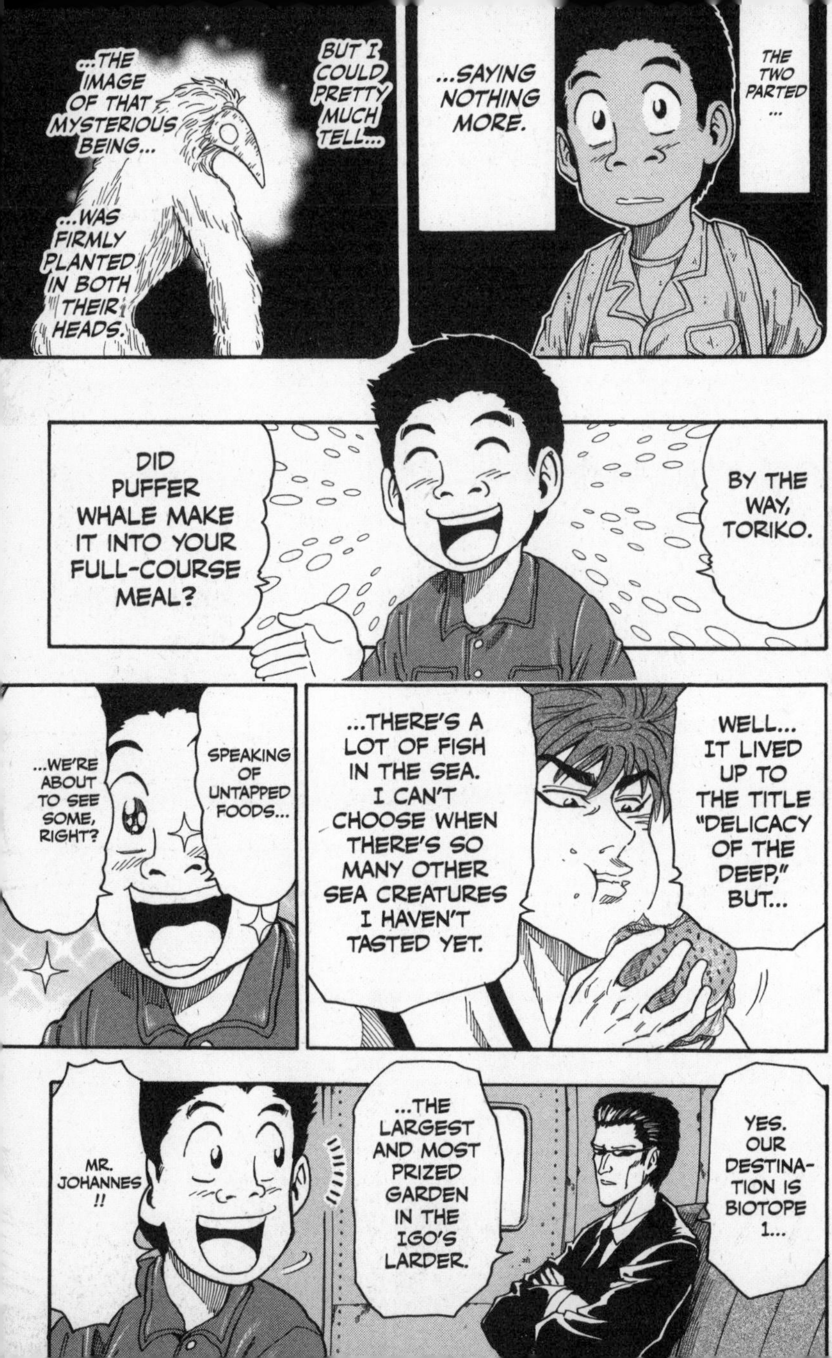
THE TWO PARTED...
...SAYING NOTHING MORE.
BUT I COULD PRETTY MUCH TELL...
...THE IMAGE OF THAT MYSTERIOUS BEING...
...WAS FIRMLY PLANTED IN BOTH THEIR HEADS.
BY THE WAY, TORIKO.
DID PUFFER WHALE MAKE IT INTO YOUR FULL-COURSE MEAL?
WELL... IT LIVED UP TO THE TITLE "DELICACY OF THE DEEP," BUT...
...THERE'S A LOT OF FISH IN THE SEA. I CAN'T CHOOSE WHEN THERE'S SO MANY OTHER SEA CREATURES I HAVEN'T TASTED YET.
SPEAKING OF UNTAPPED FOODS...
...WE'RE ABOUT TO SEE SOME, RIGHT?
YES. OUR DESTINATION IS BIOTOPE 1...
...THE LARGEST AND MOST PRIZED GARDEN IN THE IGO'S LARDER.
MR. JOHANNES !!

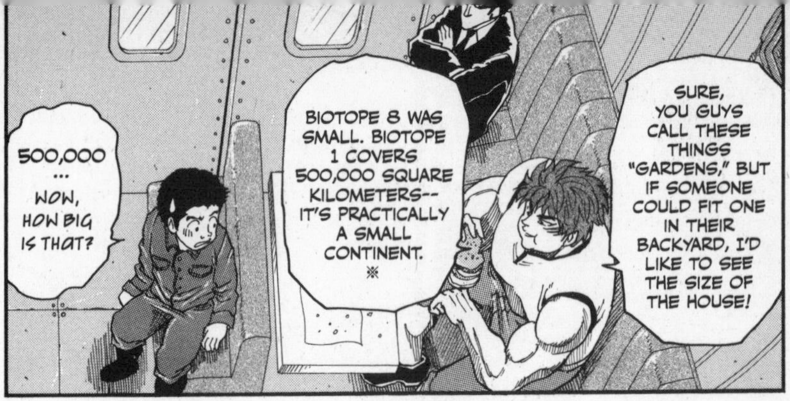
SURE, YOU GUYS CALL THESE THINGS "GARDENS," BUT IF SOMEONE COULD FIT ONE IN THEIR BACKYARD, I'D LIKE TO SEE THE SIZE OF THE HOUSE!
BIOTOPE 8 WAS SMALL. BIOTOPE 1 COVERS 500,000 SQUARE KILOMETERS-- IT'S PRACTICALLY A SMALL CONTINENT. ※
500,000 ... WOW, HOW BIG IS THAT?

※ A LITTLE SMALLER THAN THE STATE OF TEXAS

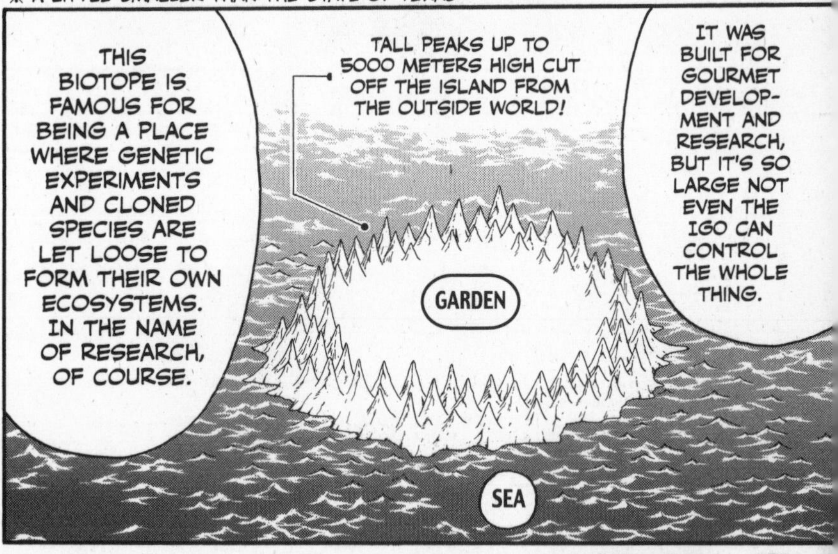
IT WAS BUILT FOR GOURMET DEVELOPMENT AND RESEARCH, BUT IT'S SO LARGE NOT EVEN THE IGO CAN CONTROL THE WHOLE THING.
TALL PEAKS UP TO 5000 METERS HIGH CUT OFF THE ISLAND FROM THE OUTSIDE WORLD!
GARDEN
SEA
THIS BIOTOPE IS FAMOUS FOR BEING A PLACE WHERE GENETIC EXPERIMENTS AND CLONED SPECIES ARE LET LOOSE TO FORM THEIR OWN ECOSYSTEMS. IN THE NAME OF RESEARCH, OF COURSE.

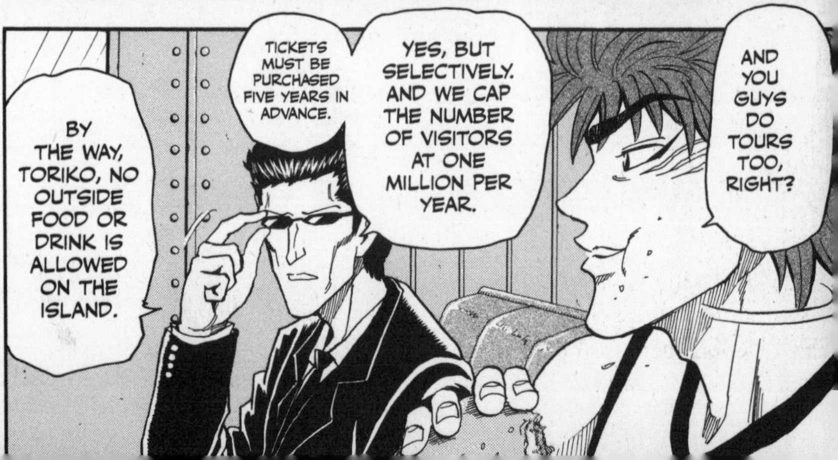
AND YOU GUYS DO TOURS TOO, RIGHT?
YES, BUT SELECTIVELY. AND WE CAP THE NUMBER OF VISITORS AT ONE MILLION PER YEAR.
TICKETS MUST BE PURCHASED FIVE YEARS IN ADVANCE.
BY THE WAY, TORIKO, NO OUTSIDE FOOD OR DRINK IS ALLOWED ON THE ISLAND.

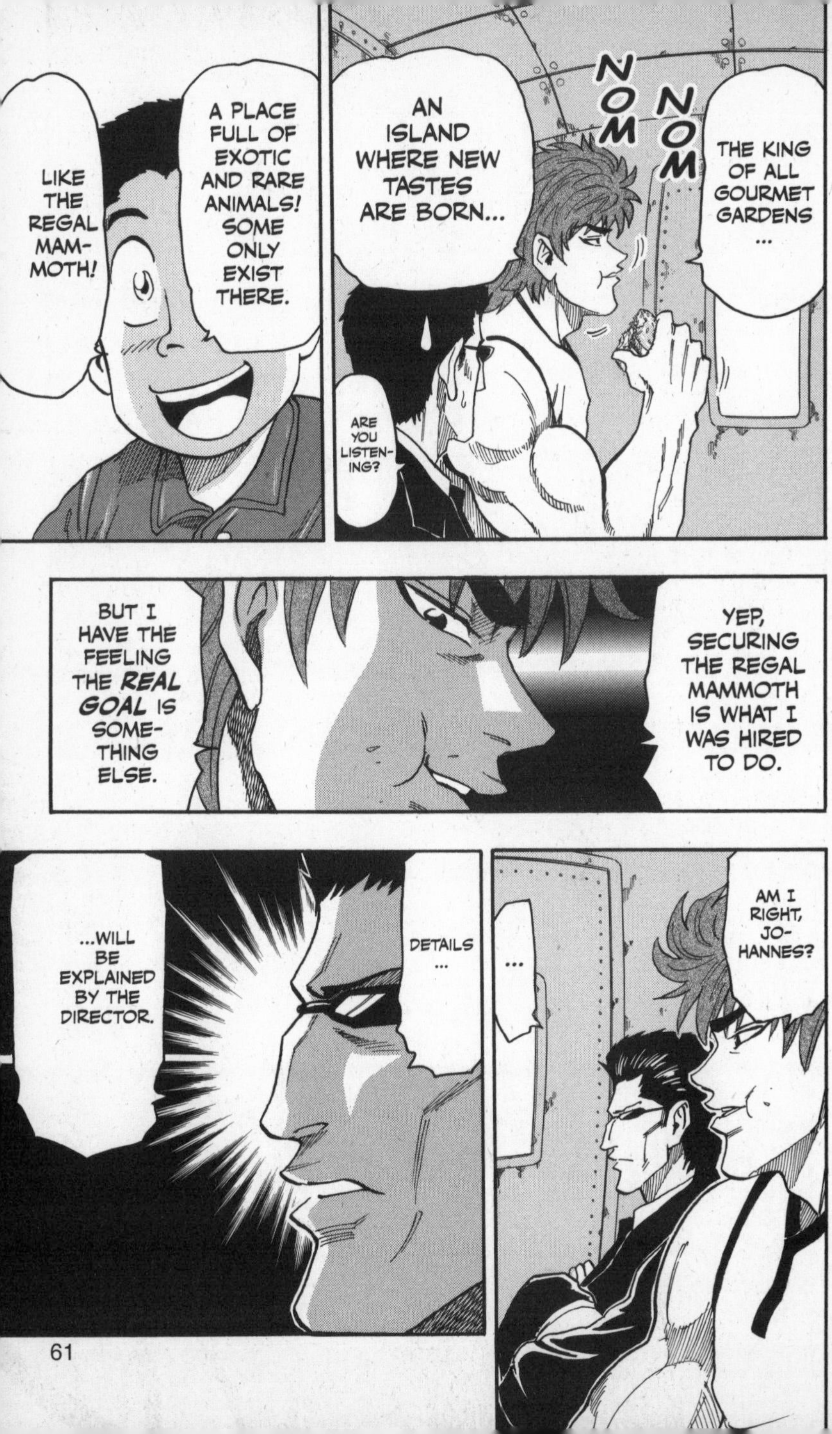
NOM NOM
THE KING OF ALL GOURMET GARDENS...
AN ISLAND WHERE NEW TASTES ARE BORN...
ARE YOU LISTENING?
A PLACE FULL OF EXOTIC AND RARE ANIMALS! SOME ONLY EXIST THERE.
LIKE THE REGAL MAMMOTH!
YEP, SECURING THE REGAL MAMMOTH IS WHAT I WAS HIRED TO DO.
BUT I HAVE THE FEELING THE *REAL GOAL* IS SOMETHING ELSE.
AM I RIGHT, JOHANNES?
...
DETAILS...
...WILL BE EXPLAINED BY THE DIRECTOR.

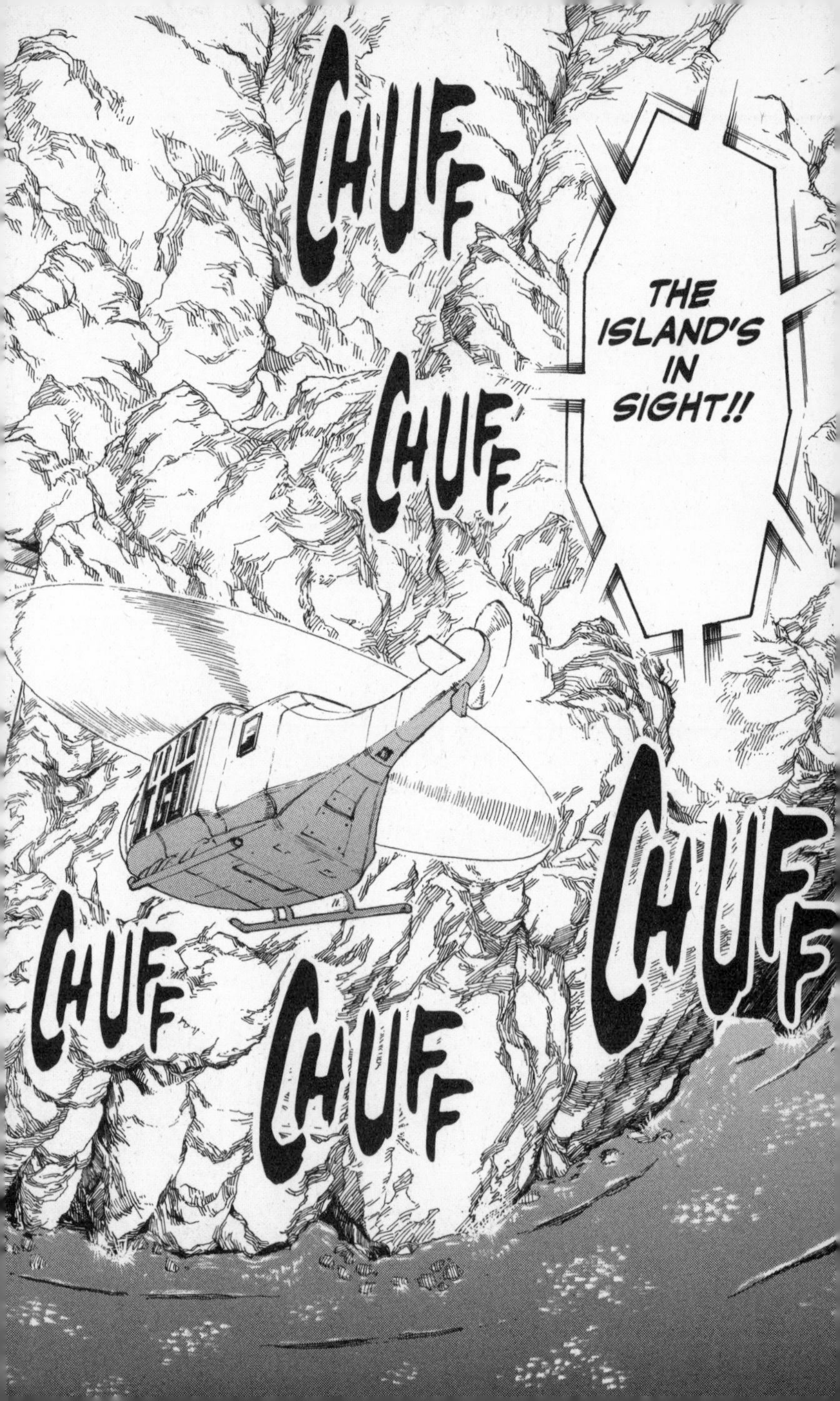
THE ISLAND'S IN SIGHT!!
CHUFF
CHUFF
CHUFF
CHUFF
CHUFF

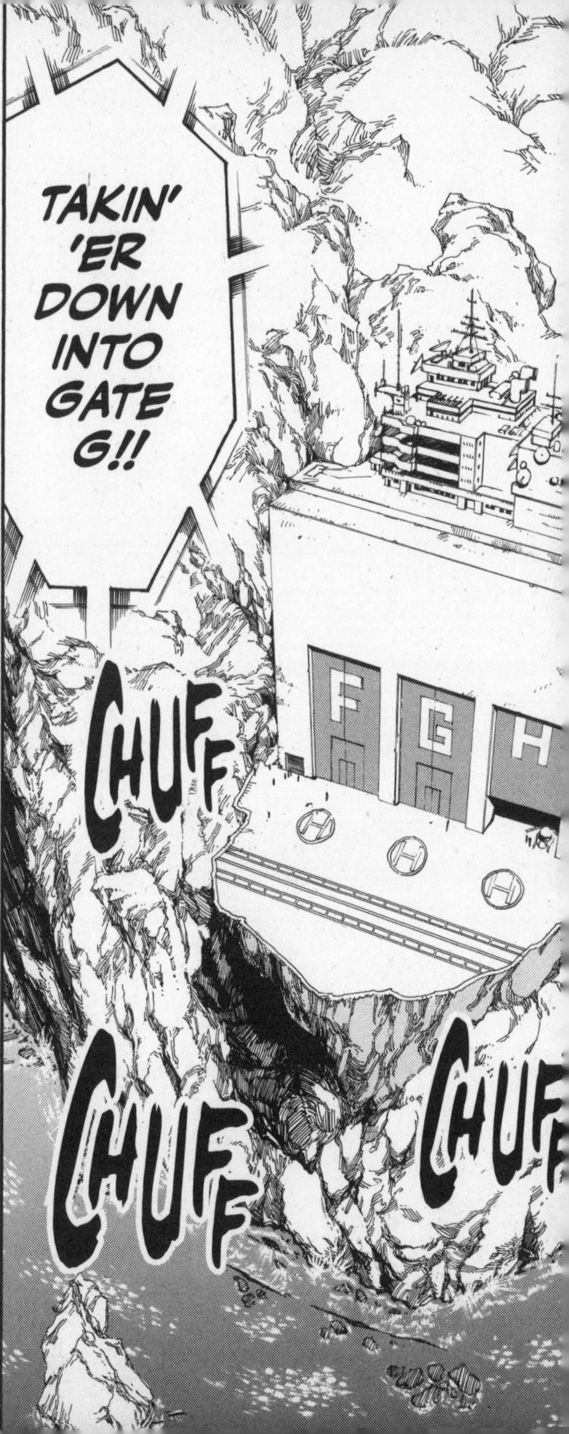
TAKIN' 'ER DOWN INTO GATE G!!
F
G
H
CHUFF
CHUFF
CHUFF

Menu 4. REGAL MAMMOTH

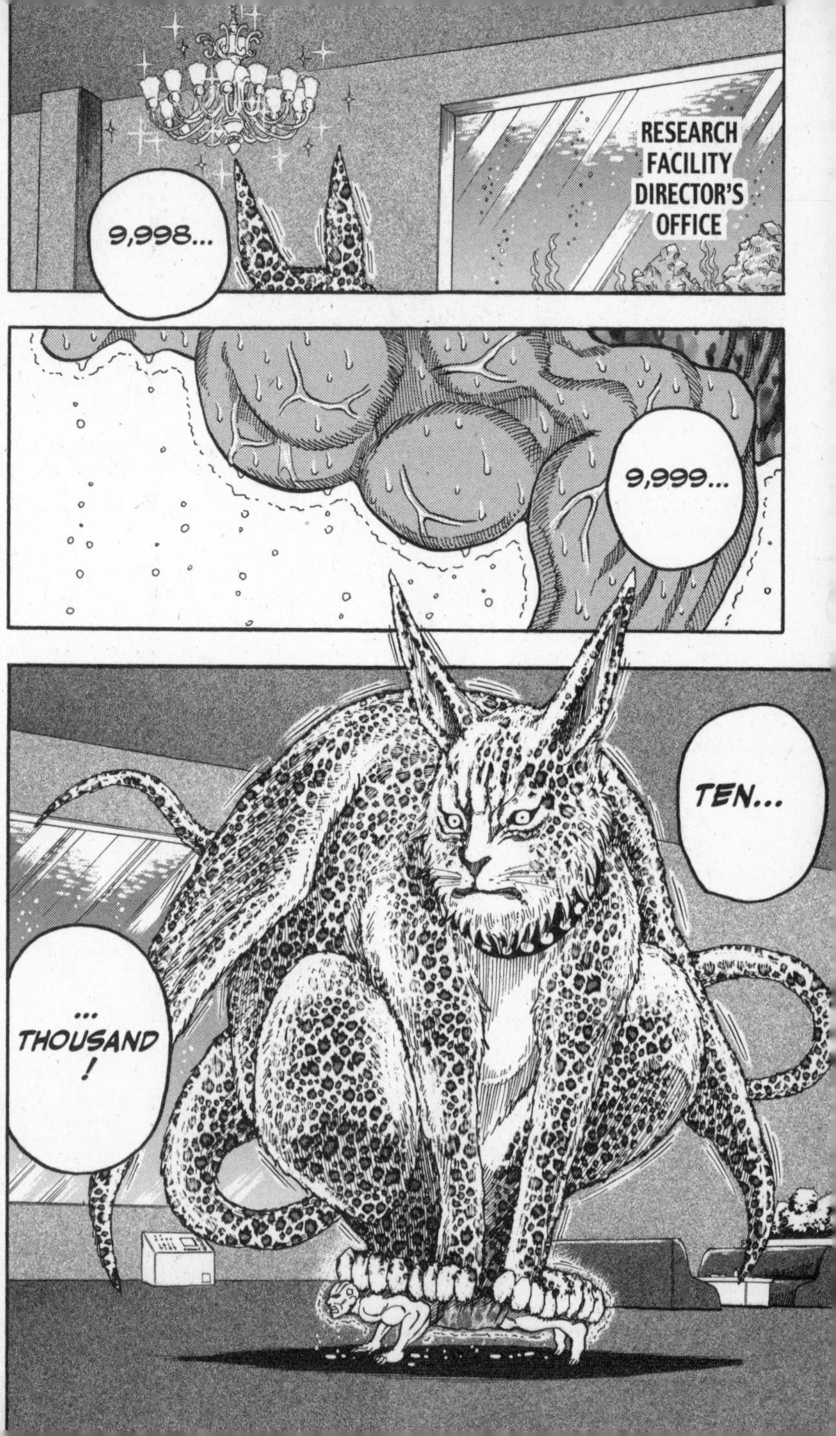
RESEARCH FACILITY DIRECTOR'S OFFICE
9,998...
9,999...
TEN...
...THOUSAND!

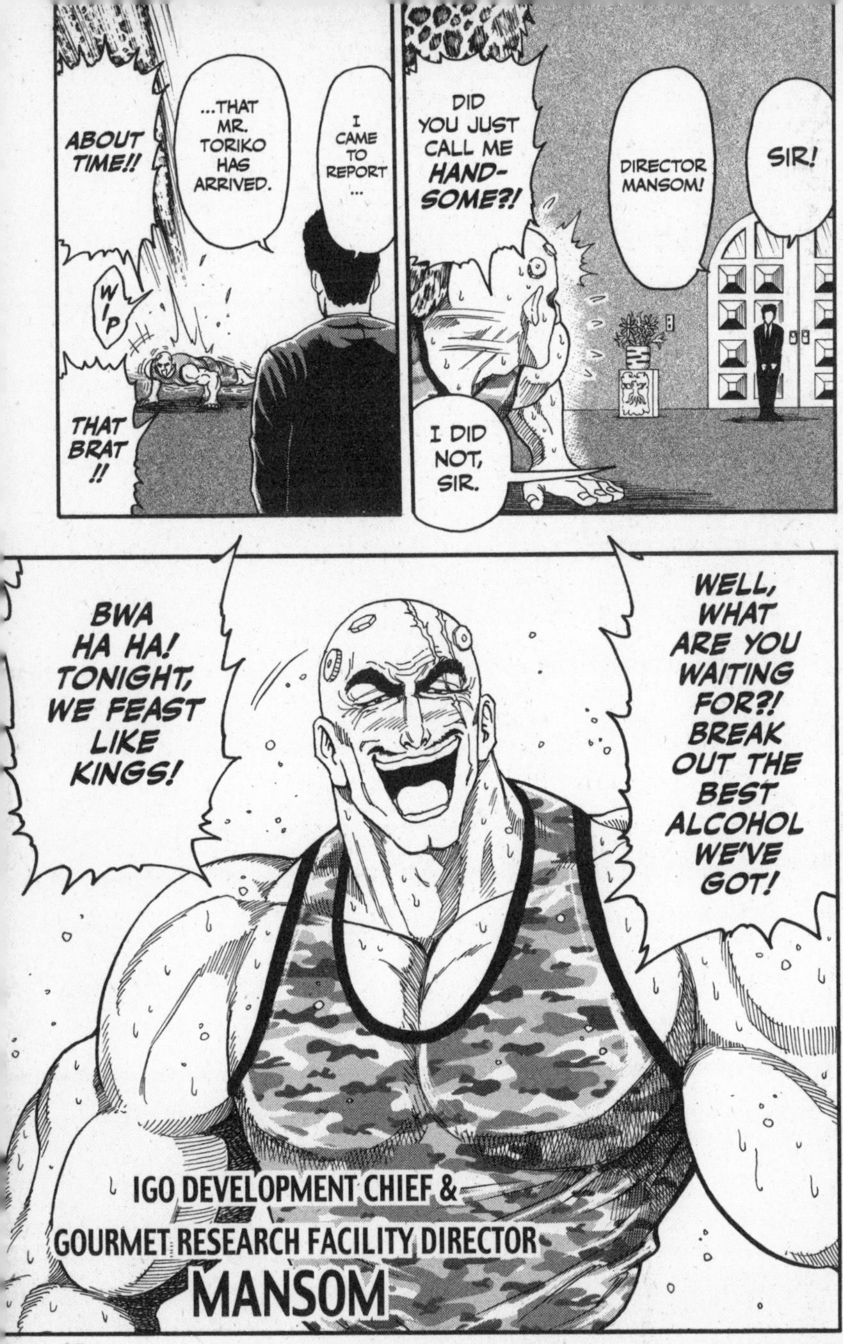
SIR!
DIRECTOR MANSOM!
DID YOU JUST CALL ME HANDSOME?!
I DID NOT, SIR.
I CAME TO REPORT ...
...THAT MR. TORIKO HAS ARRIVED.
ABOUT TIME!!
THAT BRAT!!
WELL, WHAT ARE YOU WAITING FOR?! BREAK OUT THE BEST ALCOHOL WE'VE GOT!
BWA HA HA! TONIGHT, WE FEAST LIKE KINGS!
IGO DEVELOPMENT CHIEF &
GOURMET RESEARCH FACILITY DIRECTOR
MANSOM

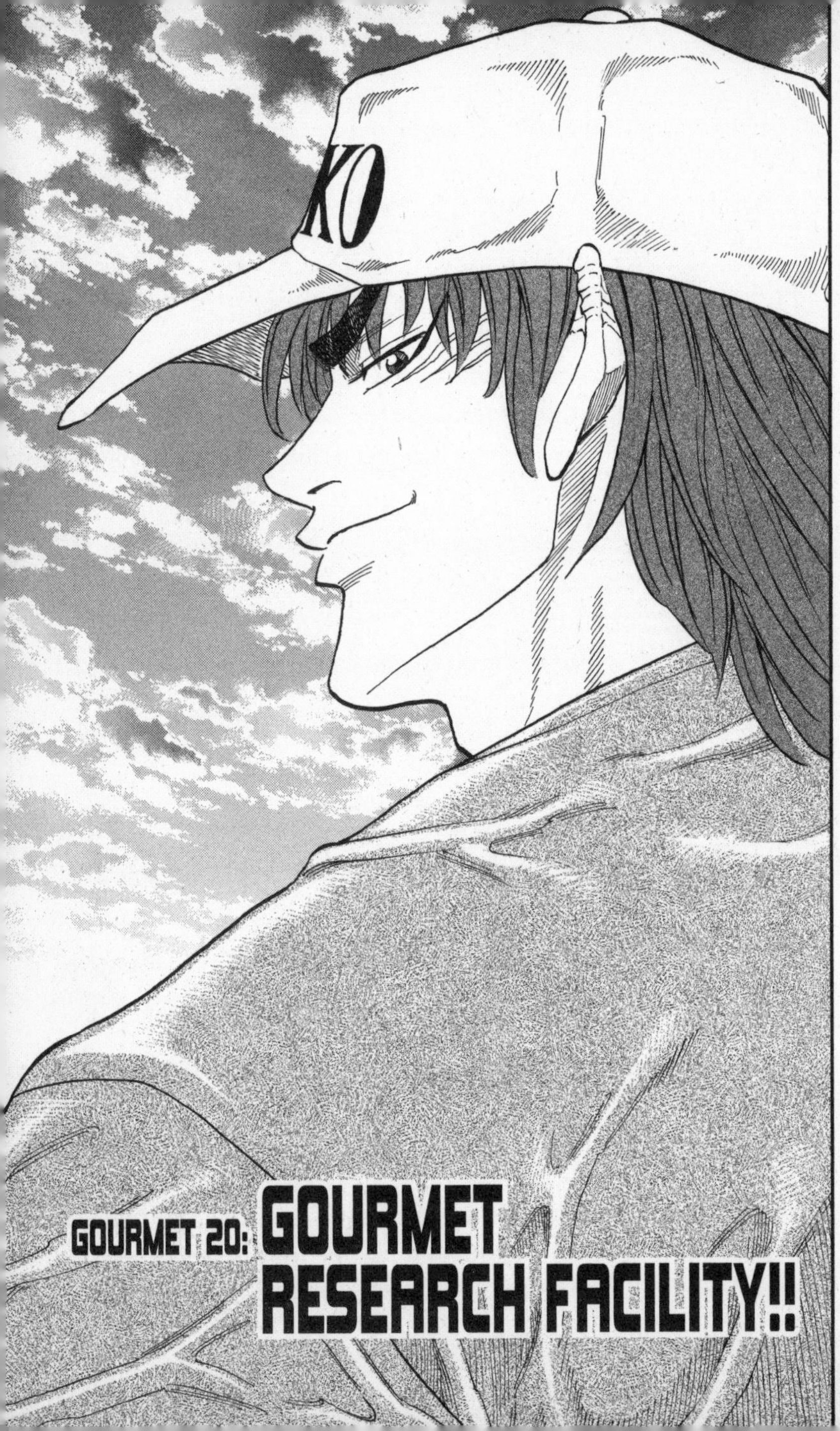
GOURMET 20: GOURMET RESEARCH FACILITY!!

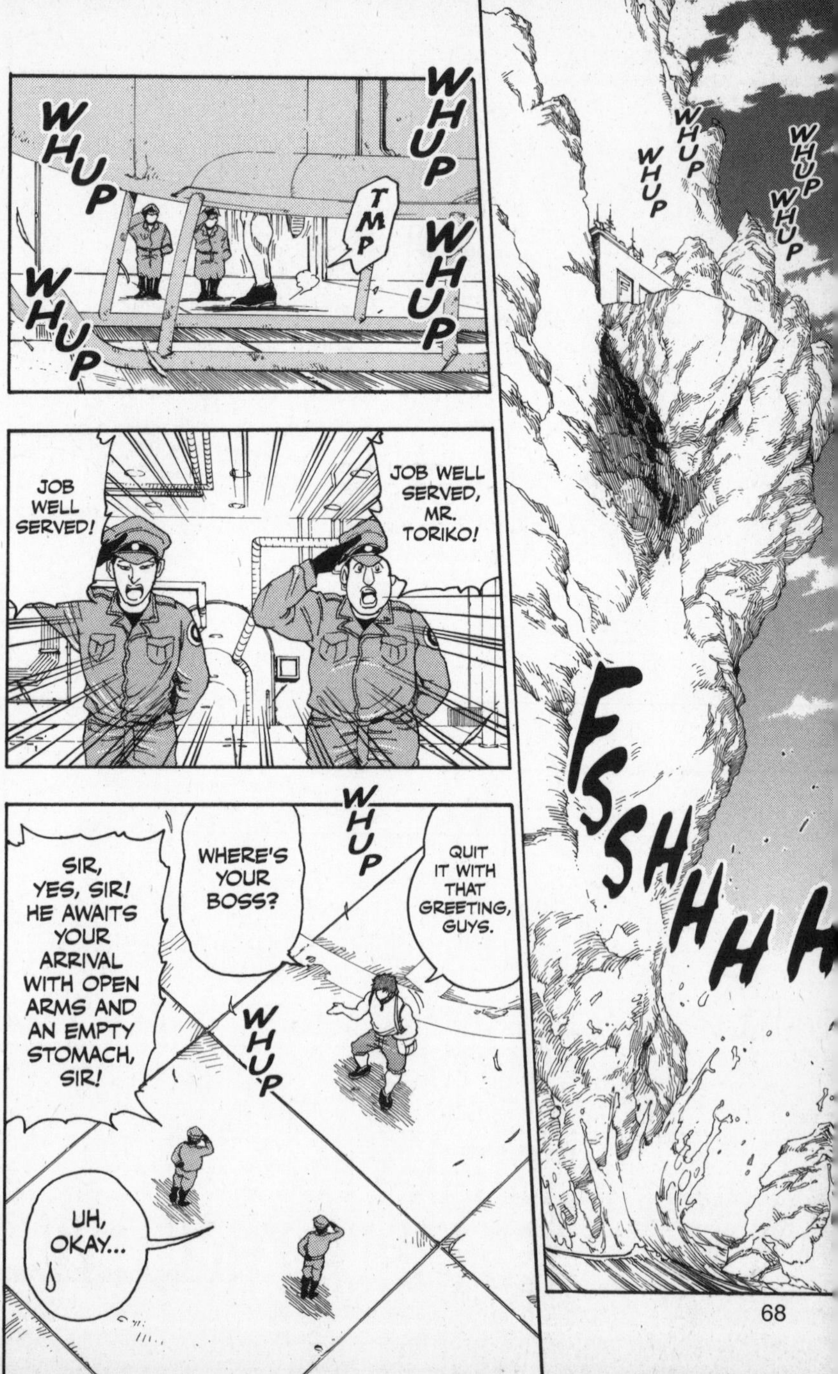
WHUP WHUP
WHUP
WHUP
FSSHHHH
WHUP
WHUP
TMP
WHUP
WHUP
WHUP
JOB WELL SERVED, MR. TORIKO!
JOB WELL SERVED!
WHUP
QUIT IT WITH THAT GREETING, GUYS.
WHERE'S YOUR BOSS?
SIR, YES, SIR! HE AWAITS YOUR ARRIVAL WITH OPEN ARMS AND AN EMPTY STOMACH, SIR!
WHUP
UH, OKAY...

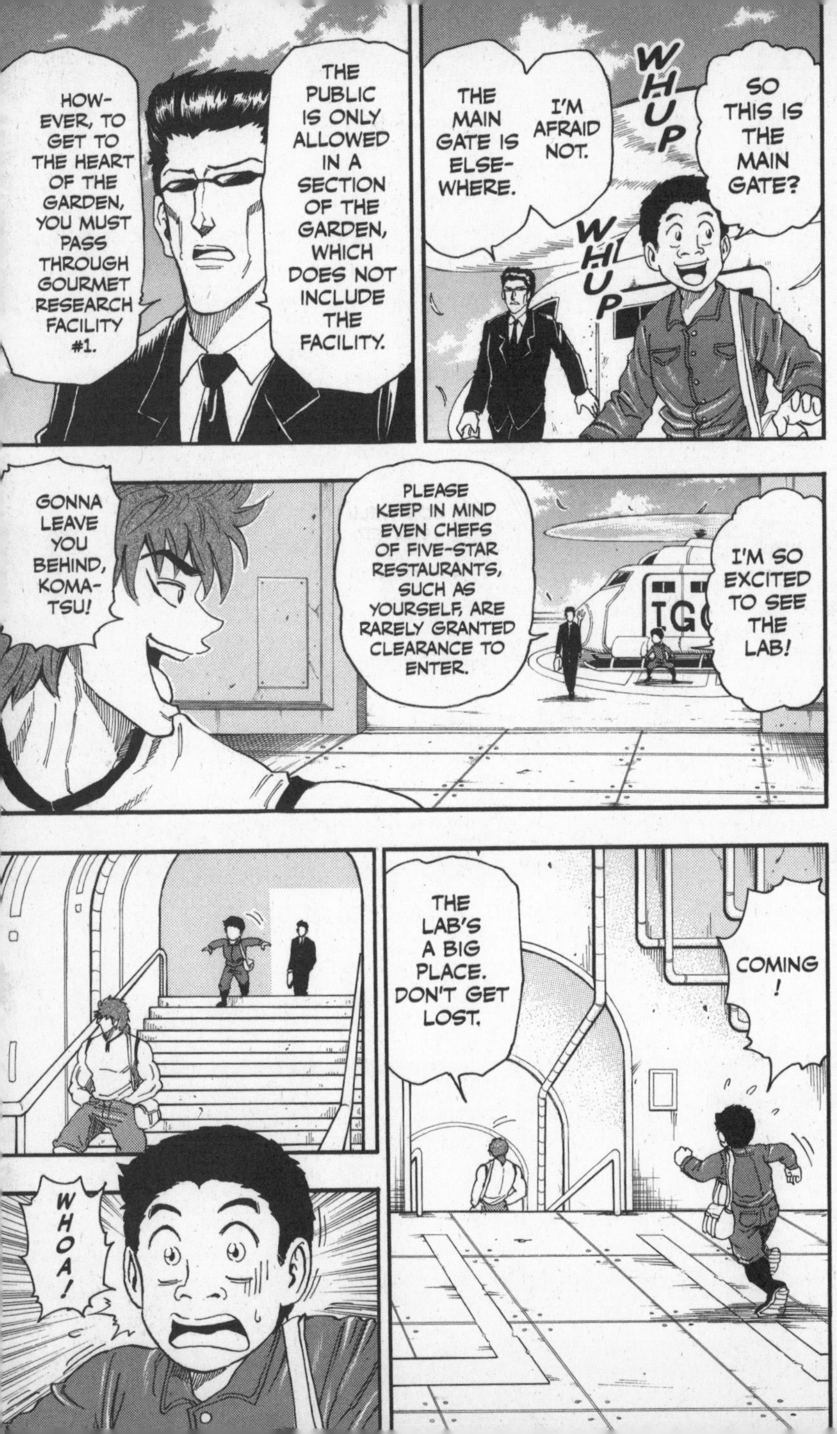
SO THIS IS THE MAIN GATE?
WHUP
WHUP
I'M AFRAID NOT.
THE MAIN GATE IS ELSE-WHERE.
THE PUBLIC IS ONLY ALLOWED IN A SECTION OF THE GARDEN, WHICH DOES NOT INCLUDE THE FACILITY.
HOW-EVER, TO GET TO THE HEART OF THE GARDEN, YOU MUST PASS THROUGH GOURMET RESEARCH FACILITY #1.
I'M SO EXCITED TO SEE THE LAB!
IGO
PLEASE KEEP IN MIND EVEN CHEFS OF FIVE-STAR RESTAURANTS, SUCH AS YOURSELF, ARE RARELY GRANTED CLEARANCE TO ENTER.
GONNA LEAVE YOU BEHIND, KOMA-TSU!
THE LAB'S A BIG PLACE. DON'T GET LOST.
COMING!
WHOA!

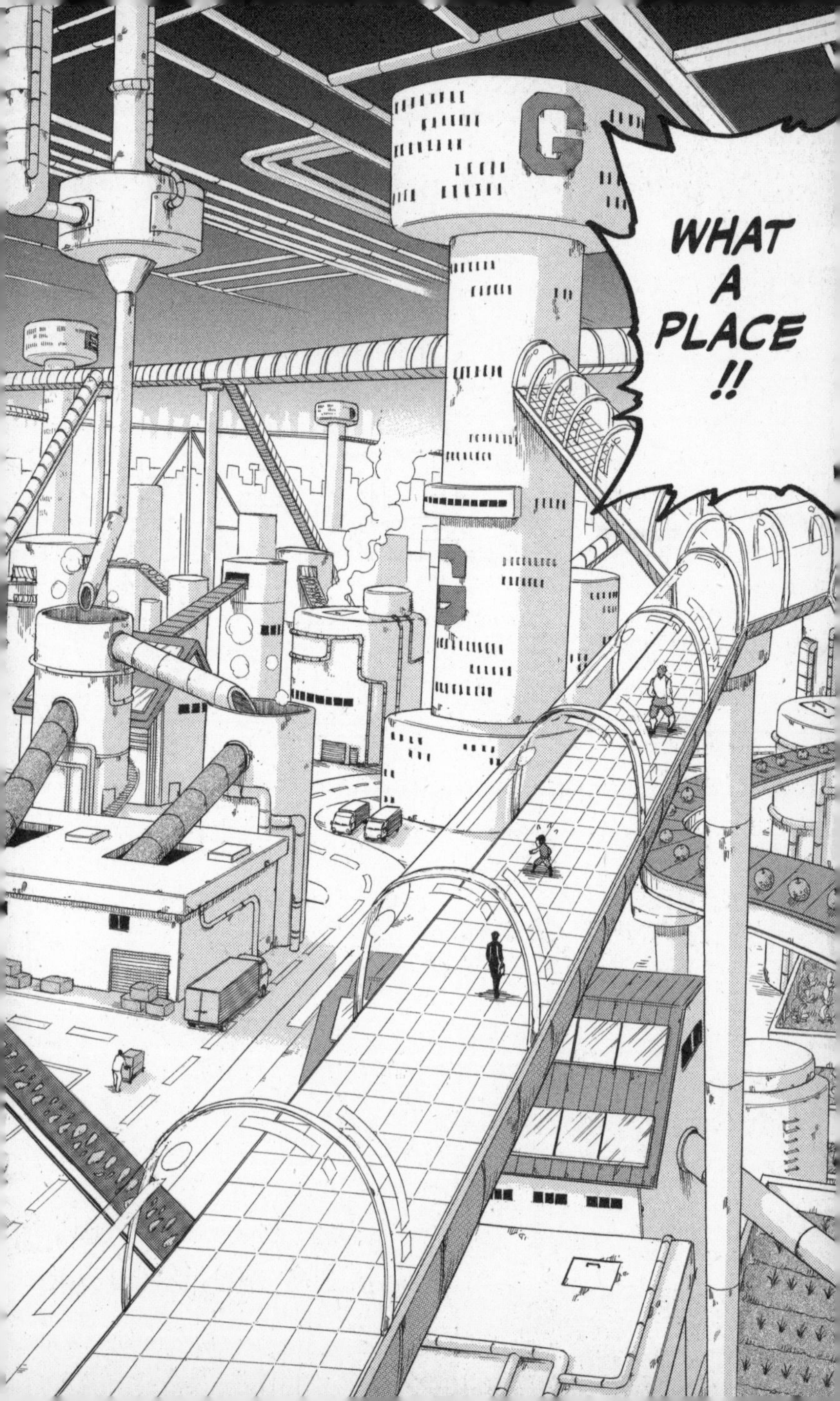
WHAT A PLACE !!

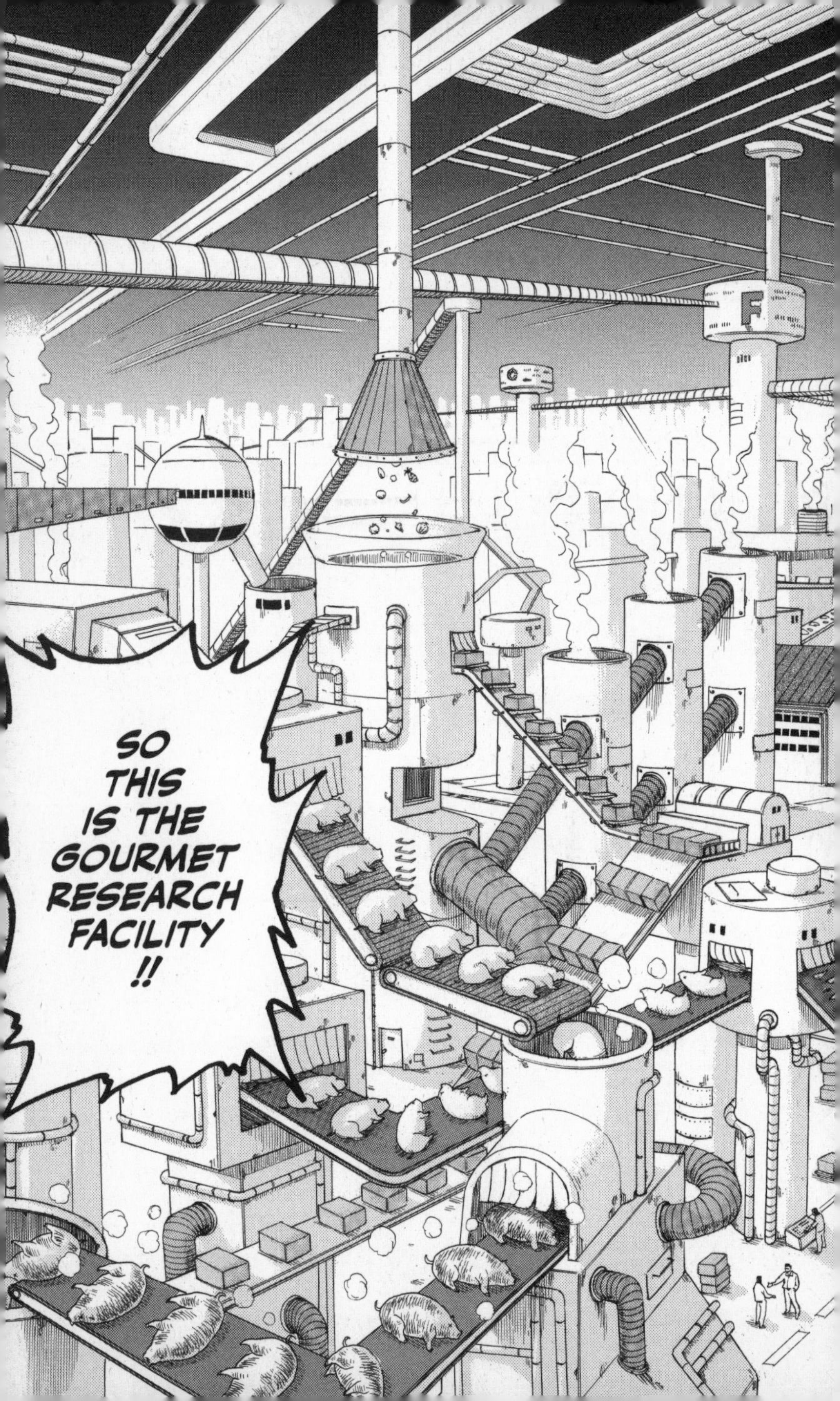
SO THIS IS THE GOURMET RESEARCH FACILITY !!

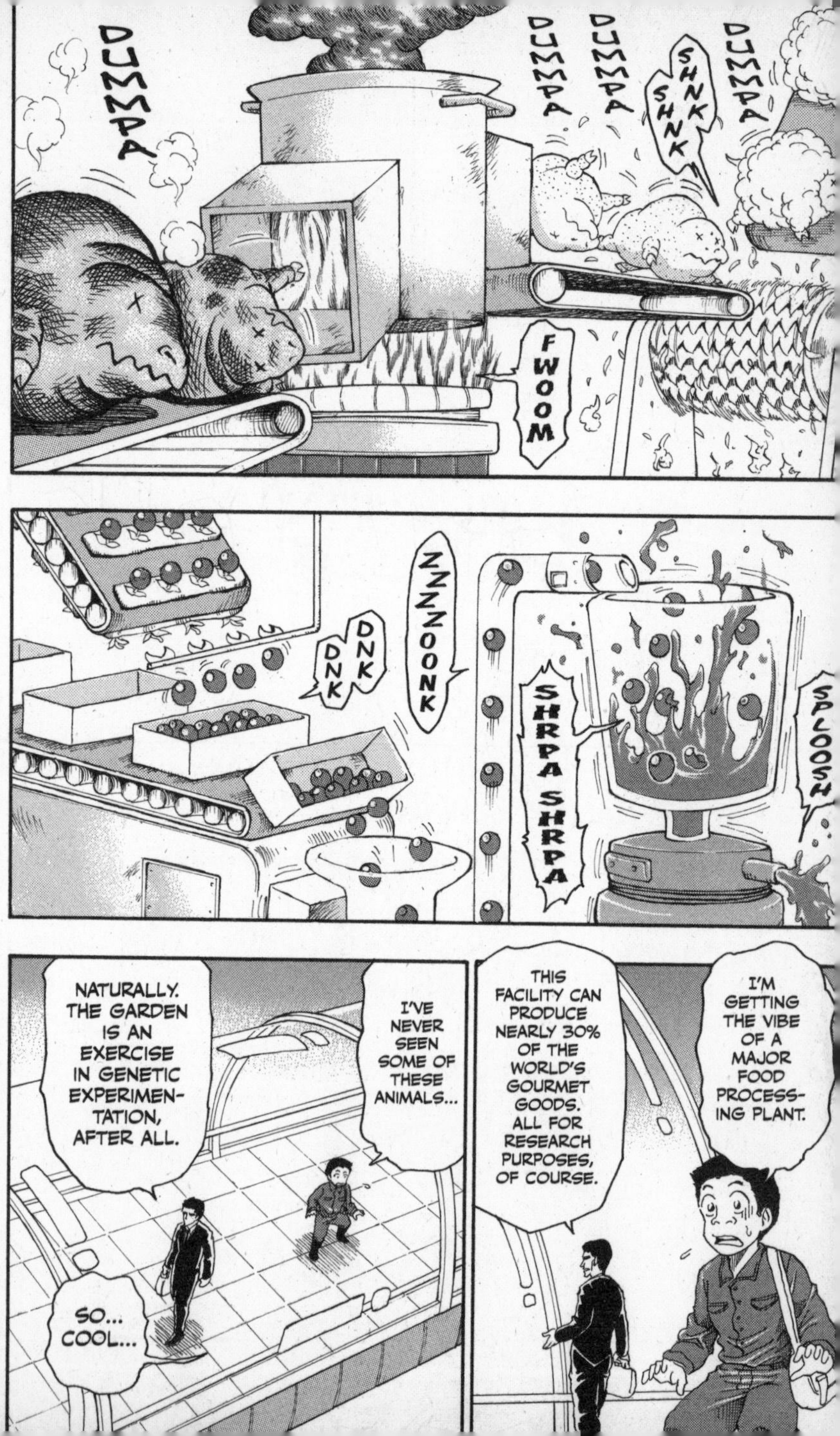
DUMMPA
SHNK SHNK
DUMMPA
DUMMPA
DUMMPA
FWOOM
SPLOOSH
SHRPA SHRPA
ZZZOOONK
DNK DNK
I'M GETTING THE VIBE OF A MAJOR FOOD PROCESSING PLANT.
THIS FACILITY CAN PRODUCE NEARLY 30% OF THE WORLD'S GOURMET GOODS. ALL FOR RESEARCH PURPOSES, OF COURSE.
I'VE NEVER SEEN SOME OF THESE ANIMALS...
NATURALLY. THE GARDEN IS AN EXERCISE IN GENETIC EXPERIMENTATION, AFTER ALL.
SO... COOL...

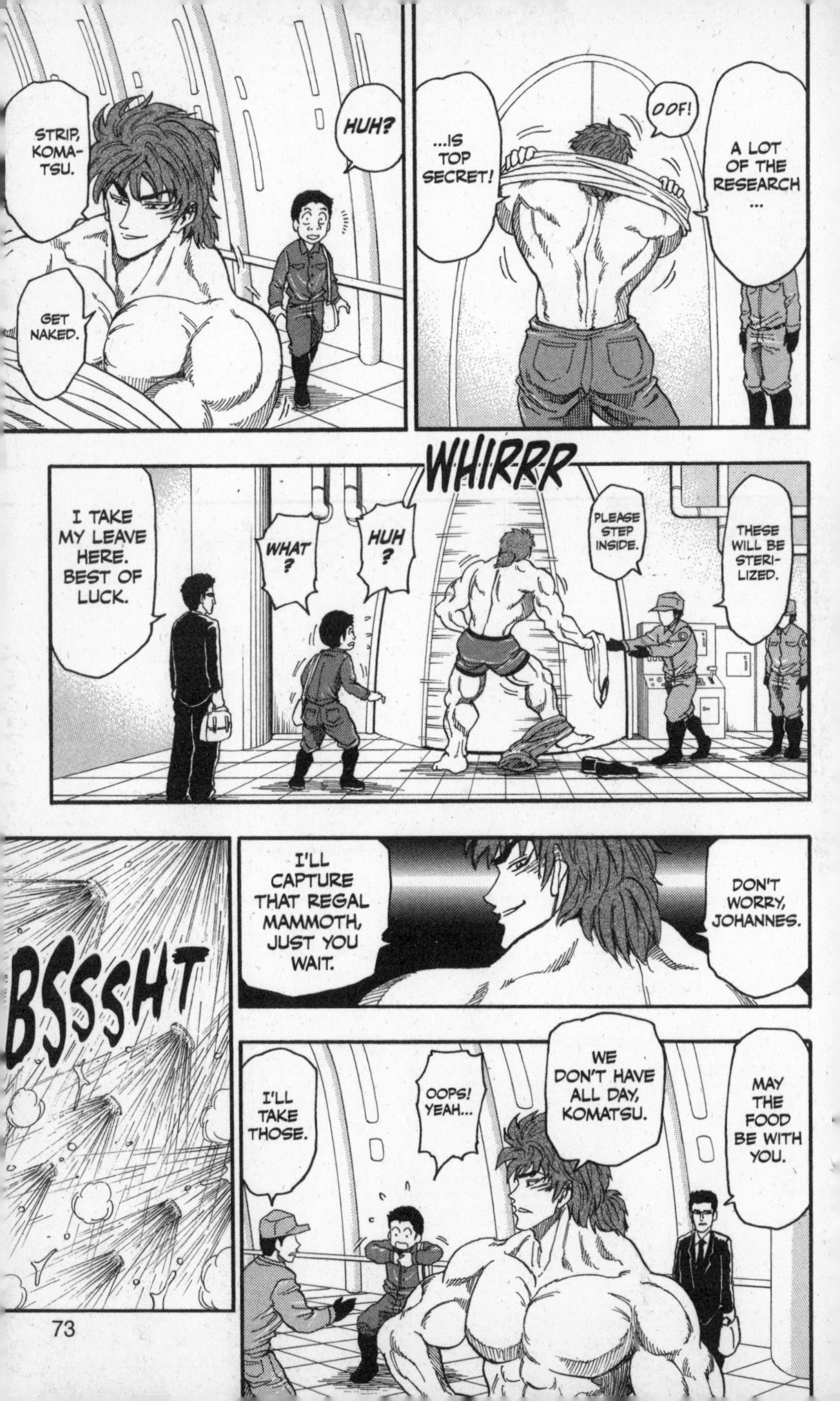
A LOT OF THE RESEARCH ...
OOF!
...IS TOP SECRET!
HUH?
STRIP, KOMA-TSU.
GET NAKED.
WHIRRR
THESE WILL BE STERI-LIZED.
PLEASE STEP INSIDE.
HUH ?
WHAT ?
I TAKE MY LEAVE HERE. BEST OF LUCK.
DON'T WORRY, JOHANNES.
I'LL CAPTURE THAT REGAL MAMMOTH, JUST YOU WAIT.
MAY THE FOOD BE WITH YOU.
WE DON'T HAVE ALL DAY, KOMATSU.
OOPS! YEAH...
I'LL TAKE THOSE.
BSSSHT

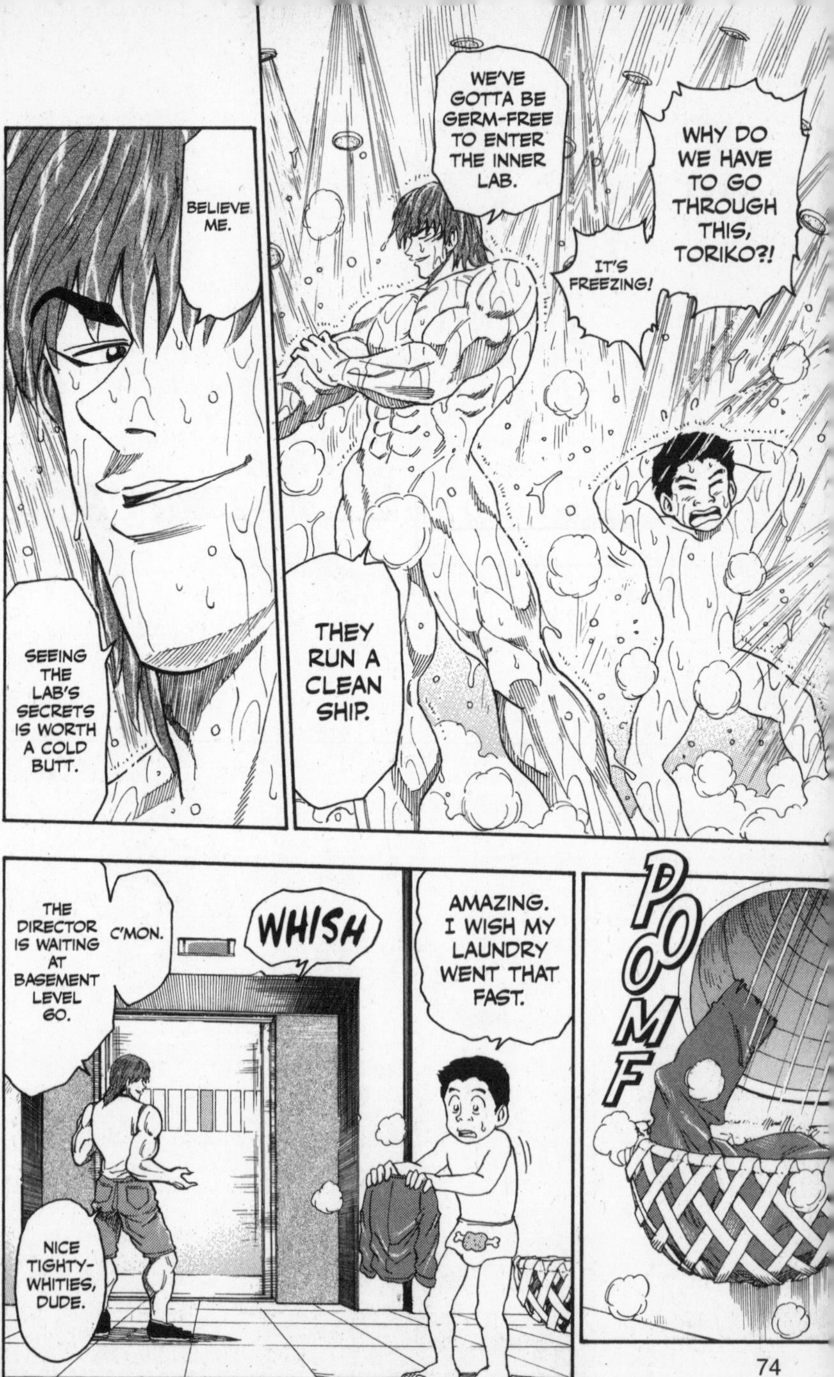
WHY DO WE HAVE TO GO THROUGH THIS, TORIKO?!
IT'S FREEZING!
WE'VE GOTTA BE GERM-FREE TO ENTER THE INNER LAB.
THEY RUN A CLEAN SHIP.
BELIEVE ME.
SEEING THE LAB'S SECRETS IS WORTH A COLD BUTT.
POOMF
AMAZING. I WISH MY LAUNDRY WENT THAT FAST.
WHISH
C'MON.
THE DIRECTOR IS WAITING AT BASEMENT LEVEL 60.
NICE TIGHTY-WHITIES, DUDE.

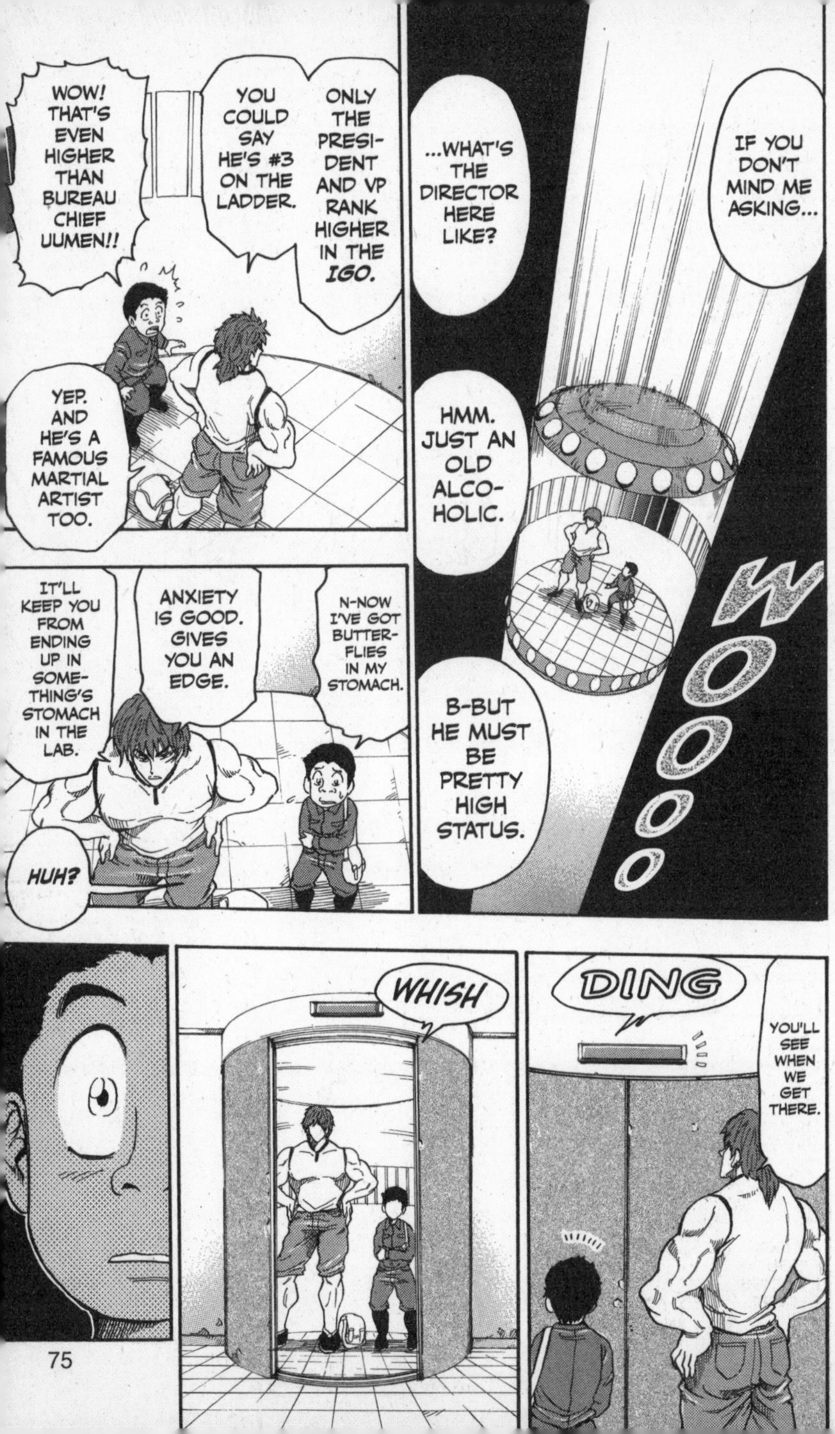
IF YOU DON'T MIND ME ASKING...
...WHAT'S THE DIRECTOR HERE LIKE?
HMM. JUST AN OLD ALCO-HOLIC.
B-BUT HE MUST BE PRETTY HIGH STATUS.
WOOOOO
ONLY THE PRESI-DENT AND VP RANK HIGHER IN THE *IGO.*
YOU COULD SAY HE'S #3 ON THE LADDER.
WOW! THAT'S EVEN HIGHER THAN BUREAU CHIEF UUMEN!!
YEP. AND HE'S A FAMOUS MARTIAL ARTIST TOO.
N-NOW I'VE GOT BUTTER-FLIES IN MY STOMACH.
ANXIETY IS GOOD. GIVES YOU AN EDGE.
IT'LL KEEP YOU FROM ENDING UP IN SOME-THING'S STOMACH IN THE LAB.
HUH?
DING
YOU'LL SEE WHEN WE GET THERE.
WHISH

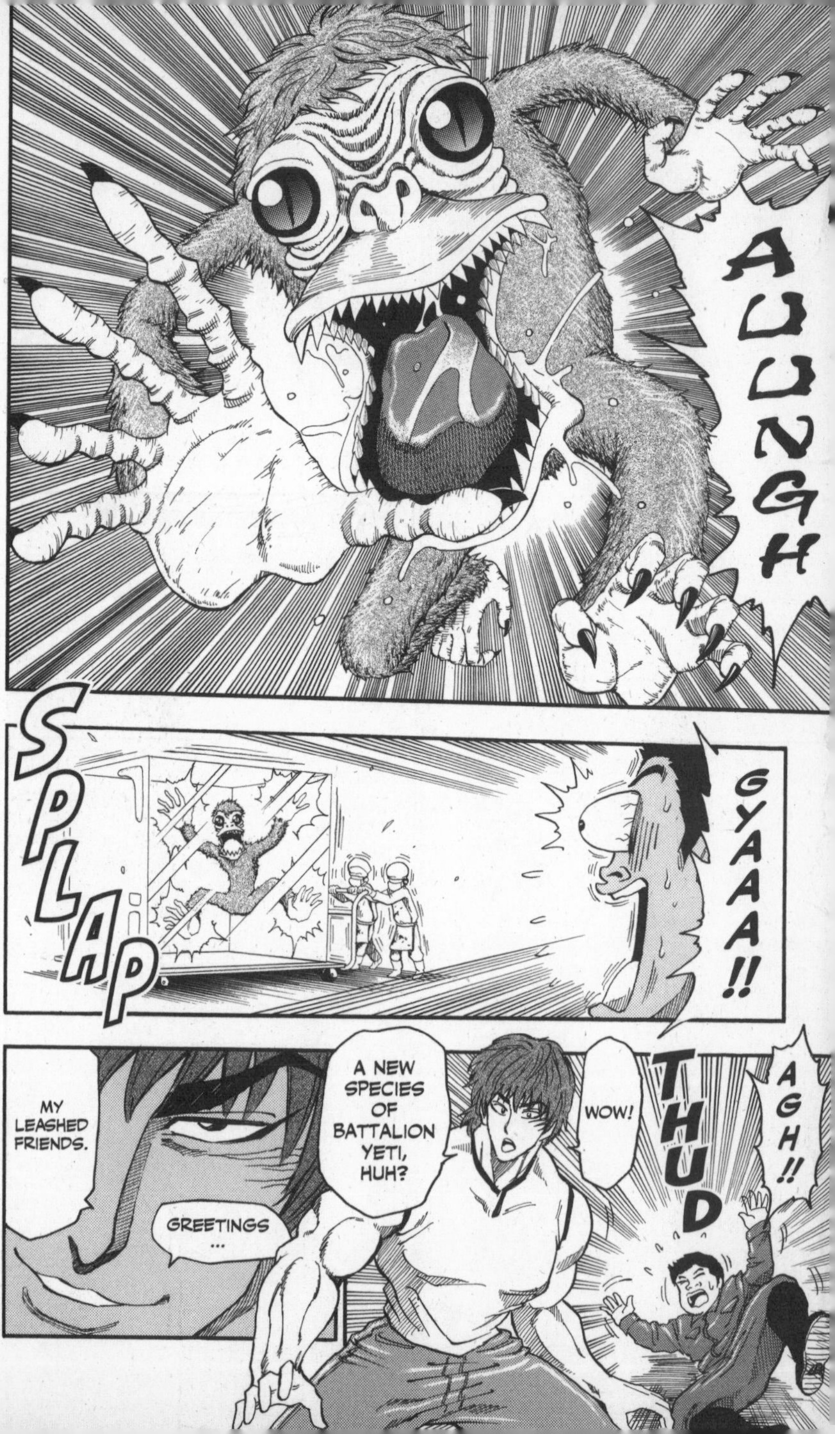
AUUNGH
GYAAAA!!
SPLAP
AGH!!
THUD
WOW!
A NEW SPECIES OF BATTALION YETI, HUH?
GREETINGS ...
MY LEASHED FRIENDS.

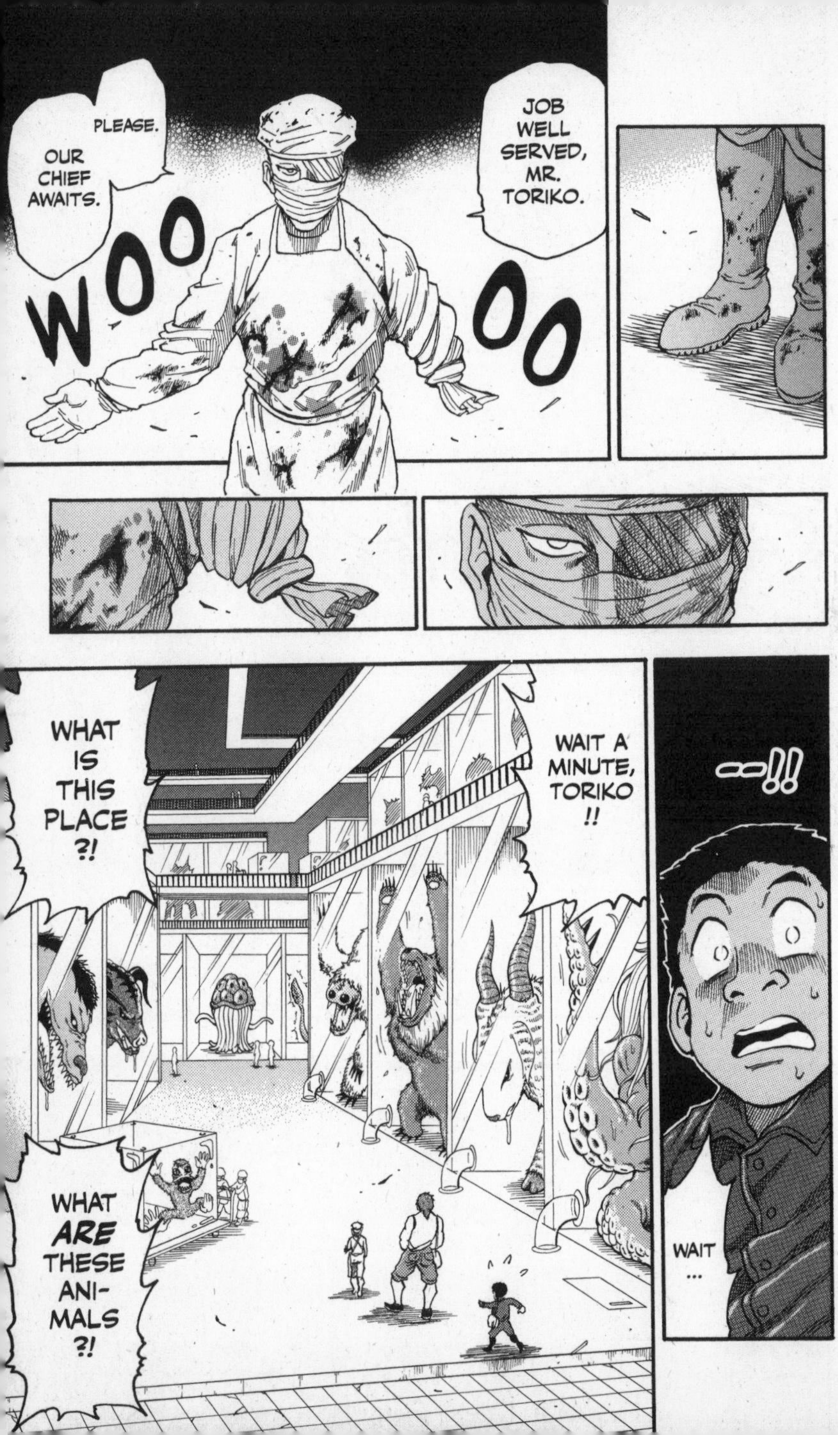
JOB WELL SERVED, MR. TORIKO.
PLEASE.
OUR CHIEF AWAITS.
WOO
OO
--!!
WAIT ...
WAIT A MINUTE, TORIKO !!
WHAT IS THIS PLACE ?!
WHAT *ARE* THESE ANI-MALS ?!

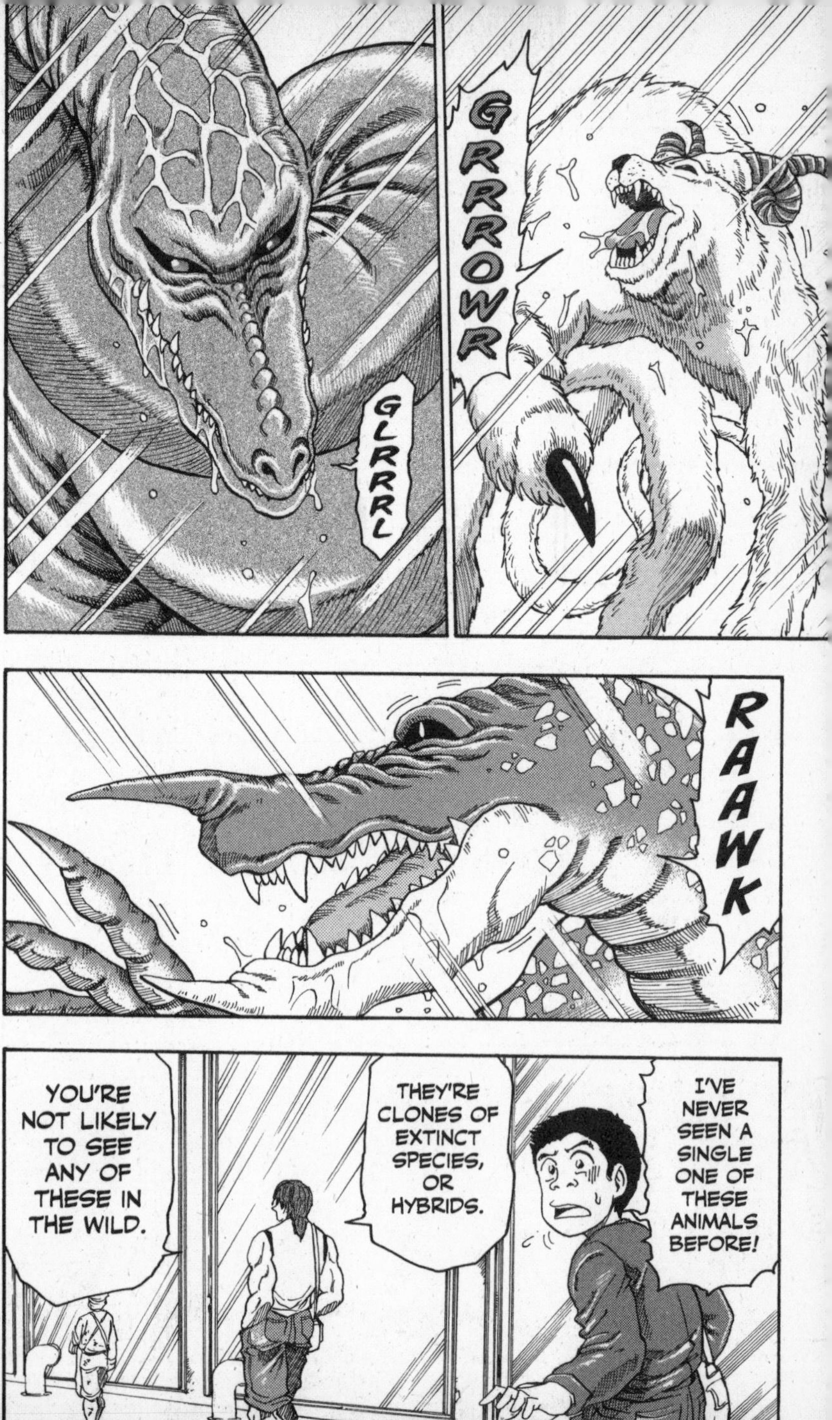
GRRROWR
GLRRRL
RAAAWK
I'VE NEVER SEEN A SINGLE ONE OF THESE ANIMALS BEFORE!
THEY'RE CLONES OF EXTINCT SPECIES, OR HYBRIDS.
YOU'RE NOT LIKELY TO SEE ANY OF THESE IN THE WILD.

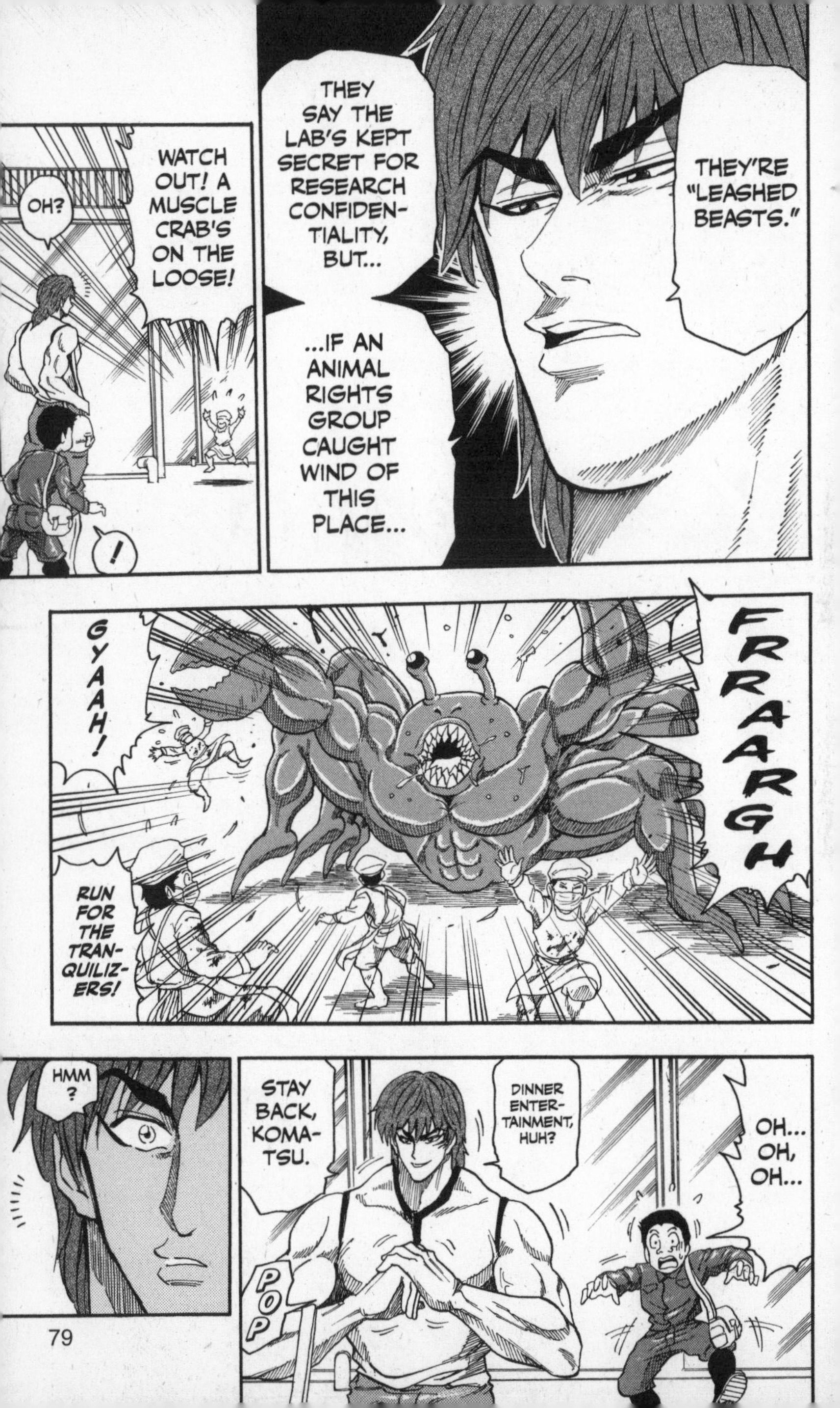
THEY'RE "LEASHED BEASTS."
THEY SAY THE LAB'S KEPT SECRET FOR RESEARCH CONFIDENTIALITY, BUT...
...IF AN ANIMAL RIGHTS GROUP CAUGHT WIND OF THIS PLACE...
WATCH OUT! A MUSCLE CRAB'S ON THE LOOSE!
OH?
!
FRRAARGH
GYAAAH!
RUN FOR THE TRANQUILIZERS!
OH... OH, OH...
DINNER ENTERTAINMENT, HUH?
STAY BACK, KOMATSU.
POP
HMM ?

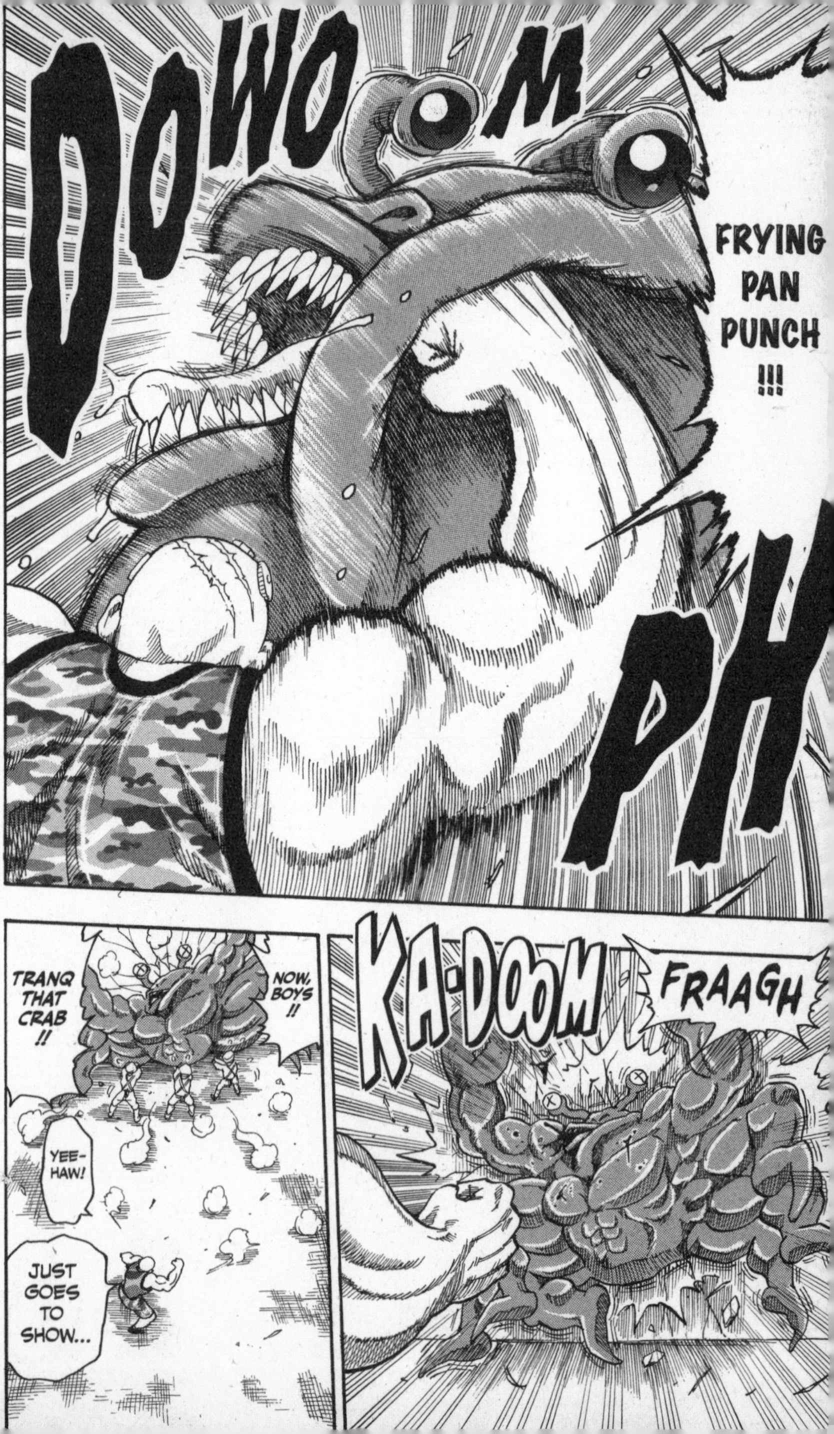
FRYING PAN PUNCH !!!
PH
KA-DOOM
FRAAGH
NOW, BOYS !!
TRANQ THAT CRAB !!
YEE-HAW!
JUST GOES TO SHOW...

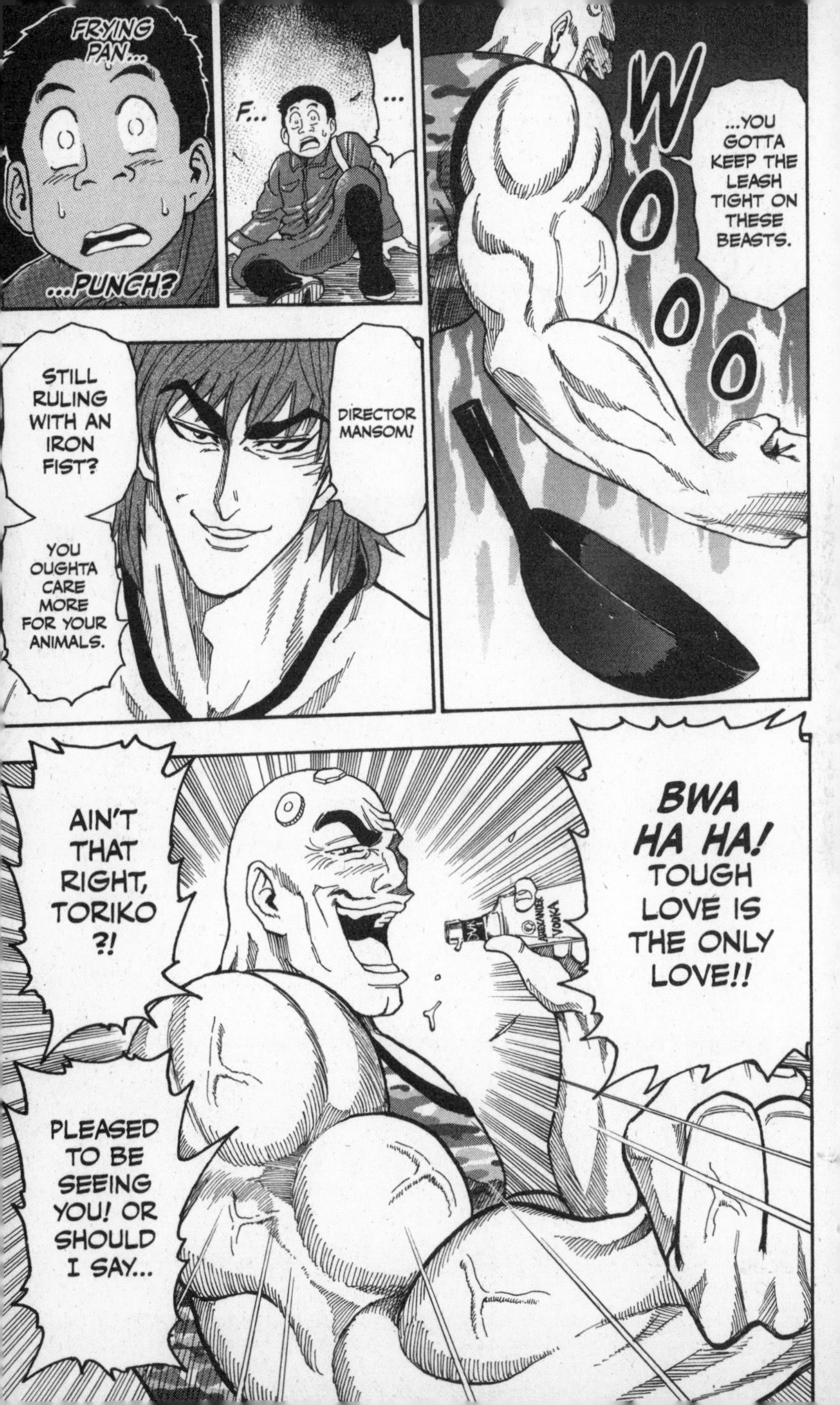
WOOOO
...YOU GOTTA KEEP THE LEASH TIGHT ON THESE BEASTS.
F...
...
FRYING PAN...
...PUNCH?
DIRECTOR MANSOM!
STILL RULING WITH AN IRON FIST?
YOU OUGHTA CARE MORE FOR YOUR ANIMALS.
BWA HA HA! TOUGH LOVE IS THE ONLY LOVE!!
ALEXANDER VODKA
AIN'T THAT RIGHT, TORIKO?!
PLEASED TO BE SEEING YOU! OR SHOULD I SAY...

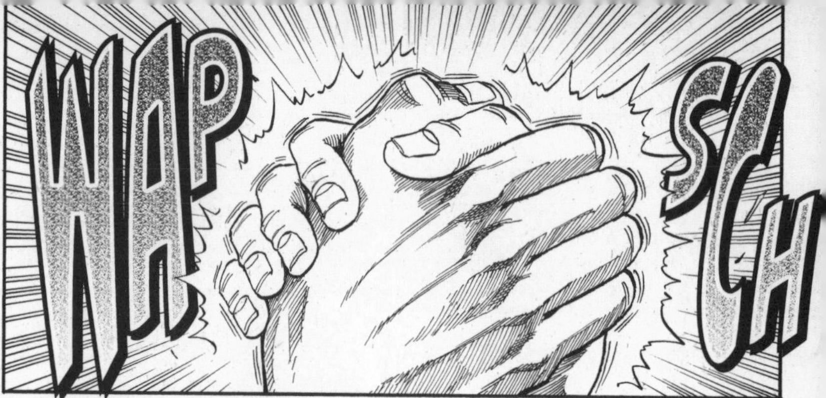
SCH
WAP
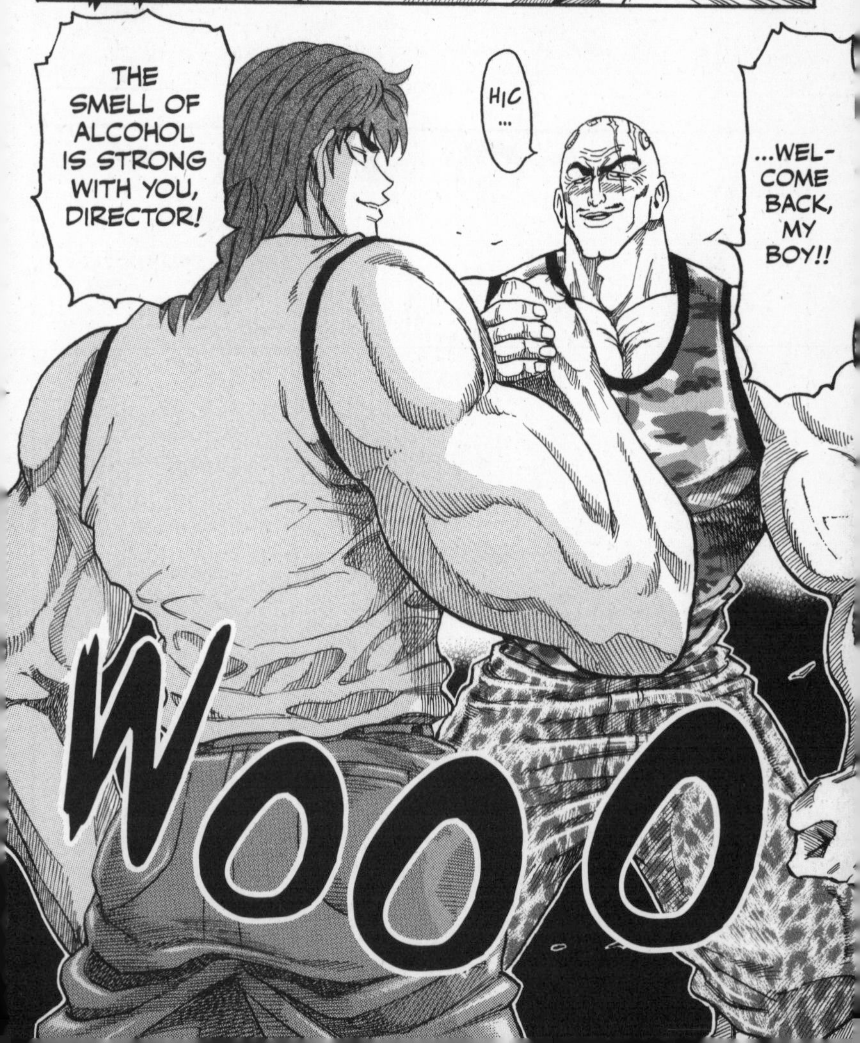
...WEL-COME BACK, MY BOY!!
HIC ...
THE SMELL OF ALCOHOL IS STRONG WITH YOU, DIRECTOR!
WOOO

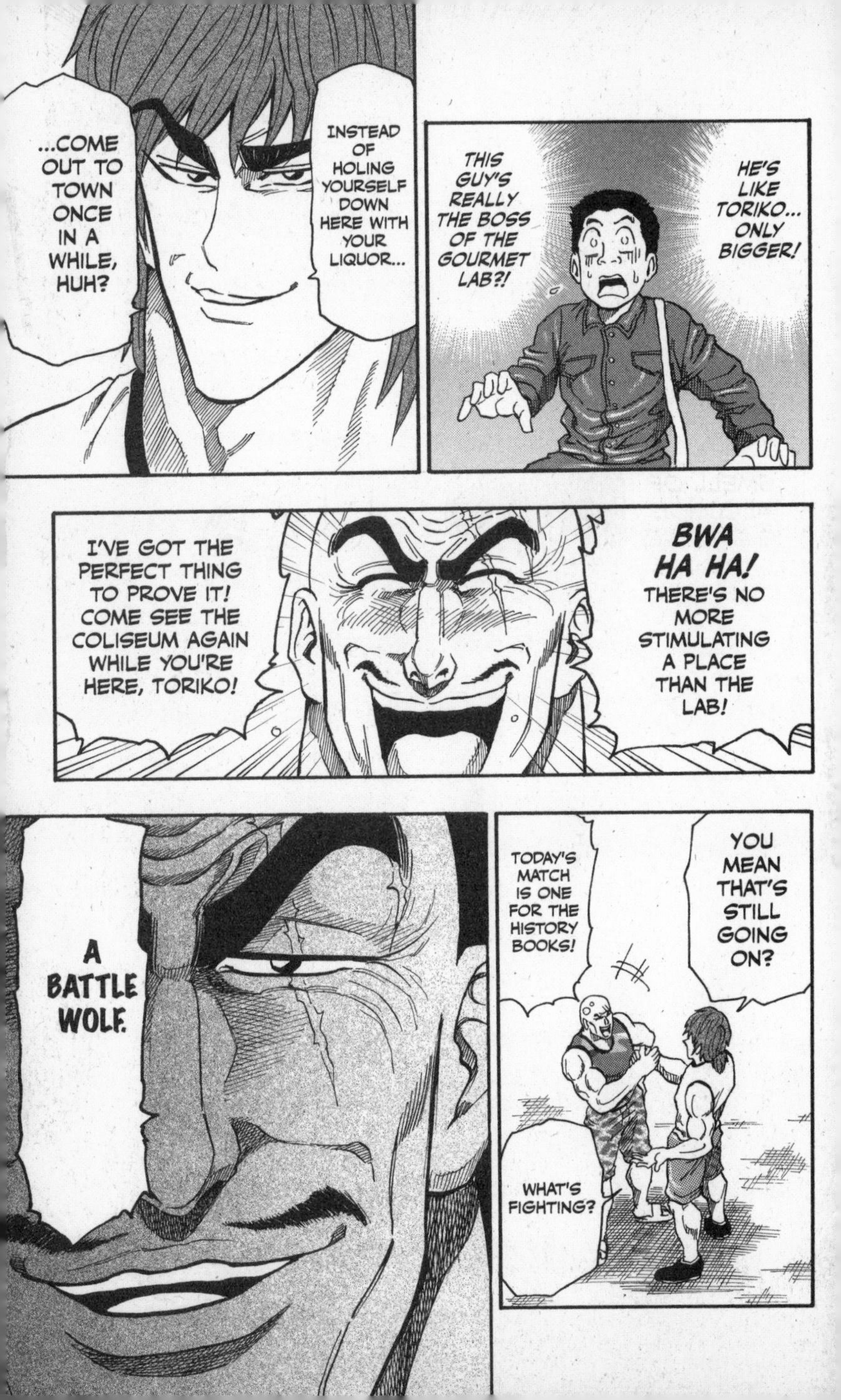
HE'S LIKE TORIKO... ONLY BIGGER!
THIS GUY'S REALLY THE BOSS OF THE GOURMET LAB?!
INSTEAD OF HOLING YOURSELF DOWN HERE WITH YOUR LIQUOR...
...COME OUT TO TOWN ONCE IN A WHILE, HUH?
BWA HA HA! THERE'S NO MORE STIMULATING A PLACE THAN THE LAB!
I'VE GOT THE PERFECT THING TO PROVE IT! COME SEE THE COLISEUM AGAIN WHILE YOU'RE HERE, TORIKO!
YOU MEAN THAT'S STILL GOING ON?
TODAY'S MATCH IS ONE FOR THE HISTORY BOOKS!
WHAT'S FIGHTING?
A BATTLE WOLF.

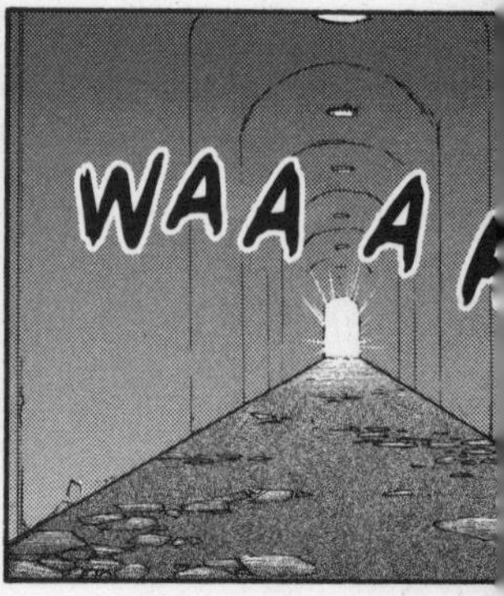
WAAAA
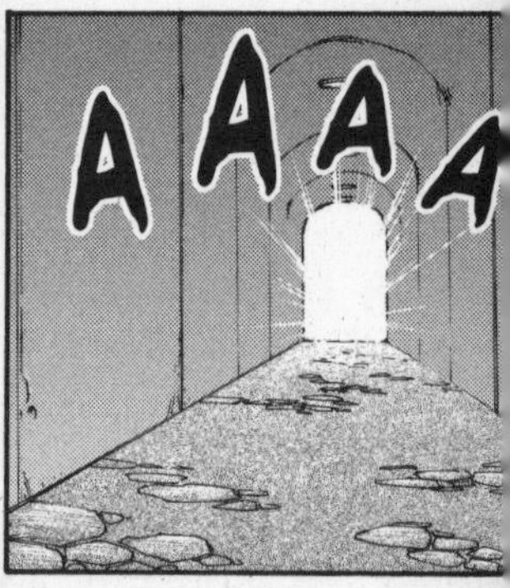
AAAA
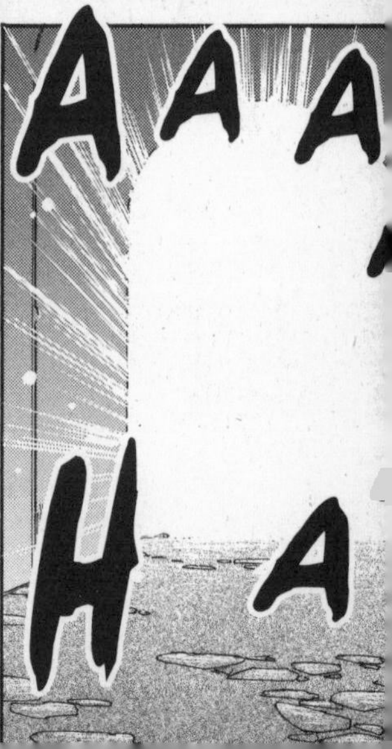
AAA
HA
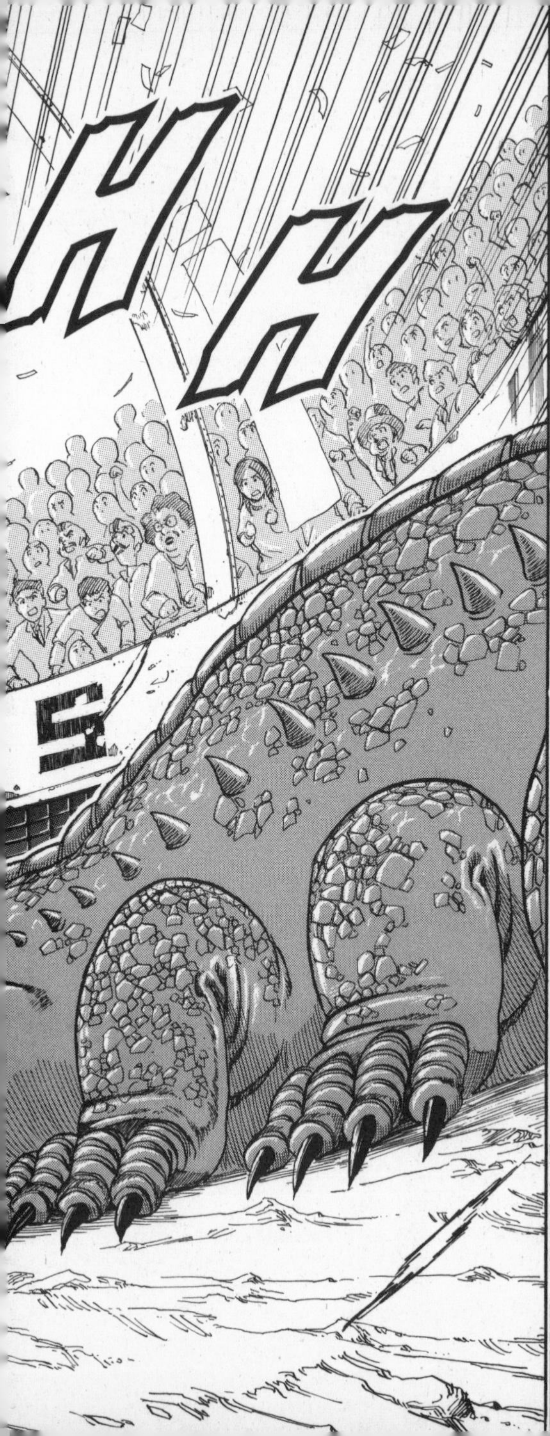
HH

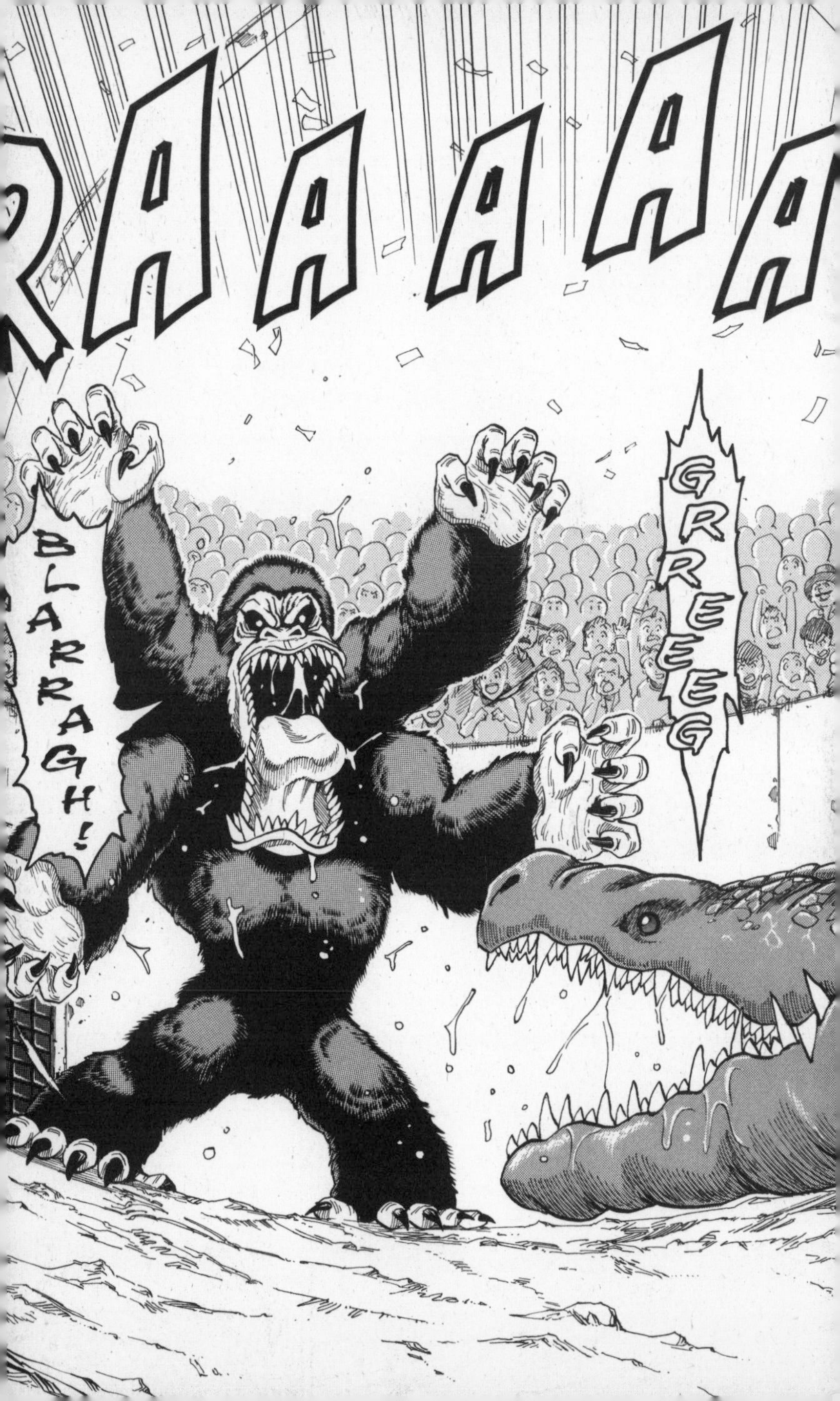
RAAAAA
GRREEG
BLARRAGH!

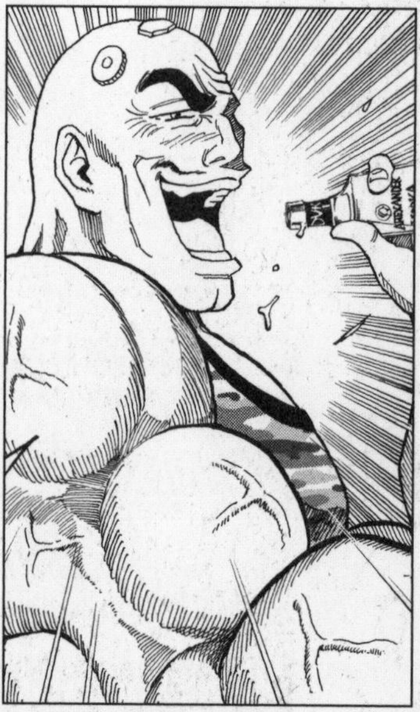
ALEXANDER

GOURMET 21: GOURMET COLISEUM!!

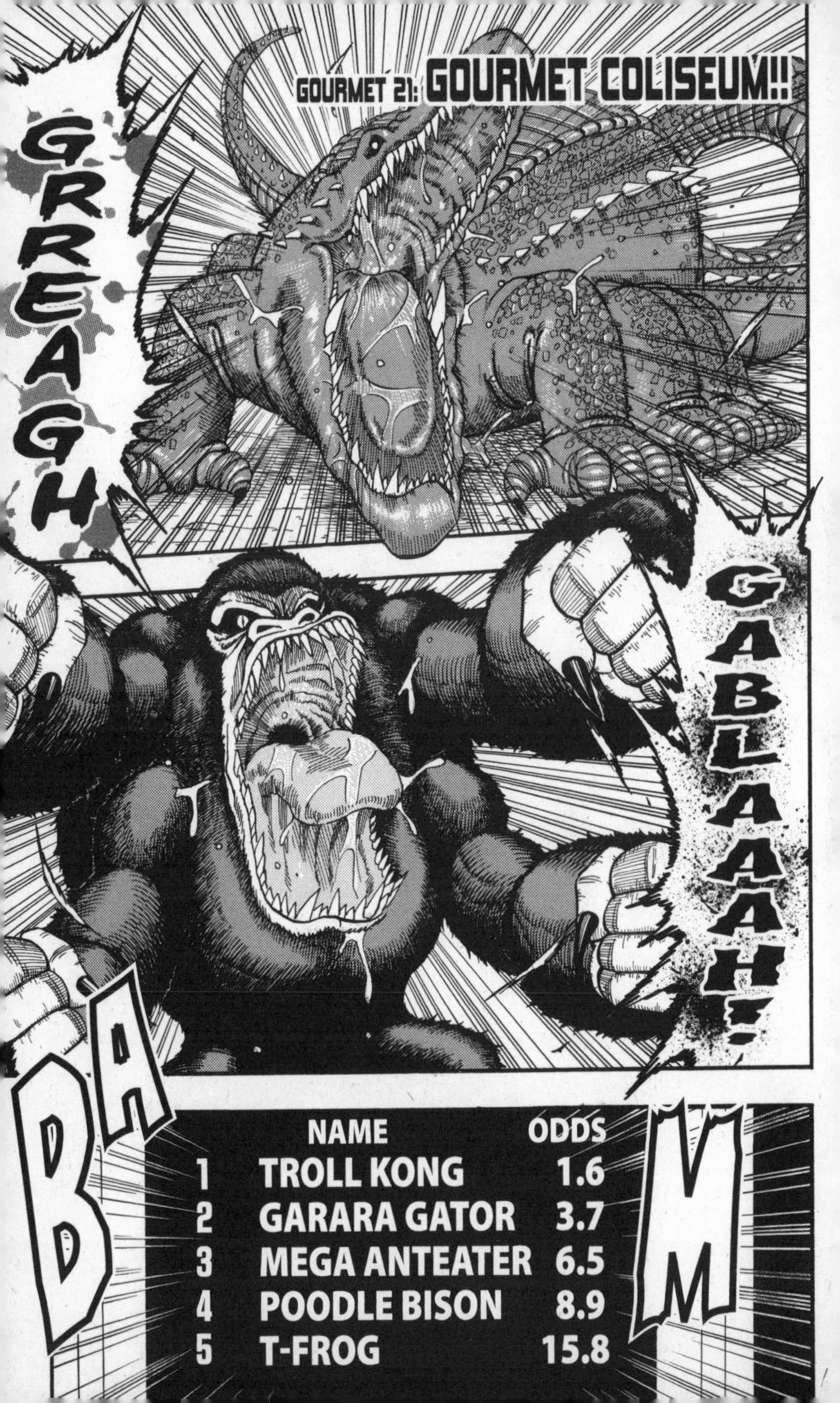
GRREAGH
GABLAAAH!!
BA
NAME ODDS
1 TROLL KONG 1.6
2 GARARA GATOR 3.7
3 MEGA ANTEATER 6.5
4 POODLE BISON 8.9
5 T-FROG 15.8
M

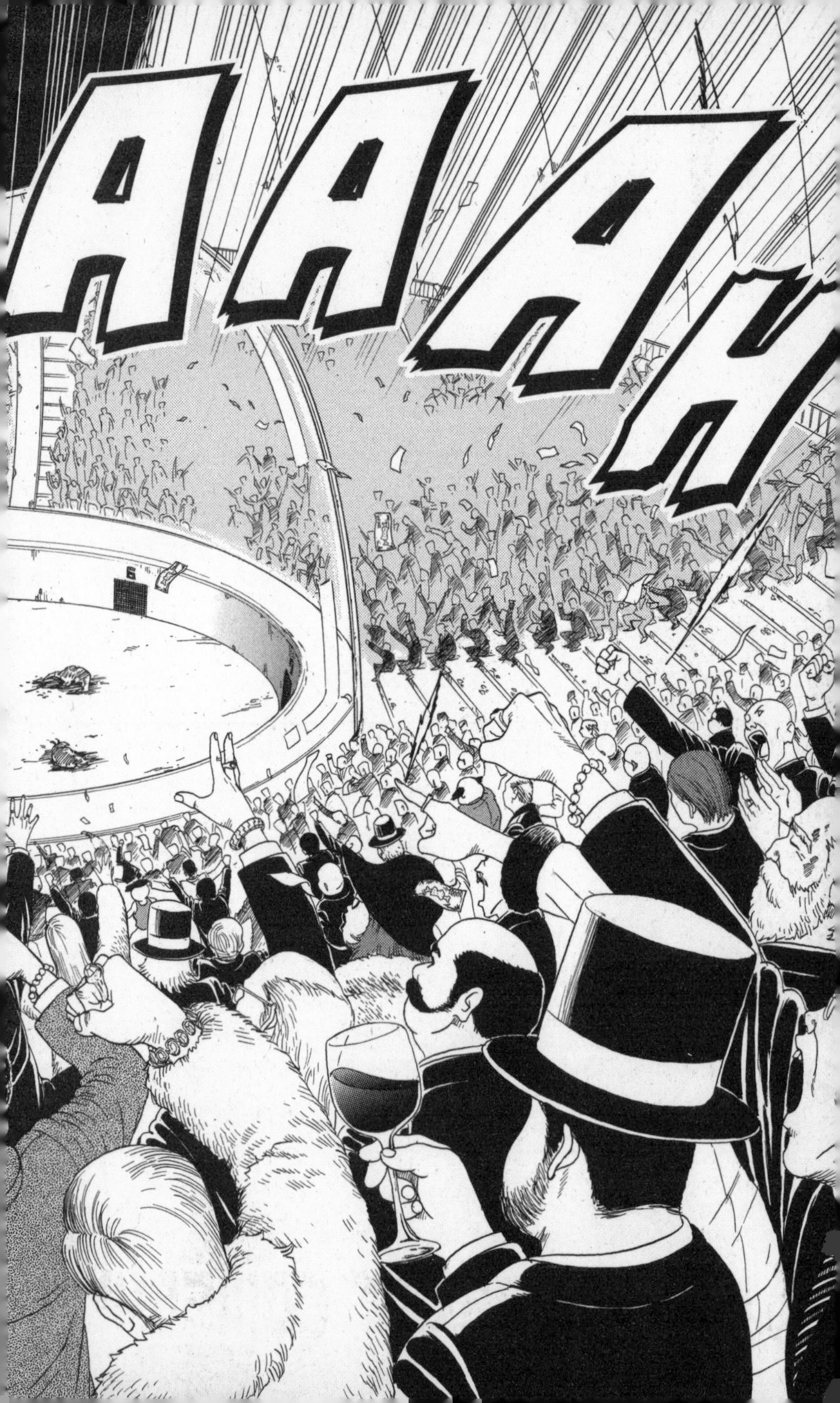
AAAH

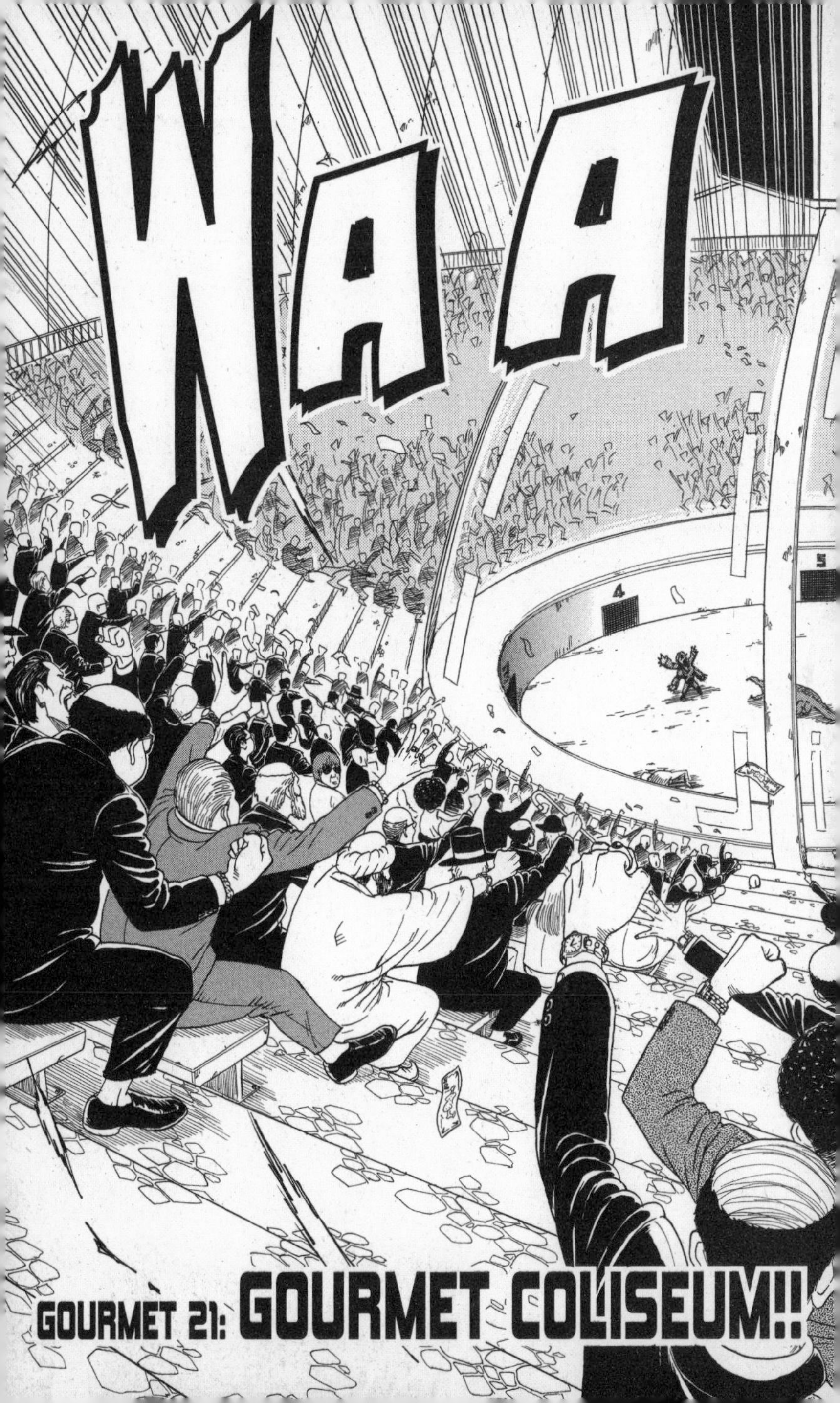
WAA
GOURMET 21: GOURMET COLISEUM!!

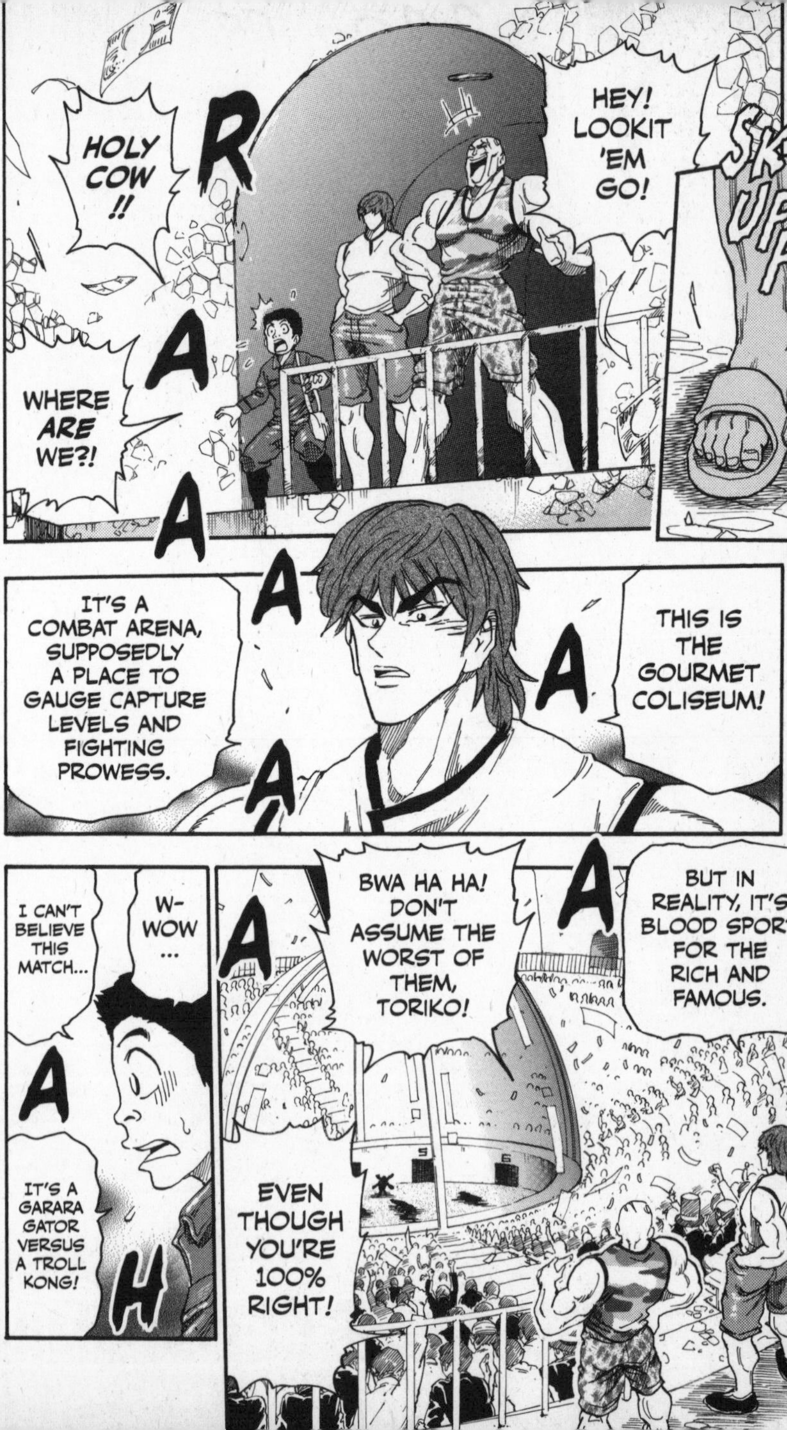
SKUFF
HEY! LOOKIT 'EM GO!
HOLY COW!!
WHERE ARE WE?!
RAAAAAAAAH
THIS IS THE GOURMET COLISEUM!
IT'S A COMBAT ARENA, SUPPOSEDLY A PLACE TO GAUGE CAPTURE LEVELS AND FIGHTING PROWESS.
BUT IN REALITY, IT'S BLOOD SPORT FOR THE RICH AND FAMOUS.
BWA HA HA! DON'T ASSUME THE WORST OF THEM, TORIKO!
EVEN THOUGH YOU'RE 100% RIGHT!
W-WOW...
I CAN'T BELIEVE THIS MATCH...
IT'S A GARARA GATOR VERSUS A TROLL KONG!

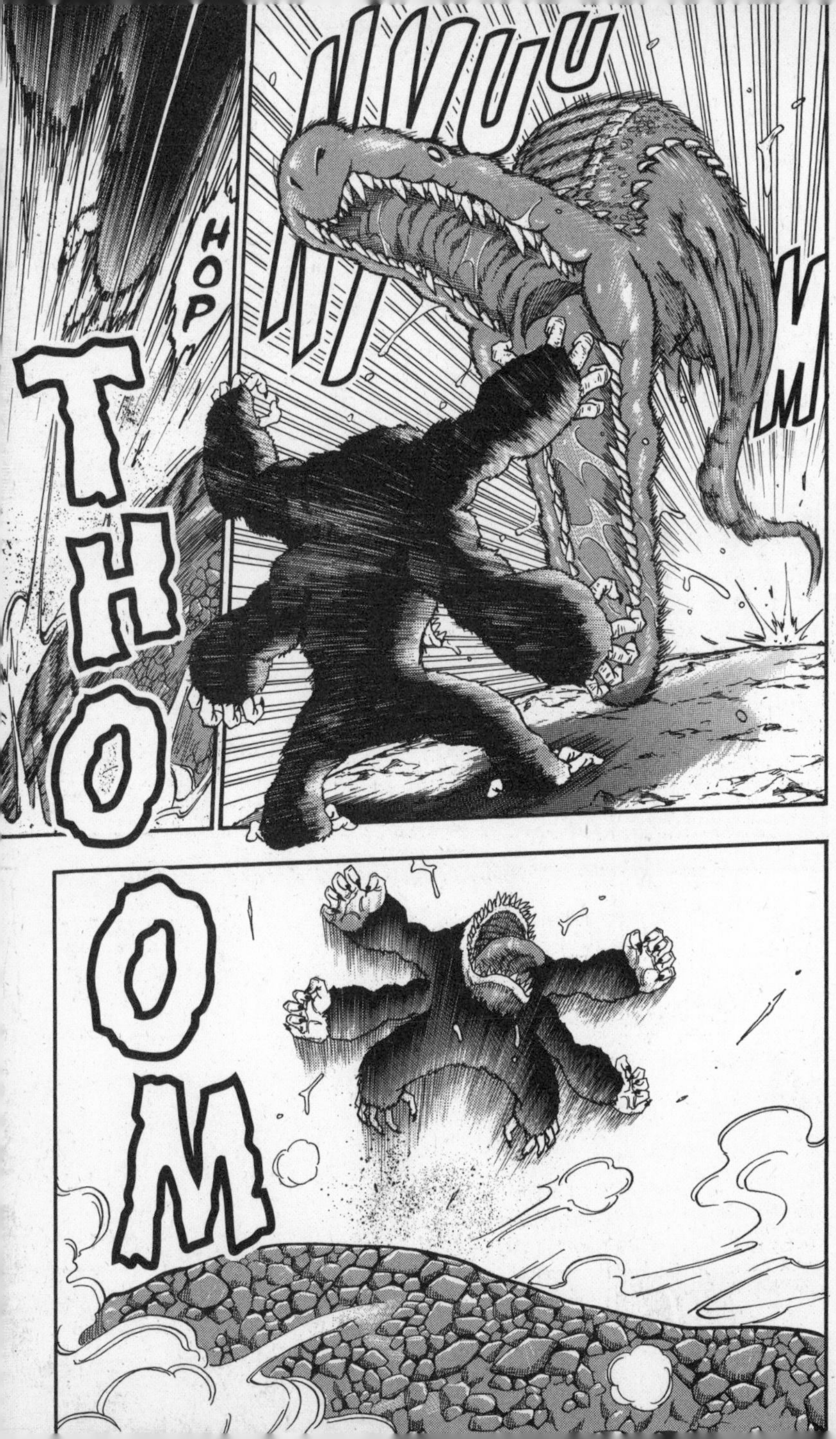
HOP
THOOM

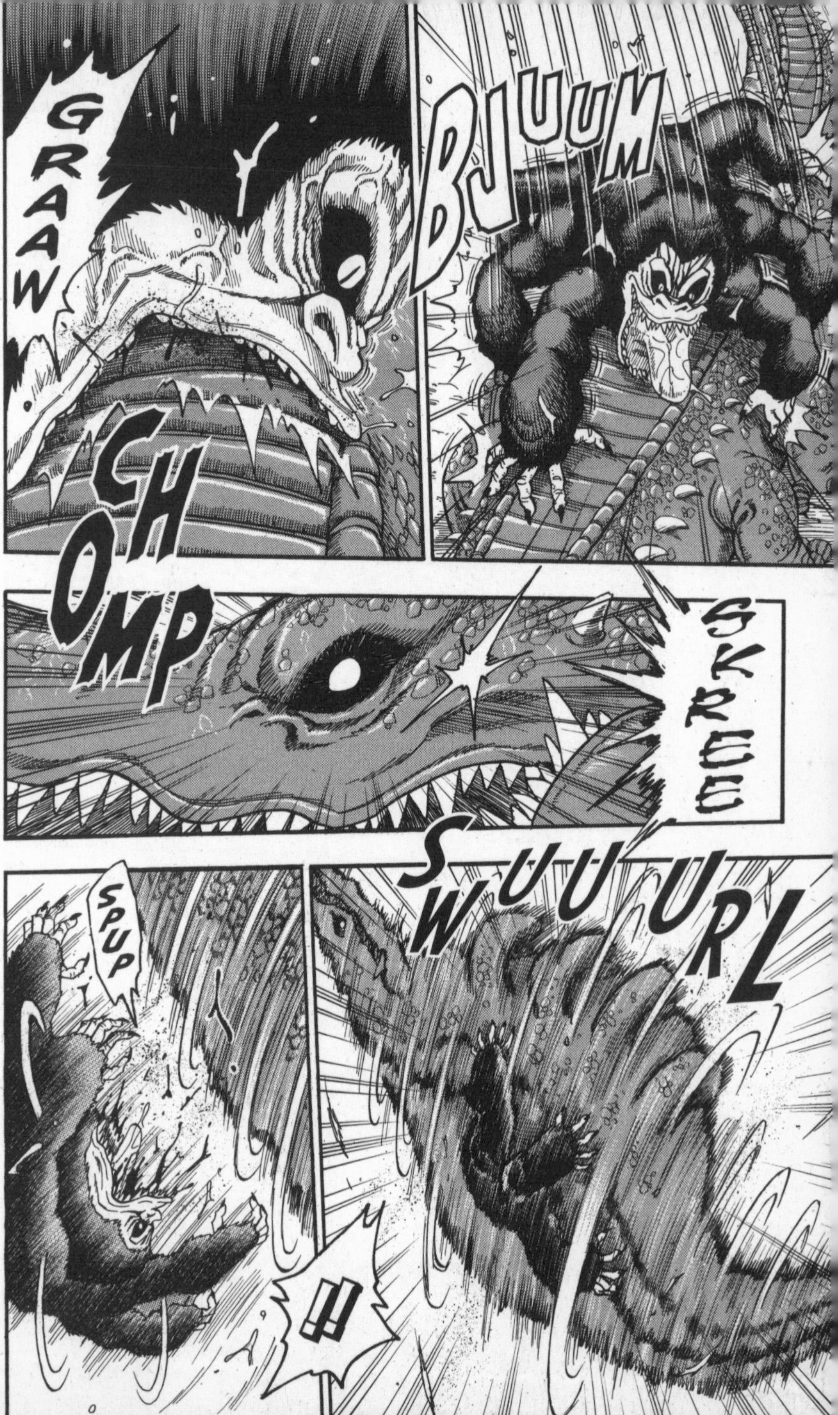
BJUUM
GRAAW
CHOMP
SKREE
SWUUURL
SPUP
!!

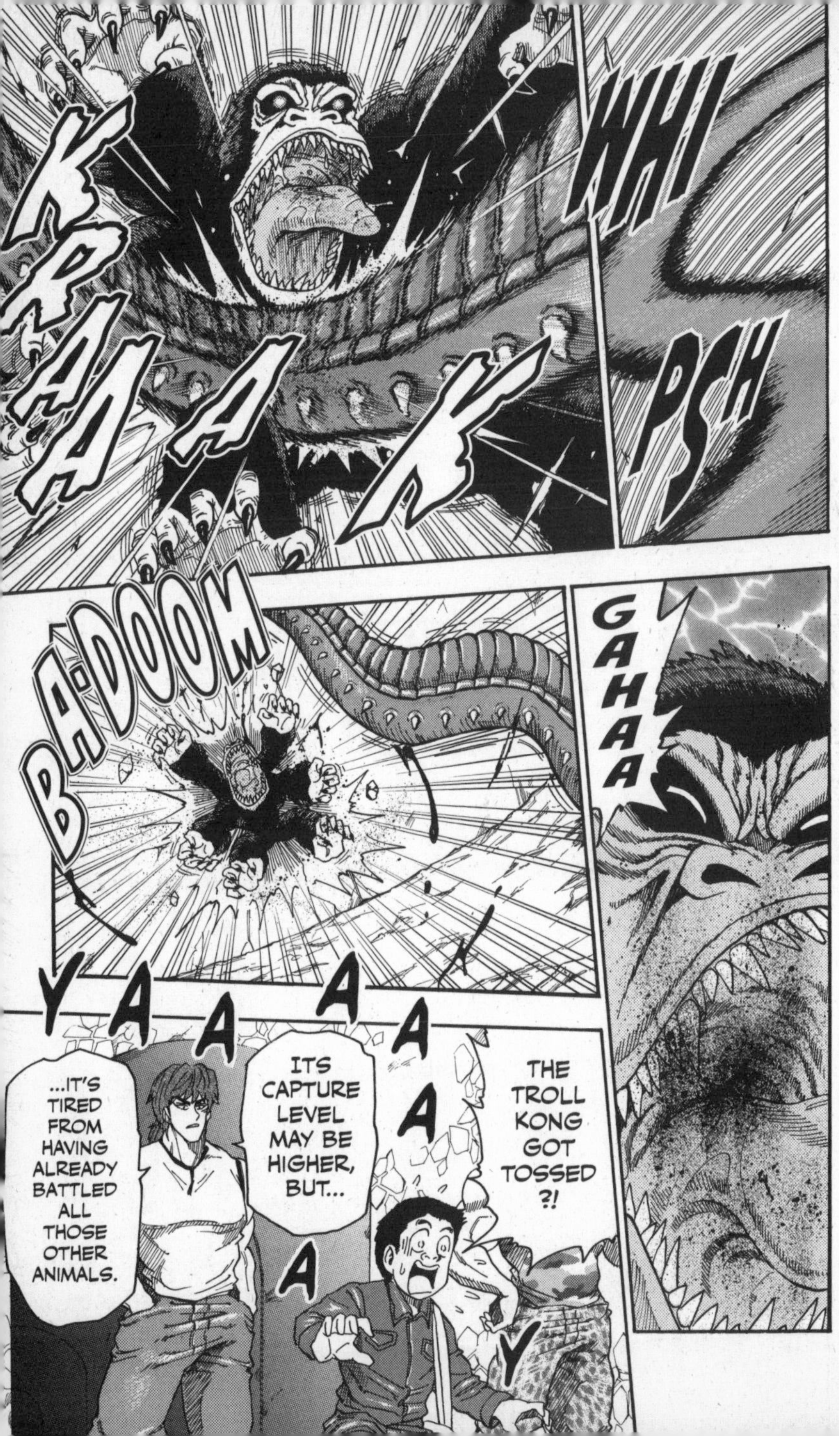

WHI
PSH
KRAAAK
GAHAAA
BA-DOOM
YAAAAAAAY
THE TROLL KONG GOT TOSSED?!
ITS CAPTURE LEVEL MAY BE HIGHER, BUT...
...IT'S TIRED FROM HAVING ALREADY BATTLED ALL THOSE OTHER ANIMALS.

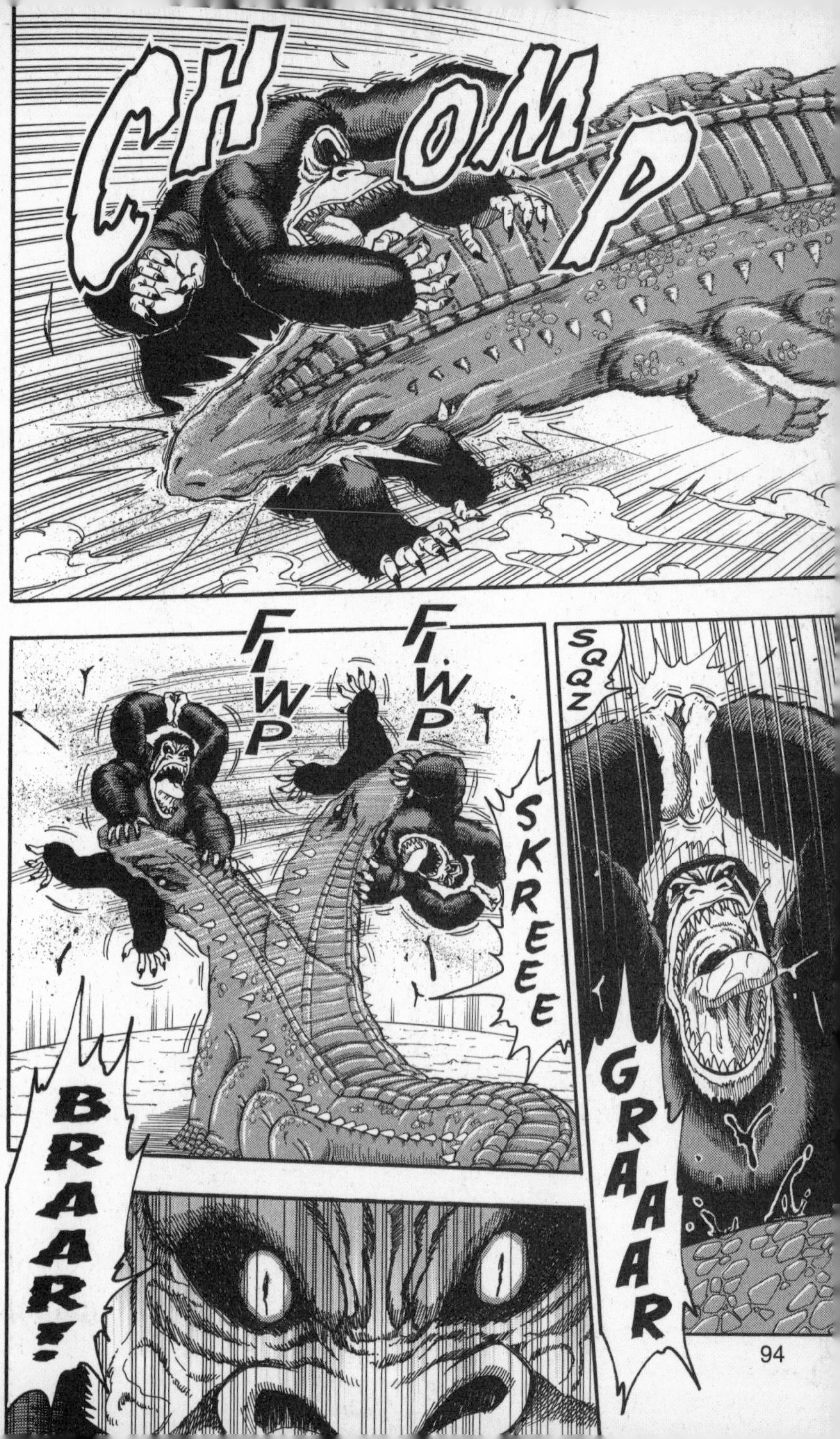

CHOMP
SQQZ
GRAAR
FIWP
FIWP
SKREEE
BRAAR!!

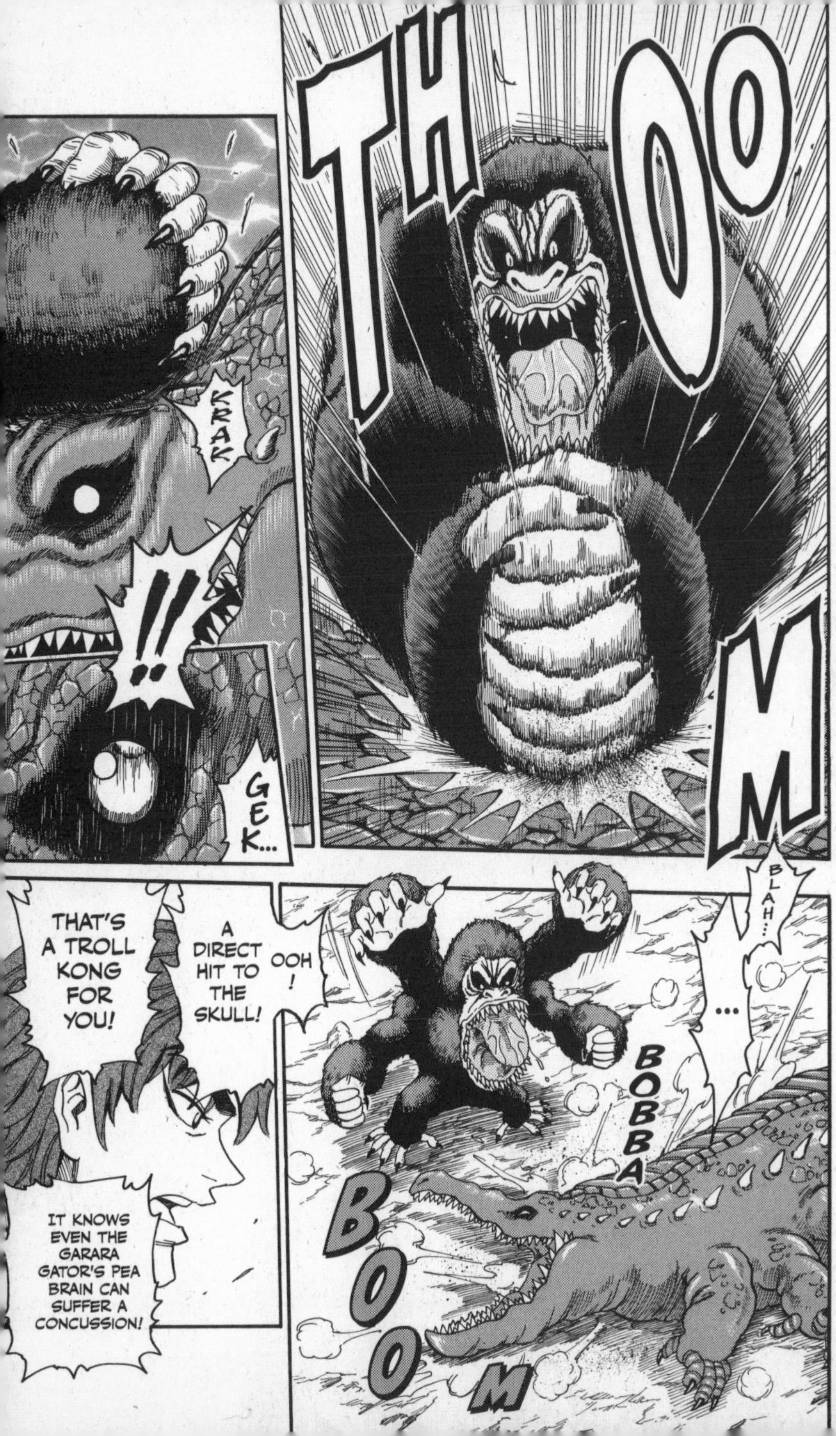

THOOM
KRAK
!!
GEK...
BLAH...
...
OOH!
BOBBA
BOOOM
A DIRECT HIT TO THE SKULL!
THAT'S A TROLL KONG FOR YOU!
IT KNOWS EVEN THE GARARA GATOR'S PEA BRAIN CAN SUFFER A CONCUSSION!

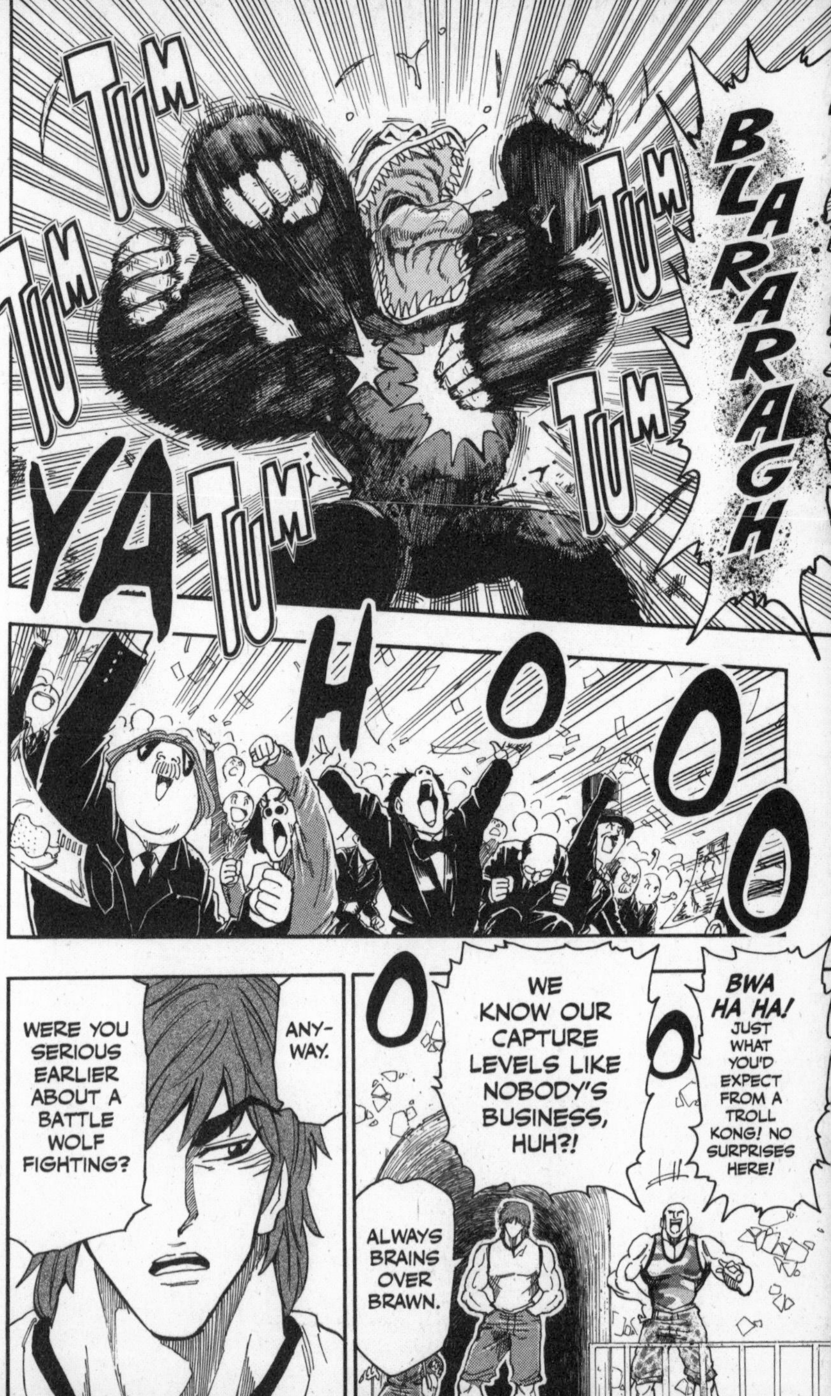

BLARAGH
TUM
TUM
TUM
TUM
TUM
TUM
YAHOOOOOO
BWA HA HA! JUST WHAT YOU'D EXPECT FROM A TROLL KONG! NO SURPRISES HERE!
WE KNOW OUR CAPTURE LEVELS LIKE NOBODY'S BUSINESS, HUH?!
ALWAYS BRAINS OVER BRAWN.
ANY-WAY.
WERE YOU SERIOUS EARLIER ABOUT A BATTLE WOLF FIGHTING?

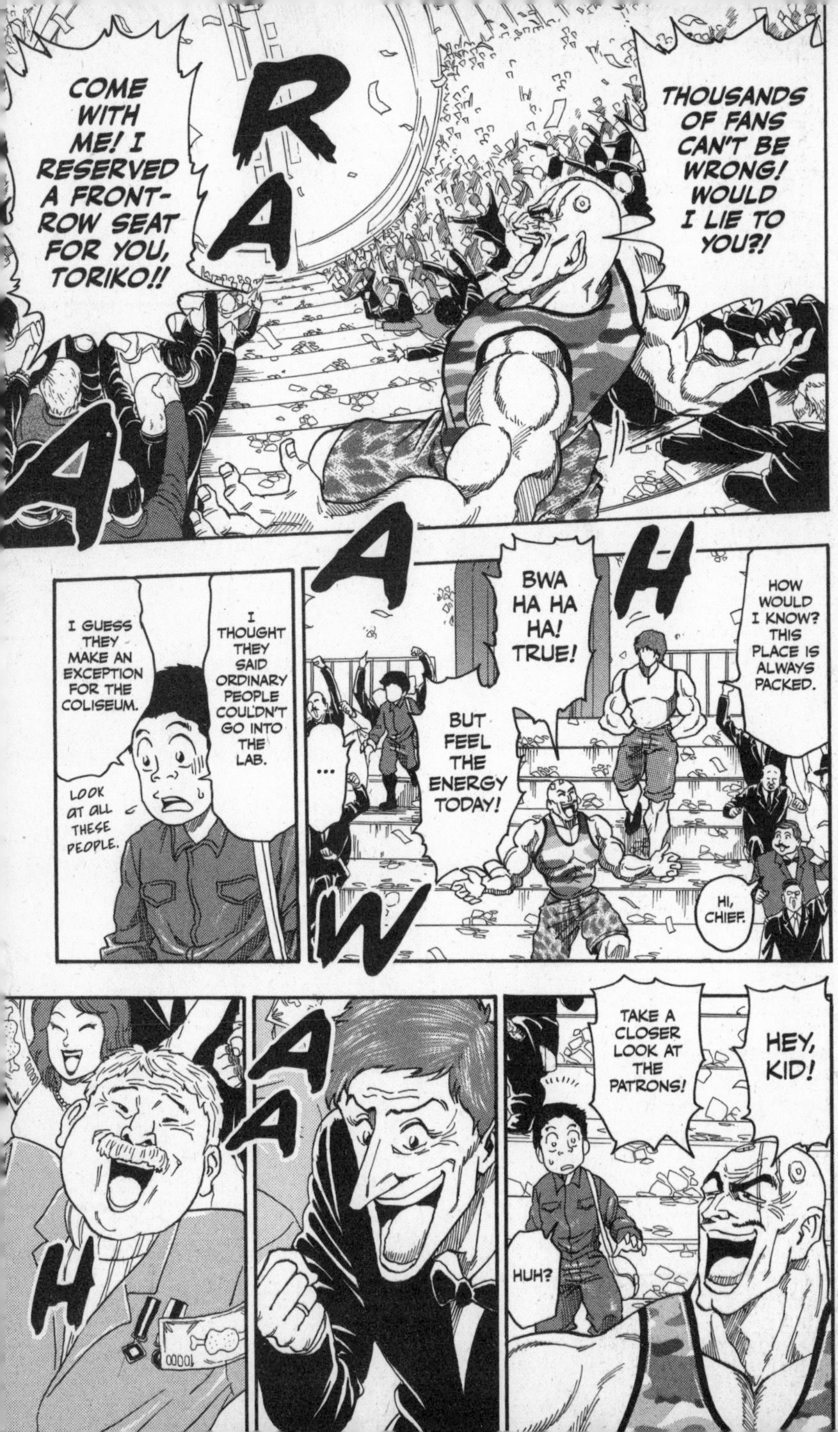
THOUSANDS OF FANS CAN'T BE WRONG! WOULD I LIE TO YOU?!
COME WITH ME! I RESERVED A FRONT-ROW SEAT FOR YOU, TORIKO!!
R
A
A
A
H
HOW WOULD I KNOW? THIS PLACE IS ALWAYS PACKED.
BWA HA HA HA! TRUE!
BUT FEEL THE ENERGY TODAY!
HI, CHIEF.
...
W
I THOUGHT THEY SAID ORDINARY PEOPLE COULDN'T GO INTO THE LAB.
I GUESS THEY MAKE AN EXCEPTION FOR THE COLISEUM.
LOOK AT ALL THESE PEOPLE.
HEY, KID!
TAKE A CLOSER LOOK AT THE PATRONS!
HUH?
A
A
H

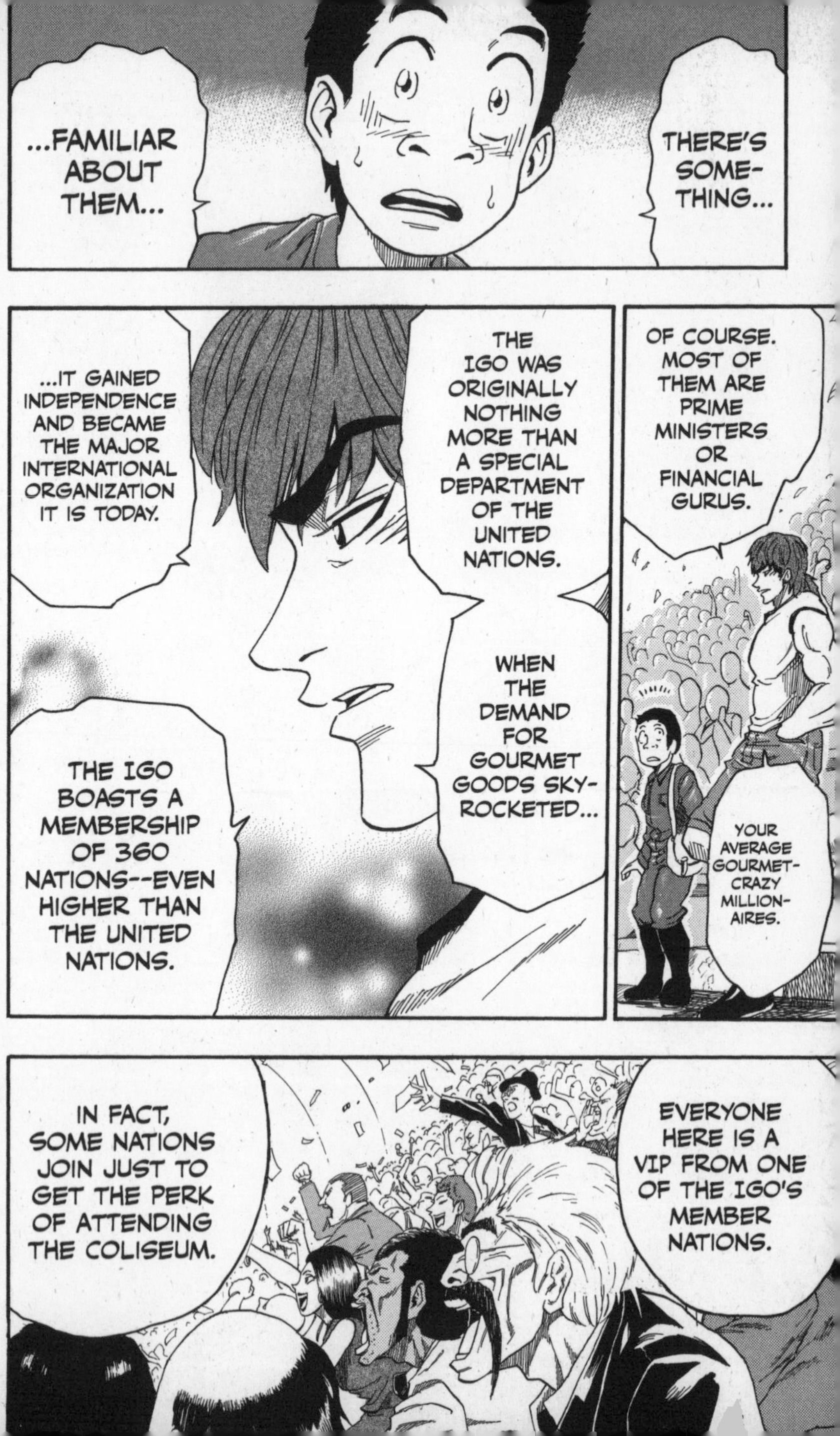
THERE'S SOME-THING...
...FAMILIAR ABOUT THEM...
OF COURSE. MOST OF THEM ARE PRIME MINISTERS OR FINANCIAL GURUS.
YOUR AVERAGE GOURMET-CRAZY MILLION-AIRES.
THE IGO WAS ORIGINALLY NOTHING MORE THAN A SPECIAL DEPARTMENT OF THE UNITED NATIONS.
WHEN THE DEMAND FOR GOURMET GOODS SKY-ROCKETED...
...IT GAINED INDEPENDENCE AND BECAME THE MAJOR INTERNATIONAL ORGANIZATION IT IS TODAY.
THE IGO BOASTS A MEMBERSHIP OF 360 NATIONS--EVEN HIGHER THAN THE UNITED NATIONS.
EVERYONE HERE IS A VIP FROM ONE OF THE IGO'S MEMBER NATIONS.
IN FACT, SOME NATIONS JOIN JUST TO GET THE PERK OF ATTENDING THE COLISEUM.

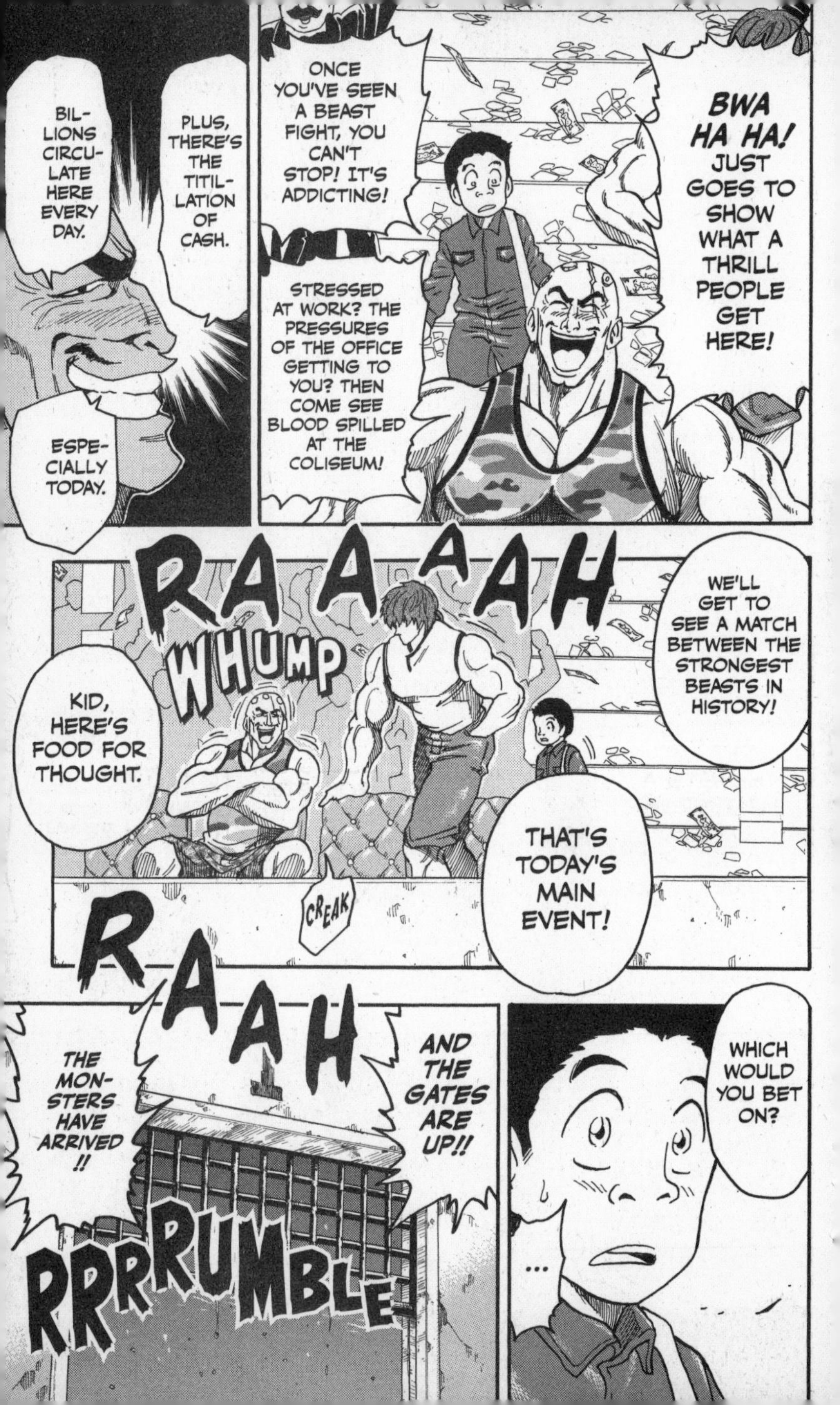
BWA HA HA! JUST GOES TO SHOW WHAT A THRILL PEOPLE GET HERE!
ONCE YOU'VE SEEN A BEAST FIGHT, YOU CAN'T STOP! IT'S ADDICTING!
STRESSED AT WORK? THE PRESSURES OF THE OFFICE GETTING TO YOU? THEN COME SEE BLOOD SPILLED AT THE COLISEUM!
PLUS, THERE'S THE TITILLATION OF CASH.
BILLIONS CIRCULATE HERE EVERY DAY.
ESPECIALLY TODAY.
RAAAAH
WE'LL GET TO SEE A MATCH BETWEEN THE STRONGEST BEASTS IN HISTORY!
WHUMP
KID, HERE'S FOOD FOR THOUGHT.
THAT'S TODAY'S MAIN EVENT!
CREAK
RAAH
WHICH WOULD YOU BET ON?
...
AND THE GATES ARE UP!!
THE MONSTERS HAVE ARRIVED!!
RRRRUMBLE

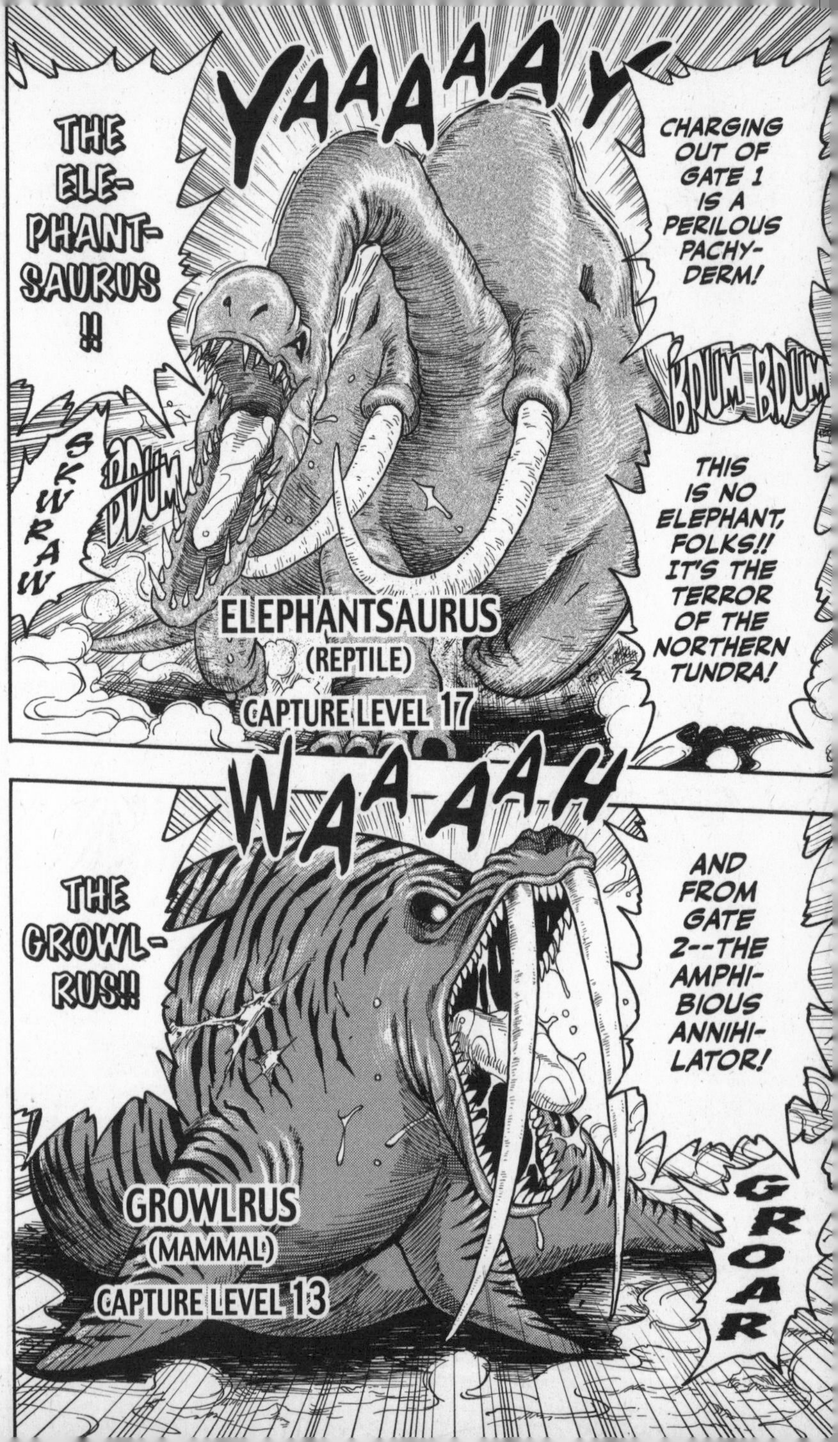
YAAAAAY
CHARGING OUT OF GATE 1 IS A PERILOUS PACHY-DERM!
THE ELE-PHANT-SAURUS!!
BDUM BDUM
THIS IS NO ELEPHANT, FOLKS!! IT'S THE TERROR OF THE NORTHERN TUNDRA!
BDUM
SKWRAW
ELEPHANTSAURUS
(REPTILE)
CAPTURE LEVEL 17
WAAAAH
AND FROM GATE 2--THE AMPHI-BIOUS ANNIHI-LATOR!
THE GROWL-RUS!!
GROAR
GROWLRUS
(MAMMAL)
CAPTURE LEVEL 13

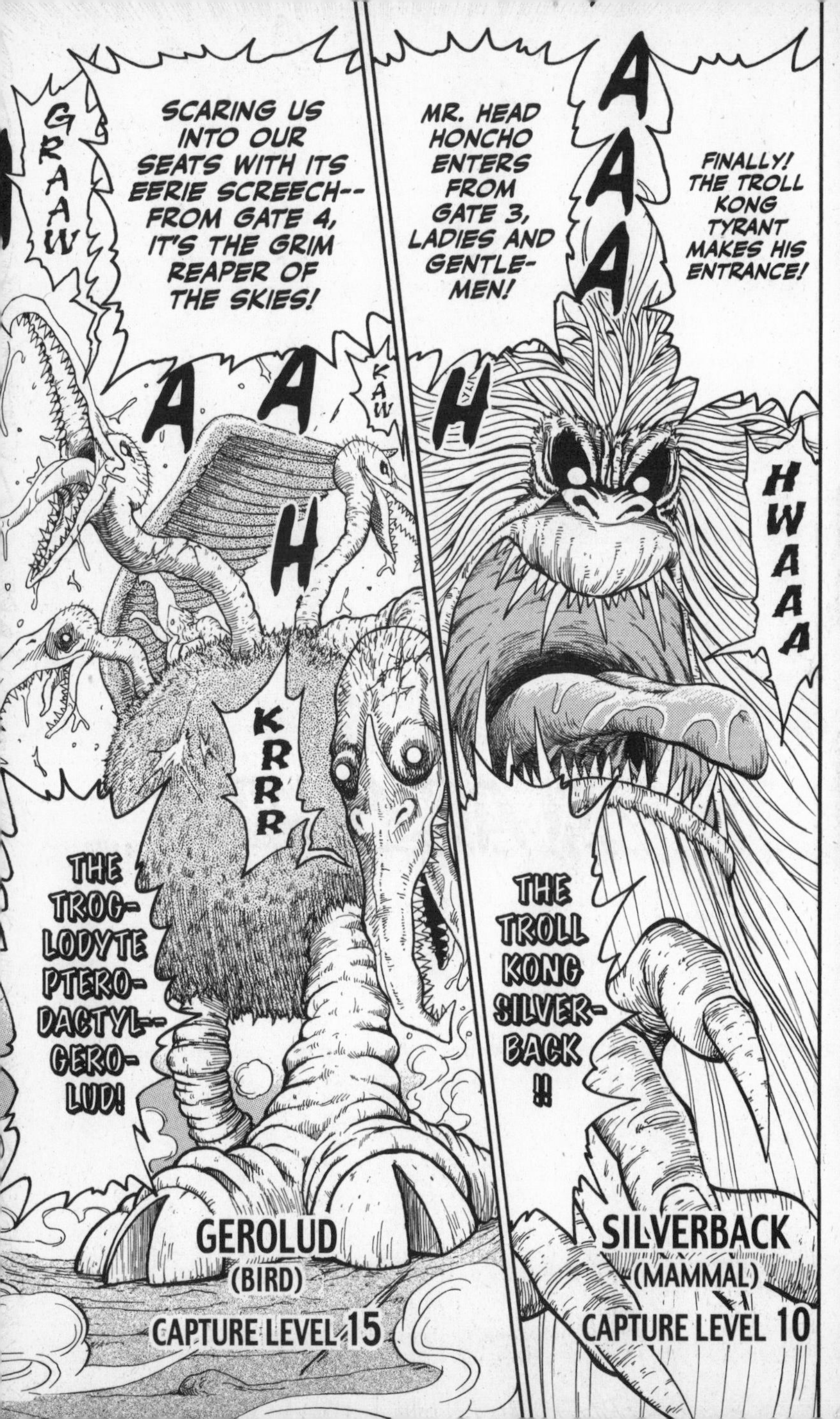
FINALLY! THE TROLL KONG TYRANT MAKES HIS ENTRANCE!
AAA
MR. HEAD HONCHO ENTERS FROM GATE 3, LADIES AND GENTLEMEN!
HWAAAA
H
THE TROLL KONG SILVERBACK!!
SILVERBACK
(MAMMAL)
CAPTURE LEVEL 10
SCARING US INTO OUR SEATS WITH ITS EERIE SCREECH-- FROM GATE 4, IT'S THE GRIM REAPER OF THE SKIES!
GRAAW
KAW
AAH
KRRR
THE TROGLODYTE PTERODACTYL-- GEROLUD!
GEROLUD
(BIRD)
CAPTURE LEVEL 15

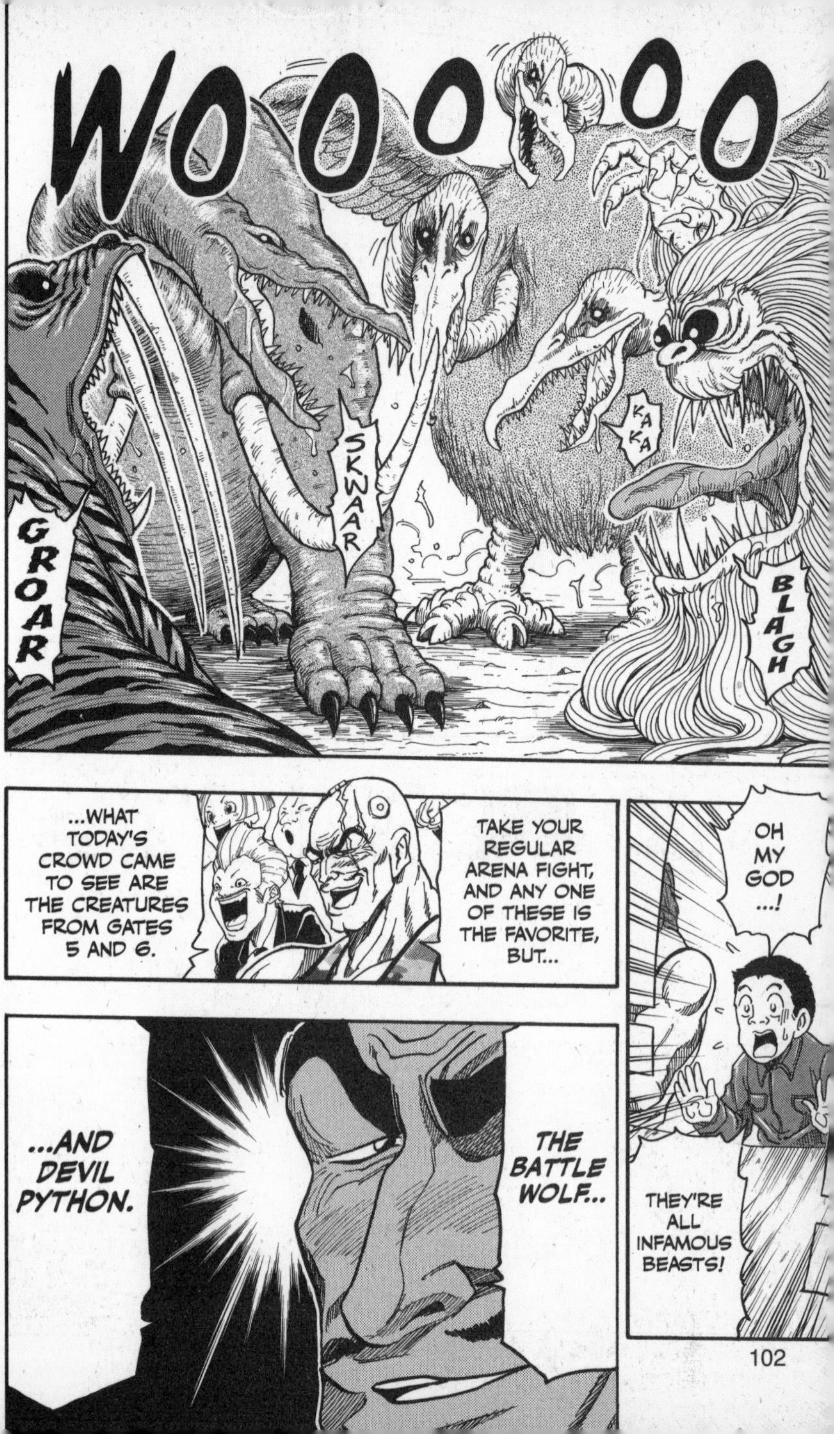
WOOOOOO
BLAGH
KAKA
SKWAAR
GROAR
OH MY GOD ...!
THEY'RE ALL INFAMOUS BEASTS!
TAKE YOUR REGULAR ARENA FIGHT, AND ANY ONE OF THESE IS THE FAVORITE, BUT...
...WHAT TODAY'S CROWD CAME TO SEE ARE THE CREATURES FROM GATES 5 AND 6.
THE BATTLE WOLF...
...AND DEVIL PYTHON.

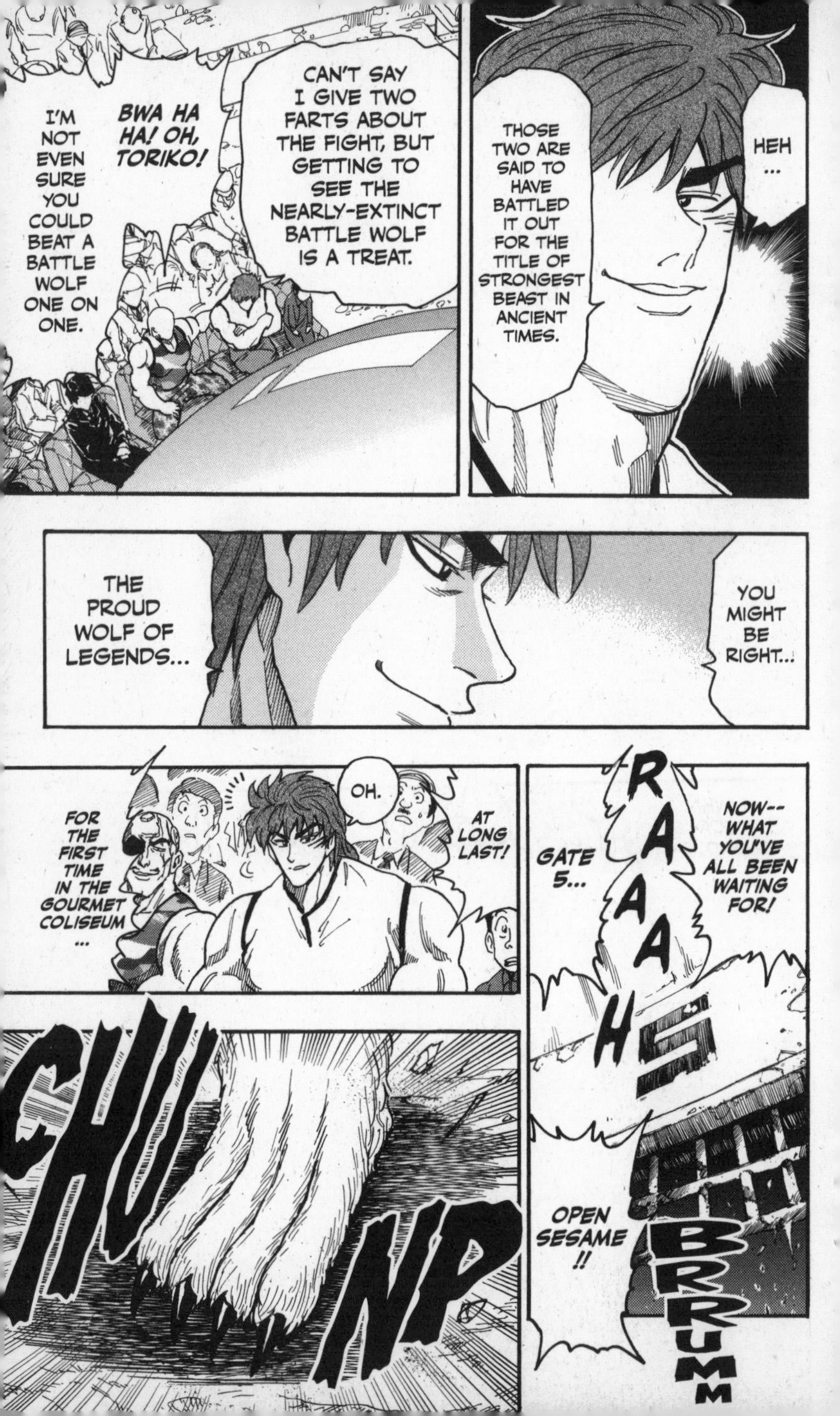
HEH ...
THOSE TWO ARE SAID TO HAVE BATTLED IT OUT FOR THE TITLE OF STRONGEST BEAST IN ANCIENT TIMES.
CAN'T SAY I GIVE TWO FARTS ABOUT THE FIGHT, BUT GETTING TO SEE THE NEARLY-EXTINCT BATTLE WOLF IS A TREAT.
BWA HA HA! OH, TORIKO!
I'M NOT EVEN SURE YOU COULD BEAT A BATTLE WOLF ONE ON ONE.
YOU MIGHT BE RIGHT...
THE PROUD WOLF OF LEGENDS...
RAAAAHS
NOW-- WHAT YOU'VE ALL BEEN WAITING FOR!
GATE 5...
OPEN SESAME !!
BRRUMM
AT LONG LAST!
OH.
FOR THE FIRST TIME IN THE GOURMET COLISEUM ...
CHUNP

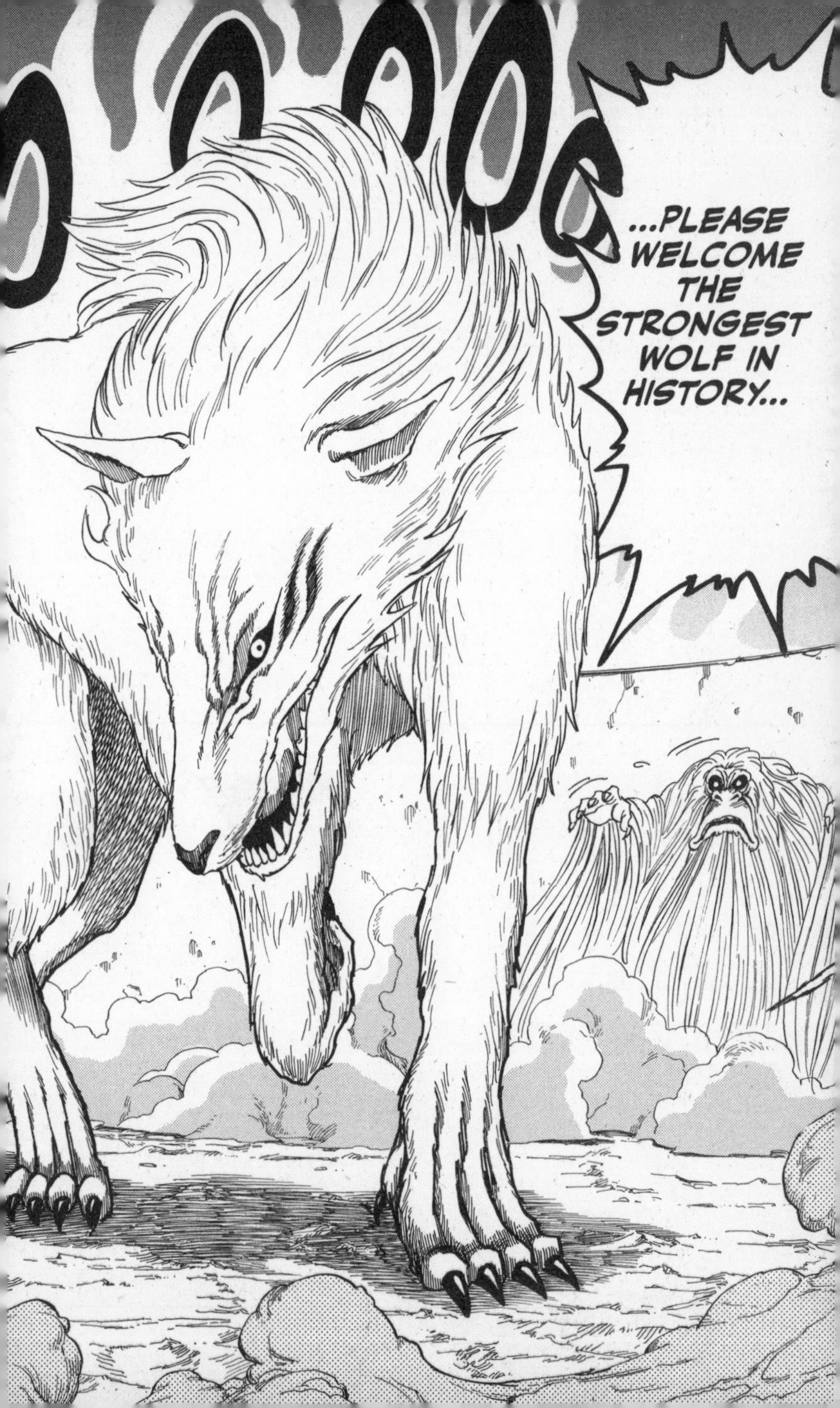
...PLEASE WELCOME THE STRONGEST WOLF IN HISTORY...

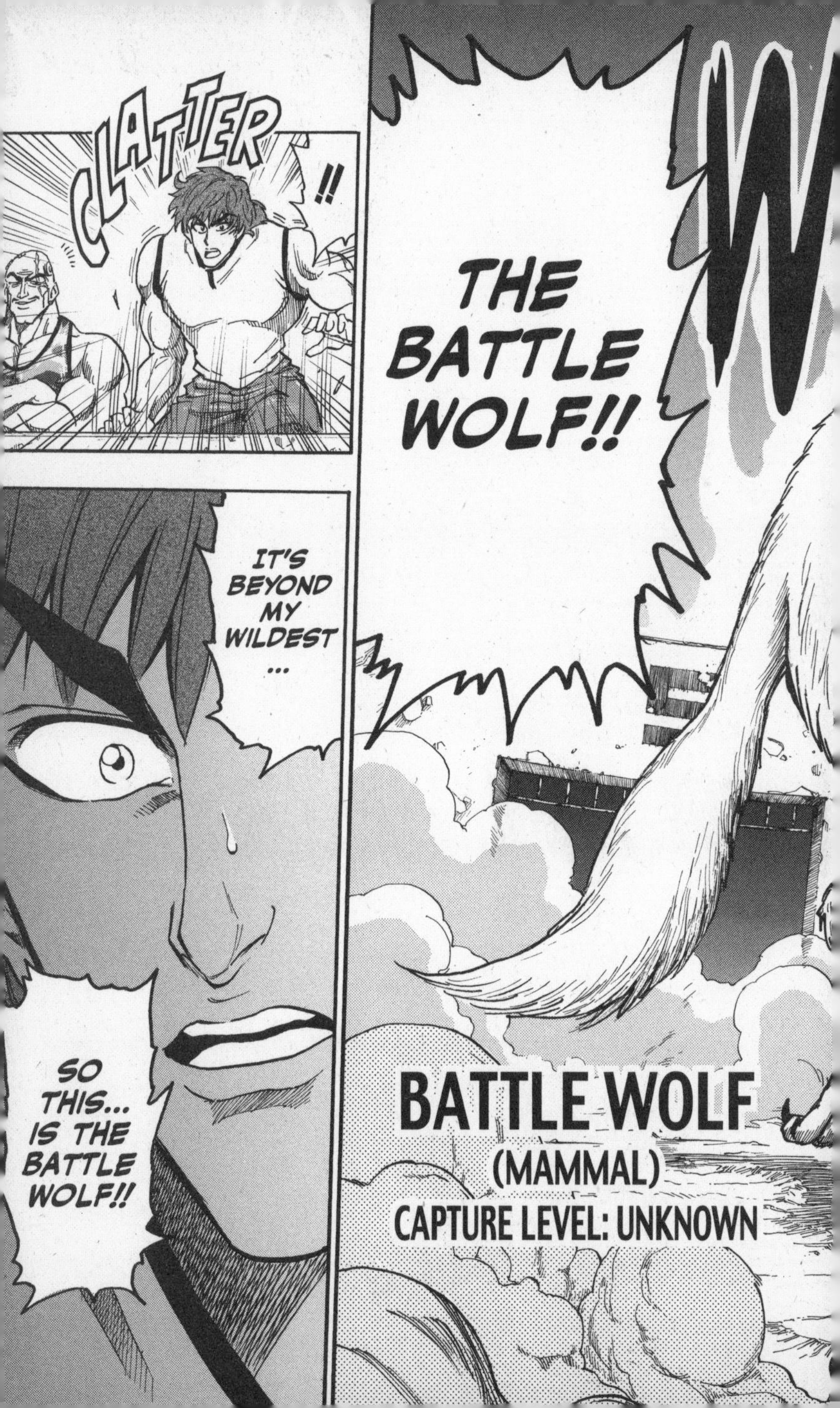
THE BATTLE WOLF!!
BATTLE WOLF
(MAMMAL)
CAPTURE LEVEL: UNKNOWN
CLATTER
!!
IT'S BEYOND MY WILDEST ...
SO THIS... IS THE BATTLE WOLF!!

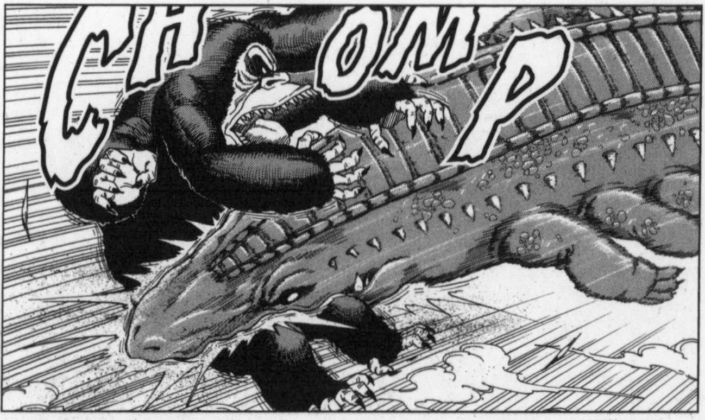
CH OM P

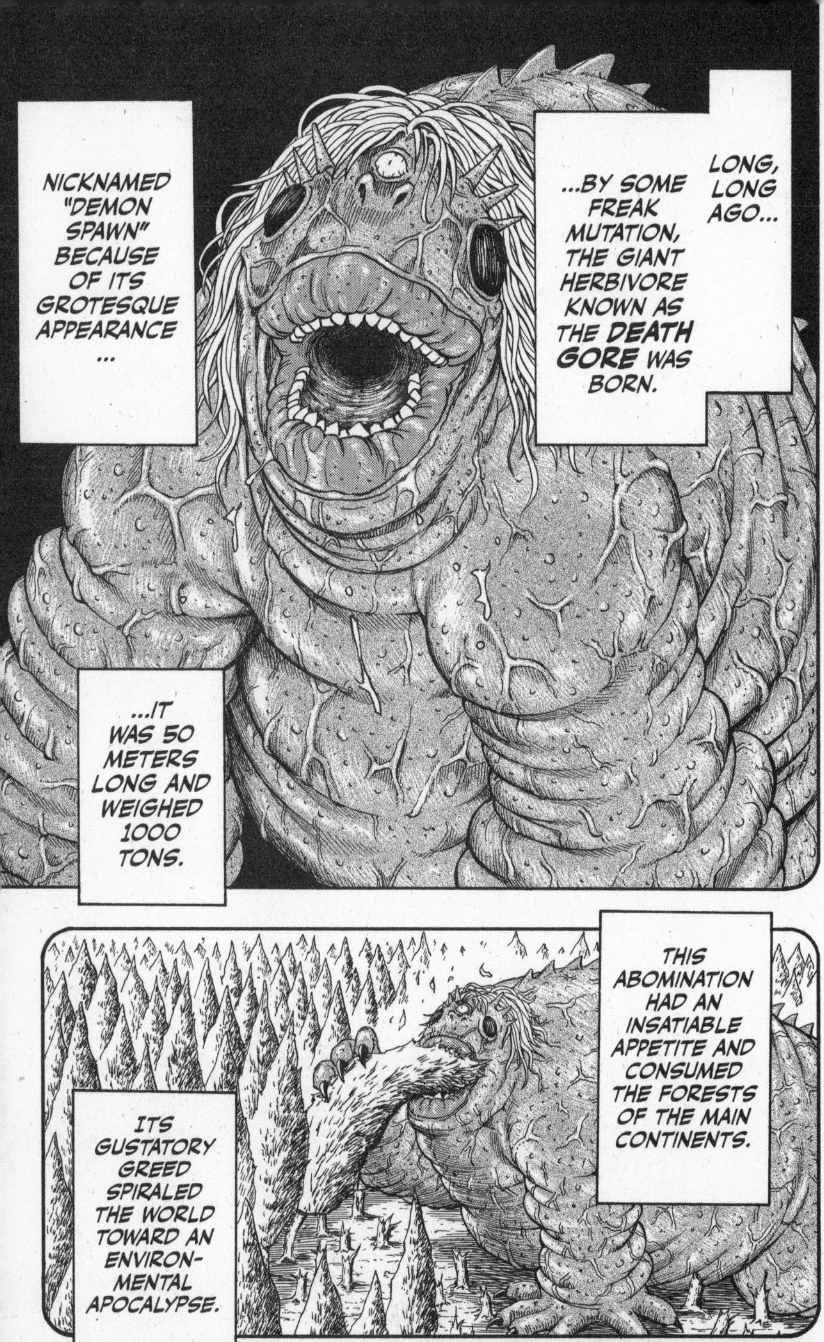
LONG, LONG AGO...
...BY SOME FREAK MUTATION, THE GIANT HERBIVORE KNOWN AS THE DEATH GORE WAS BORN.
NICKNAMED "DEMON SPAWN" BECAUSE OF ITS GROTESQUE APPEARANCE ...
...IT WAS 50 METERS LONG AND WEIGHED 1000 TONS.
THIS ABOMINATION HAD AN INSATIABLE APPETITE AND CONSUMED THE FORESTS OF THE MAIN CONTINENTS.
ITS GUSTATORY GREED SPIRALED THE WORLD TOWARD AN ENVIRON-MENTAL APOCALYPSE.

GOURMET 22: THE BATTLE WOLF!!

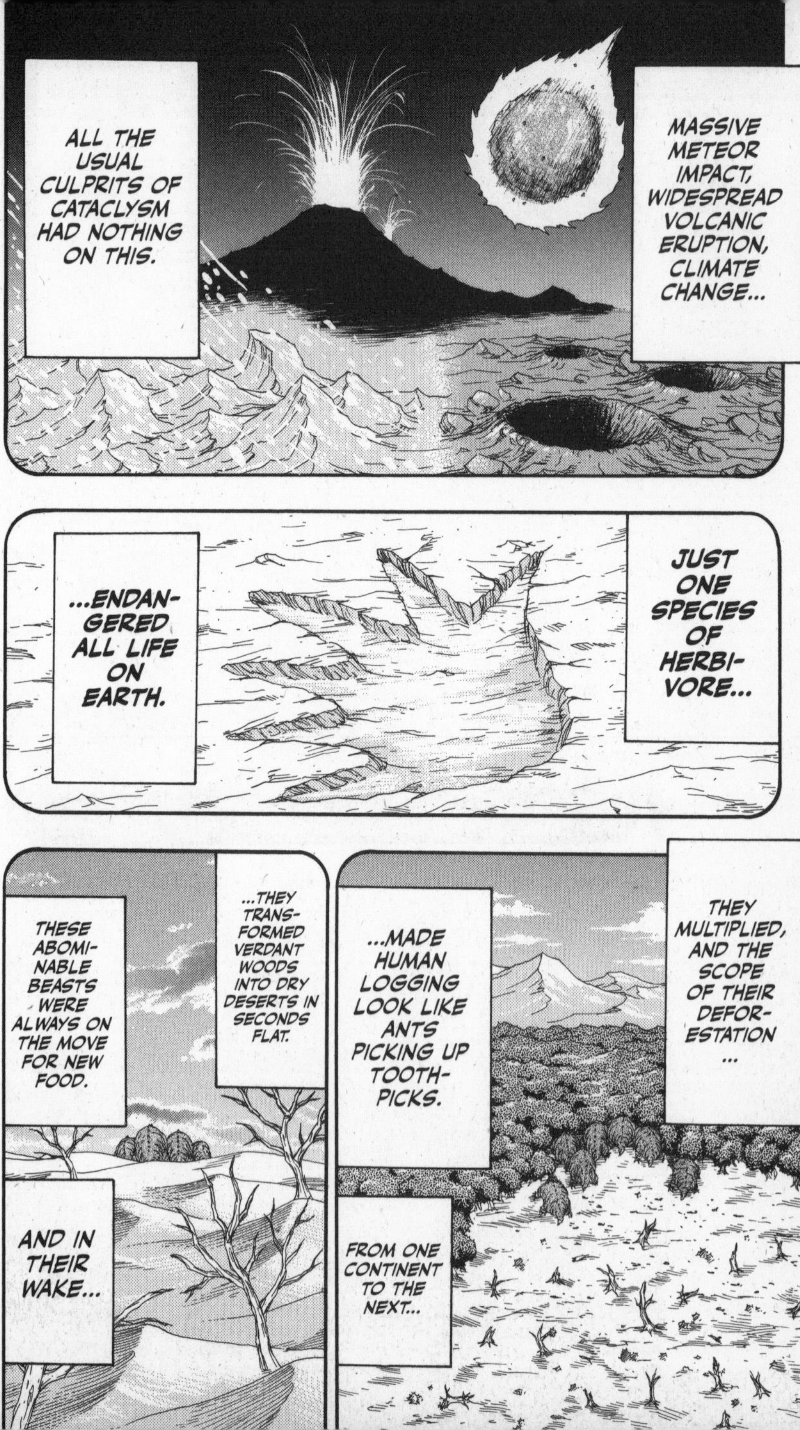
MASSIVE METEOR IMPACT, WIDESPREAD VOLCANIC ERUPTION, CLIMATE CHANGE...
ALL THE USUAL CULPRITS OF CATACLYSM HAD NOTHING ON THIS.
JUST ONE SPECIES OF HERBIVORE...
...ENDANGERED ALL LIFE ON EARTH.
THEY MULTIPLIED, AND THE SCOPE OF THEIR DEFORESTATION...
...MADE HUMAN LOGGING LOOK LIKE ANTS PICKING UP TOOTHPICKS.
FROM ONE CONTINENT TO THE NEXT...
...THEY TRANSFORMED VERDANT WOODS INTO DRY DESERTS IN SECONDS FLAT.
THESE ABOMINABLE BEASTS WERE ALWAYS ON THE MOVE FOR NEW FOOD.
AND IN THEIR WAKE...

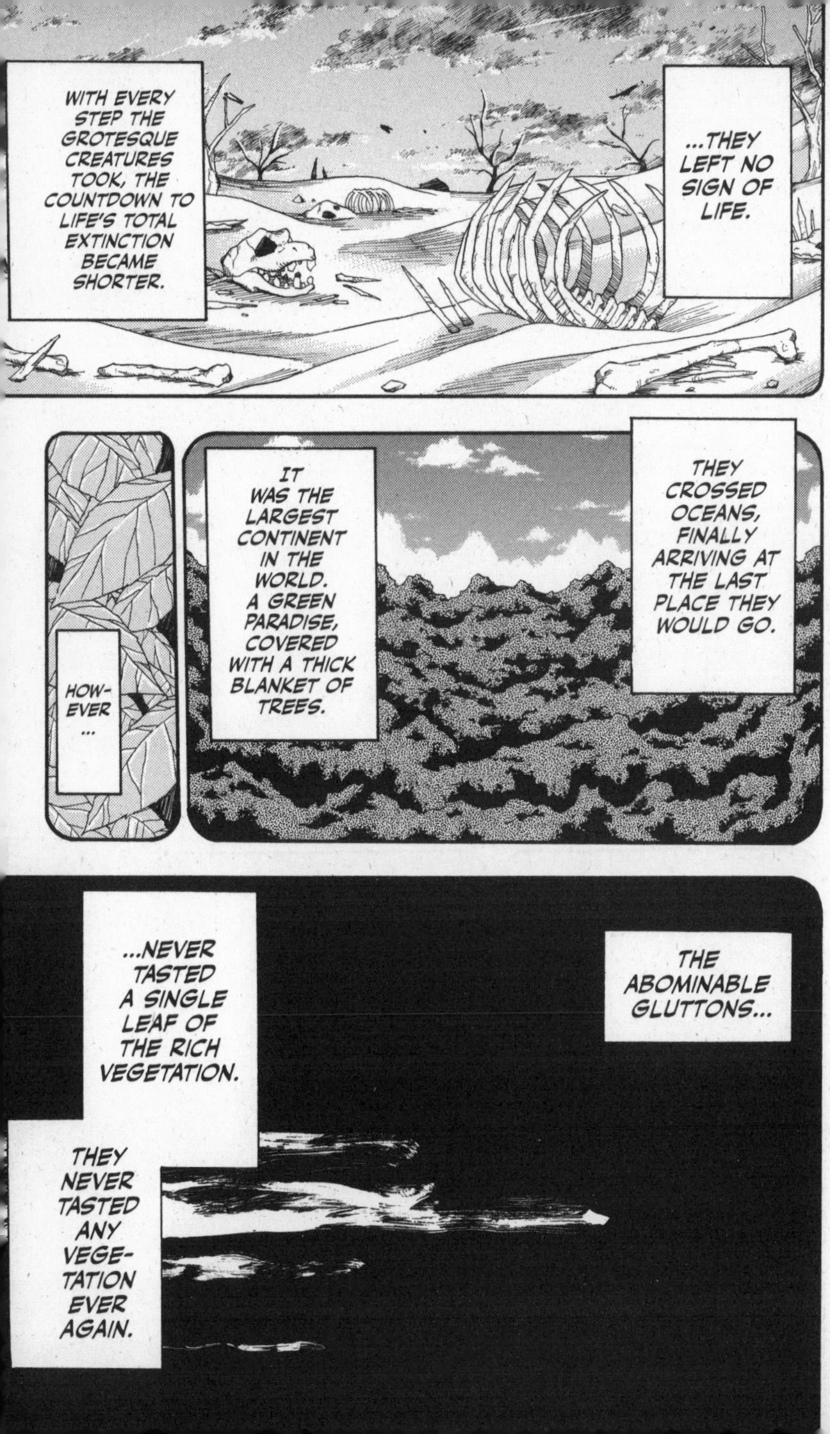
...THEY LEFT NO SIGN OF LIFE.
WITH EVERY STEP THE GROTESQUE CREATURES TOOK, THE COUNTDOWN TO LIFE'S TOTAL EXTINCTION BECAME SHORTER.
THEY CROSSED OCEANS, FINALLY ARRIVING AT THE LAST PLACE THEY WOULD GO.
IT WAS THE LARGEST CONTINENT IN THE WORLD. A GREEN PARADISE, COVERED WITH A THICK BLANKET OF TREES.
HOW-EVER ...
THE ABOMINABLE GLUTTONS...
...NEVER TASTED A SINGLE LEAF OF THE RICH VEGETATION.
THEY NEVER TASTED ANY VEGE-TATION EVER AGAIN.

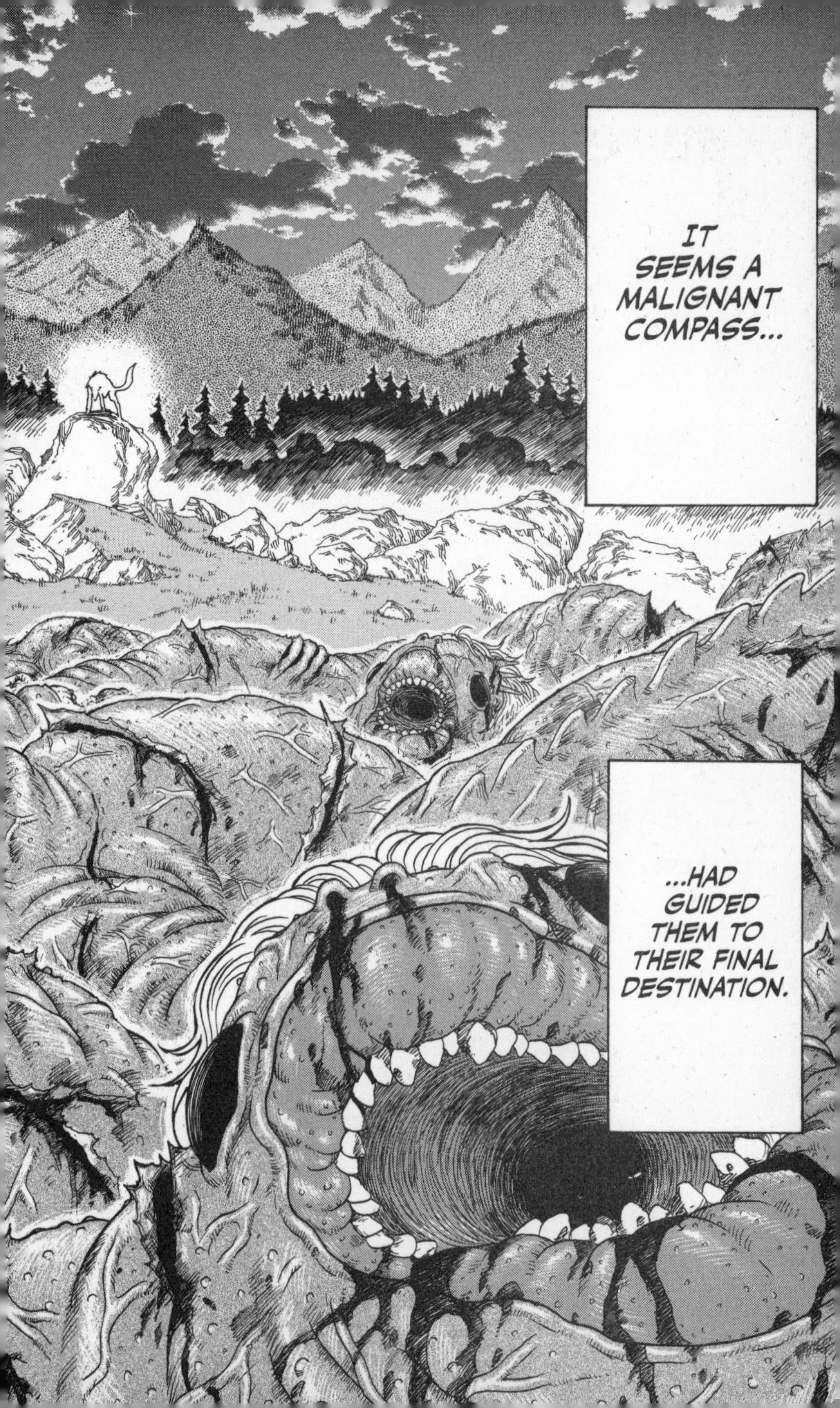
IT SEEMS A MALIGNANT COMPASS...
...HAD GUIDED THEM TO THEIR FINAL DESTINATION.

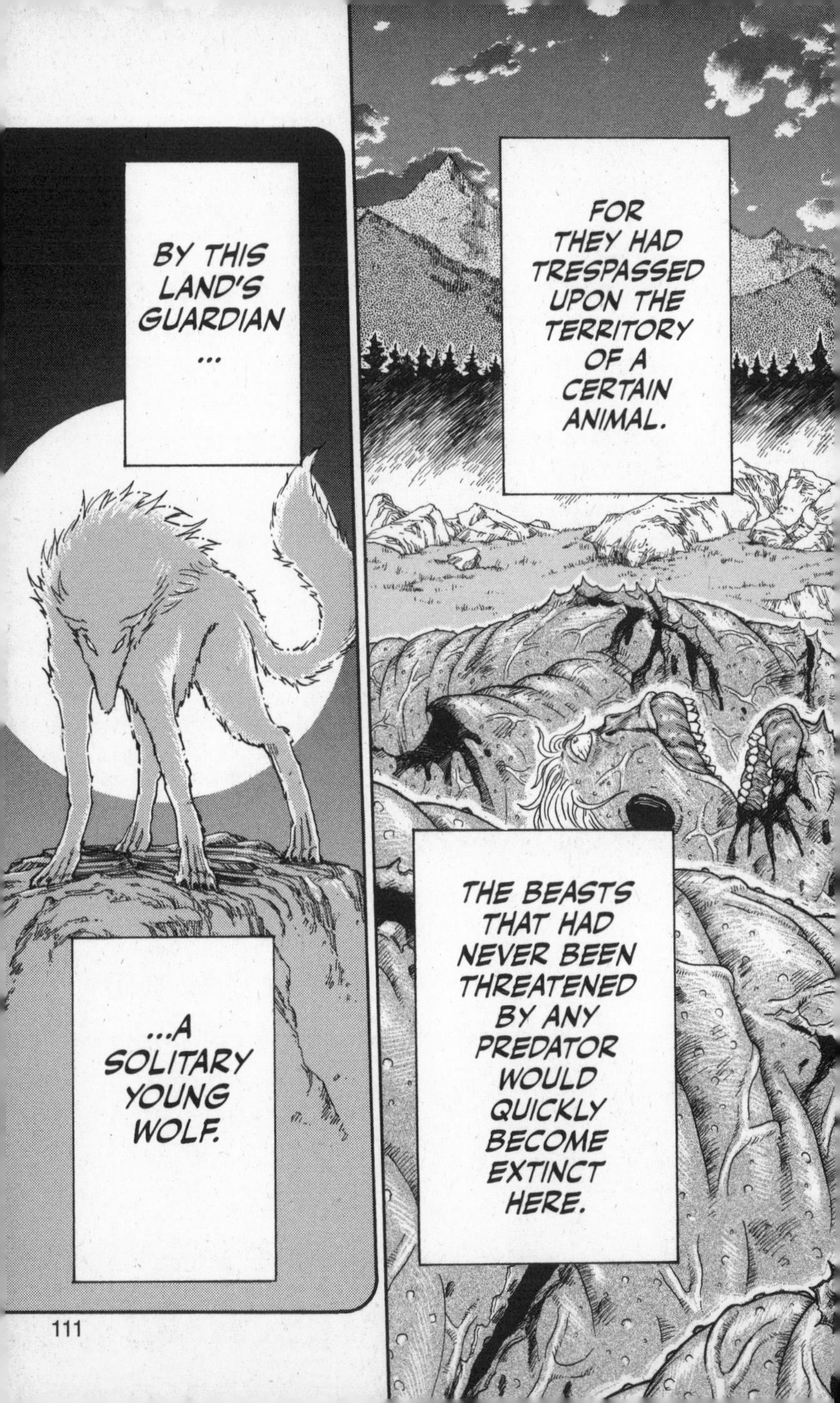
FOR THEY HAD TRESPASSED UPON THE TERRITORY OF A CERTAIN ANIMAL.
THE BEASTS THAT HAD NEVER BEEN THREATENED BY ANY PREDATOR WOULD QUICKLY BECOME EXTINCT HERE.
BY THIS LAND'S GUARDIAN ...
...A SOLITARY YOUNG WOLF.

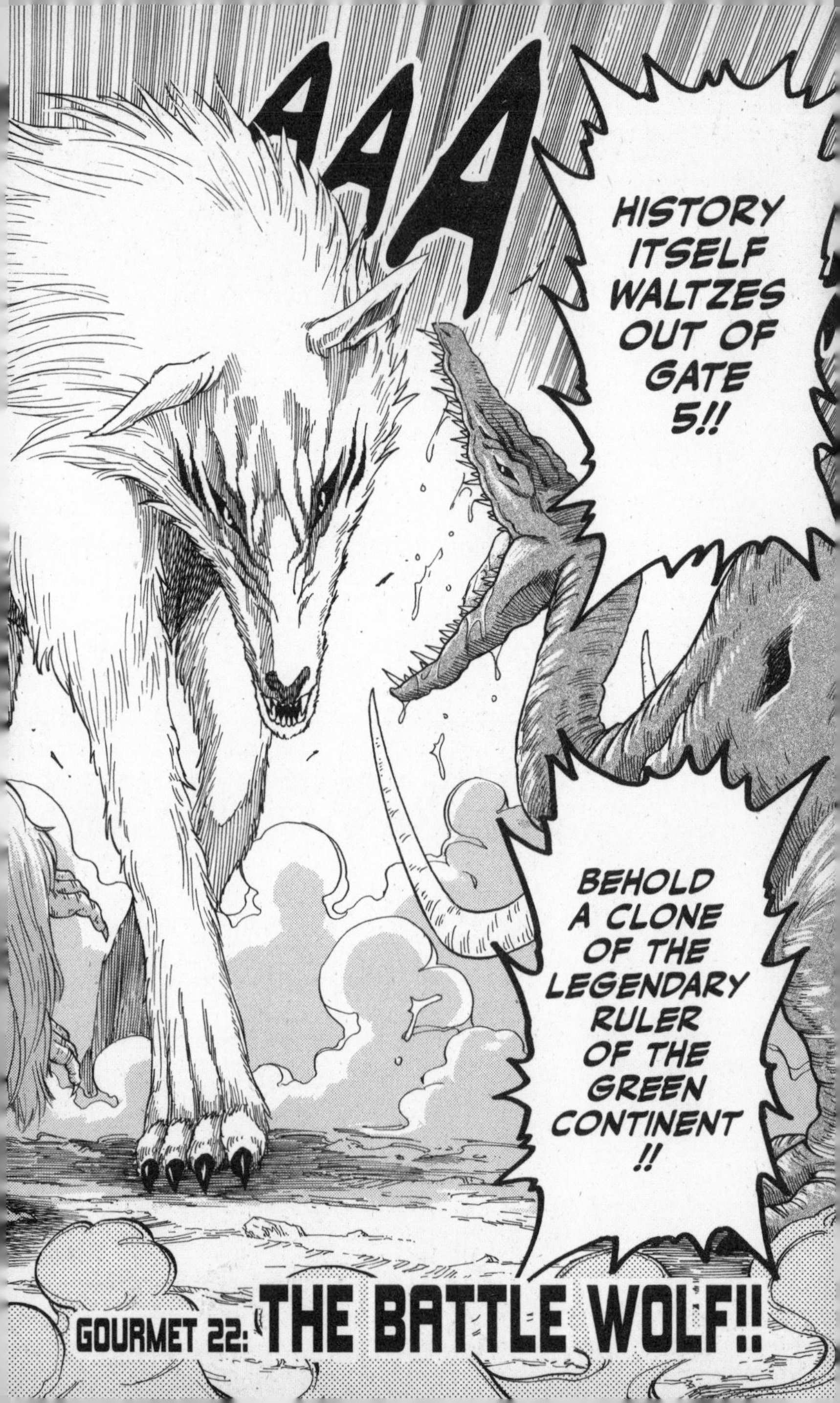
AAA
HISTORY ITSELF WALTZES OUT OF GATE 5!!
BEHOLD A CLONE OF THE LEGENDARY RULER OF THE GREEN CONTINENT!!
GOURMET 22: THE BATTLE WOLF!!

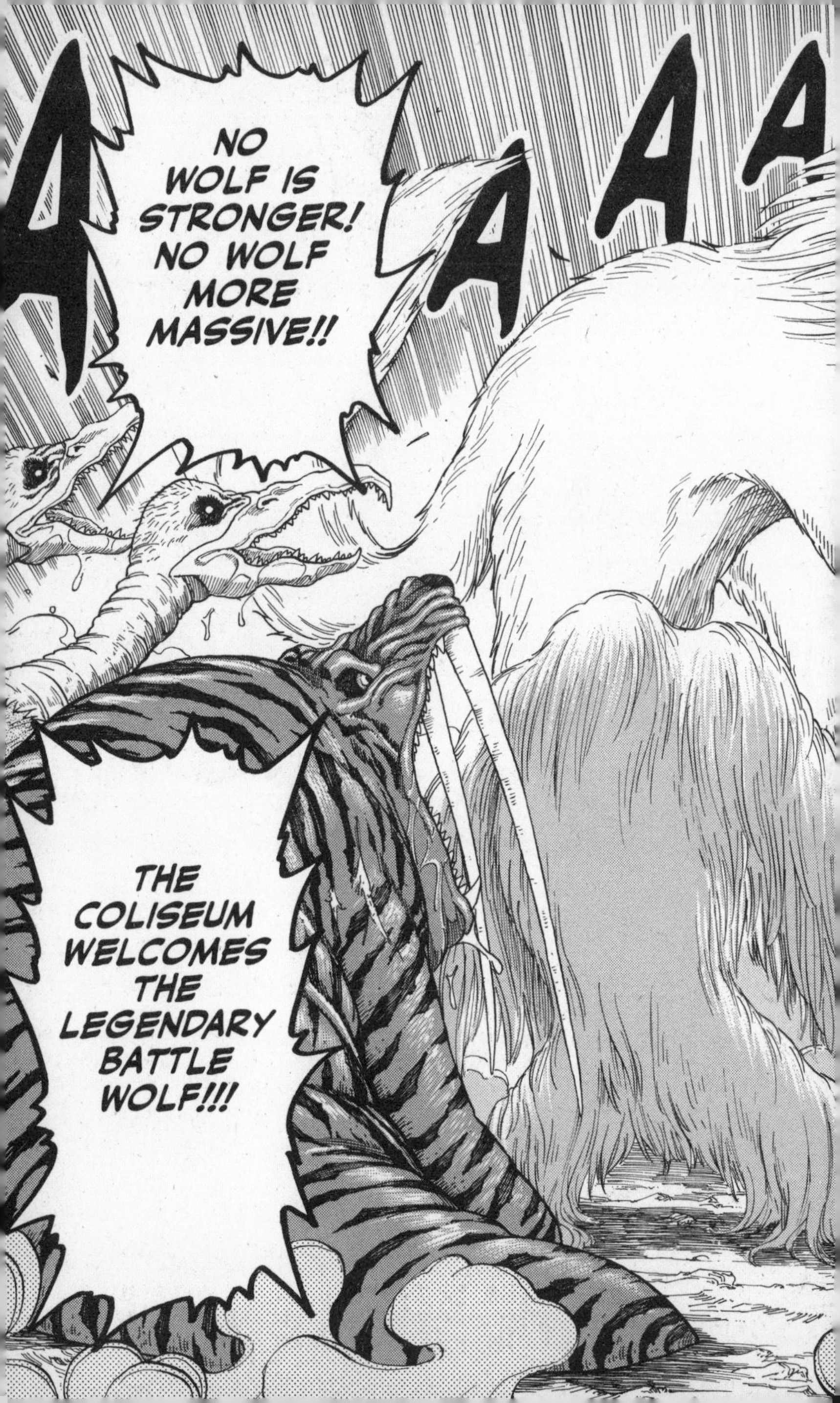

AAAA
NO WOLF IS STRONGER! NO WOLF MORE MASSIVE!!
THE COLISEUM WELCOMES THE LEGENDARY BATTLE WOLF!!!

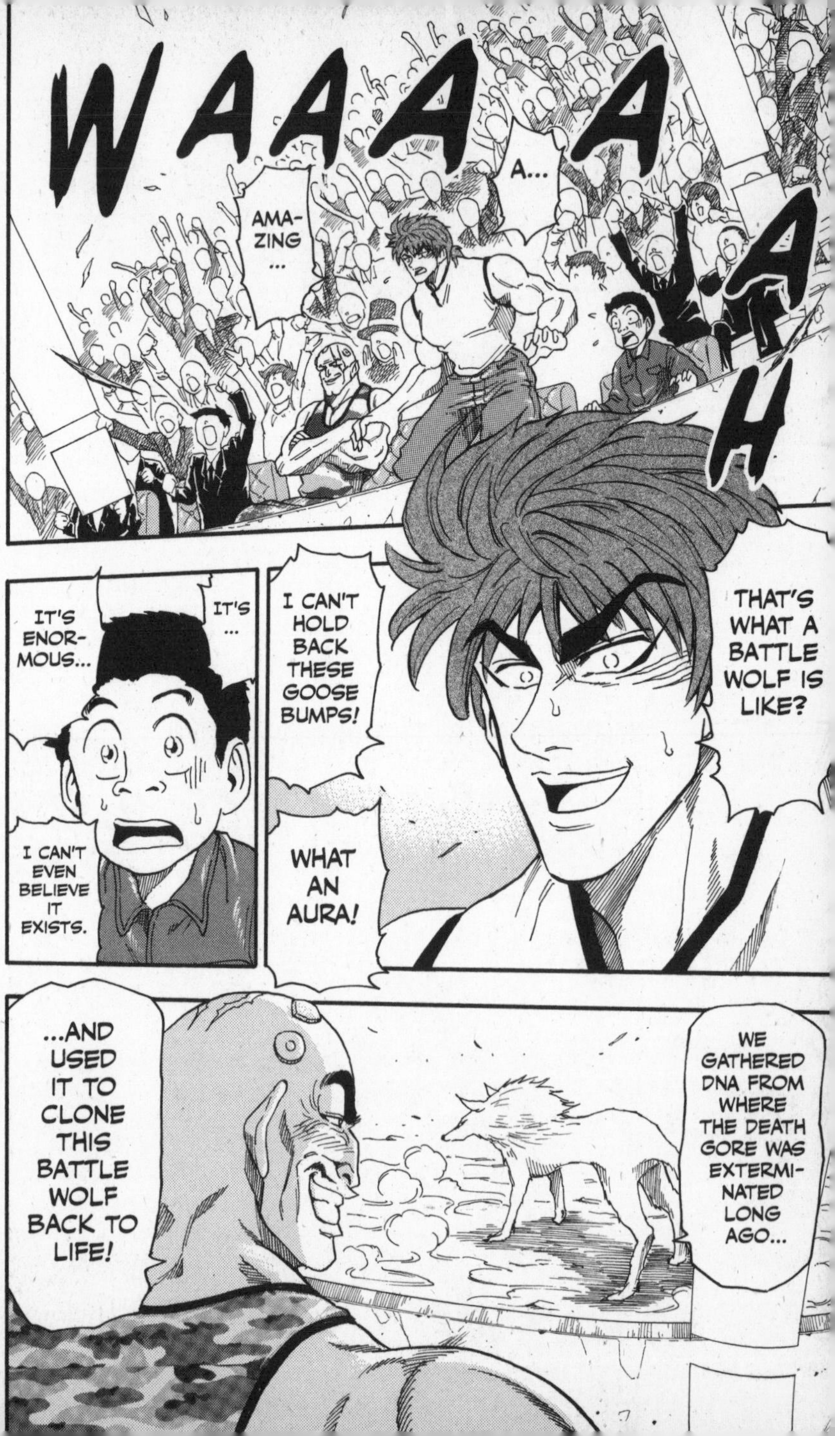
WAAAAAAH
A...
AMA-ZING...
THAT'S WHAT A BATTLE WOLF IS LIKE?
I CAN'T HOLD BACK THESE GOOSE BUMPS!
WHAT AN AURA!
IT'S...
IT'S ENOR-MOUS...
I CAN'T EVEN BELIEVE IT EXISTS.
WE GATHERED DNA FROM WHERE THE DEATH GORE WAS EXTERMI-NATED LONG AGO...
...AND USED IT TO CLONE THIS BATTLE WOLF BACK TO LIFE!

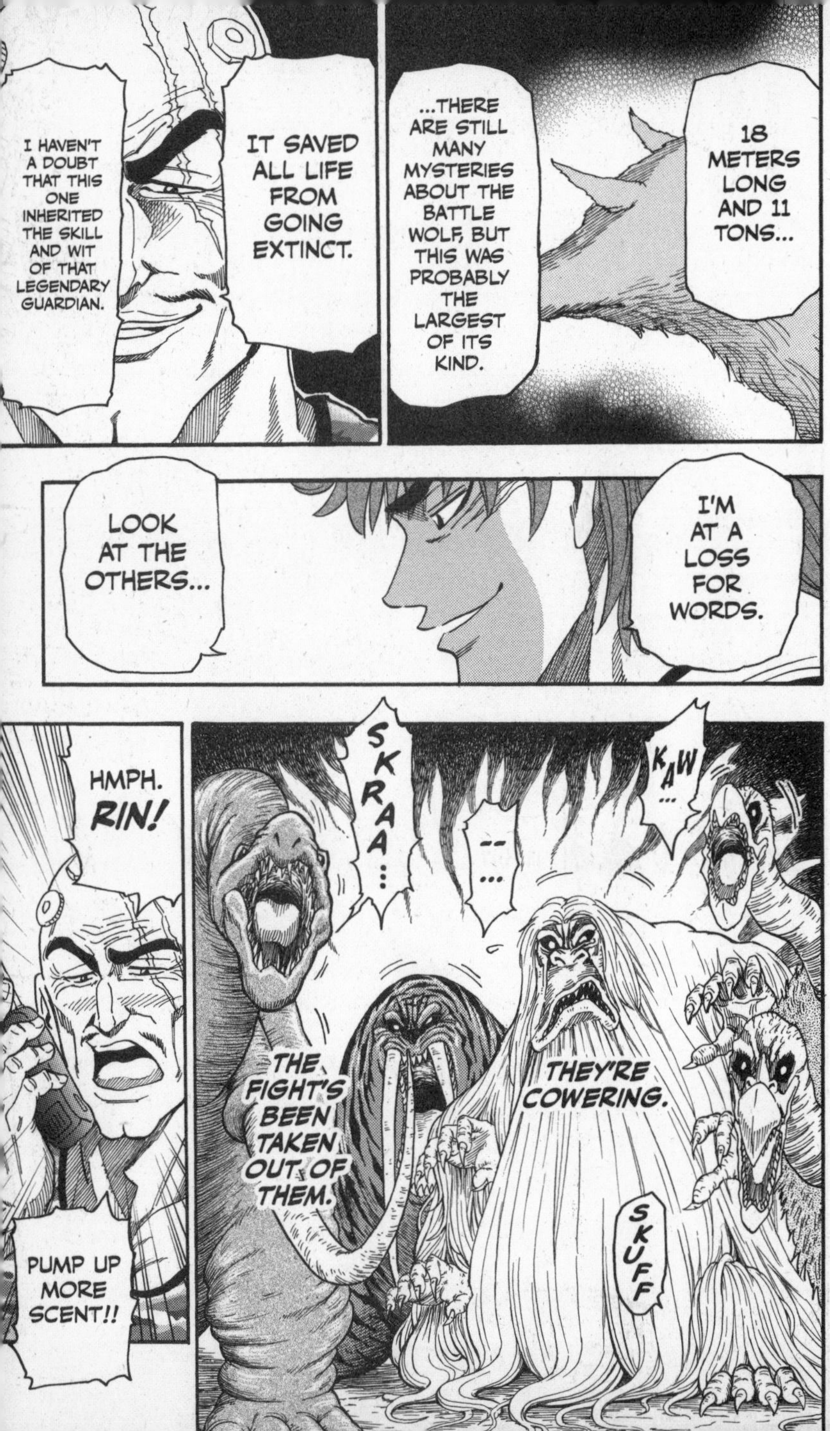

18 METERS LONG AND 11 TONS...
...THERE ARE STILL MANY MYSTERIES ABOUT THE BATTLE WOLF, BUT THIS WAS PROBABLY THE LARGEST OF ITS KIND.
IT SAVED ALL LIFE FROM GOING EXTINCT.
I HAVEN'T A DOUBT THAT THIS ONE INHERITED THE SKILL AND WIT OF THAT LEGENDARY GUARDIAN.
I'M AT A LOSS FOR WORDS.
LOOK AT THE OTHERS...
KAW...
SKRAA...
--...
THEY'RE COWERING.
THE FIGHT'S BEEN TAKEN OUT OF THEM.
SKUFF
HMPH. RIN!
PUMP UP MORE SCENT!!

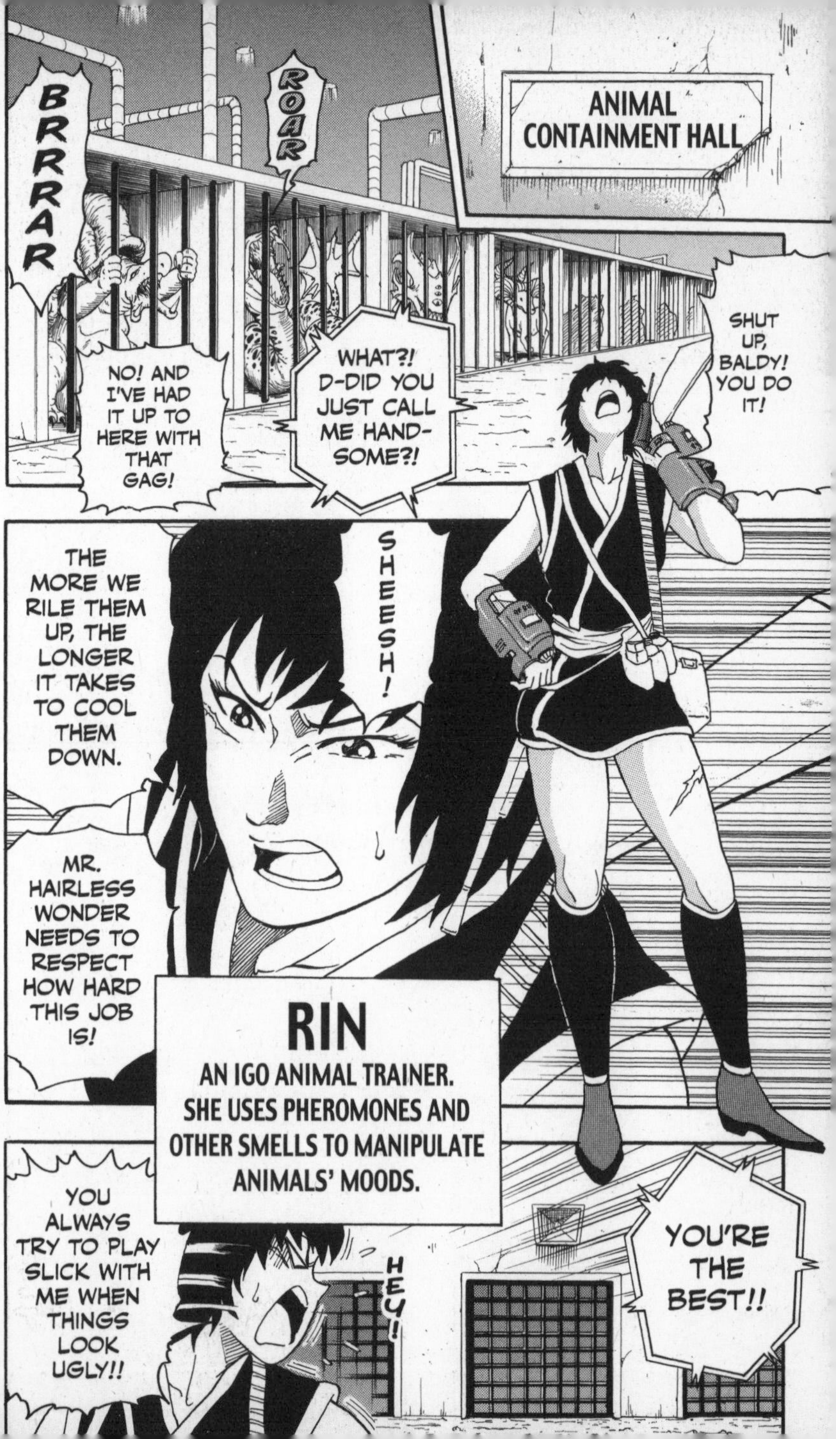
ANIMAL CONTAINMENT HALL
SHUT UP, BALDY! YOU DO IT!
ROAR
WHAT?! D-DID YOU JUST CALL ME HANDSOME?!
BRRRAR
NO! AND I'VE HAD IT UP TO HERE WITH THAT GAG!
SHEESH!
THE MORE WE RILE THEM UP, THE LONGER IT TAKES TO COOL THEM DOWN.
MR. HAIRLESS WONDER NEEDS TO RESPECT HOW HARD THIS JOB IS!
RIN
AN IGO ANIMAL TRAINER. SHE USES PHEROMONES AND OTHER SMELLS TO MANIPULATE ANIMALS' MOODS.
YOU'RE THE BEST!!
HEY!
YOU ALWAYS TRY TO PLAY SLICK WITH ME WHEN THINGS LOOK UGLY!!

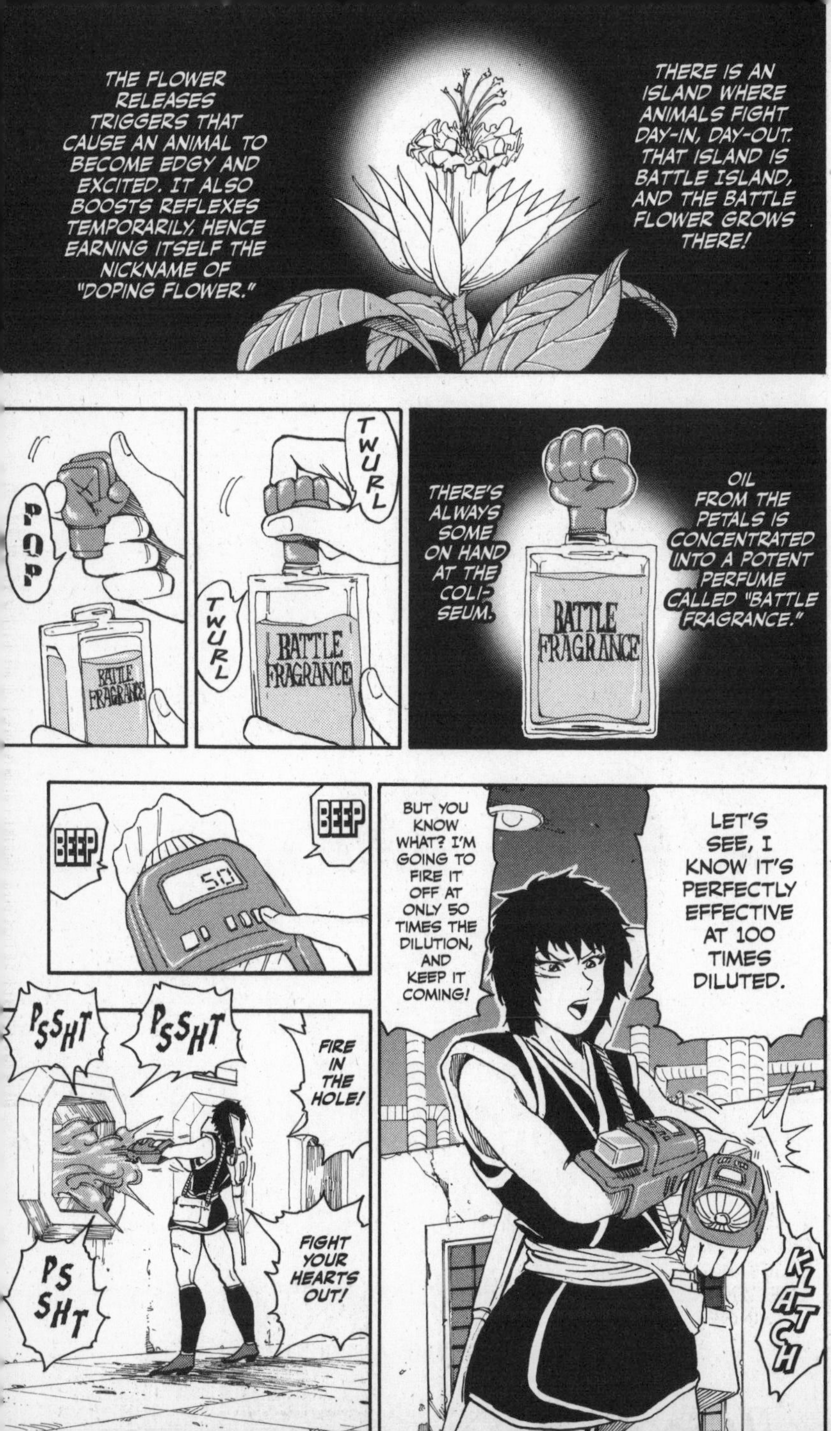
THERE IS AN ISLAND WHERE ANIMALS FIGHT DAY-IN, DAY-OUT. THAT ISLAND IS BATTLE ISLAND, AND THE BATTLE FLOWER GROWS THERE!
THE FLOWER RELEASES TRIGGERS THAT CAUSE AN ANIMAL TO BECOME EDGY AND EXCITED. IT ALSO BOOSTS REFLEXES TEMPORARILY, HENCE EARNING ITSELF THE NICKNAME OF "DOPING FLOWER."
OIL FROM THE PETALS IS CONCENTRATED INTO A POTENT PERFUME CALLED "BATTLE FRAGRANCE."
THERE'S ALWAYS SOME ON HAND AT THE COLI-SEUM.
BATTLE FRAGRANCE
TWURL
TWURL
BATTLE FRAGRANCE
POP
BATTLE FRAGRANCE
LET'S SEE, I KNOW IT'S PERFECTLY EFFECTIVE AT 100 TIMES DILUTED.
BUT YOU KNOW WHAT? I'M GOING TO FIRE IT OFF AT ONLY 50 TIMES THE DILUTION, AND KEEP IT COMING!
KLATCH
BEEP
BEEP
50
FIRE IN THE HOLE!
PSSHT
PSSHT
FIGHT YOUR HEARTS OUT!
PS SHT

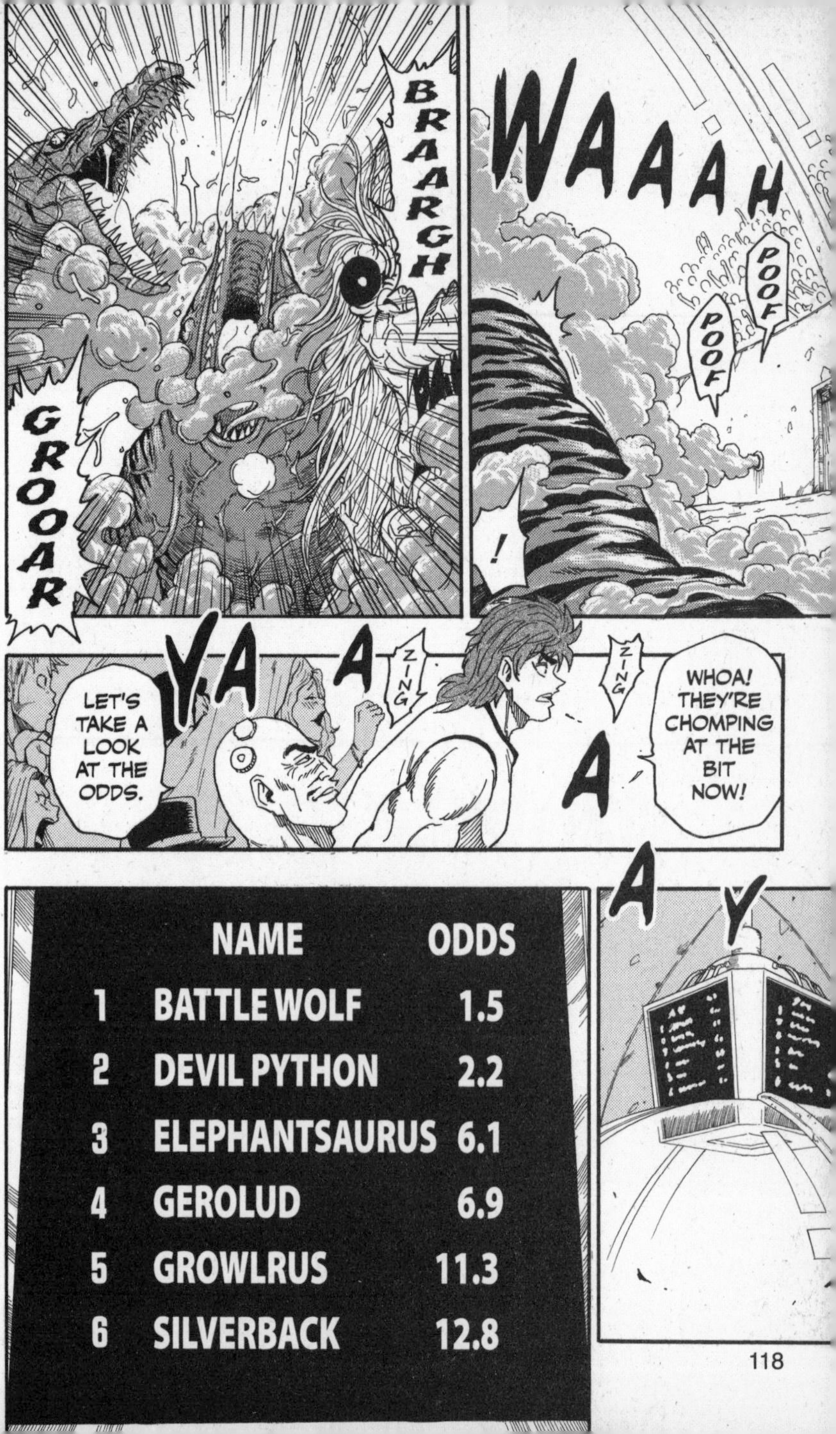
WAAAH
POOF
POOF
!
BRAARGH
GROOAR
WHOA! THEY'RE CHOMPING AT THE BIT NOW!
ZING
ZING
YAAAAY
LET'S TAKE A LOOK AT THE ODDS.
NAME ODDS
1 BATTLE WOLF 1.5
2 DEVIL PYTHON 2.2
3 ELEPHANTSAURUS 6.1
4 GEROLUD 6.9
5 GROWLRUS 11.3
6 SILVERBACK 12.8

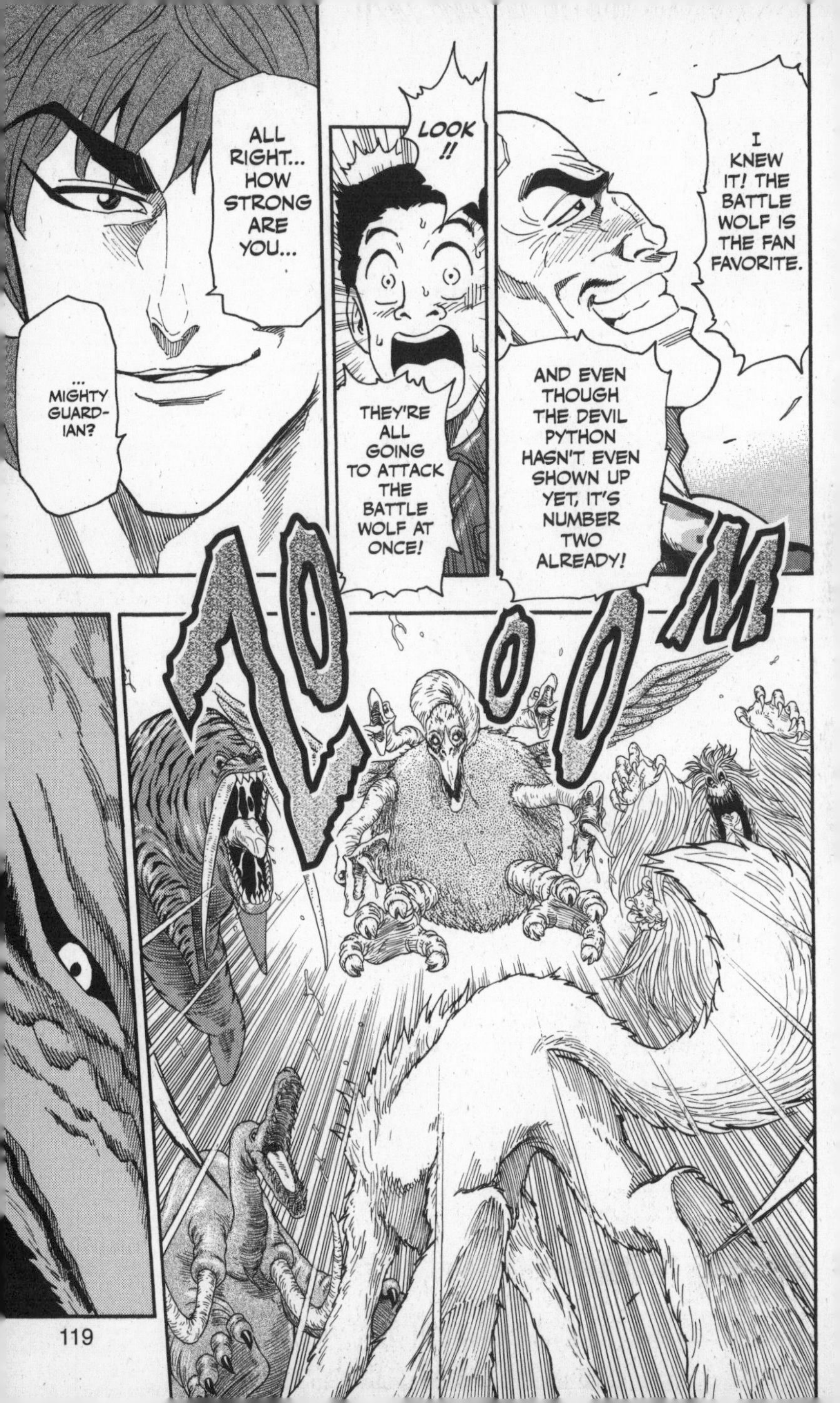

I KNEW IT! THE BATTLE WOLF IS THE FAN FAVORITE.
AND EVEN THOUGH THE DEVIL PYTHON HASN'T EVEN SHOWN UP YET, IT'S NUMBER TWO ALREADY!
LOOK!!
THEY'RE ALL GOING TO ATTACK THE BATTLE WOLF AT ONCE!
ALL RIGHT... HOW STRONG ARE YOU...
...MIGHTY GUARDIAN?
ZOOOOM

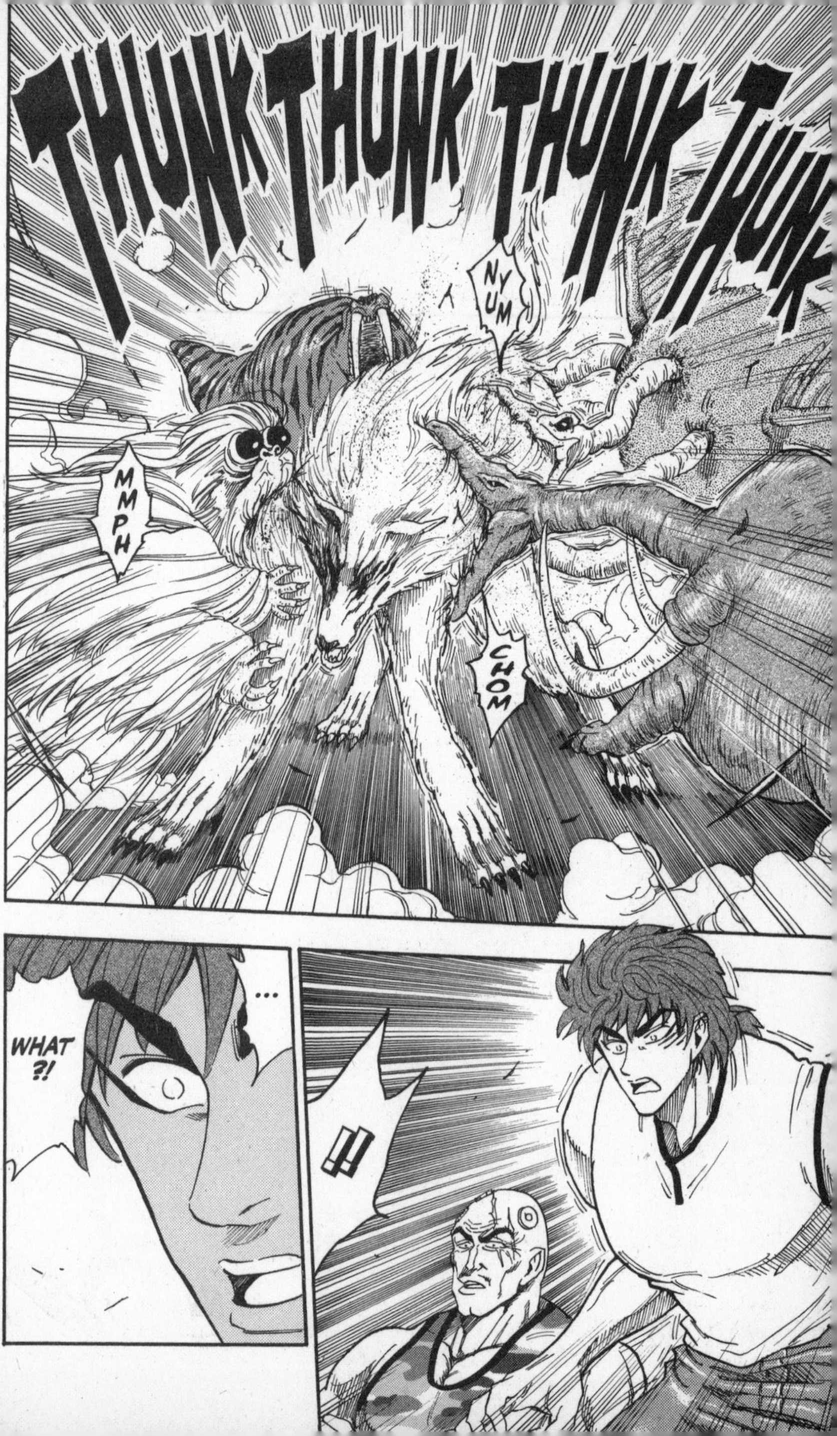
THUNK THUNK THUNK THUNK
NYUM
MMPH
CHOM
!!
...
WHAT?!

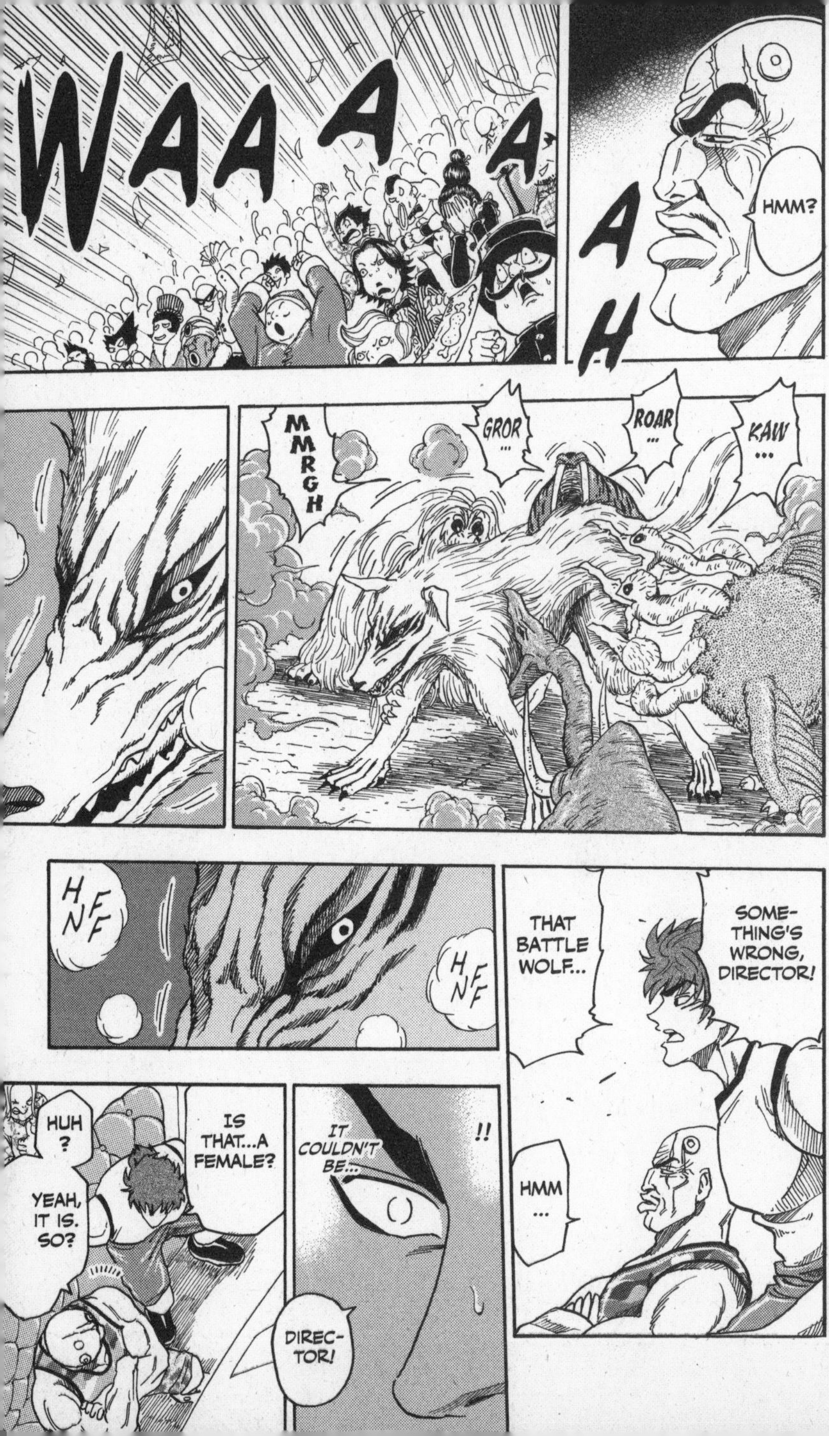
HMM?
WAAAAAAH
KAW...
ROAR...
GROR...
MMRGH
SOMETHING'S WRONG, DIRECTOR!
THAT BATTLE WOLF...
HMM...
HNFF
HNFF
!!
IT COULDN'T BE...
DIRECTOR!
IS THAT...A FEMALE?
HUH?
YEAH, IT IS. SO?

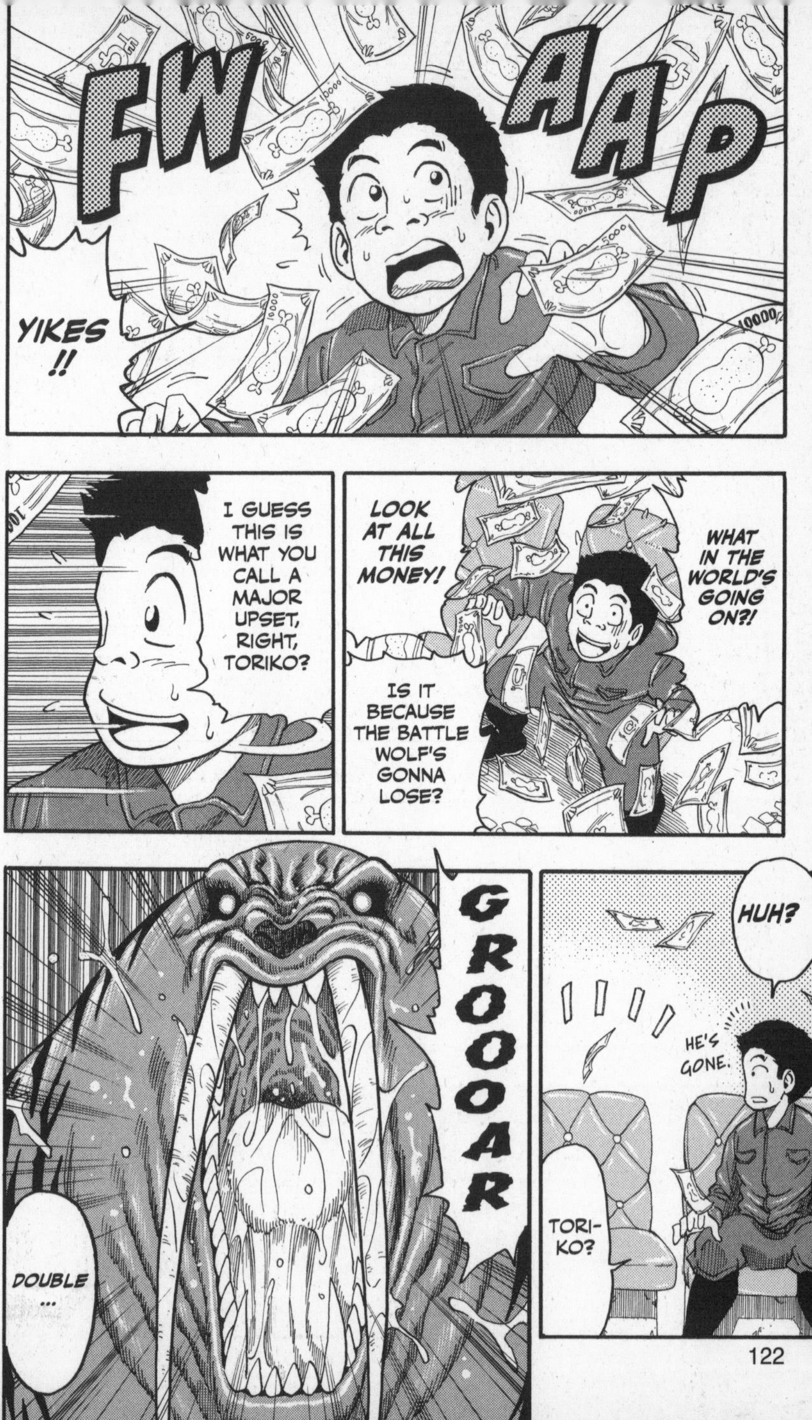
FWAAAP
YIKES!!
WHAT IN THE WORLD'S GOING ON?!
LOOK AT ALL THIS MONEY!
IS IT BECAUSE THE BATTLE WOLF'S GONNA LOSE?
I GUESS THIS IS WHAT YOU CALL A MAJOR UPSET, RIGHT, TORIKO?
HUH?
HE'S GONE.
TORI-KO?
GROOOAR
DOUBLE...

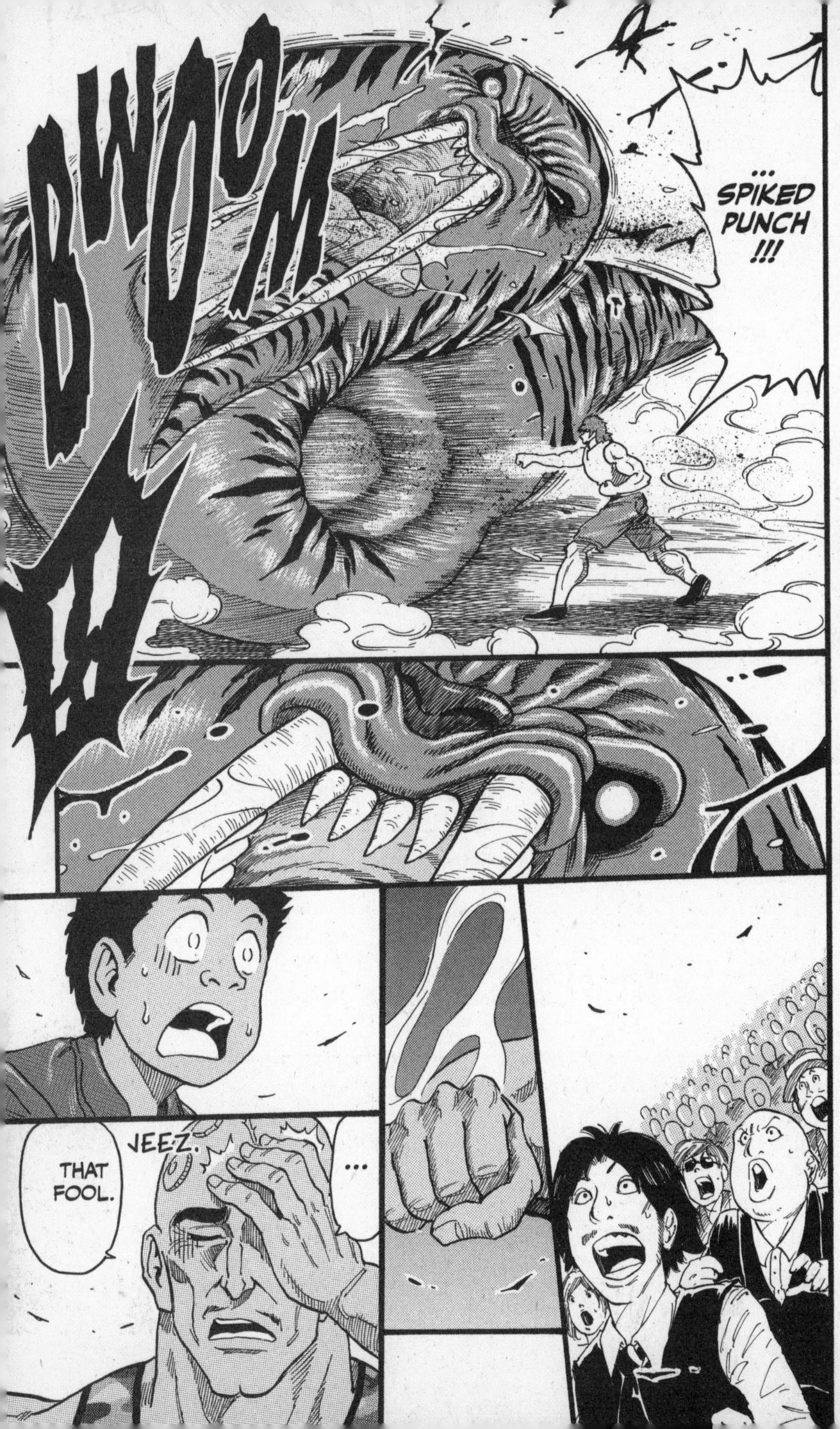
... SPIKED PUNCH !!!
BWOOM
...
JEEZ.
THAT FOOL.

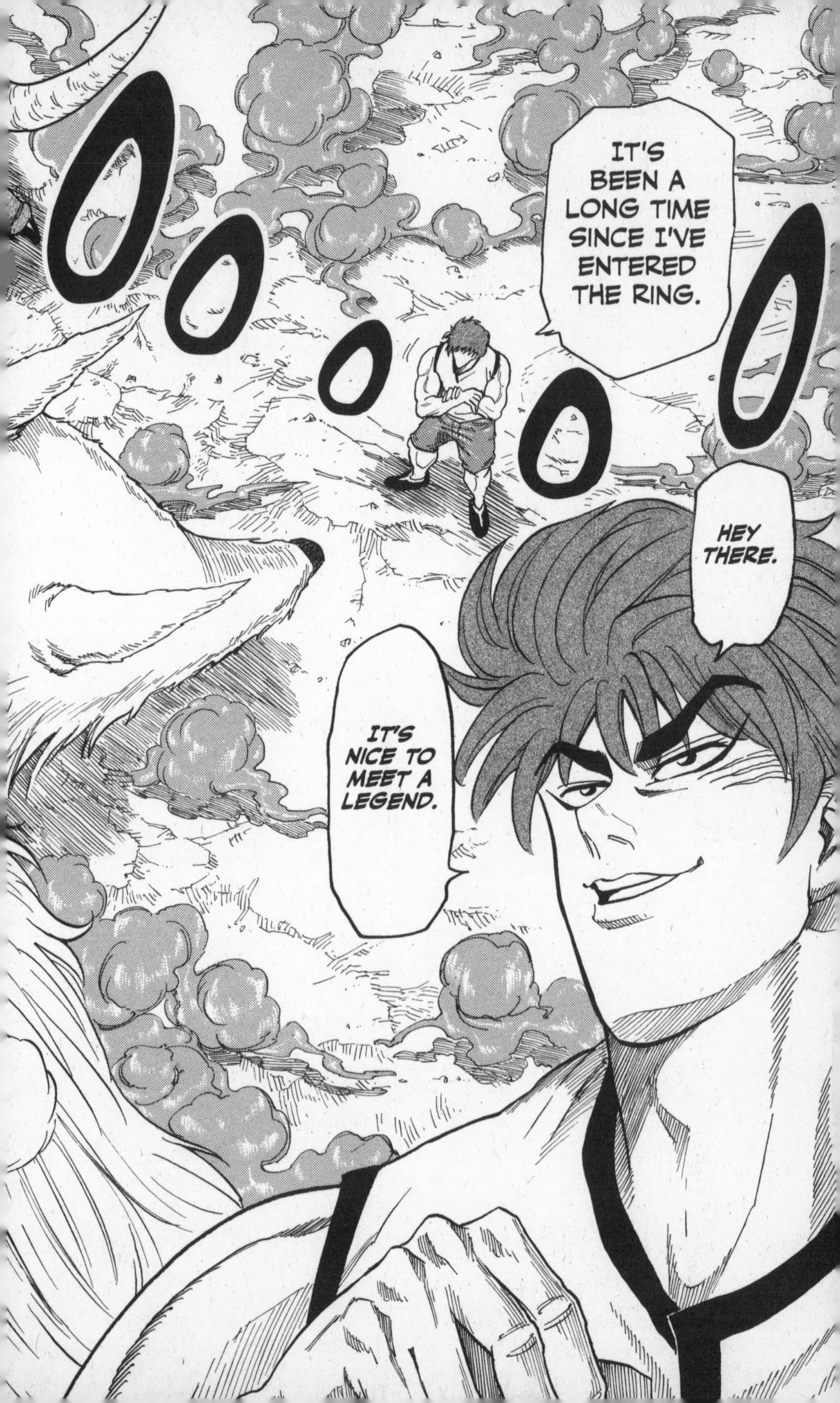
IT'S BEEN A LONG TIME SINCE I'VE ENTERED THE RING.
OOOOO
HEY THERE.
IT'S NICE TO MEET A LEGEND.

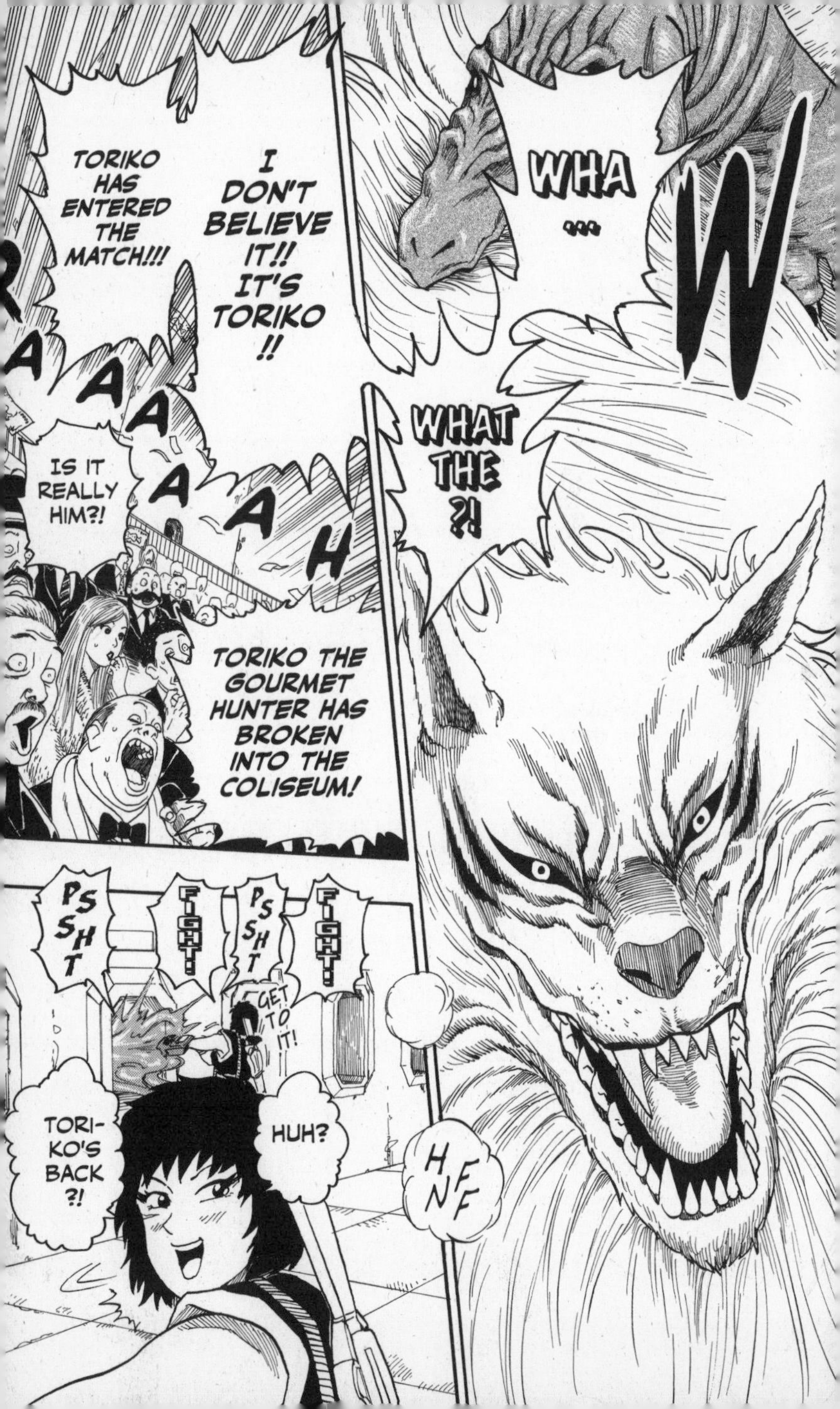
WHA ...
W
WHAT THE ?!
I DON'T BELIEVE IT!! IT'S TORIKO !!
TORIKO HAS ENTERED THE MATCH!!!
RAAAAAAH
IS IT REALLY HIM?!
TORIKO THE GOURMET HUNTER HAS BROKEN INTO THE COLISEUM!
HFNF
FIGHT!
PSSHT
GET TO IT!
FIGHT!
PSSHT
HUH?
TORIKO'S BACK ?!

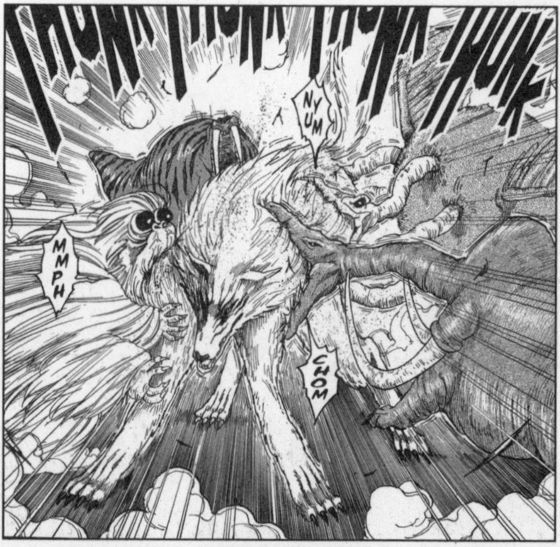
NYUM
CHOM
MMPH

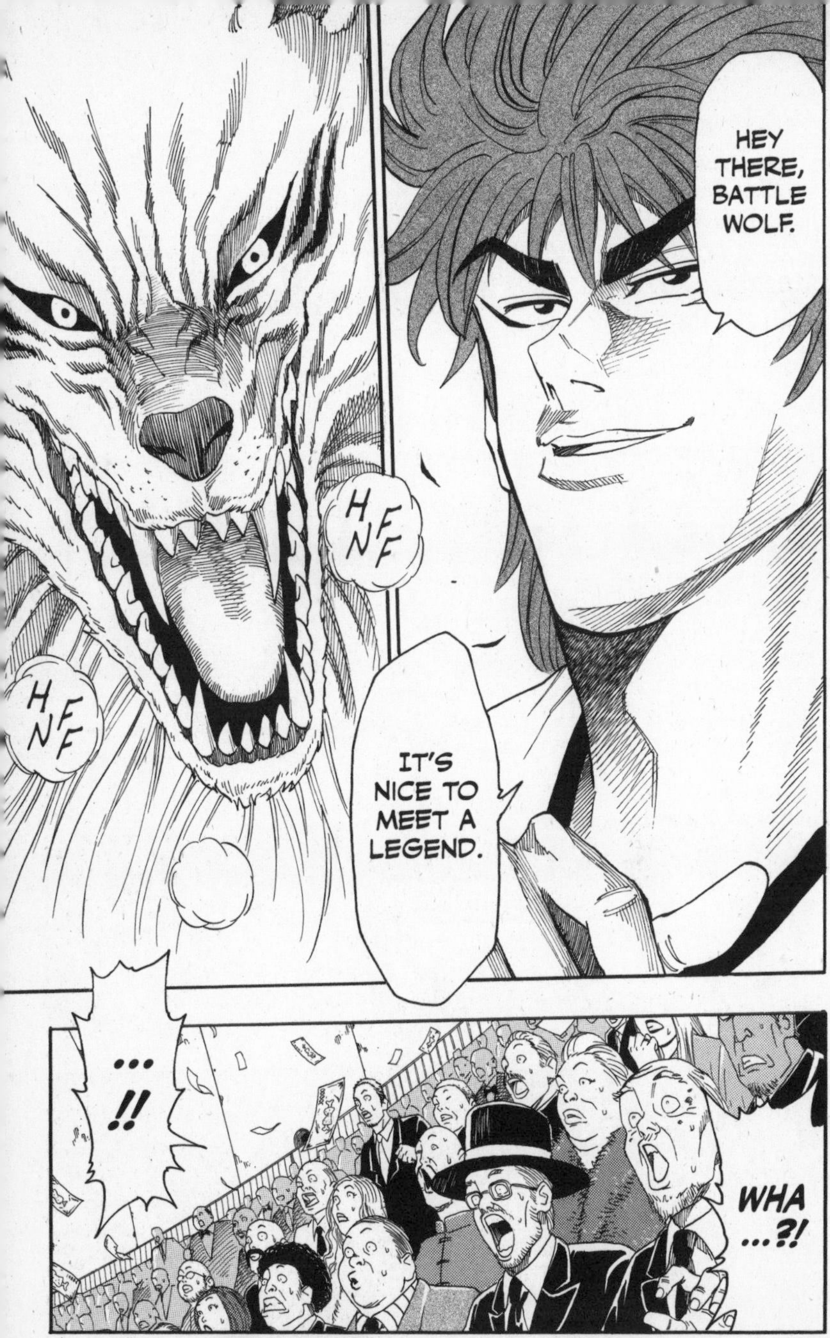
HEY THERE, BATTLE WOLF.
IT'S NICE TO MEET A LEGEND.
HNFF
HNFF
WHA ...?!
...!!

GOURMET 23: WELCOME!!

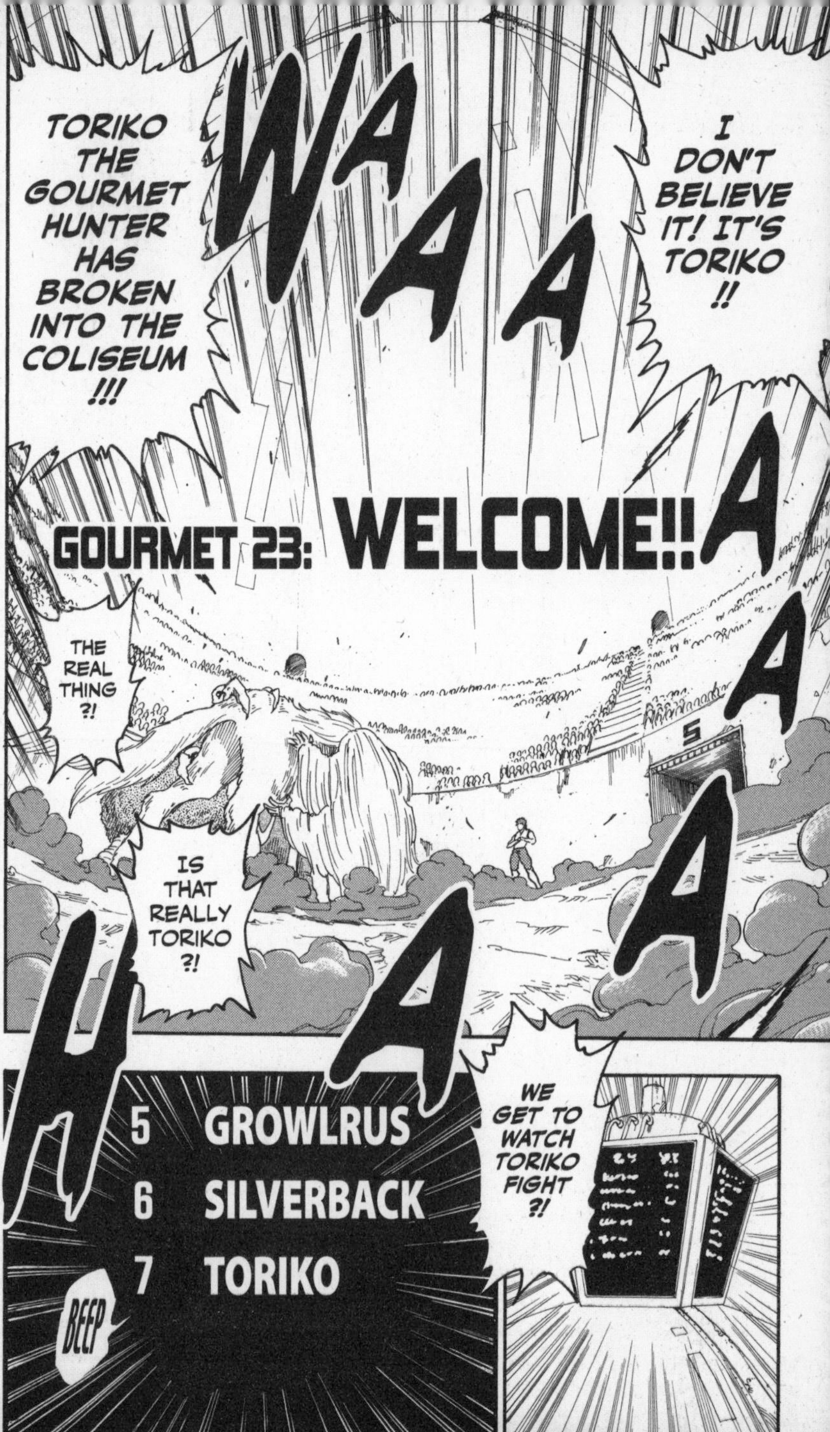
I DON'T BELIEVE IT! IT'S TORIKO!!
TORIKO THE GOURMET HUNTER HAS BROKEN INTO THE COLISEUM!!!
WAAAAAAAA
GOURMET 23: WELCOME!!
THE REAL THING?!
IS THAT REALLY TORIKO?!
HAA
WE GET TO WATCH TORIKO FIGHT?!
5 GROWLRUS
6 SILVERBACK
7 TORIKO
BEEP

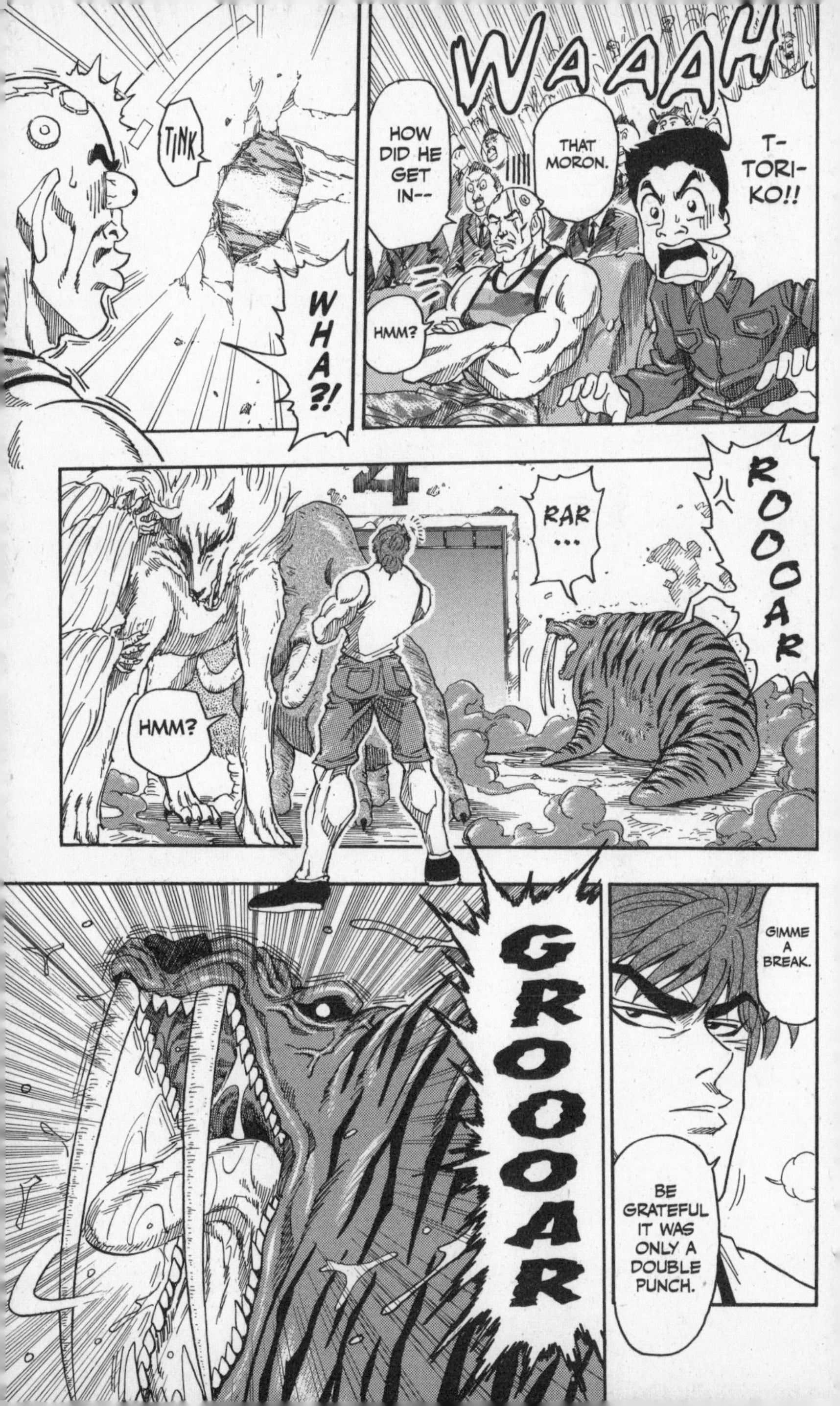
WAAAH
T-TORIKO!!
THAT MORON.
HOW DID HE GET IN--
HMM?
TINK
WHA?!
ROOOOAR
RAR...
4
HMM?
GIMME A BREAK.
BE GRATEFUL IT WAS ONLY A DOUBLE PUNCH.
GROOOOAR

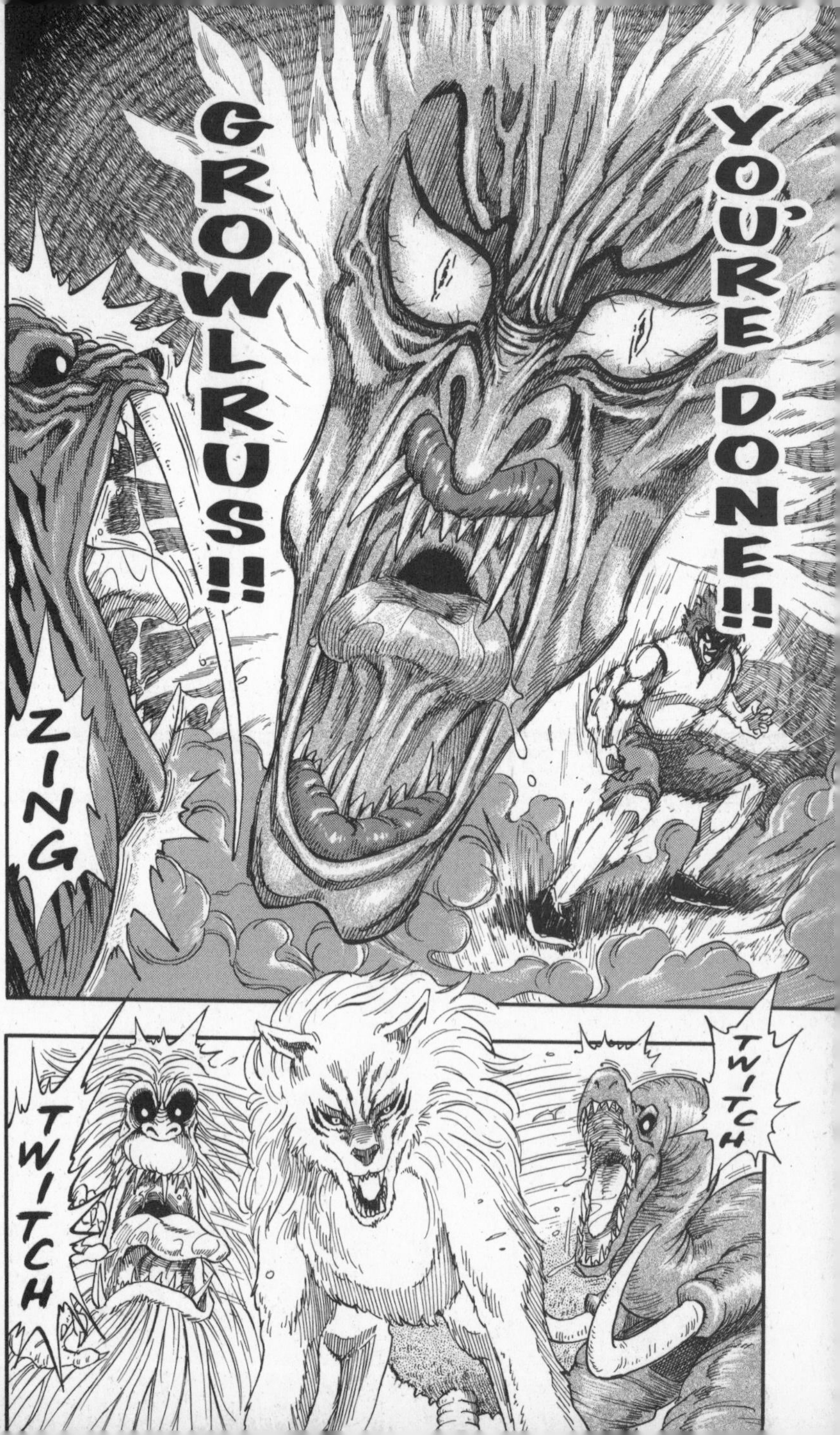
YOU'RE DONE!!
GROWLRUS!!
ZING
TWITCH
TWITCH

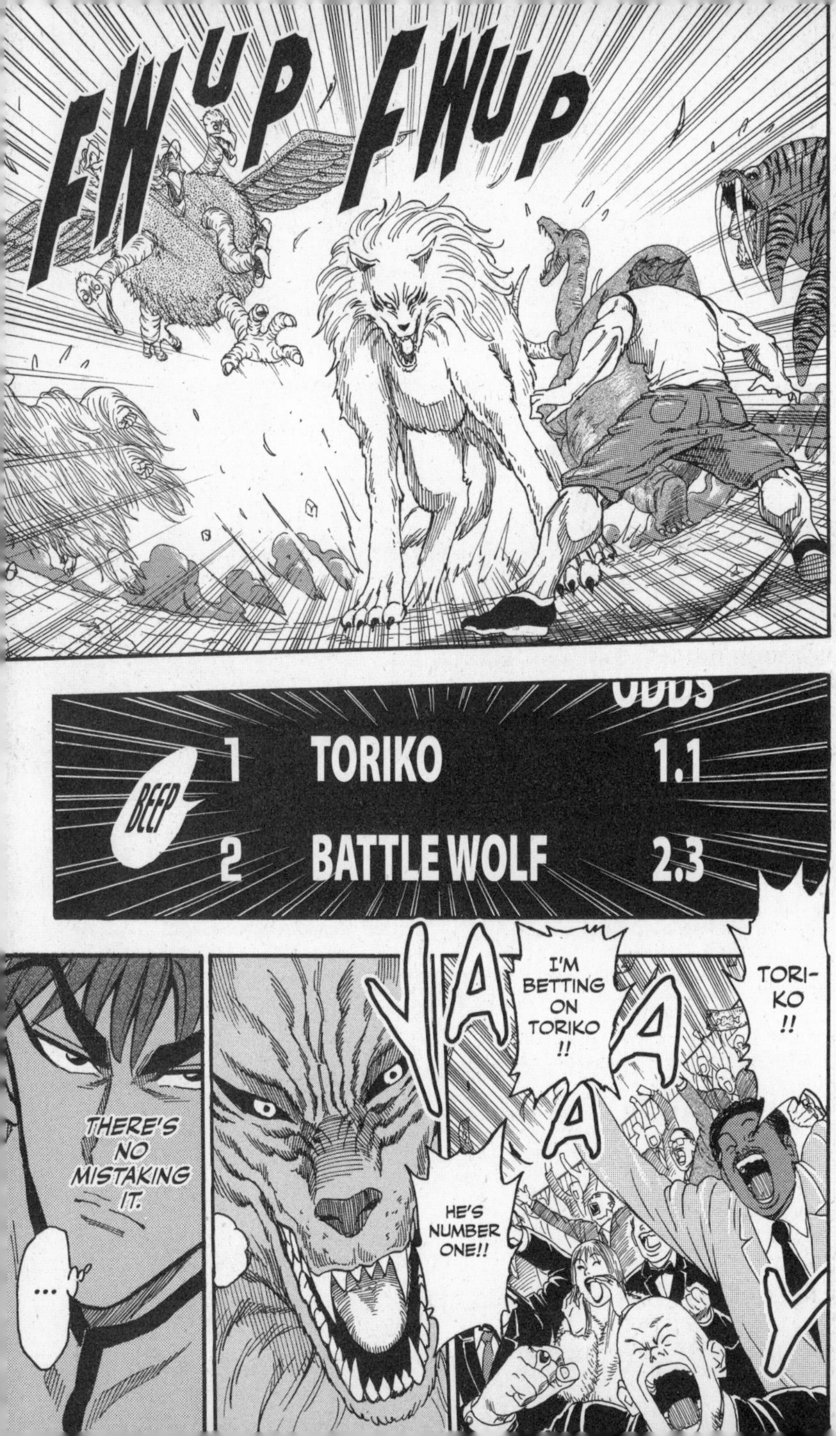
FWUP FWUP
ODDS
1 TORIKO 1.1
2 BATTLE WOLF 2.3
BEEP
YAAAAY
TORI-KO!!
I'M BETTING ON TORIKO!!
HE'S NUMBER ONE!!
THERE'S NO MISTAKING IT.
...

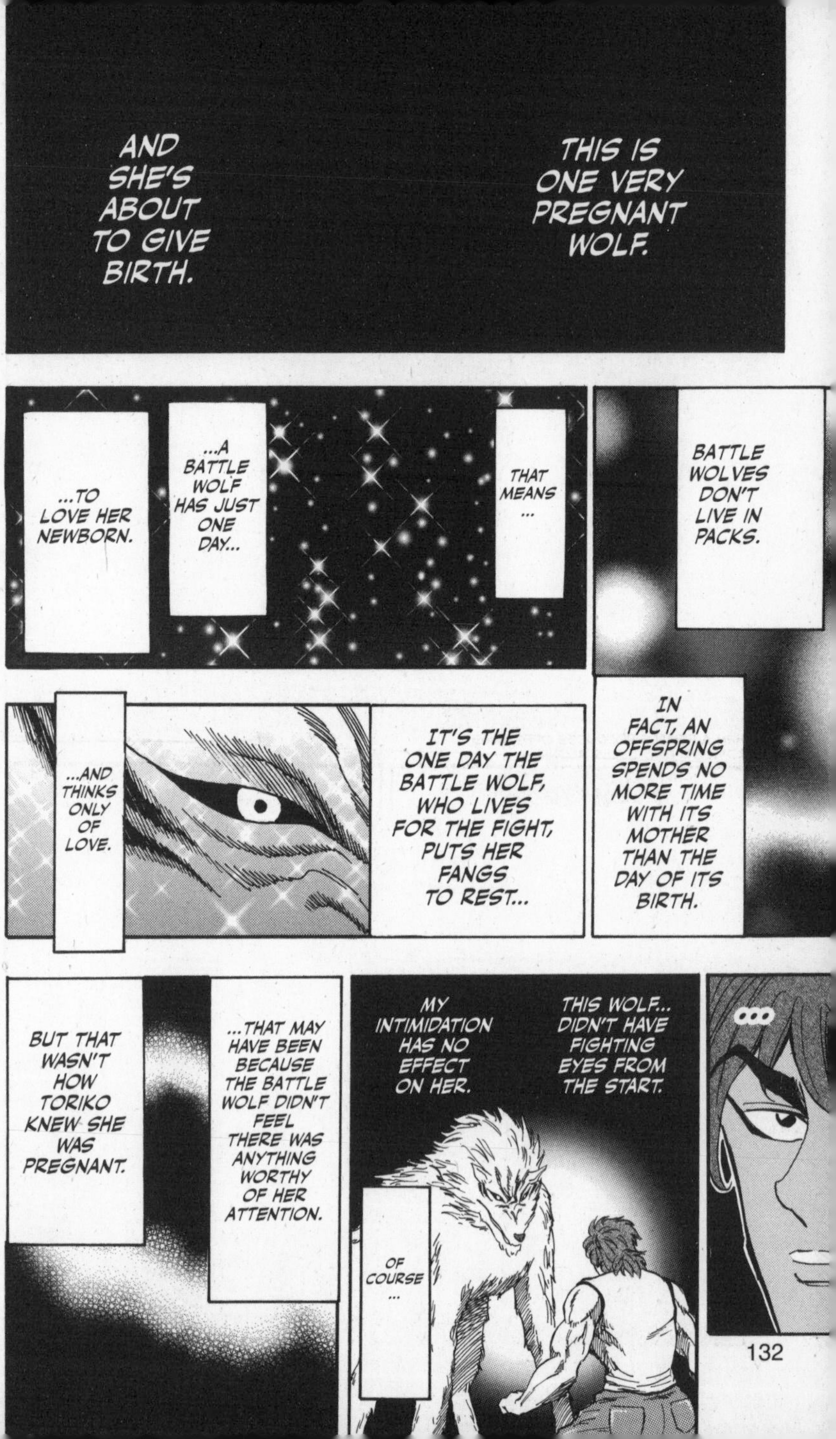
THIS IS ONE VERY PREGNANT WOLF.
AND SHE'S ABOUT TO GIVE BIRTH.
BATTLE WOLVES DON'T LIVE IN PACKS.
THAT MEANS...
...A BATTLE WOLF HAS JUST ONE DAY...
...TO LOVE HER NEWBORN.
IN FACT, AN OFFSPRING SPENDS NO MORE TIME WITH ITS MOTHER THAN THE DAY OF ITS BIRTH.
IT'S THE ONE DAY THE BATTLE WOLF, WHO LIVES FOR THE FIGHT, PUTS HER FANGS TO REST...
...AND THINKS ONLY OF LOVE.
...
THIS WOLF... DIDN'T HAVE FIGHTING EYES FROM THE START.
MY INTIMIDATION HAS NO EFFECT ON HER.
OF COURSE...
...THAT MAY HAVE BEEN BECAUSE THE BATTLE WOLF DIDN'T FEEL THERE WAS ANYTHING WORTHY OF HER ATTENTION.
BUT THAT WASN'T HOW TORIKO KNEW SHE WAS PREGNANT.

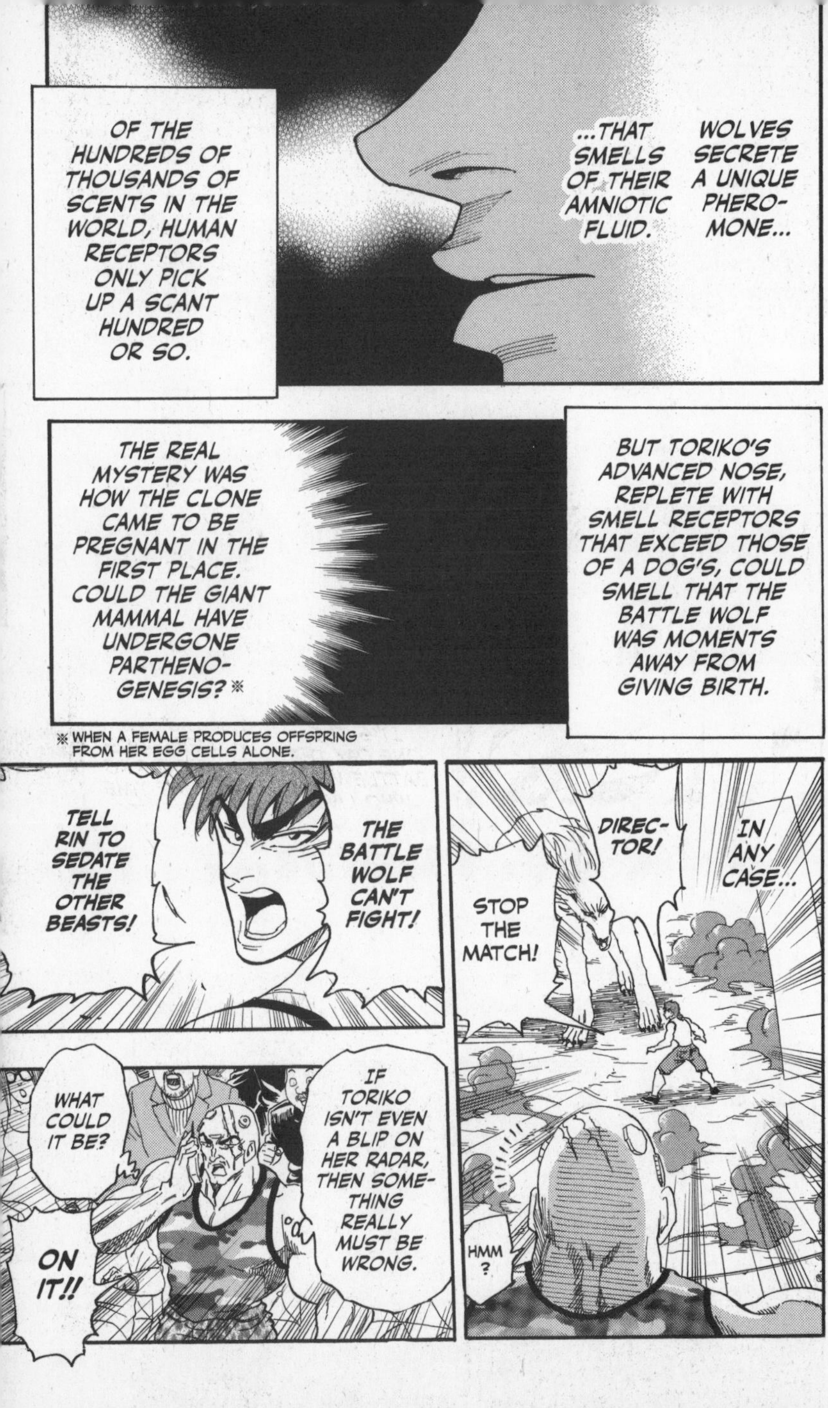
WOLVES SECRETE A UNIQUE PHEROMONE...
...THAT SMELLS OF THEIR AMNIOTIC FLUID.
OF THE HUNDREDS OF THOUSANDS OF SCENTS IN THE WORLD, HUMAN RECEPTORS ONLY PICK UP A SCANT HUNDRED OR SO.
BUT TORIKO'S ADVANCED NOSE, REPLETE WITH SMELL RECEPTORS THAT EXCEED THOSE OF A DOG'S, COULD SMELL THAT THE BATTLE WOLF WAS MOMENTS AWAY FROM GIVING BIRTH.
THE REAL MYSTERY WAS HOW THE CLONE CAME TO BE PREGNANT IN THE FIRST PLACE. COULD THE GIANT MAMMAL HAVE UNDERGONE PARTHENO-GENESIS? ※
IN ANY CASE...
DIRECTOR!
STOP THE MATCH!
HMM ?
THE BATTLE WOLF CAN'T FIGHT!
TELL RIN TO SEDATE THE OTHER BEASTS!
IF TORIKO ISN'T EVEN A BLIP ON HER RADAR, THEN SOME-THING REALLY MUST BE WRONG.
WHAT COULD IT BE?
ON IT!!

※ WHEN A FEMALE PRODUCES OFFSPRING FROM HER EGG CELLS ALONE.

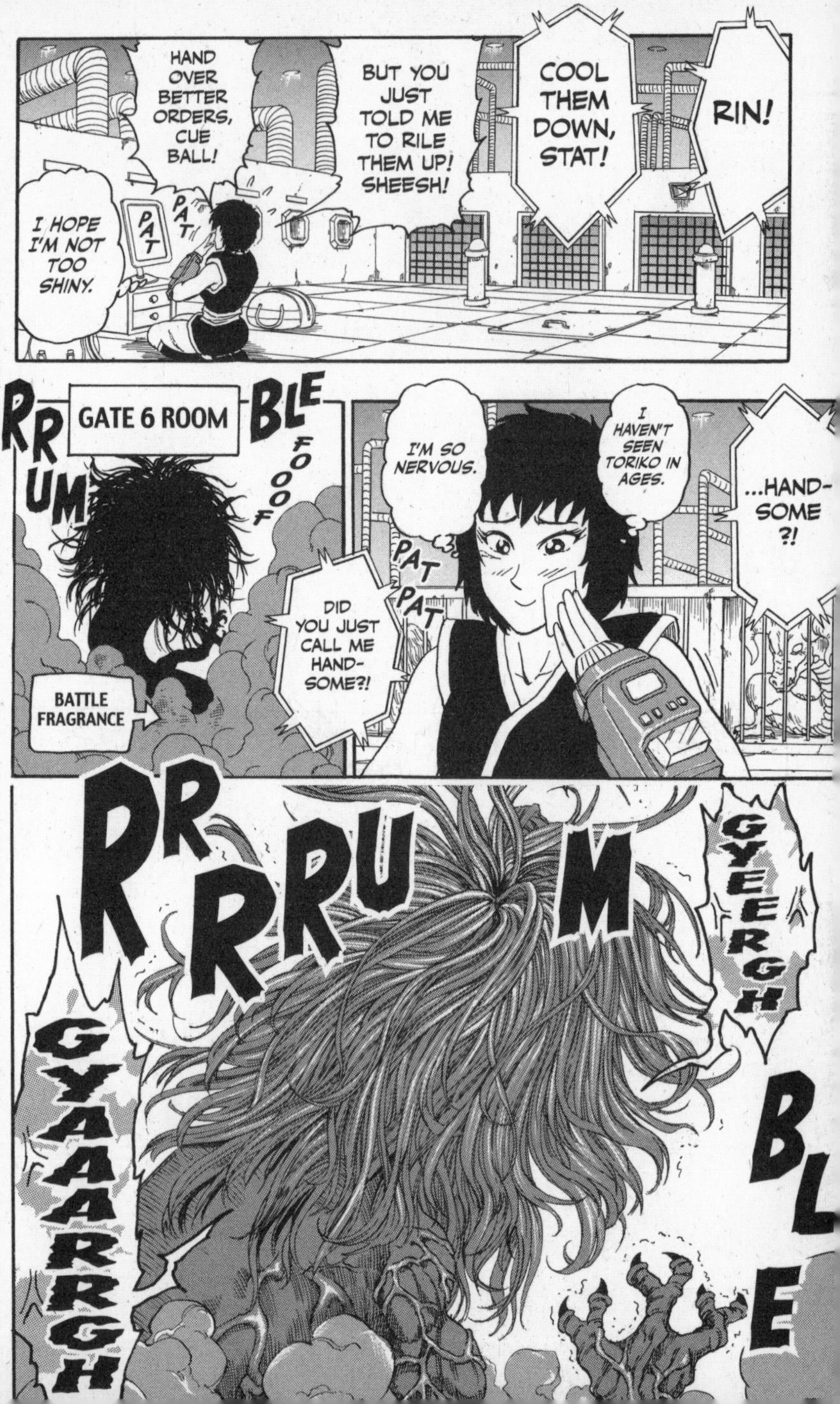
RIN!
COOL THEM DOWN, STAT!
BUT YOU JUST TOLD ME TO RILE THEM UP! SHEESH!
HAND OVER BETTER ORDERS, CUE BALL!
PAT
PAT
I HOPE I'M NOT TOO SHINY.
...HAND-SOME ?!
I HAVEN'T SEEN TORIKO IN AGES.
I'M SO NERVOUS.
PAT
PAT
DID YOU JUST CALL ME HAND-SOME?!
GATE 6 ROOM
RRUMBLE
FOOOOF
BATTLE FRAGRANCE
GYERGH
BLE
RRRRUM
GYAAARRGH

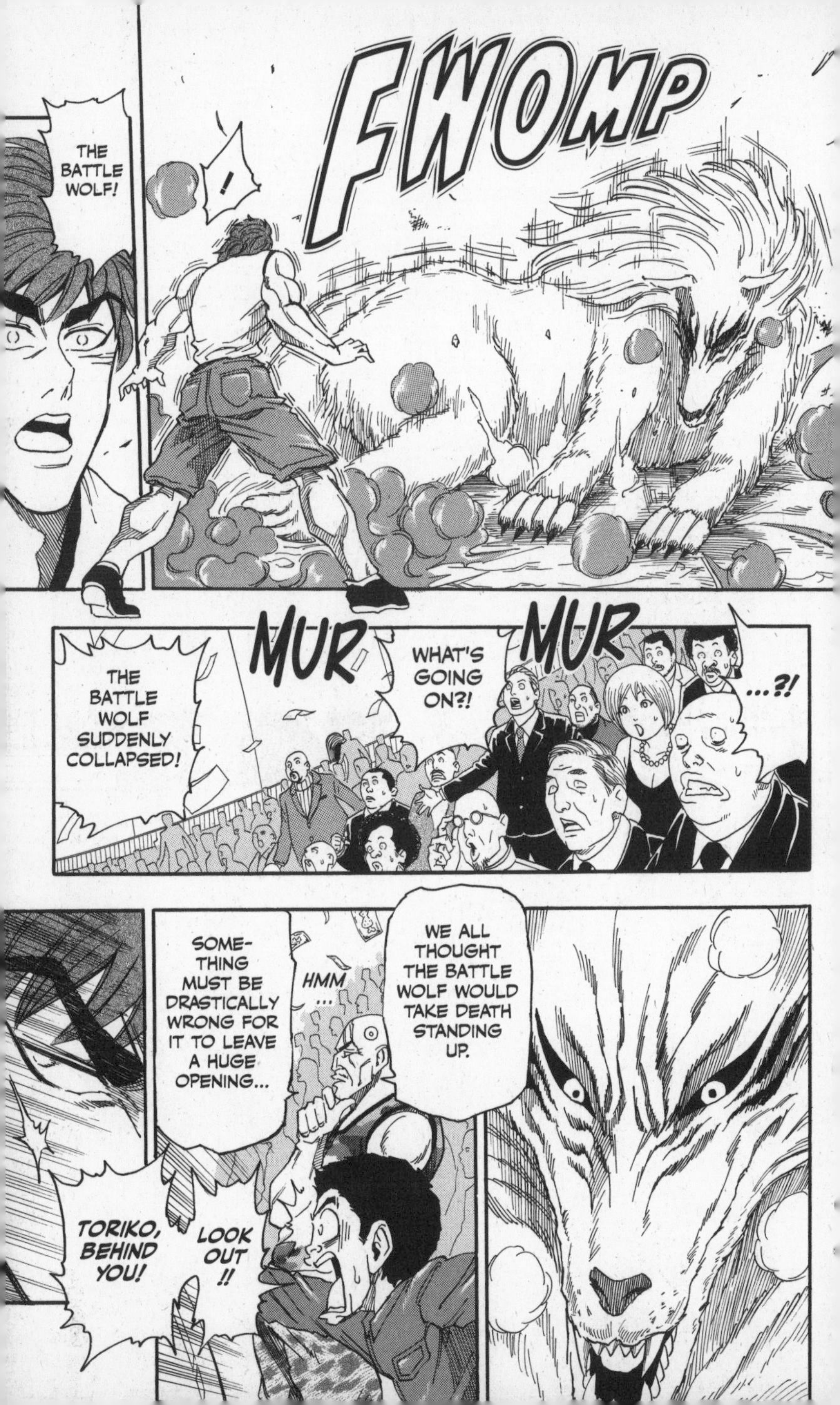
FWOMP
!
THE BATTLE WOLF!
...?!
MUR
WHAT'S GOING ON?!
MUR
THE BATTLE WOLF SUDDENLY COLLAPSED!
WE ALL THOUGHT THE BATTLE WOLF WOULD TAKE DEATH STANDING UP.
HMM...
SOME-THING MUST BE DRASTICALLY WRONG FOR IT TO LEAVE A HUGE OPENING...
LOOK OUT!!
TORIKO, BEHIND YOU!

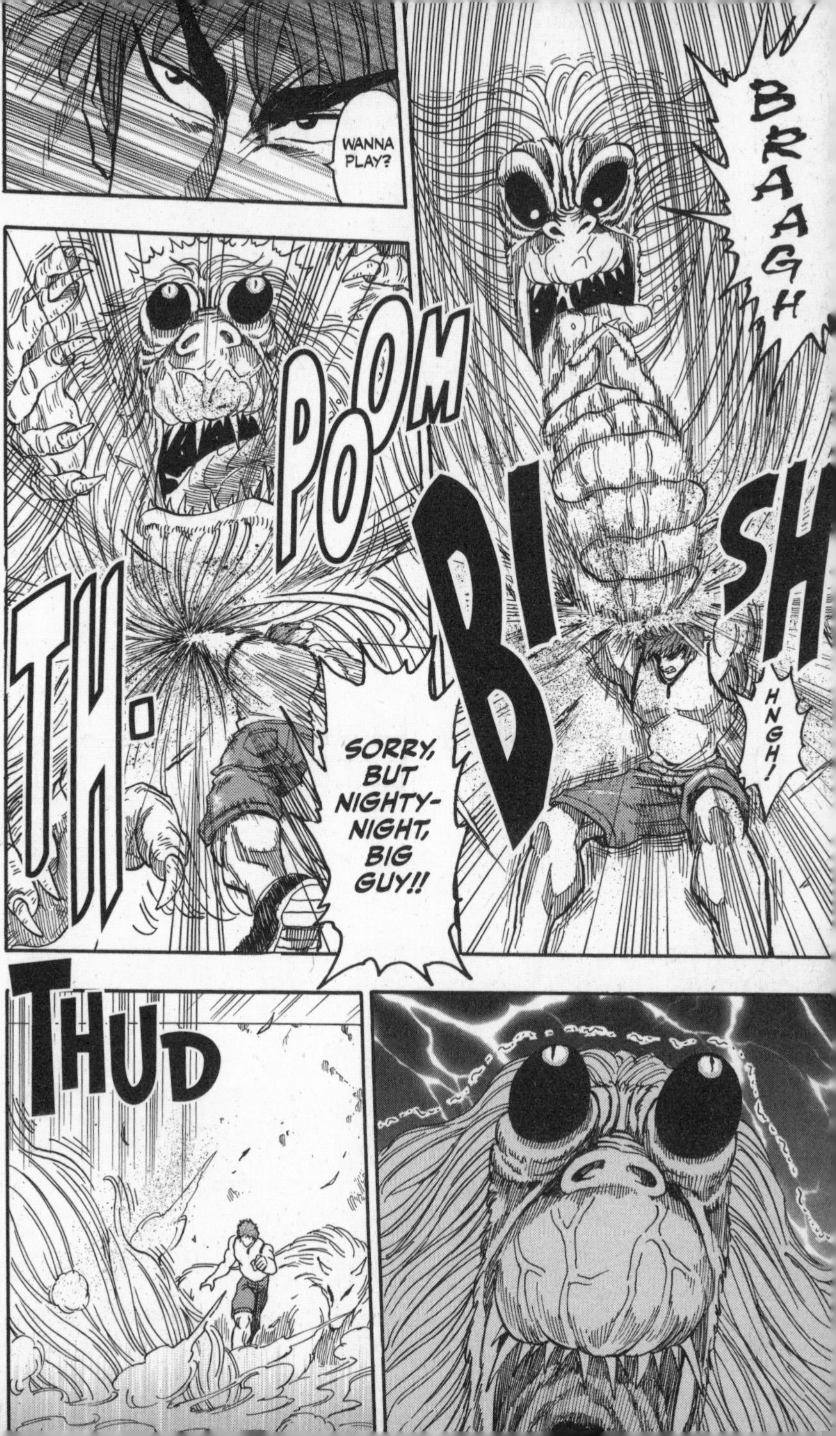
BRAAGH
BISH
HNGH!
WANNA PLAY?
POOM
TH
SORRY, BUT NIGHTY-NIGHT, BIG GUY!!
THUD

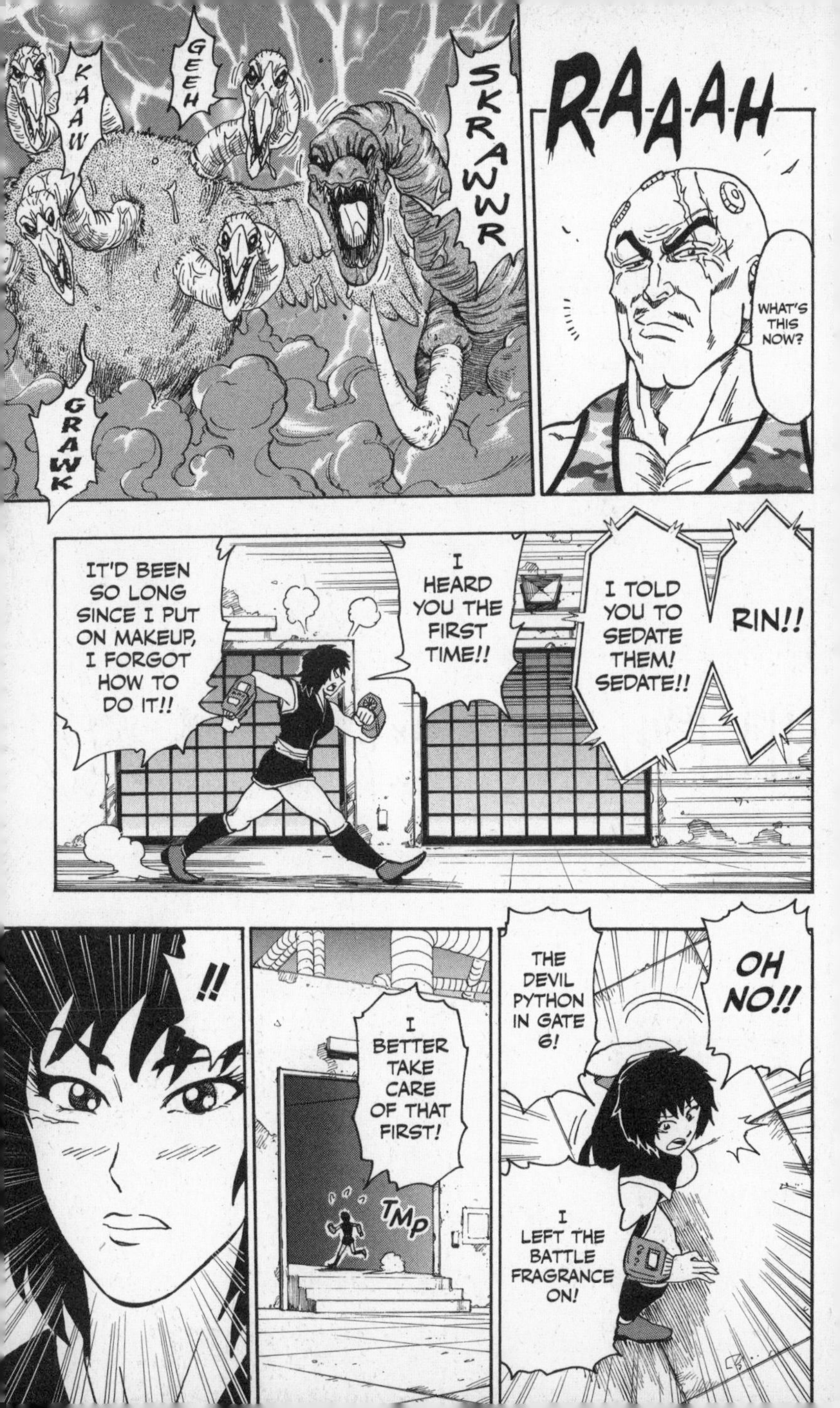
RAAAH
WHAT'S THIS NOW?
SKRAWWR
GEEH
KAAW
GRAWK
RIN!!
I TOLD YOU TO SEDATE THEM! SEDATE!!
I HEARD YOU THE FIRST TIME!!
IT'D BEEN SO LONG SINCE I PUT ON MAKEUP, I FORGOT HOW TO DO IT!!
OH NO!!
THE DEVIL PYTHON IN GATE 6!
I LEFT THE BATTLE FRAGRANCE ON!
I BETTER TAKE CARE OF THAT FIRST!
TMP
!!

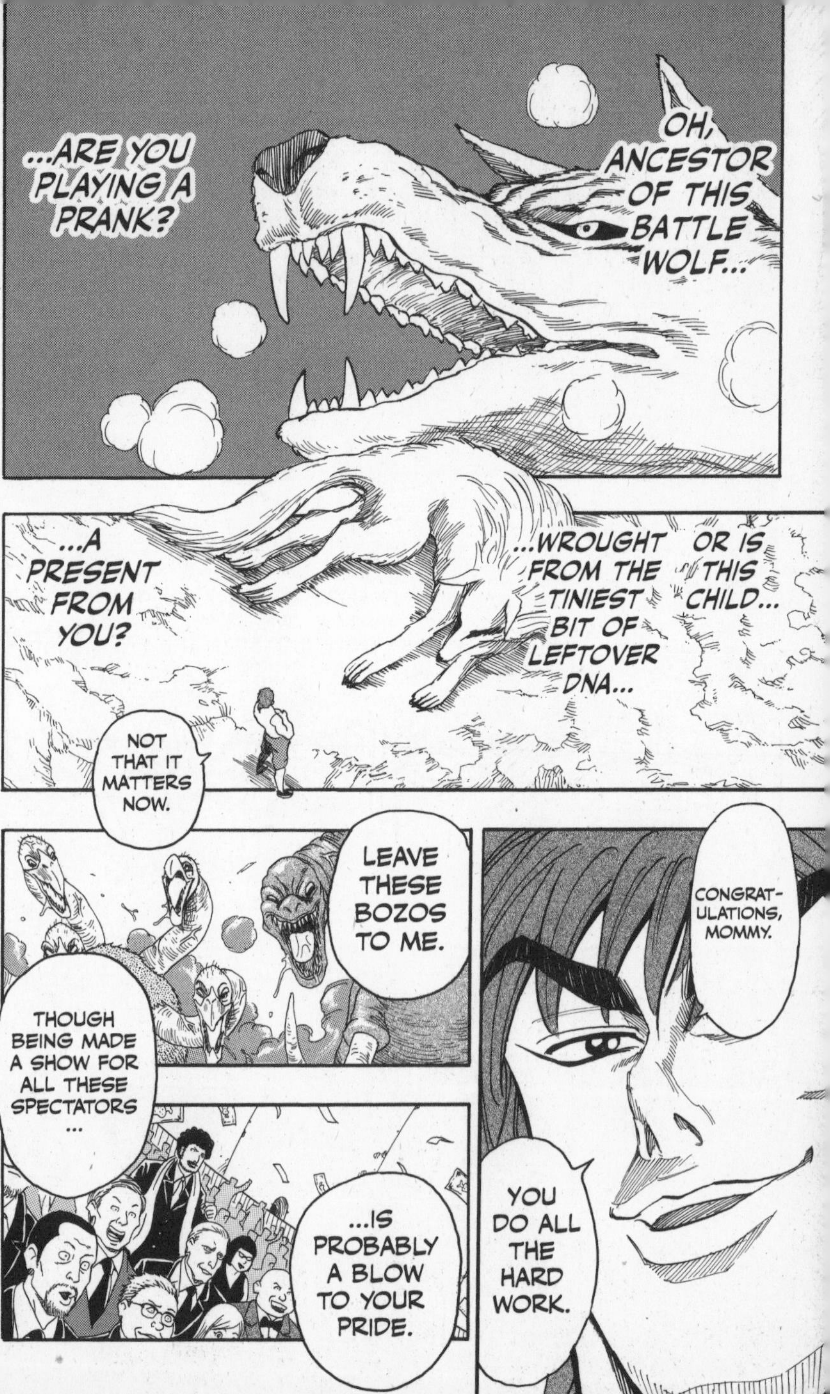

OH, ANCESTOR OF THIS BATTLE WOLF...
...ARE YOU PLAYING A PRANK?
OR IS THIS CHILD...
...WROUGHT FROM THE TINIEST BIT OF LEFTOVER DNA...
...A PRESENT FROM YOU?
NOT THAT IT MATTERS NOW.
CONGRAT-ULATIONS, MOMMY.
YOU DO ALL THE HARD WORK.
LEAVE THESE BOZOS TO ME.
THOUGH BEING MADE A SHOW FOR ALL THESE SPECTATORS...
...IS PROBABLY A BLOW TO YOUR PRIDE.

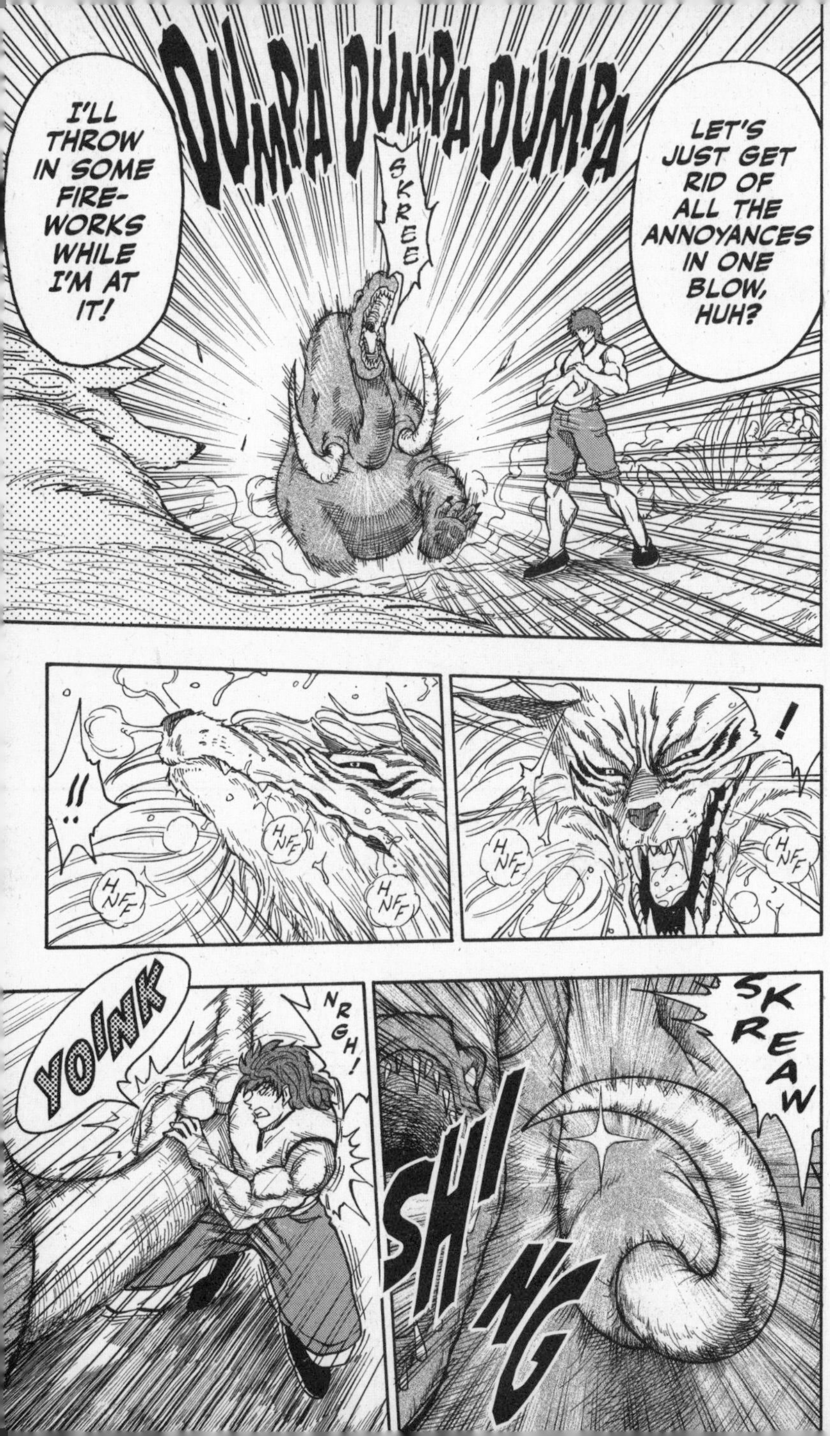
LET'S JUST GET RID OF ALL THE ANNOYANCES IN ONE BLOW, HUH?
DUMPA DUMPA DUMPA
SKREE
I'LL THROW IN SOME FIRE-WORKS WHILE I'M AT IT!
!
HNFF
HNFF
!!
HNFF
HNFF
HNFF
SKREAW
SHING
NRGH!
YOINK

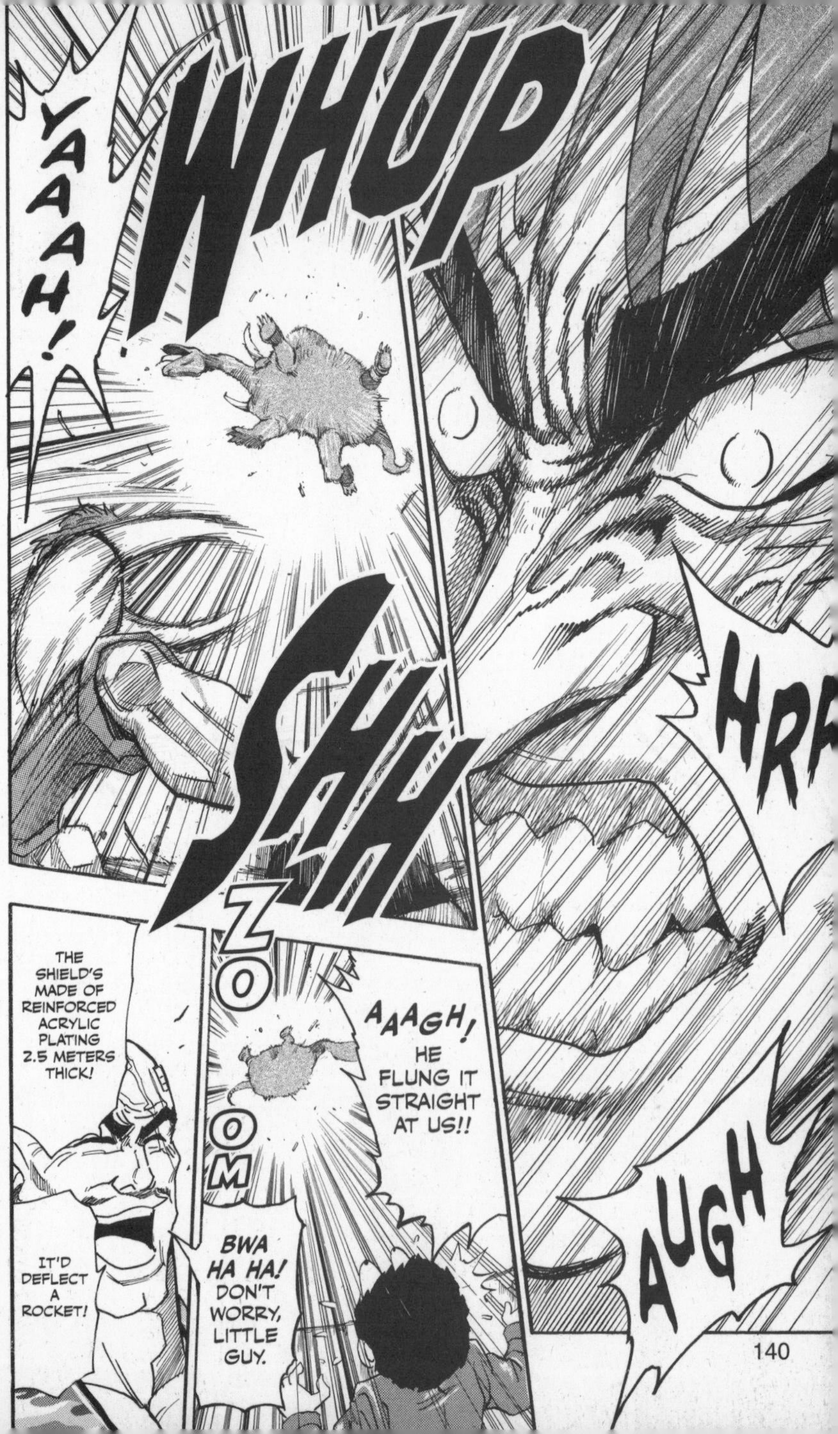
HRR
AUGH
WHUP
YAAAAH!
SHH
ZOOM
AAAGH! HE FLUNG IT STRAIGHT AT US!!
BWA HA HA! DON'T WORRY, LITTLE GUY.
THE SHIELD'S MADE OF REINFORCED ACRYLIC PLATING 2.5 METERS THICK!
IT'D DEFLECT A ROCKET!

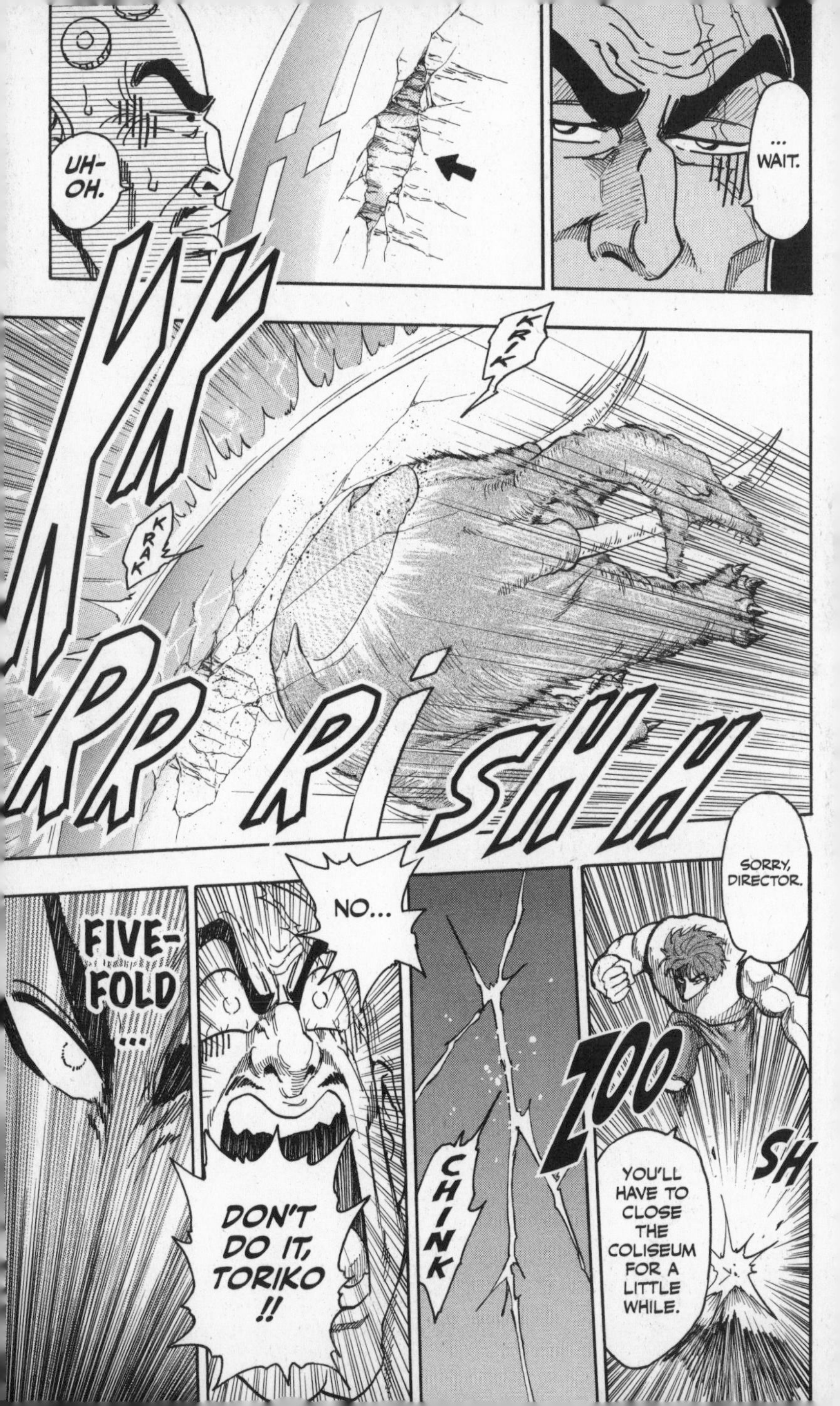

... WAIT.
UH-OH.
KRIK
KRAK
SORRY, DIRECTOR.
ZOOOSH
YOU'LL HAVE TO CLOSE THE COLISEUM FOR A LITTLE WHILE.
CHINK
NO...
DON'T DO IT, TORIKO !!
FIVE-FOLD ...

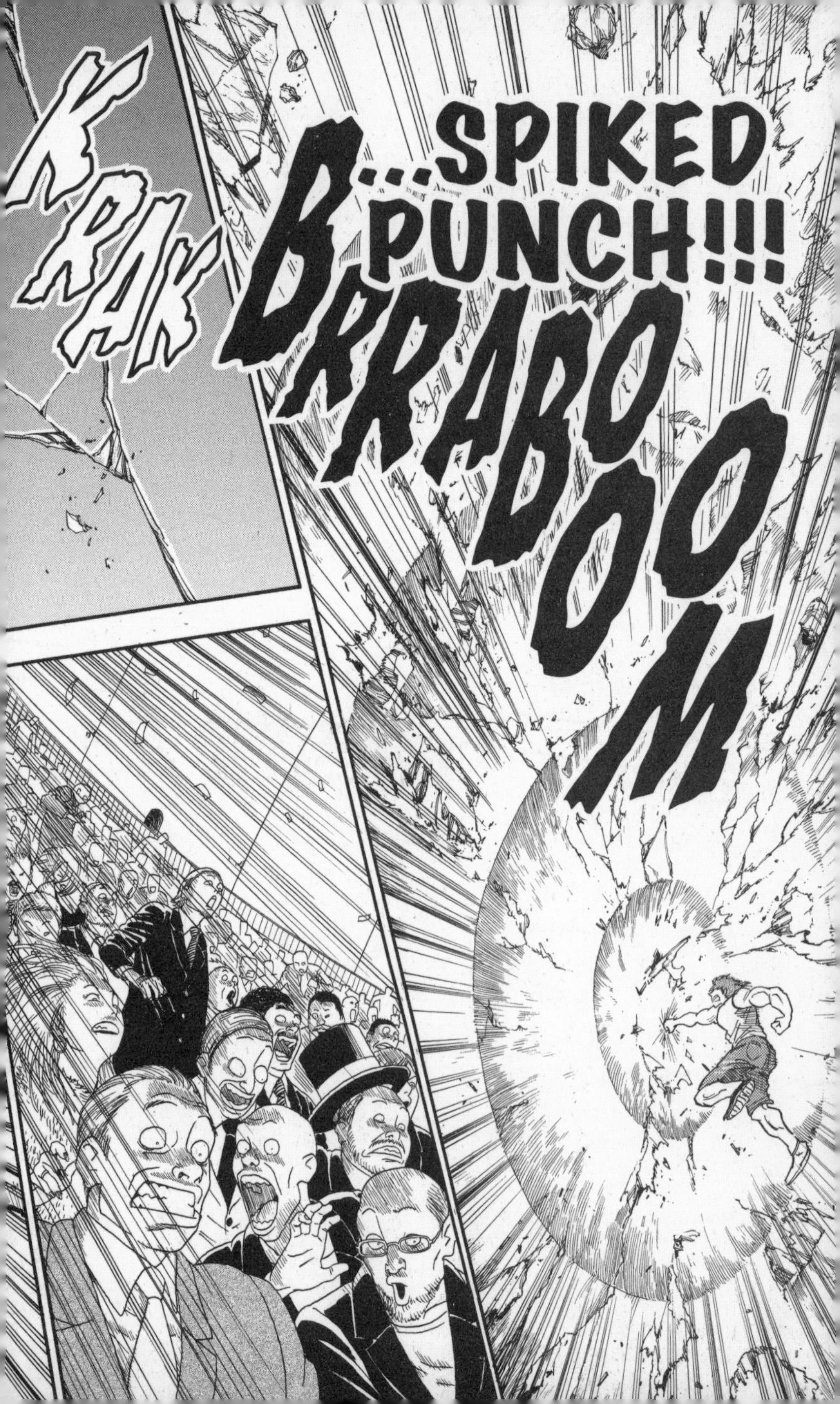
...SPIKED PUNCH!!!
BRRABOOM
KRAK

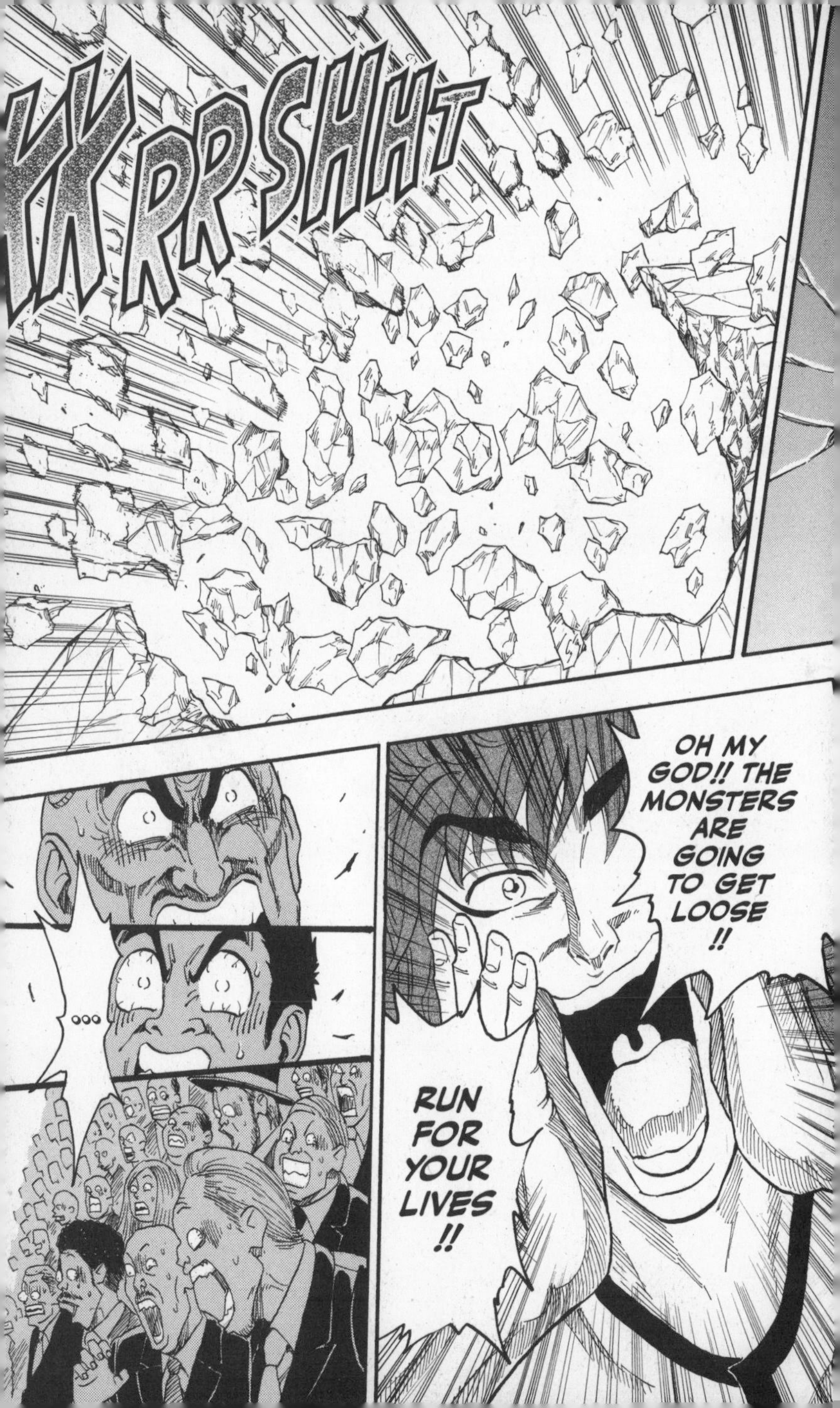
KRRSHHT
OH MY GOD!! THE MONSTERS ARE GOING TO GET LOOSE!!
RUN FOR YOUR LIVES!!
...

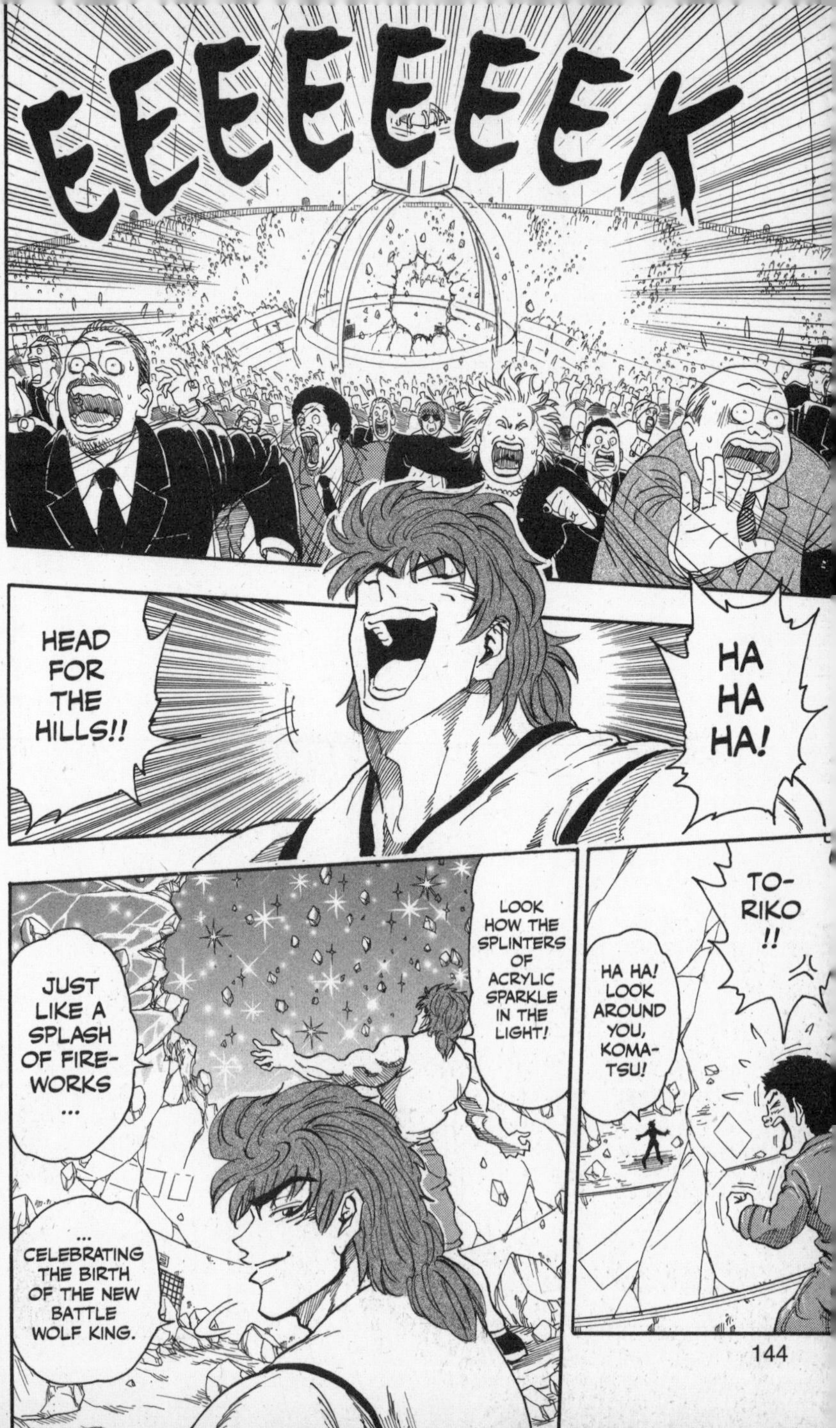
EEEEEEEK
HA HA HA!
HEAD FOR THE HILLS!!
TO-RIKO!!
HA HA! LOOK AROUND YOU, KOMATSU!
LOOK HOW THE SPLINTERS OF ACRYLIC SPARKLE IN THE LIGHT!
JUST LIKE A SPLASH OF FIRE-WORKS...
...CELEBRATING THE BIRTH OF THE NEW BATTLE WOLF KING.

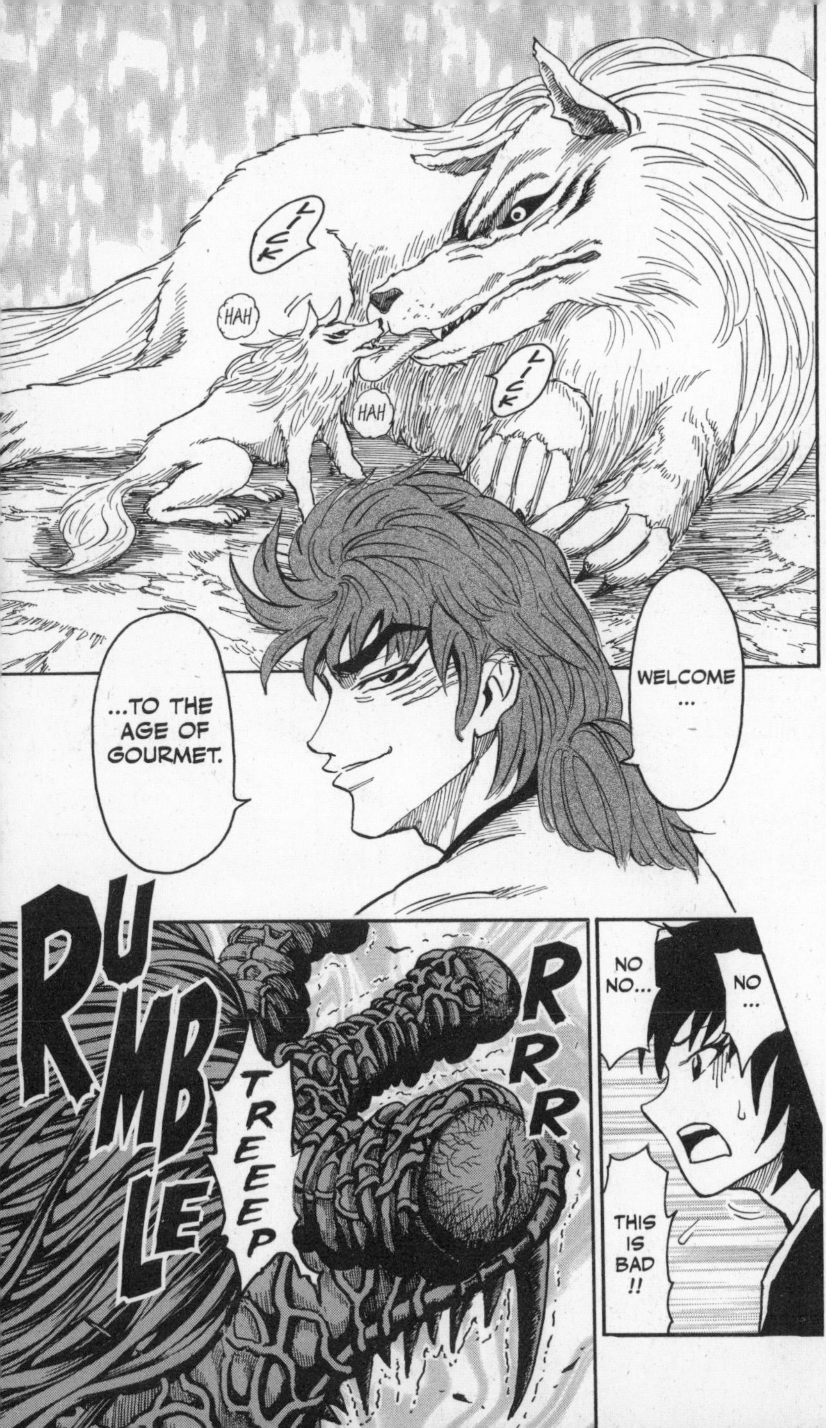
LICK
HAH
LICK
HAH
WELCOME ...
...TO THE AGE OF GOURMET.
NO ...
NO NO...
THIS IS BAD !!
RRRR
TREEEP
RUMBLE

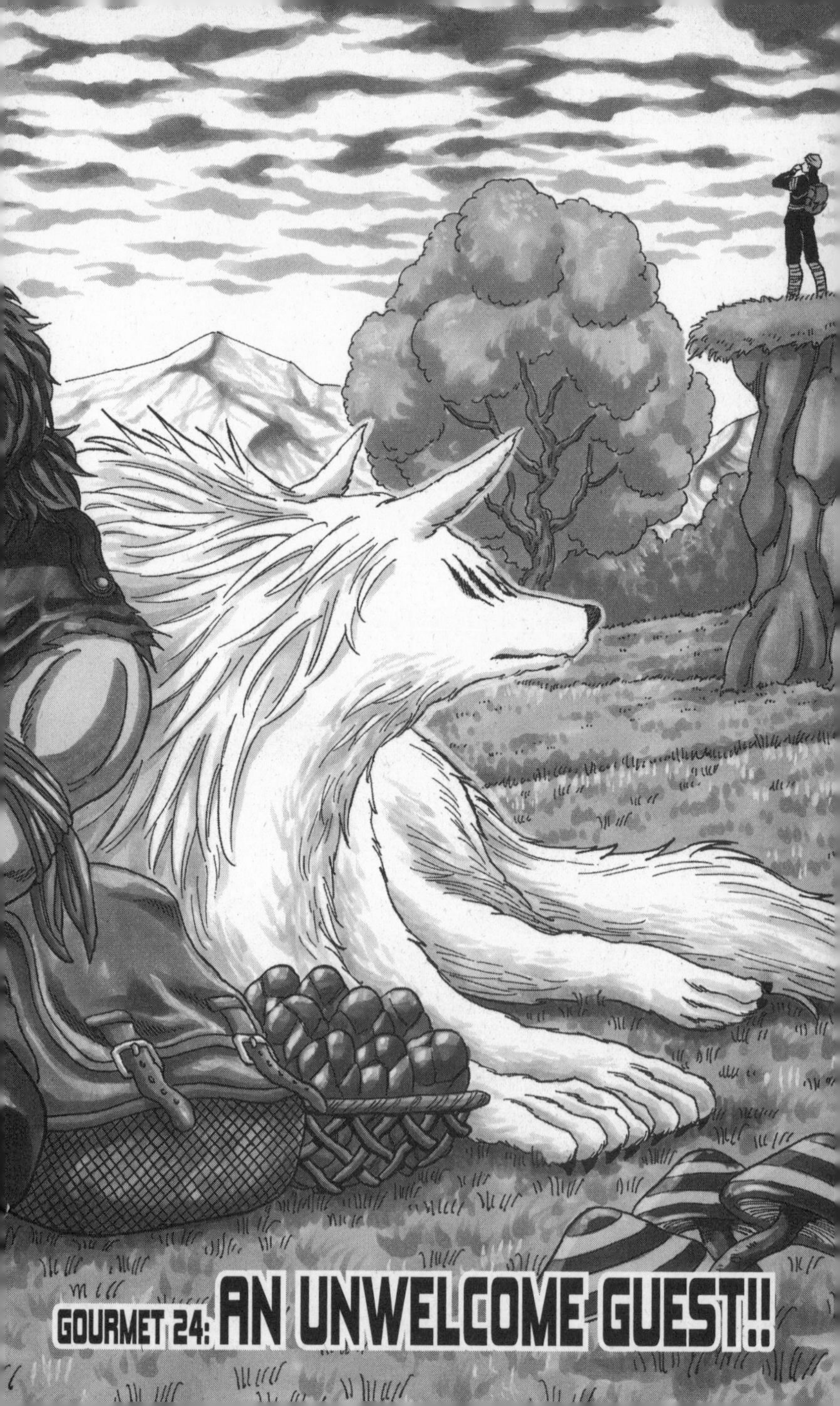
GOURMET 24: AN UNWELCOME GUEST!!

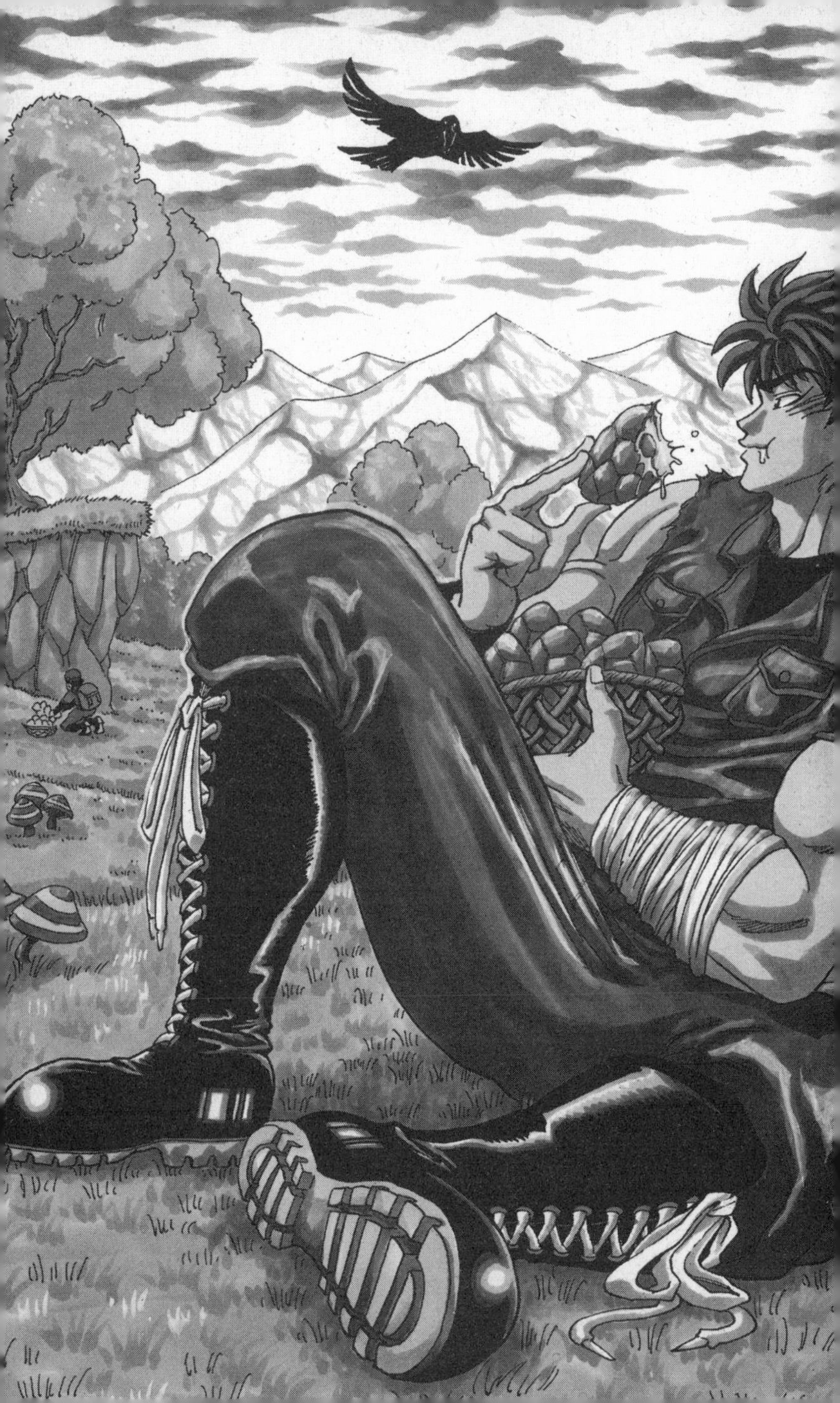

TORIKO

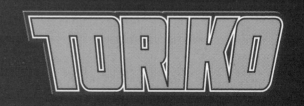

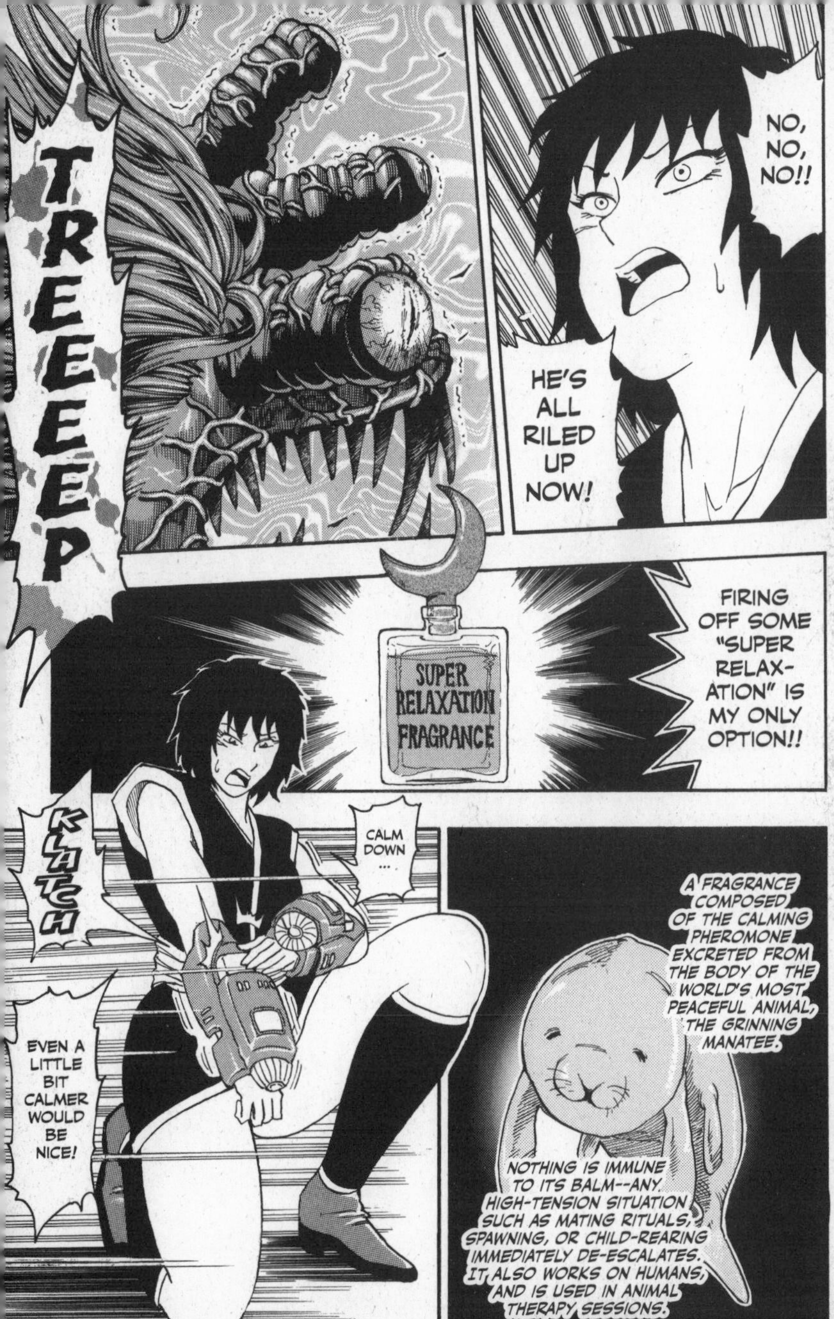
NO, NO, NO!!
HE'S ALL RILED UP NOW!
TREEEEEP
FIRING OFF SOME "SUPER RELAX-ATION" IS MY ONLY OPTION!!
SUPER RELAXATION FRAGRANCE
A FRAGRANCE COMPOSED OF THE CALMING PHEROMONE EXCRETED FROM THE BODY OF THE WORLD'S MOST PEACEFUL ANIMAL, THE GRINNING MANATEE.
NOTHING IS IMMUNE TO ITS BALM--ANY HIGH-TENSION SITUATION SUCH AS MATING RITUALS, SPAWNING, OR CHILD-REARING IMMEDIATELY DE-ESCALATES. IT ALSO WORKS ON HUMANS, AND IS USED IN ANIMAL THERAPY SESSIONS.
CALM DOWN ...
KLATCH
EVEN A LITTLE BIT CALMER WOULD BE NICE!

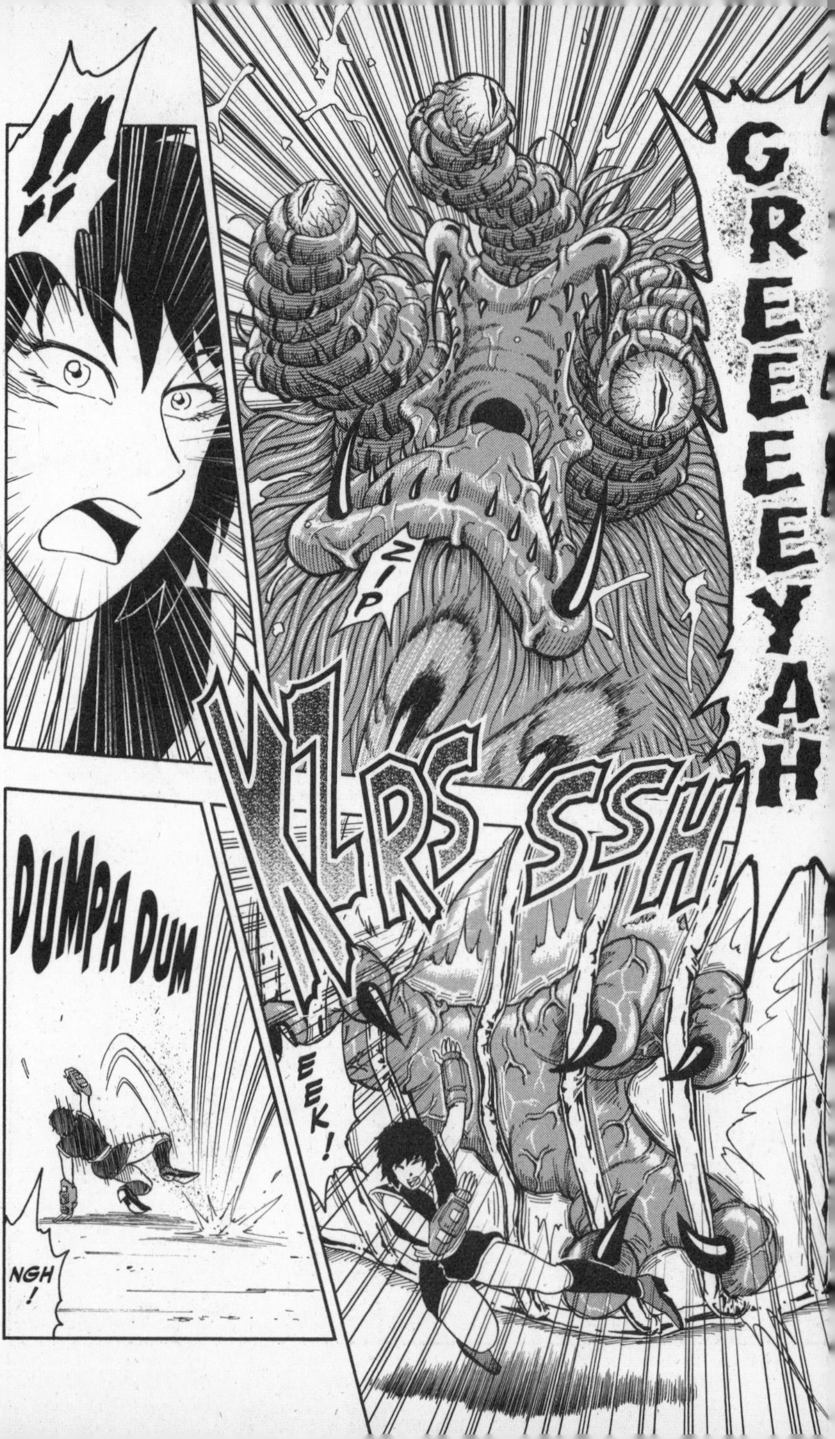

GREEEEYAH
ZIP
VLRS SSH
EEK!
!!
DUMPA DUM
NGH!

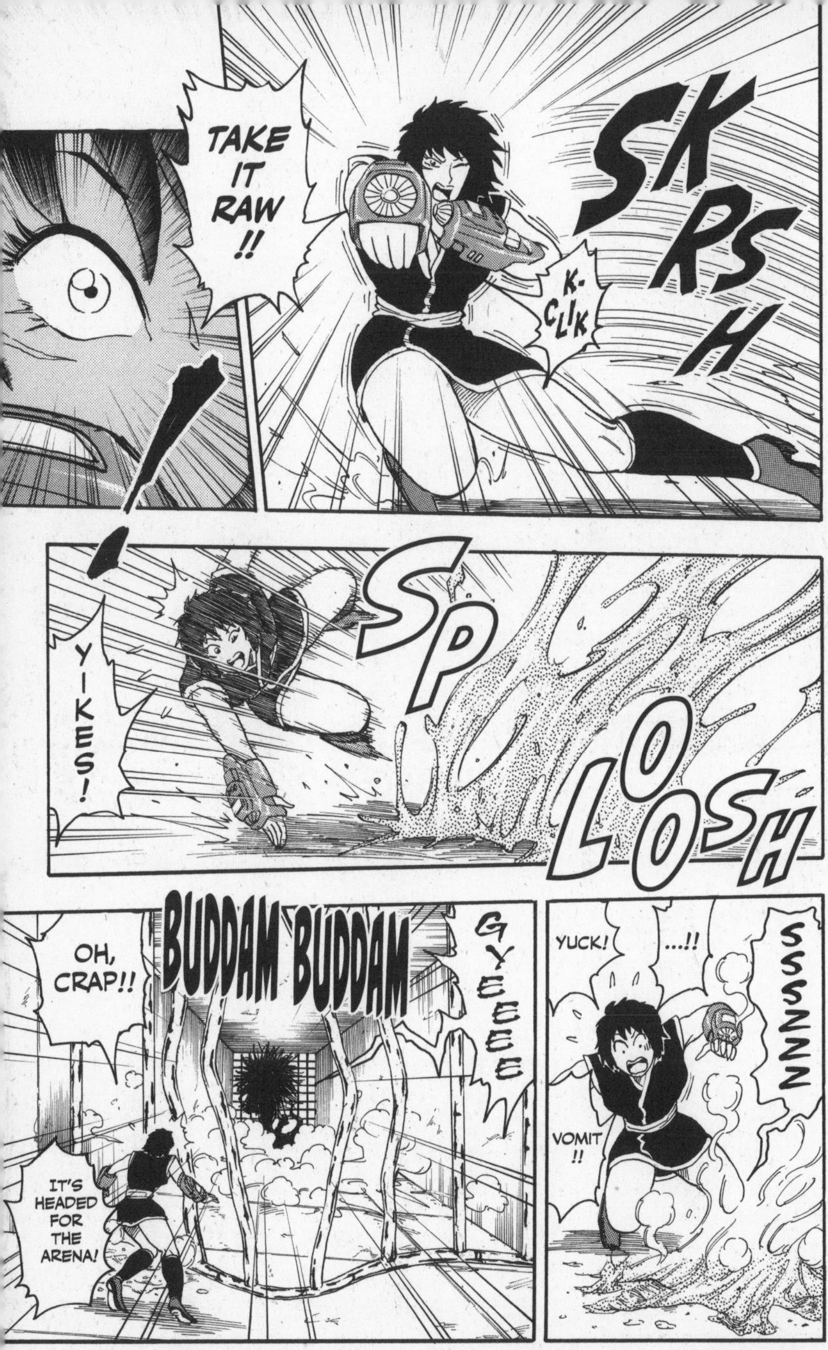
SKRSH
K-CLIK
TAKE IT RAW!!
SPLOOSH
YIKES!
SSSZZZ
...!!
YUCK!
VOMIT!!
GYEEEE
BUDDAM BUDDAM
OH, CRAP!!
IT'S HEADED FOR THE ARENA!

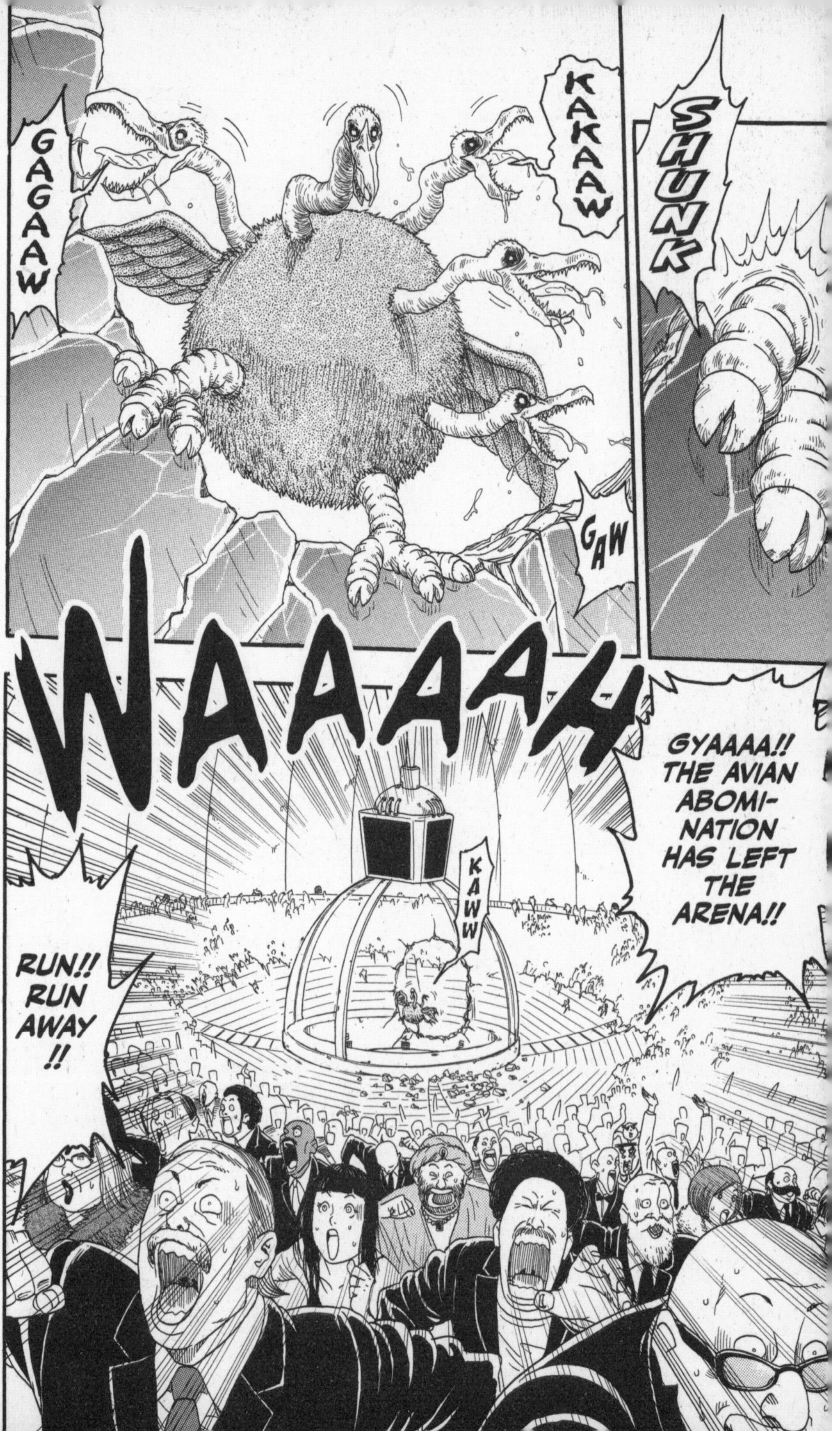
SHUNK
KAKAAW
GAGAAW
GAW
WAAAAH
GYAAAA!! THE AVIAN ABOMI-NATION HAS LEFT THE ARENA!!
KAWW
RUN!! RUN AWAY !!

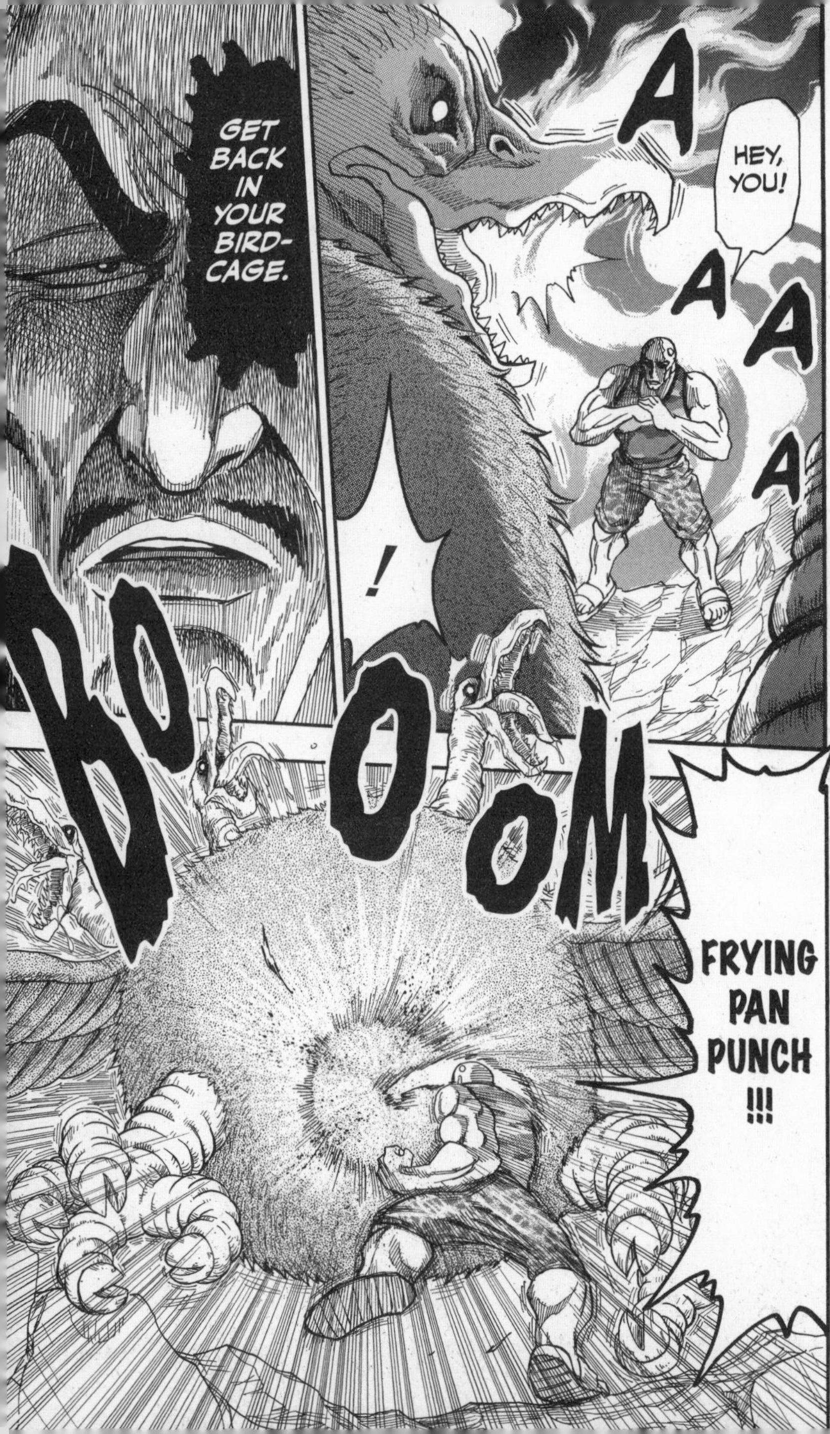
HEY, YOU!
AAAA
!
GET BACK IN YOUR BIRD-CAGE.
BOOOM
FRYING PAN PUNCH !!!

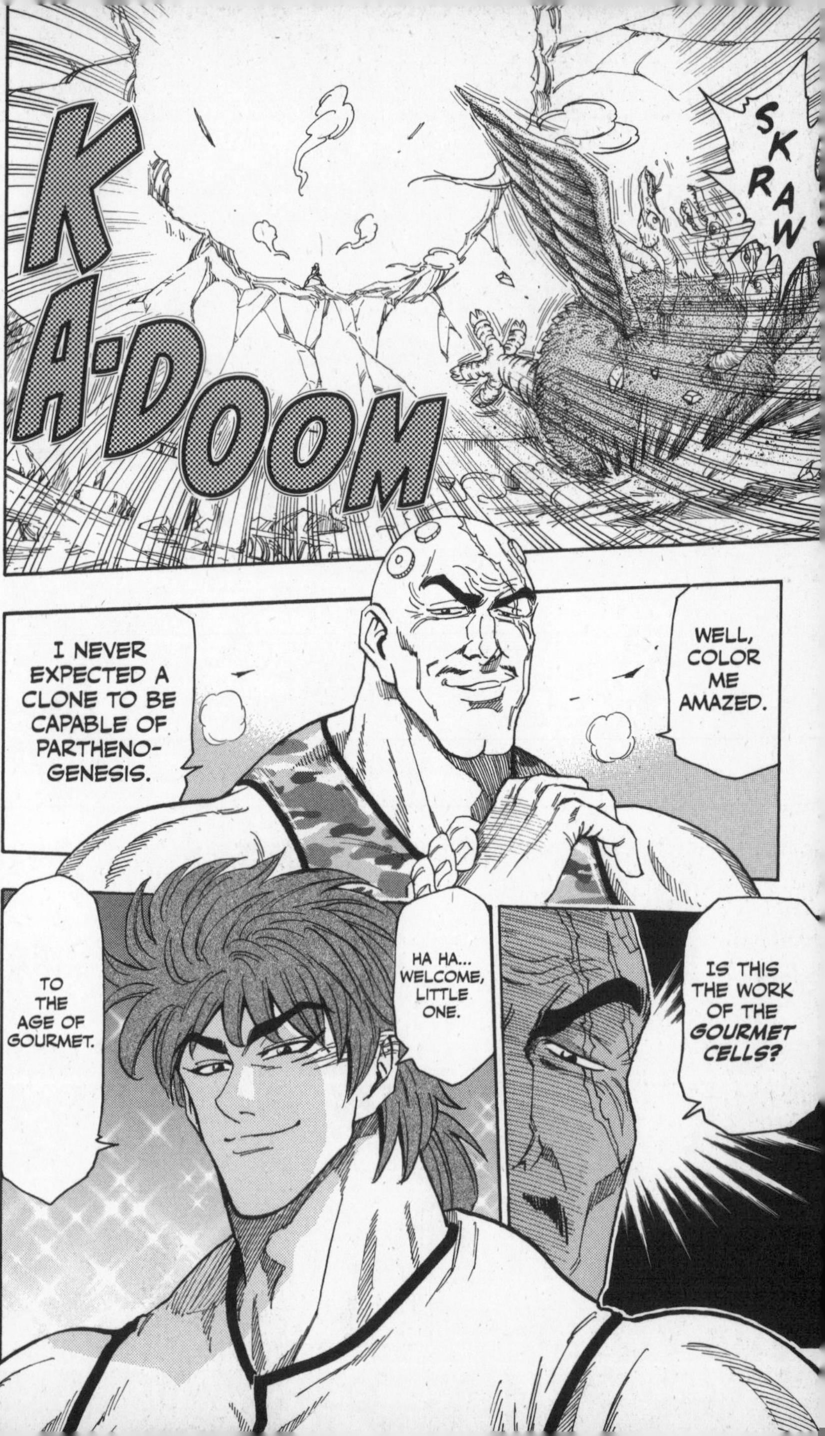
SKRAW
KA-DOOM
WELL, COLOR ME AMAZED.
I NEVER EXPECTED A CLONE TO BE CAPABLE OF PARTHENO-GENESIS.
IS THIS THE WORK OF THE *GOURMET CELLS?*
HA HA... WELCOME, LITTLE ONE.
TO THE AGE OF GOURMET.

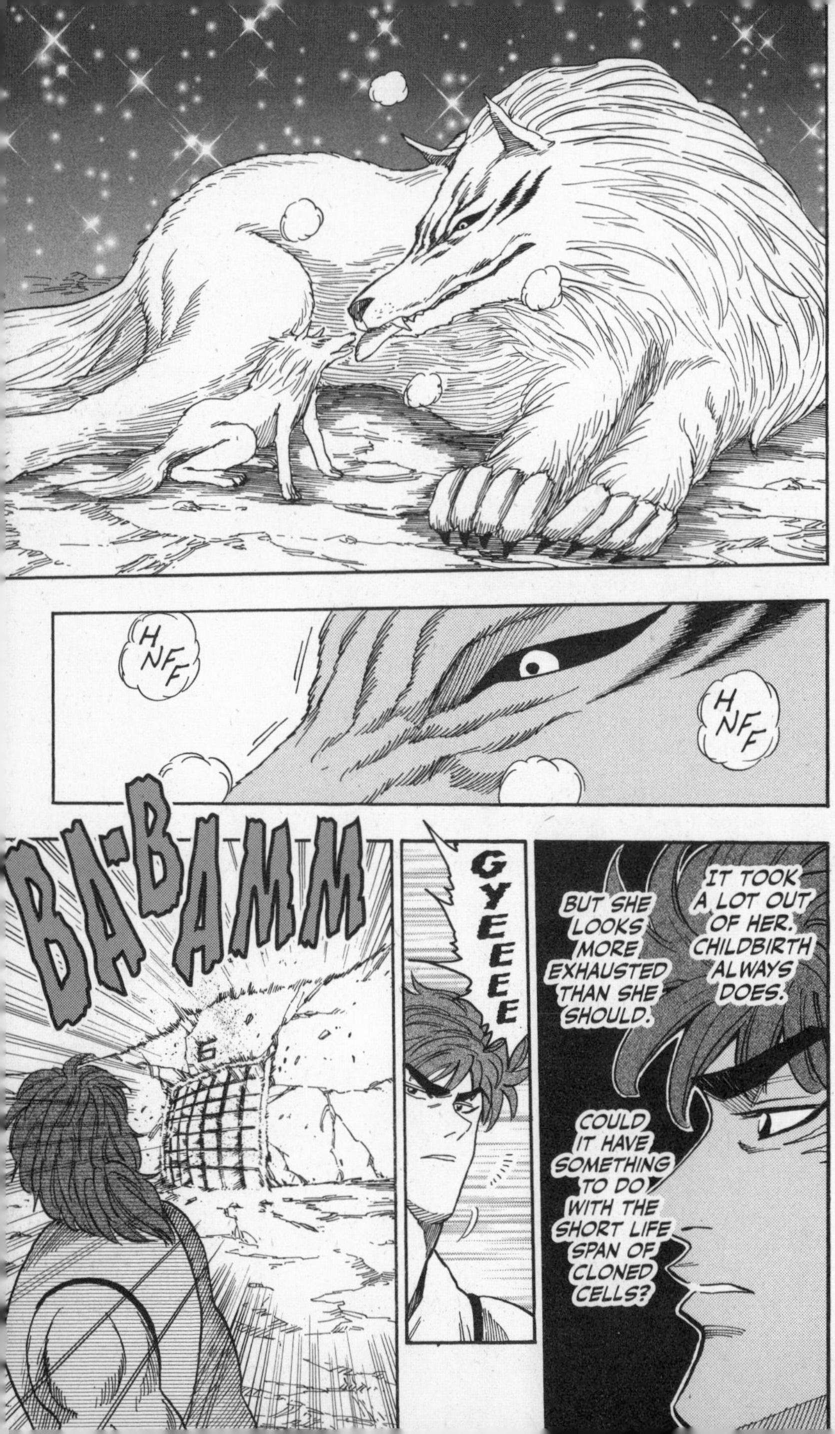

HNFF
HNFF
IT TOOK A LOT OUT OF HER. CHILDBIRTH ALWAYS DOES.
BUT SHE LOOKS MORE EXHAUSTED THAN SHE SHOULD.
COULD IT HAVE SOMETHING TO DO WITH THE SHORT LIFE SPAN OF CLONED CELLS?
GYEEEE
BA-BAMM

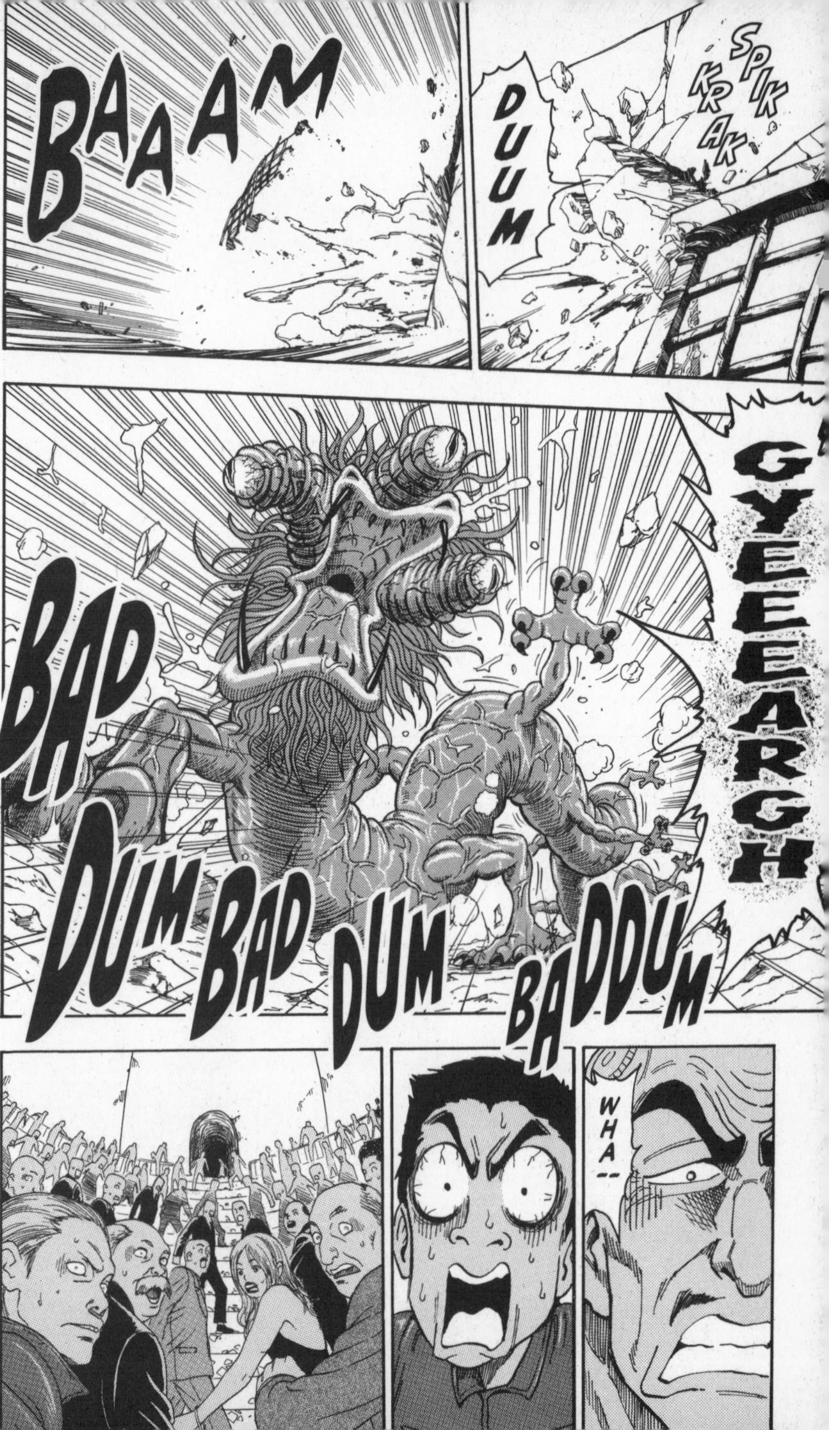
SPIK
KRAK
DUUM
BAAAM
GYEEARGH
BAD DUM BAD DUM BADDUM
WHA--

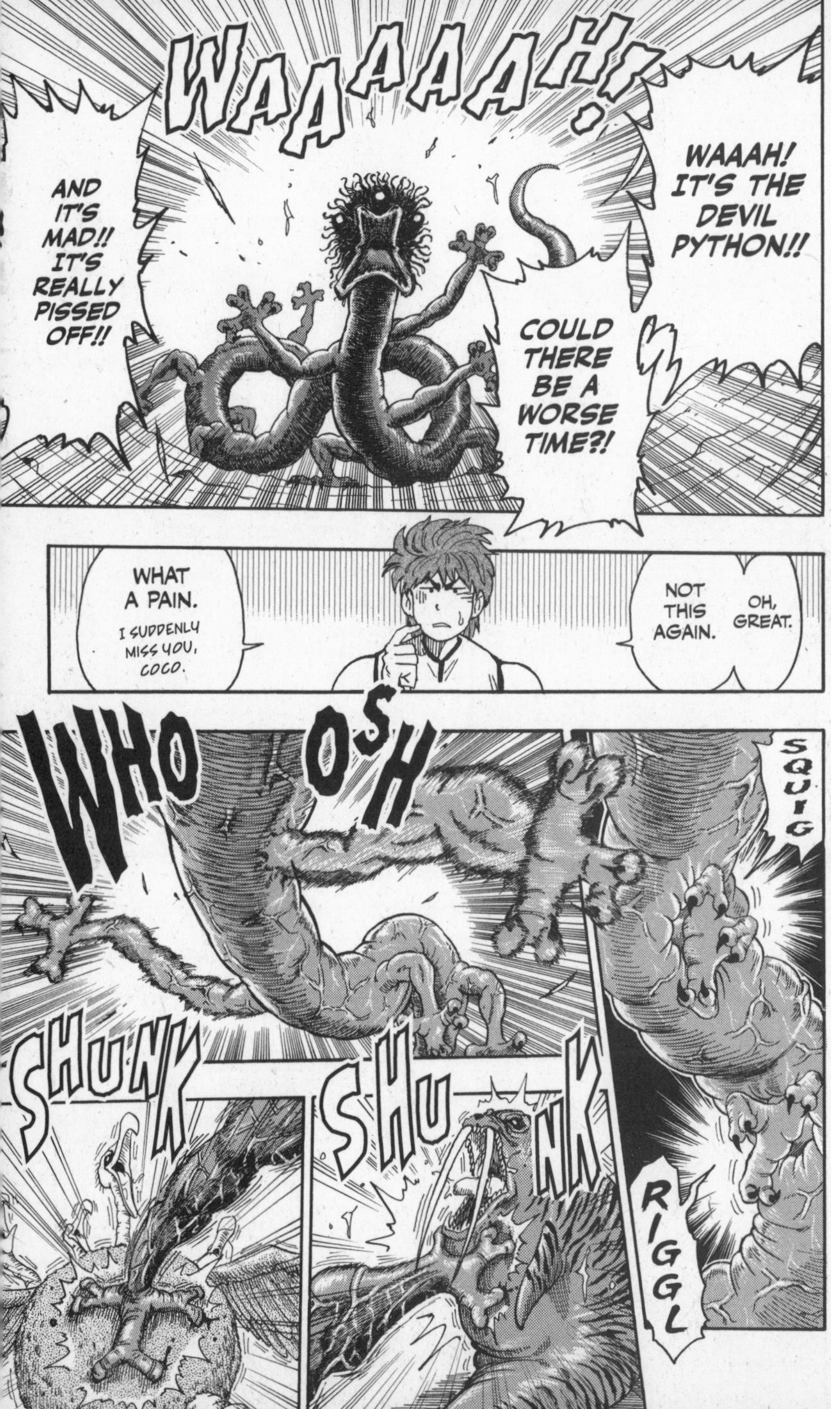
WAAAAAH!!
WAAAH! IT'S THE DEVIL PYTHON!!
COULD THERE BE A WORSE TIME?!
AND IT'S MAD!! IT'S REALLY PISSED OFF!!
OH, GREAT.
NOT THIS AGAIN.
WHAT A PAIN.
I SUDDENLY MISS YOU, COCO.
SQUIG
WHOOSH
RIGGL
SHUNK
SHUNK

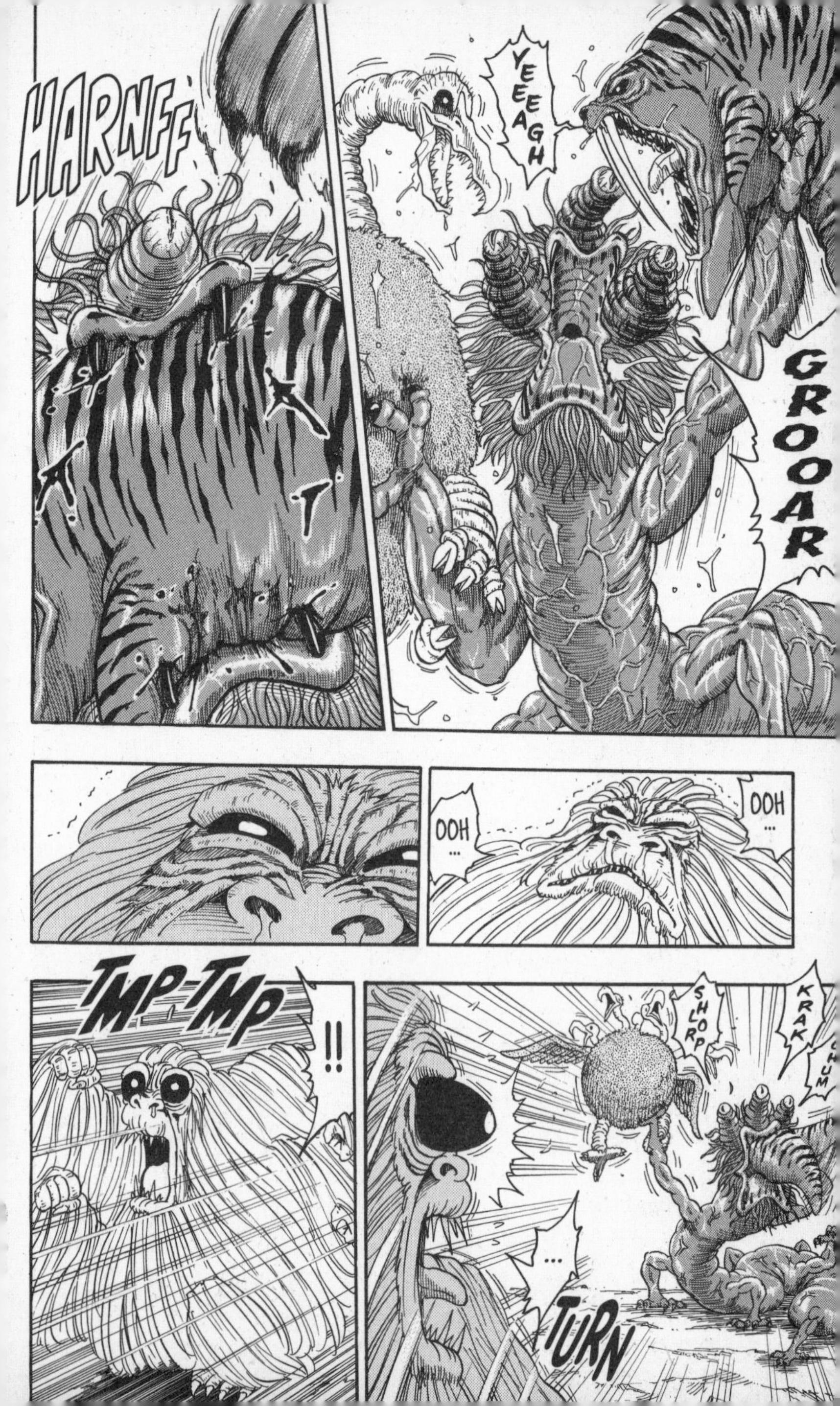

YEEEAGH
GROOOAR
HARNFF
OOH...
OOH...
KRAK
SHLORP
...
TURN
TMP-TMP
!!

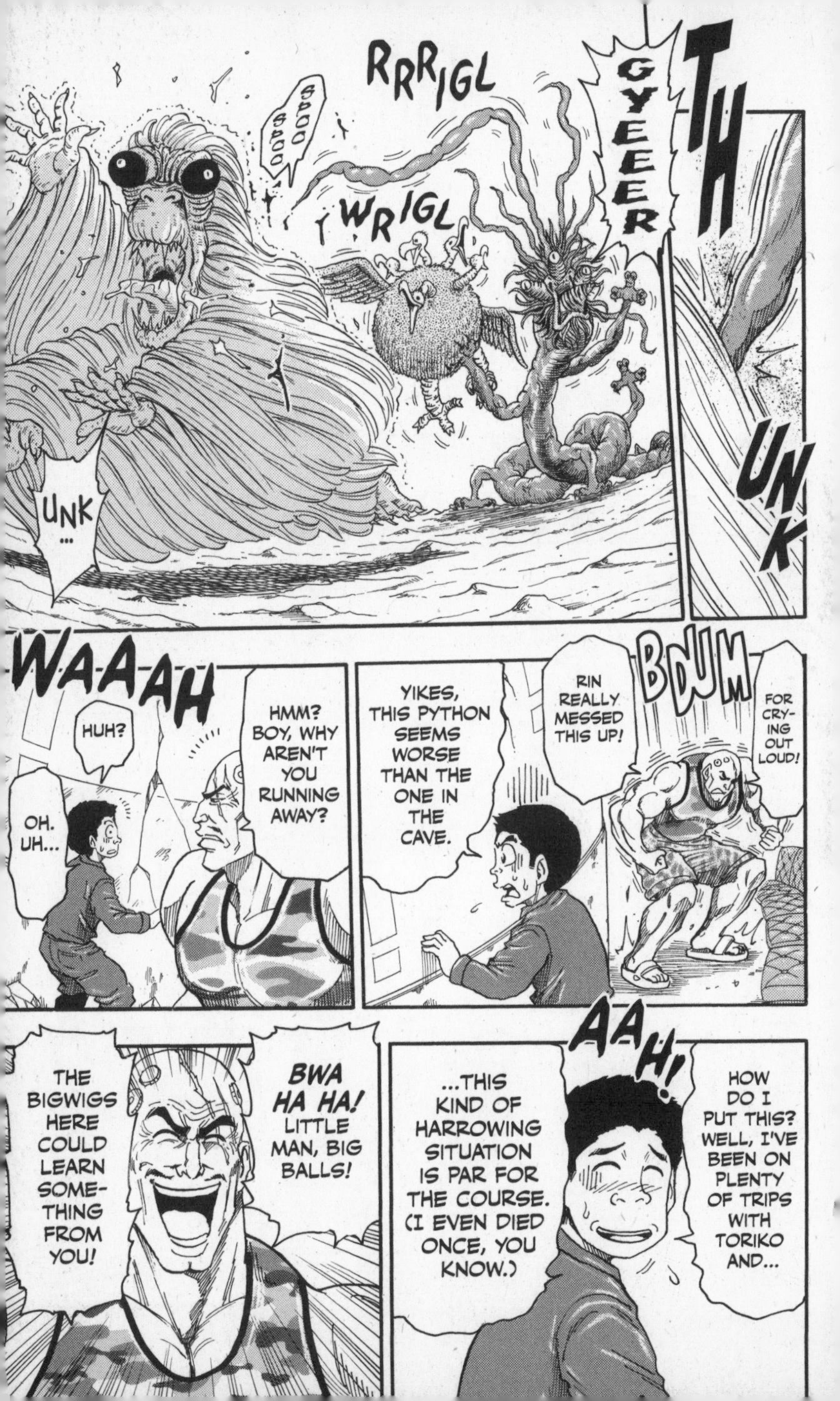
THUNK
GYEEER
RRRIGL
SPOO SPOO SPOO
WRIGL
UNK...
FOR CRY-ING OUT LOUD!
BDUM
RIN REALLY MESSED THIS UP!
YIKES, THIS PYTHON SEEMS WORSE THAN THE ONE IN THE CAVE.
HMM? BOY, WHY AREN'T YOU RUNNING AWAY?
WAAAH
HUH?
OH. UH...
AAH!
HOW DO I PUT THIS? WELL, I'VE BEEN ON PLENTY OF TRIPS WITH TORIKO AND...
...THIS KIND OF HARROWING SITUATION IS PAR FOR THE COURSE. (I EVEN DIED ONCE, YOU KNOW.)
BWA HA HA! LITTLE MAN, BIG BALLS!
THE BIGWIGS HERE COULD LEARN SOME-THING FROM YOU!

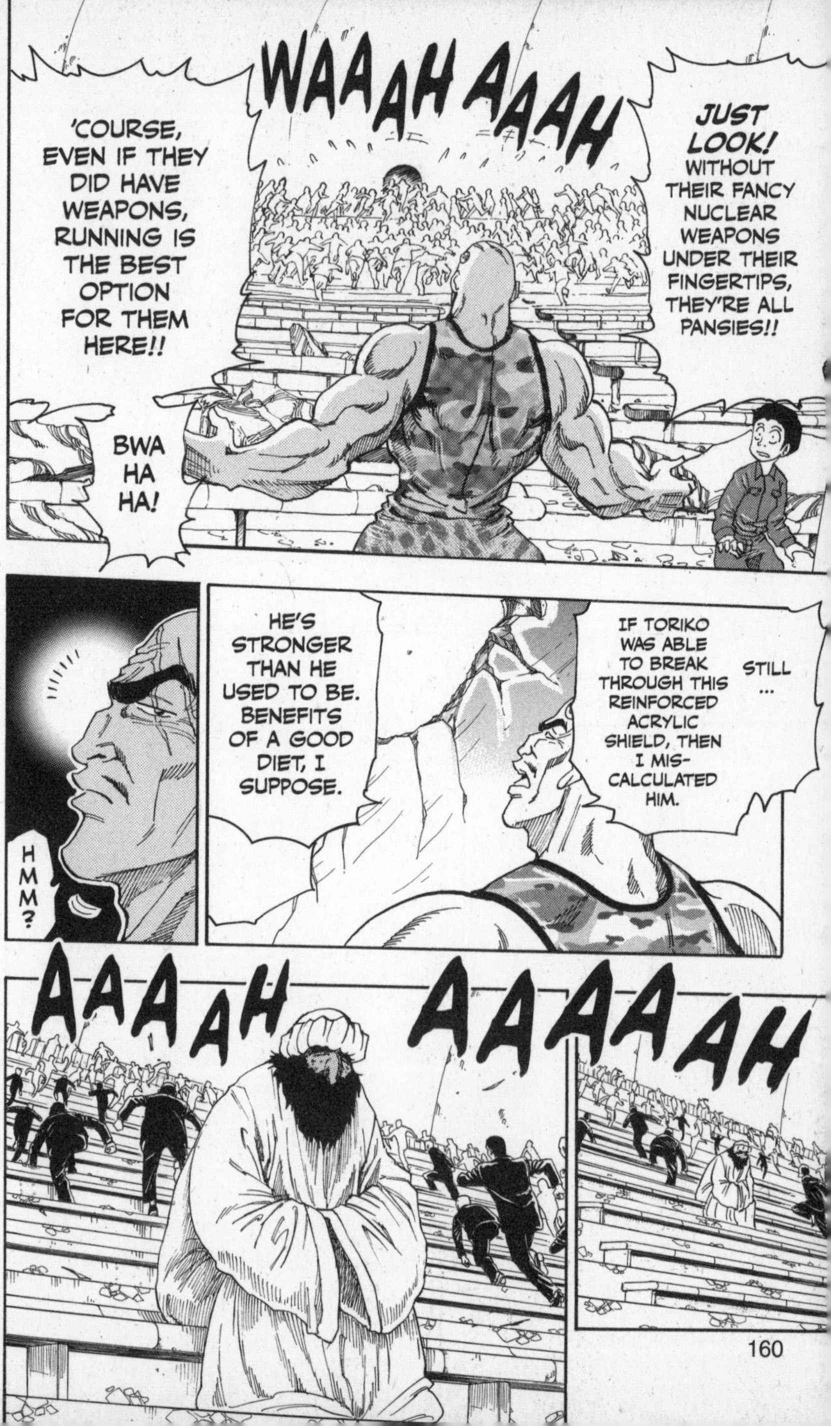
WAAAH AAAH
JUST LOOK! WITHOUT THEIR FANCY NUCLEAR WEAPONS UNDER THEIR FINGERTIPS, THEY'RE ALL PANSIES!!
'COURSE, EVEN IF THEY DID HAVE WEAPONS, RUNNING IS THE BEST OPTION FOR THEM HERE!!
BWA HA HA!
STILL ...
IF TORIKO WAS ABLE TO BREAK THROUGH THIS REINFORCED ACRYLIC SHIELD, THEN I MIS-CALCULATED HIM.
HE'S STRONGER THAN HE USED TO BE. BENEFITS OF A GOOD DIET, I SUPPOSE.
HMM?
AAAAH AAAAAAH

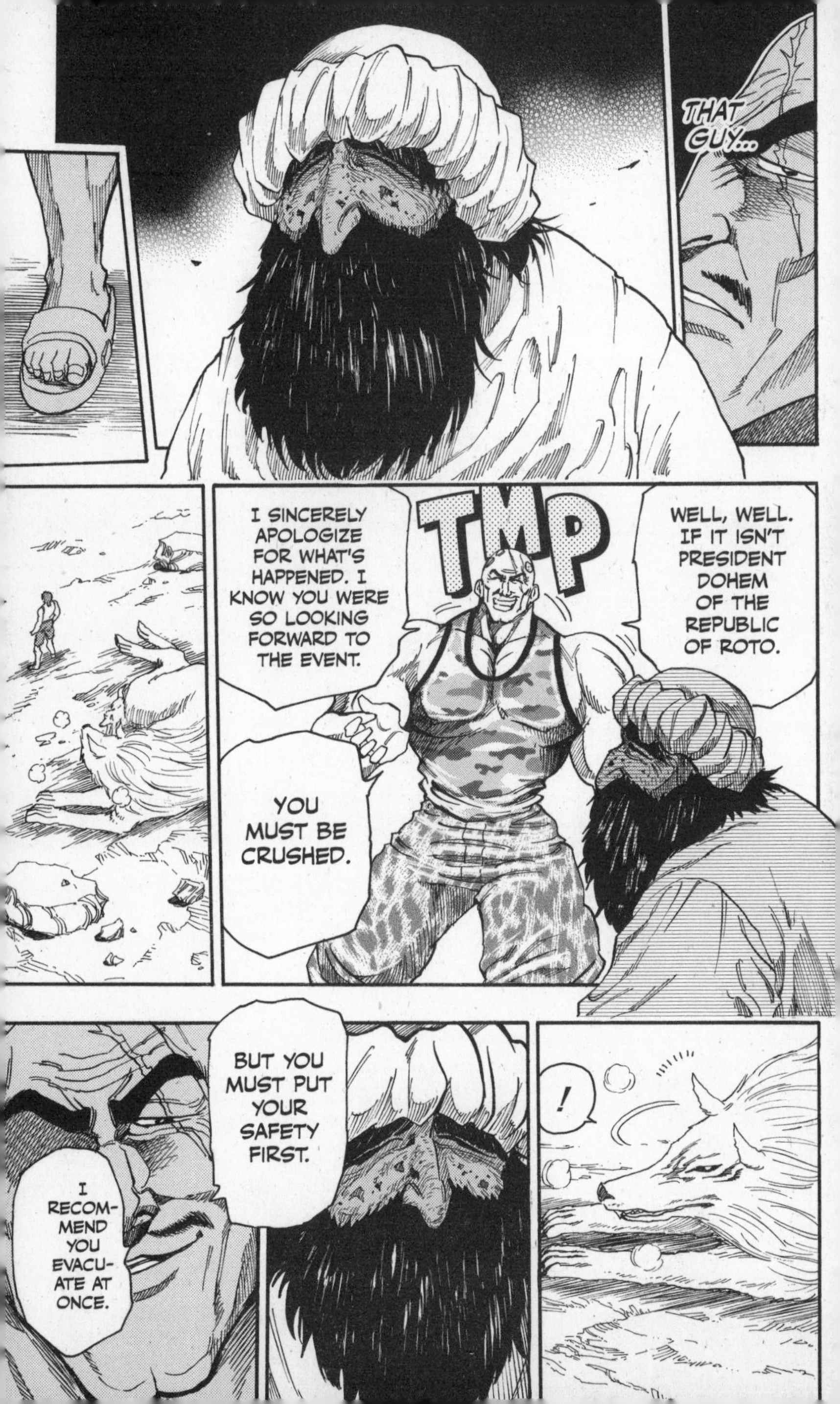
THAT GUY...
WELL, WELL. IF IT ISN'T PRESIDENT DOHEM OF THE REPUBLIC OF ROTO.
TMP
I SINCERELY APOLOGIZE FOR WHAT'S HAPPENED. I KNOW YOU WERE SO LOOKING FORWARD TO THE EVENT.
YOU MUST BE CRUSHED.
!
BUT YOU MUST PUT YOUR SAFETY FIRST.
I RECOMMEND YOU EVACUATE AT ONCE.

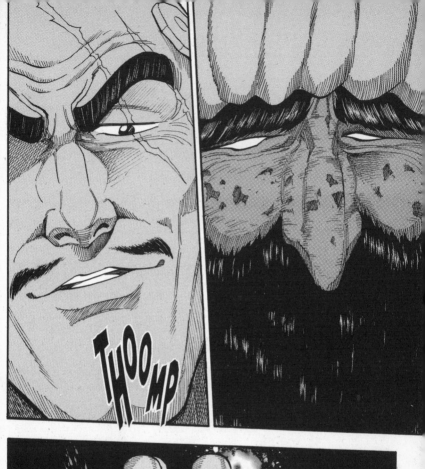

THOOMP

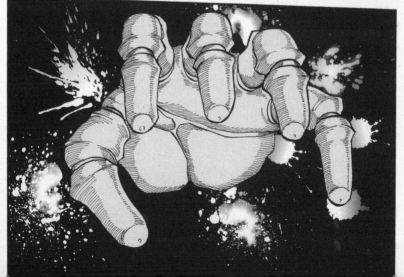

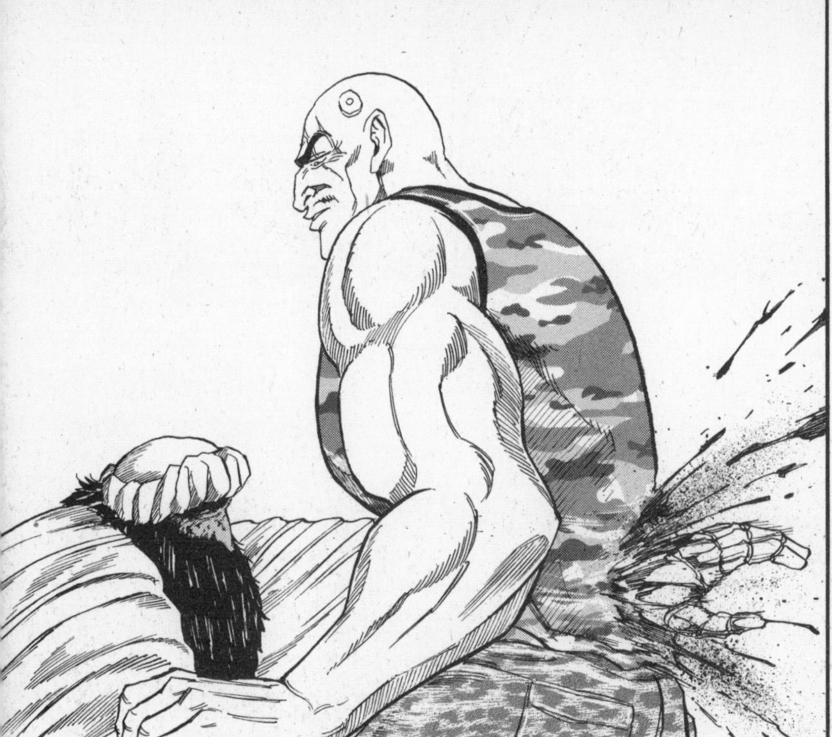

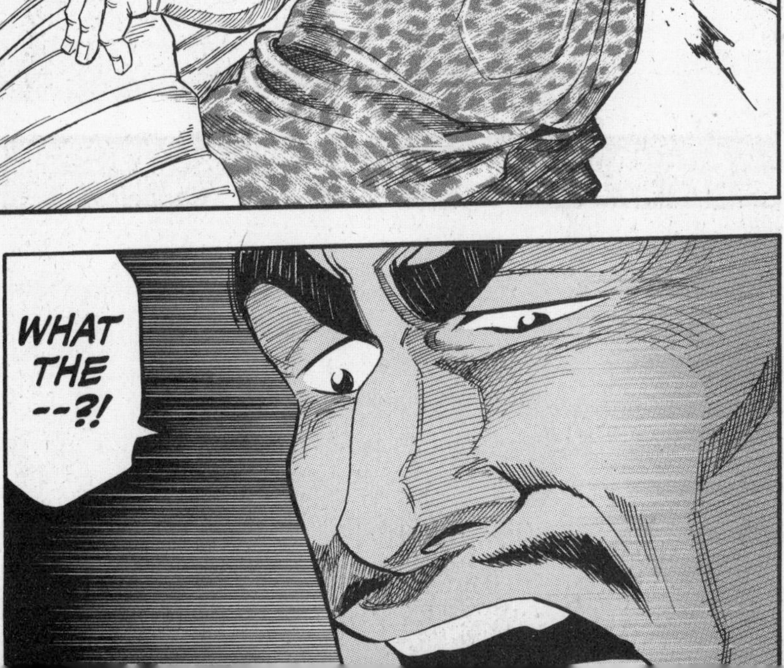
WHAT THE --?!

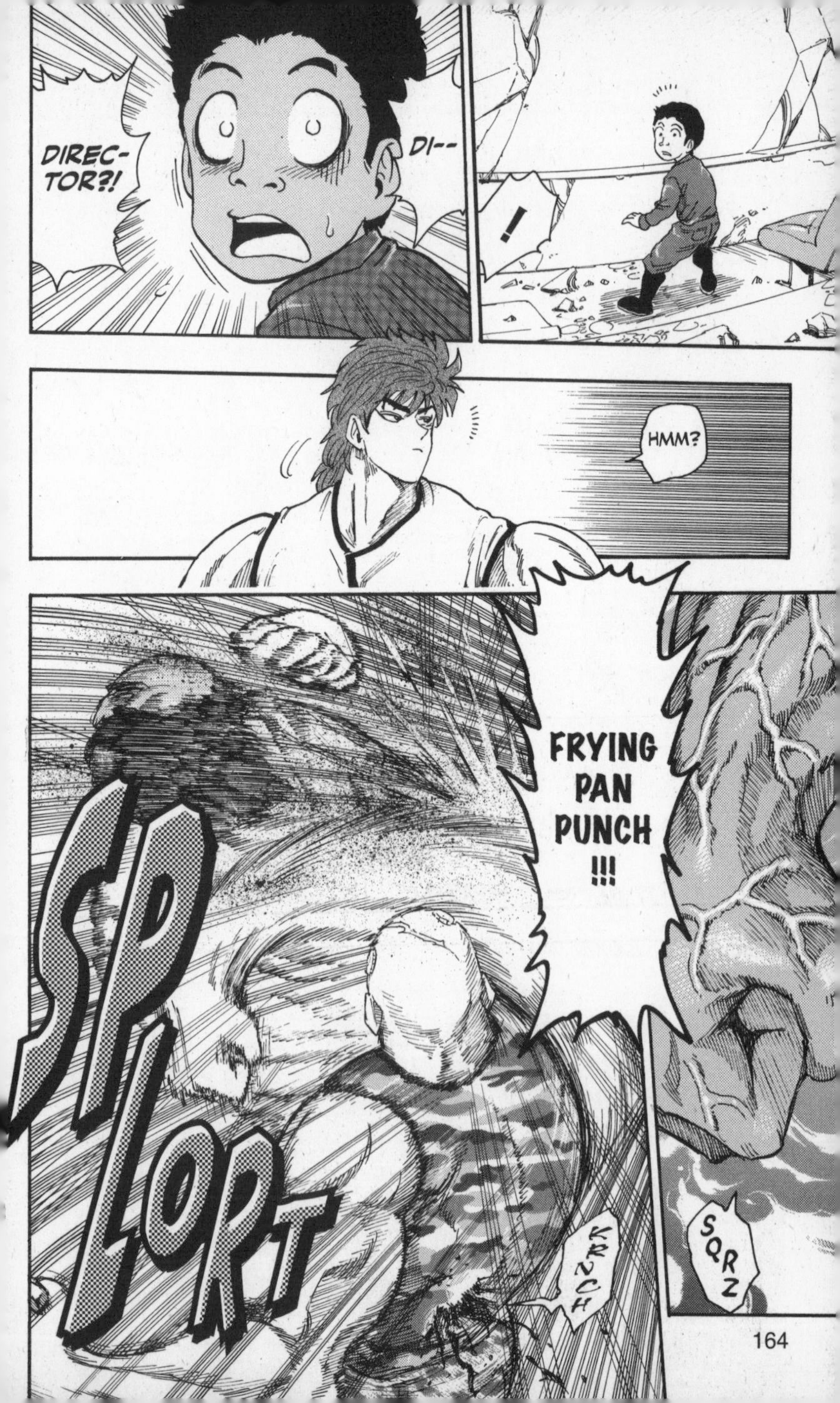
!
DI--
DIRECTOR?!
HMM?
FRYING PAN PUNCH!!!
SQRZ
KRNCH
SPLORT

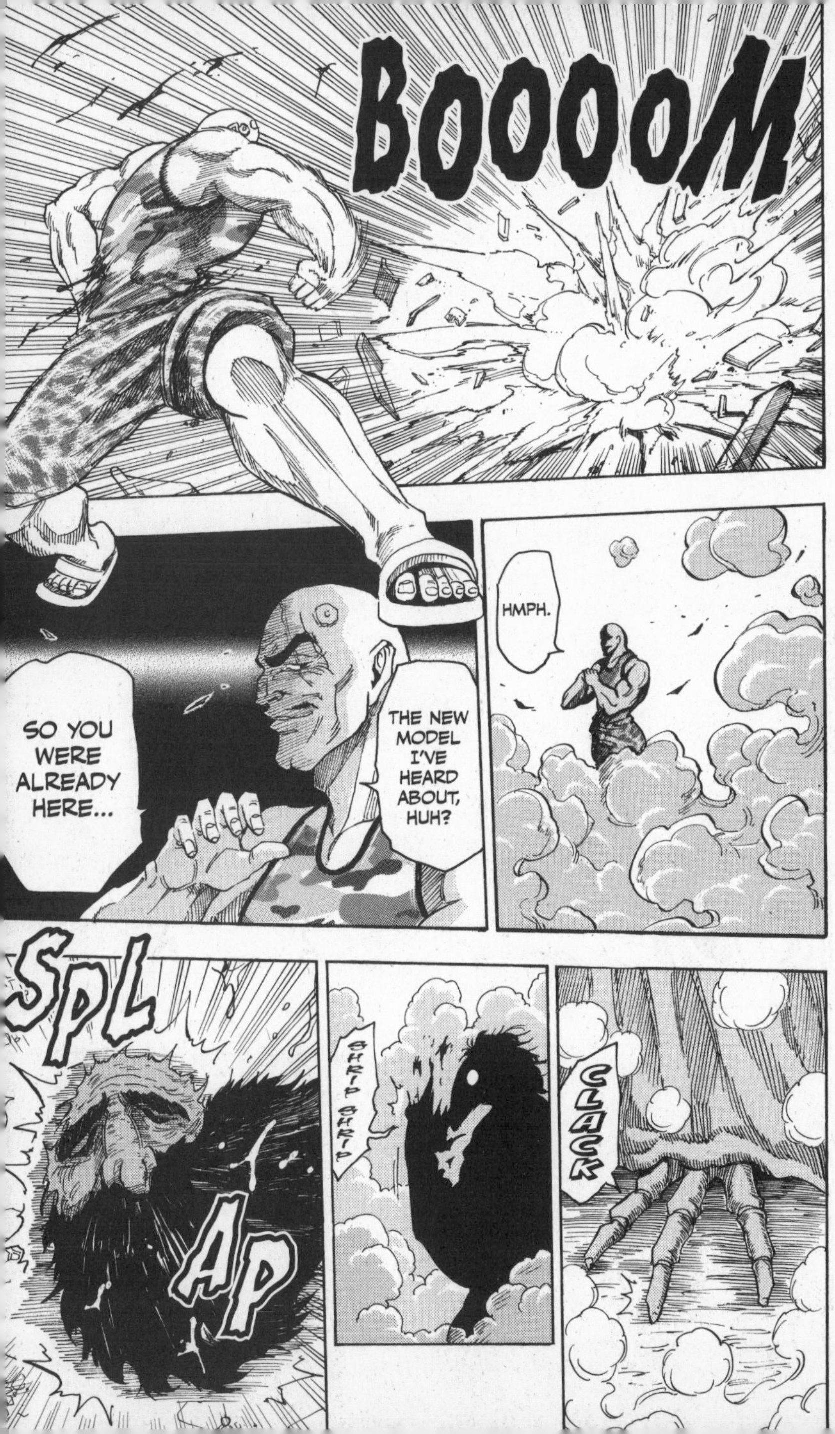
BOOOOM
HMPH.
THE NEW MODEL I'VE HEARD ABOUT, HUH?
SO YOU WERE ALREADY HERE...
CLACK
SHRIP SHRIP
SPL
AP

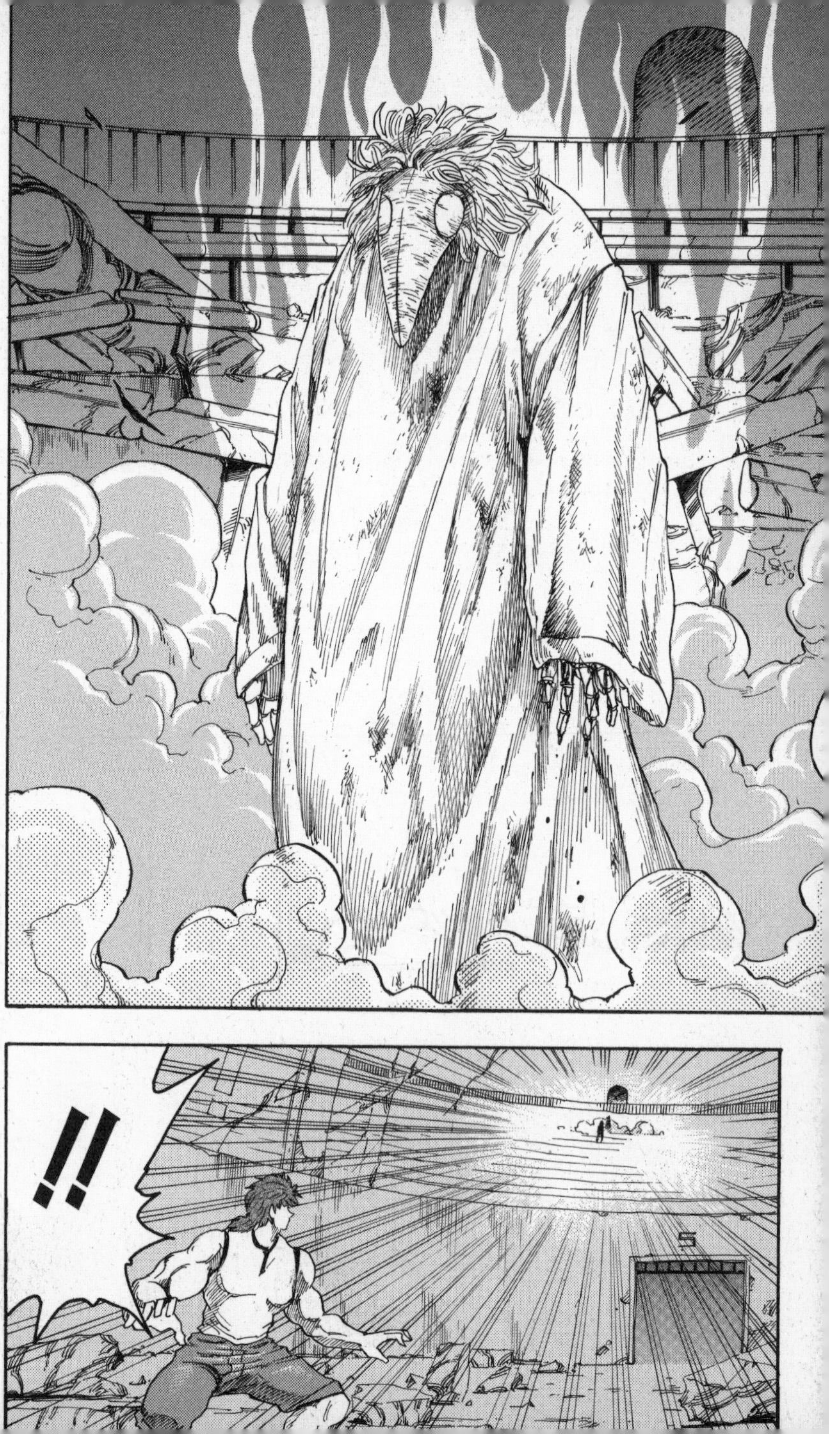
!!

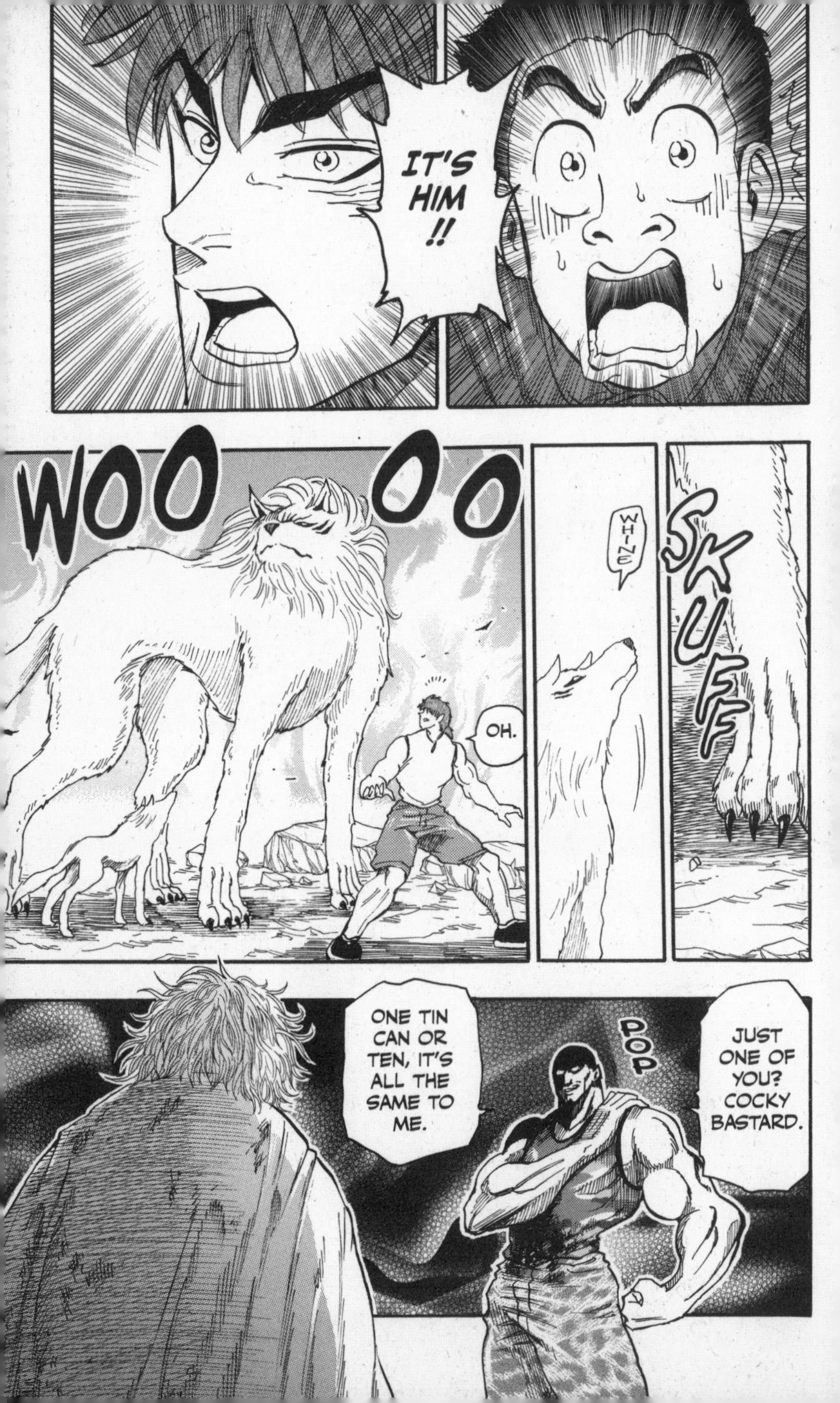
IT'S HIM!!
SKUFF
WHINE
WOOOO
OH.
JUST ONE OF YOU? COCKY BASTARD.
POP
ONE TIN CAN OR TEN, IT'S ALL THE SAME TO ME.

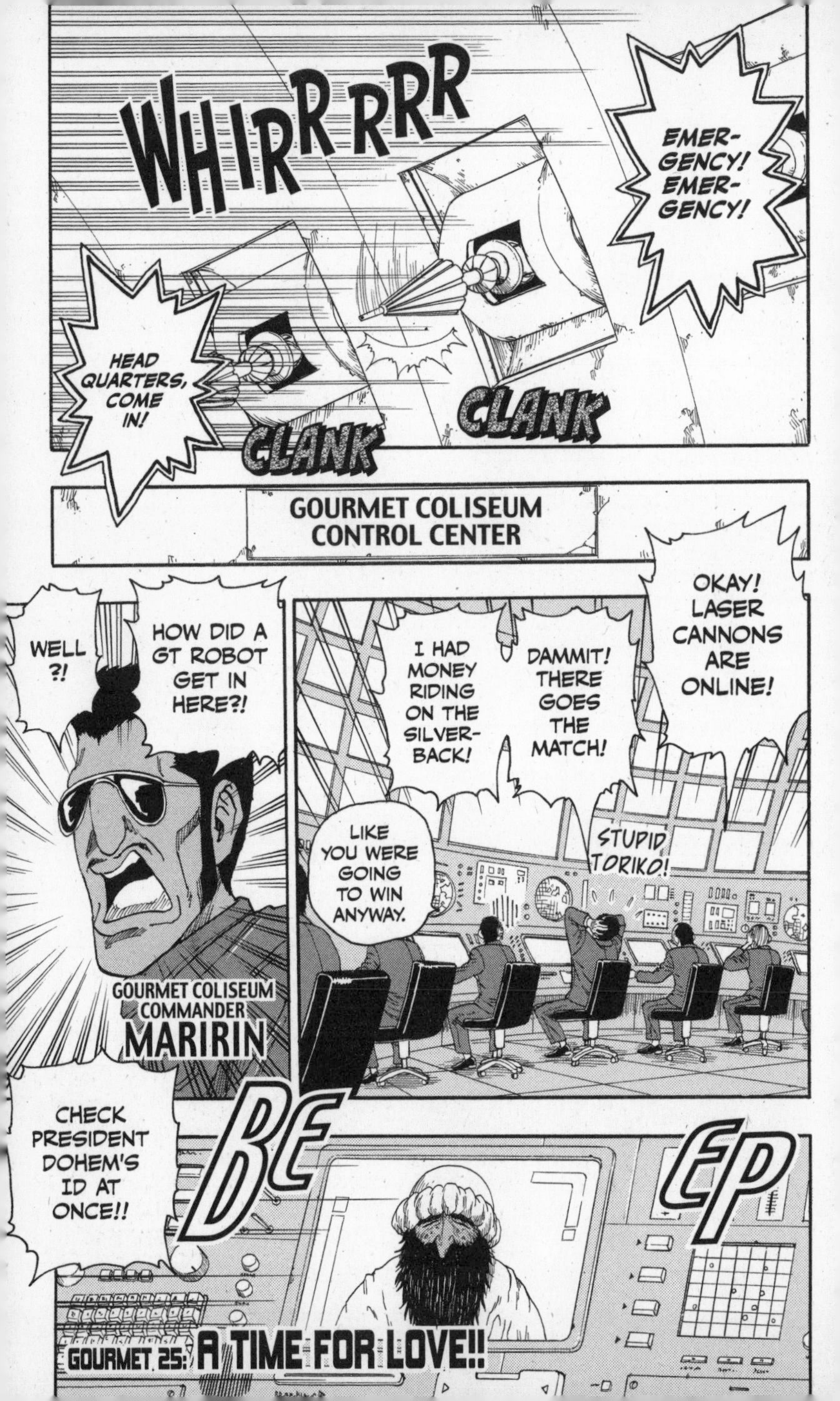
EMERGENCY! EMERGENCY!
WHIRRRRRR
CLANK
HEAD QUARTERS, COME IN!
CLANK
GOURMET COLISEUM CONTROL CENTER
OKAY! LASER CANNONS ARE ONLINE!
DAMMIT! THERE GOES THE MATCH!
I HAD MONEY RIDING ON THE SILVER-BACK!
STUPID TORIKO!
LIKE YOU WERE GOING TO WIN ANYWAY.
HOW DID A GT ROBOT GET IN HERE?!
WELL?!
GOURMET COLISEUM COMMANDER MARIRIN
BEEP
CHECK PRESIDENT DOHEM'S ID AT ONCE!!
GOURMET 25: A TIME FOR LOVE!!

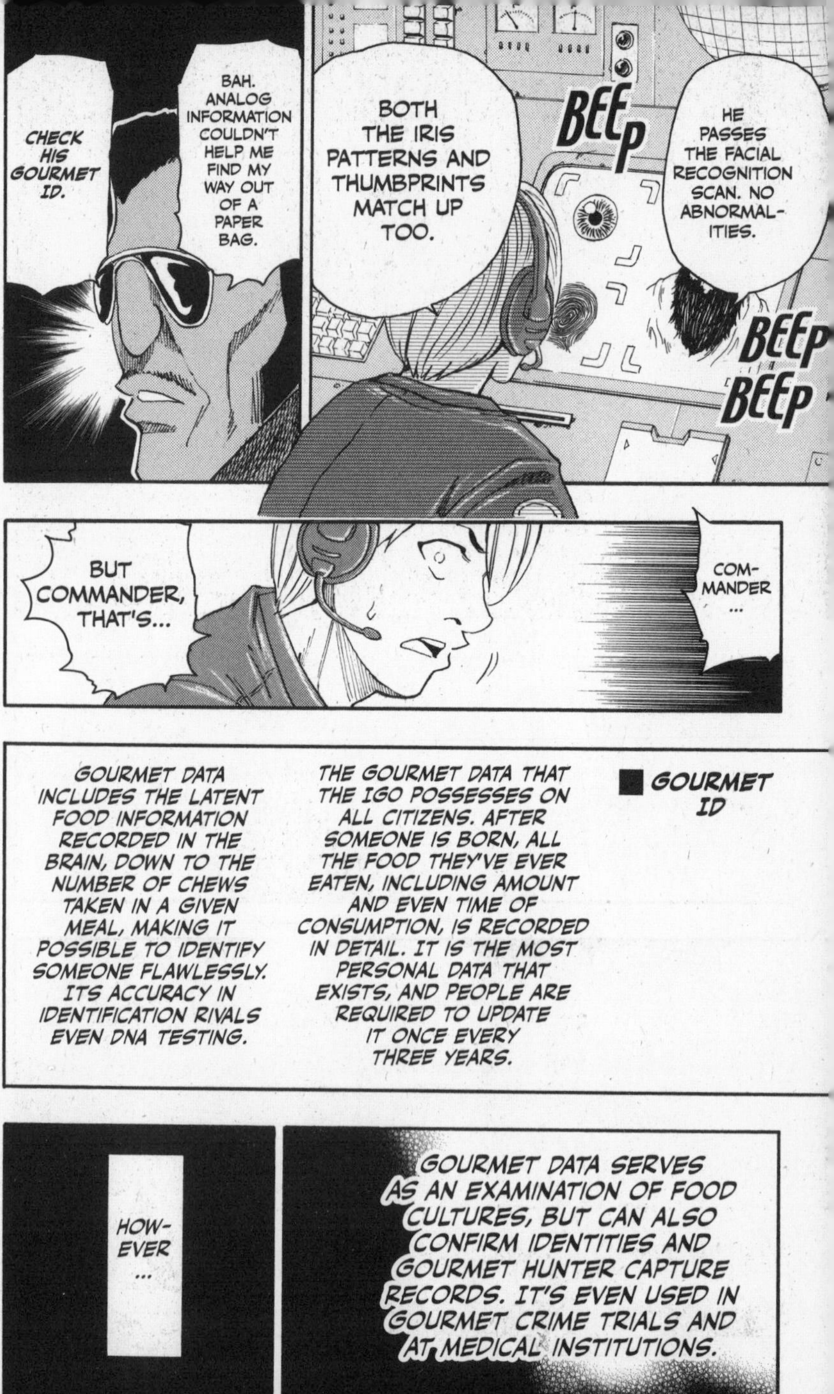
HE PASSES THE FACIAL RECOGNITION SCAN. NO ABNORMAL-ITIES.
BEEP
BOTH THE IRIS PATTERNS AND THUMBPRINTS MATCH UP TOO.
BEEP BEEP
BAH. ANALOG INFORMATION COULDN'T HELP ME FIND MY WAY OUT OF A PAPER BAG.
CHECK HIS GOURMET ID.
COM-MANDER...
BUT COMMANDER, THAT'S...
■ GOURMET ID
THE GOURMET DATA THAT THE IGO POSSESSES ON ALL CITIZENS. AFTER SOMEONE IS BORN, ALL THE FOOD THEY'VE EVER EATEN, INCLUDING AMOUNT AND EVEN TIME OF CONSUMPTION, IS RECORDED IN DETAIL. IT IS THE MOST PERSONAL DATA THAT EXISTS, AND PEOPLE ARE REQUIRED TO UPDATE IT ONCE EVERY THREE YEARS.
GOURMET DATA INCLUDES THE LATENT FOOD INFORMATION RECORDED IN THE BRAIN, DOWN TO THE NUMBER OF CHEWS TAKEN IN A GIVEN MEAL, MAKING IT POSSIBLE TO IDENTIFY SOMEONE FLAWLESSLY. ITS ACCURACY IN IDENTIFICATION RIVALS EVEN DNA TESTING.
GOURMET DATA SERVES AS AN EXAMINATION OF FOOD CULTURES, BUT CAN ALSO CONFIRM IDENTITIES AND GOURMET HUNTER CAPTURE RECORDS. IT'S EVEN USED IN GOURMET CRIME TRIALS AND AT MEDICAL INSTITUTIONS.
HOW-EVER...

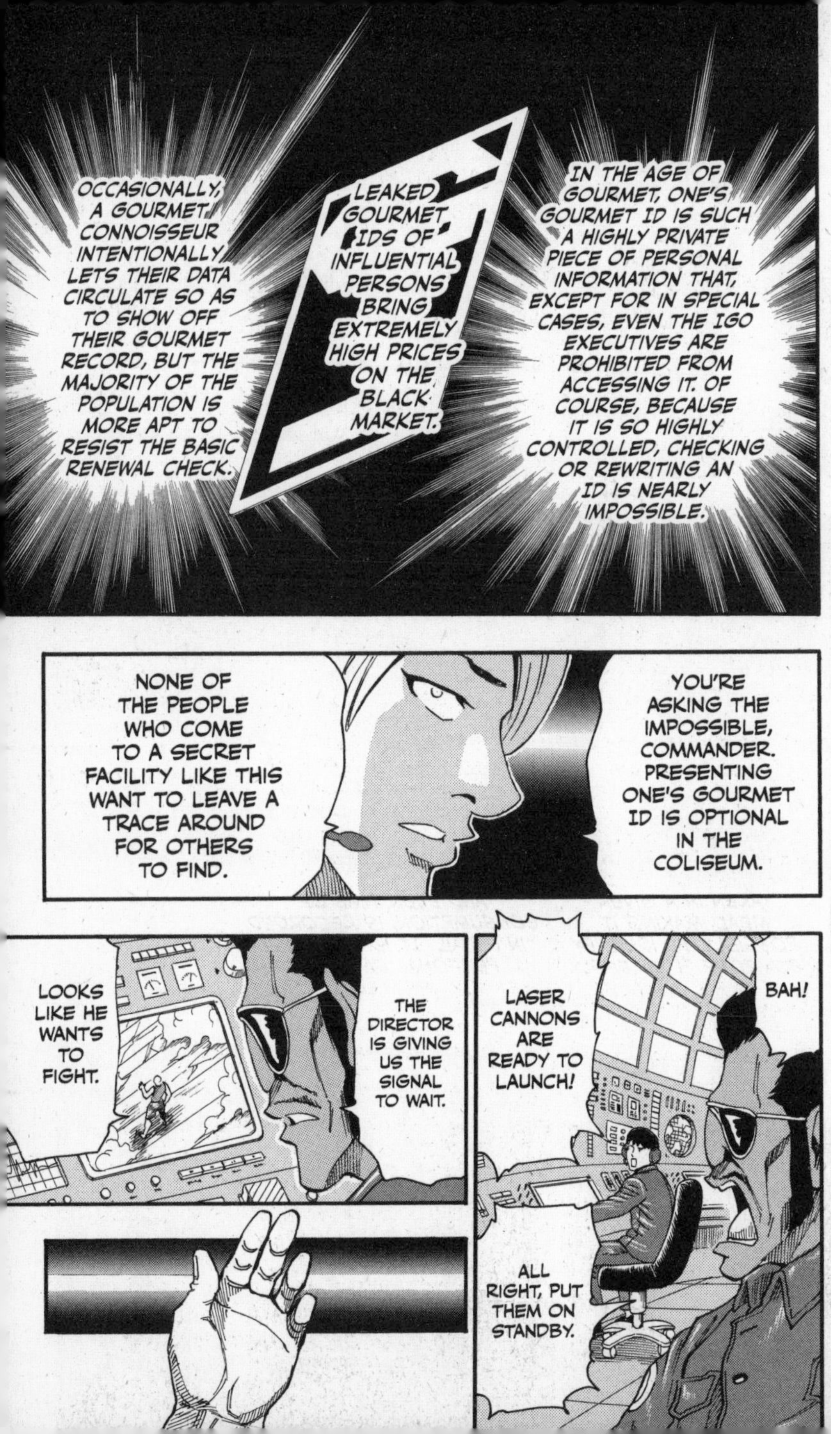
IN THE AGE OF GOURMET, ONE'S GOURMET ID IS SUCH A HIGHLY PRIVATE PIECE OF PERSONAL INFORMATION THAT, EXCEPT FOR IN SPECIAL CASES, EVEN THE IGO EXECUTIVES ARE PROHIBITED FROM ACCESSING IT. OF COURSE, BECAUSE IT IS SO HIGHLY CONTROLLED, CHECKING OR REWRITING AN ID IS NEARLY IMPOSSIBLE.
LEAKED GOURMET IDS OF INFLUENTIAL PERSONS BRING EXTREMELY HIGH PRICES ON THE BLACK MARKET.
OCCASIONALLY, A GOURMET CONNOISSEUR INTENTIONALLY LETS THEIR DATA CIRCULATE SO AS TO SHOW OFF THEIR GOURMET RECORD, BUT THE MAJORITY OF THE POPULATION IS MORE APT TO RESIST THE BASIC RENEWAL CHECK.
YOU'RE ASKING THE IMPOSSIBLE, COMMANDER. PRESENTING ONE'S GOURMET ID IS OPTIONAL IN THE COLISEUM.
NONE OF THE PEOPLE WHO COME TO A SECRET FACILITY LIKE THIS WANT TO LEAVE A TRACE AROUND FOR OTHERS TO FIND.
BAH!
LASER CANNONS ARE READY TO LAUNCH!
ALL RIGHT, PUT THEM ON STANDBY.
THE DIRECTOR IS GIVING US THE SIGNAL TO WAIT.
LOOKS LIKE HE WANTS TO FIGHT.

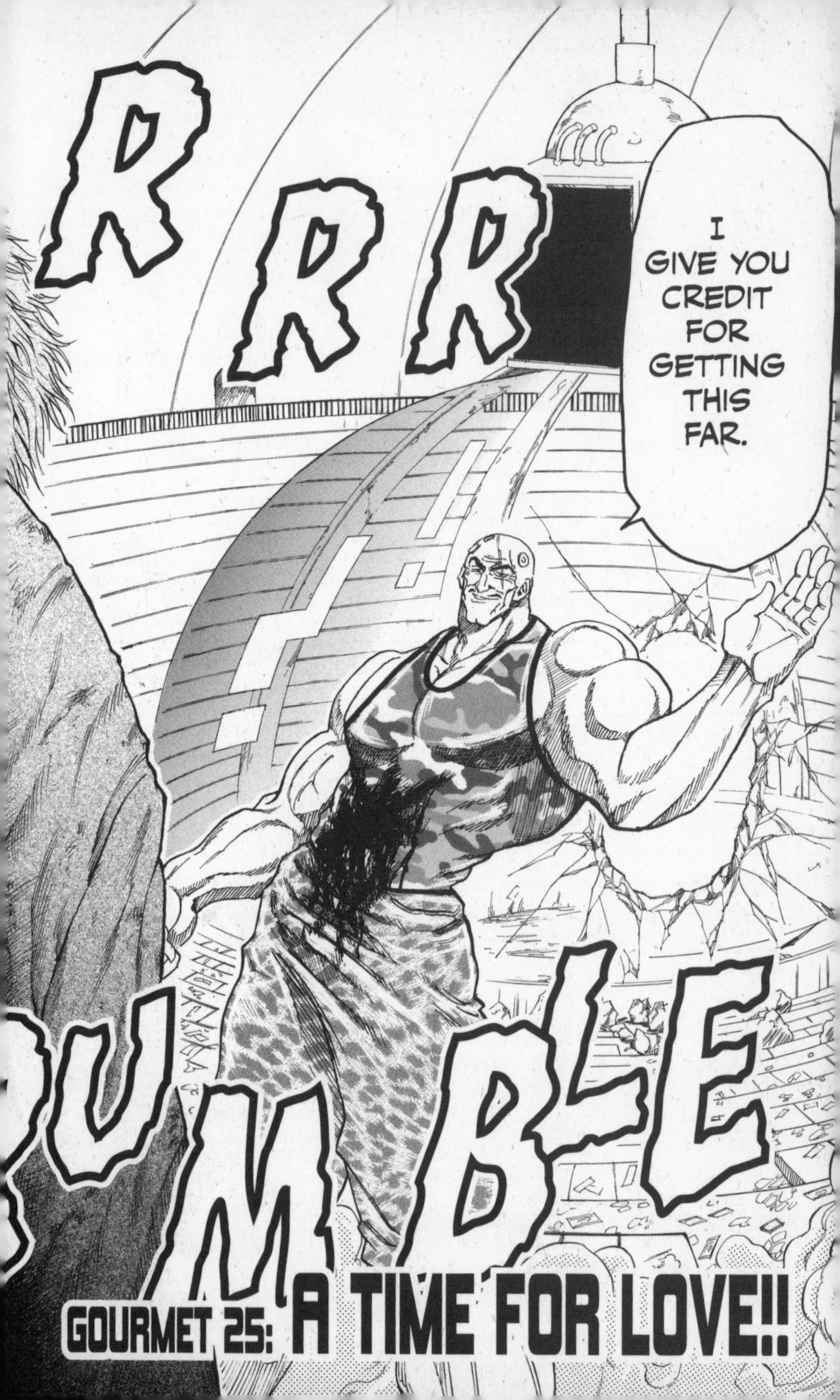
RRRUMBLE
I GIVE YOU CREDIT FOR GETTING THIS FAR.
GOURMET 25: A TIME FOR LOVE!!

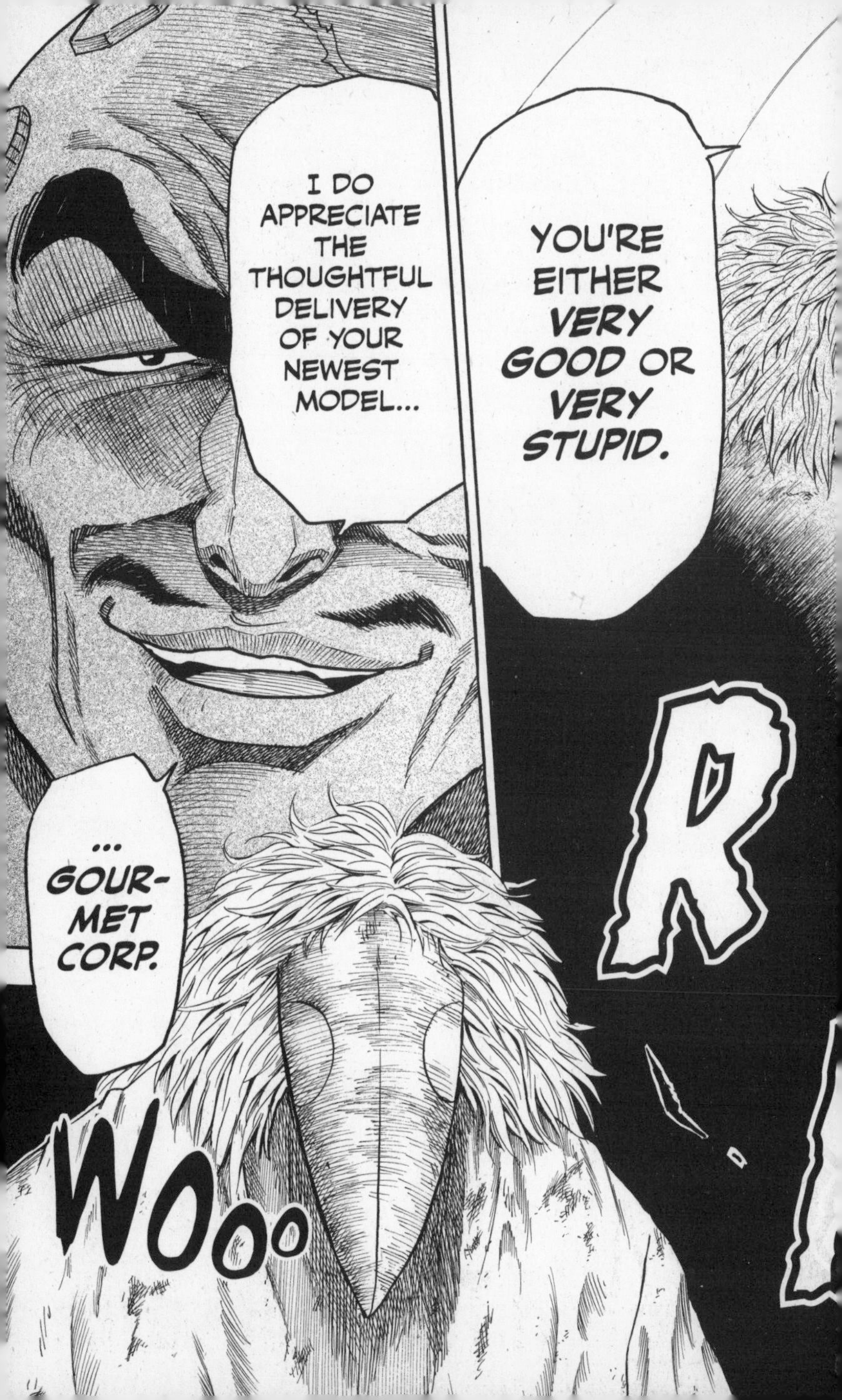
YOU'RE EITHER VERY GOOD OR VERY STUPID.
R
I DO APPRECIATE THE THOUGHTFUL DELIVERY OF YOUR NEWEST MODEL...
...GOUR-MET CORP.
WOOO

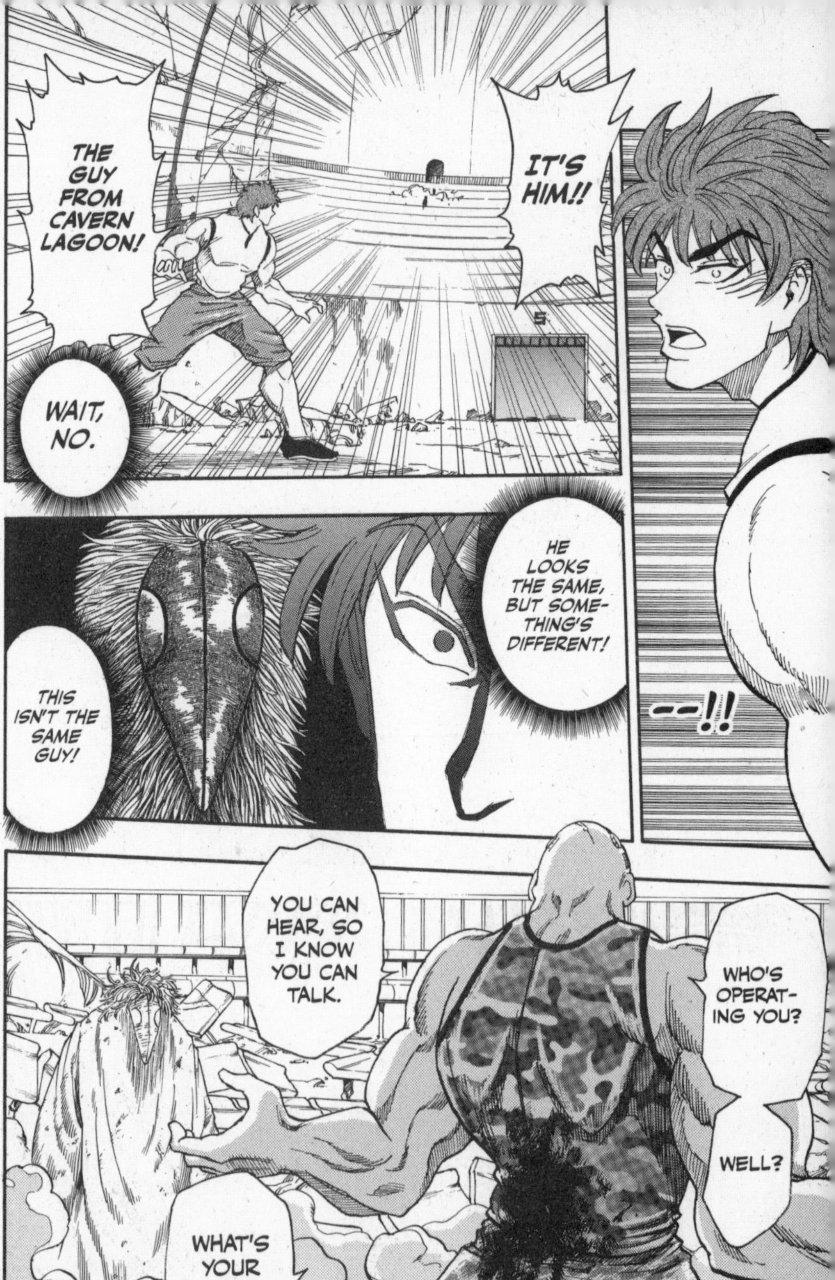

IT'S HIM!!
--!!
THE GUY FROM CAVERN LAGOON!
WAIT, NO.
HE LOOKS THE SAME, BUT SOME-THING'S DIFFERENT!
THIS ISN'T THE SAME GUY!
WHO'S OPERAT-ING YOU?
YOU CAN HEAR, SO I KNOW YOU CAN TALK.
WELL?
WHAT'S YOUR TARGET?

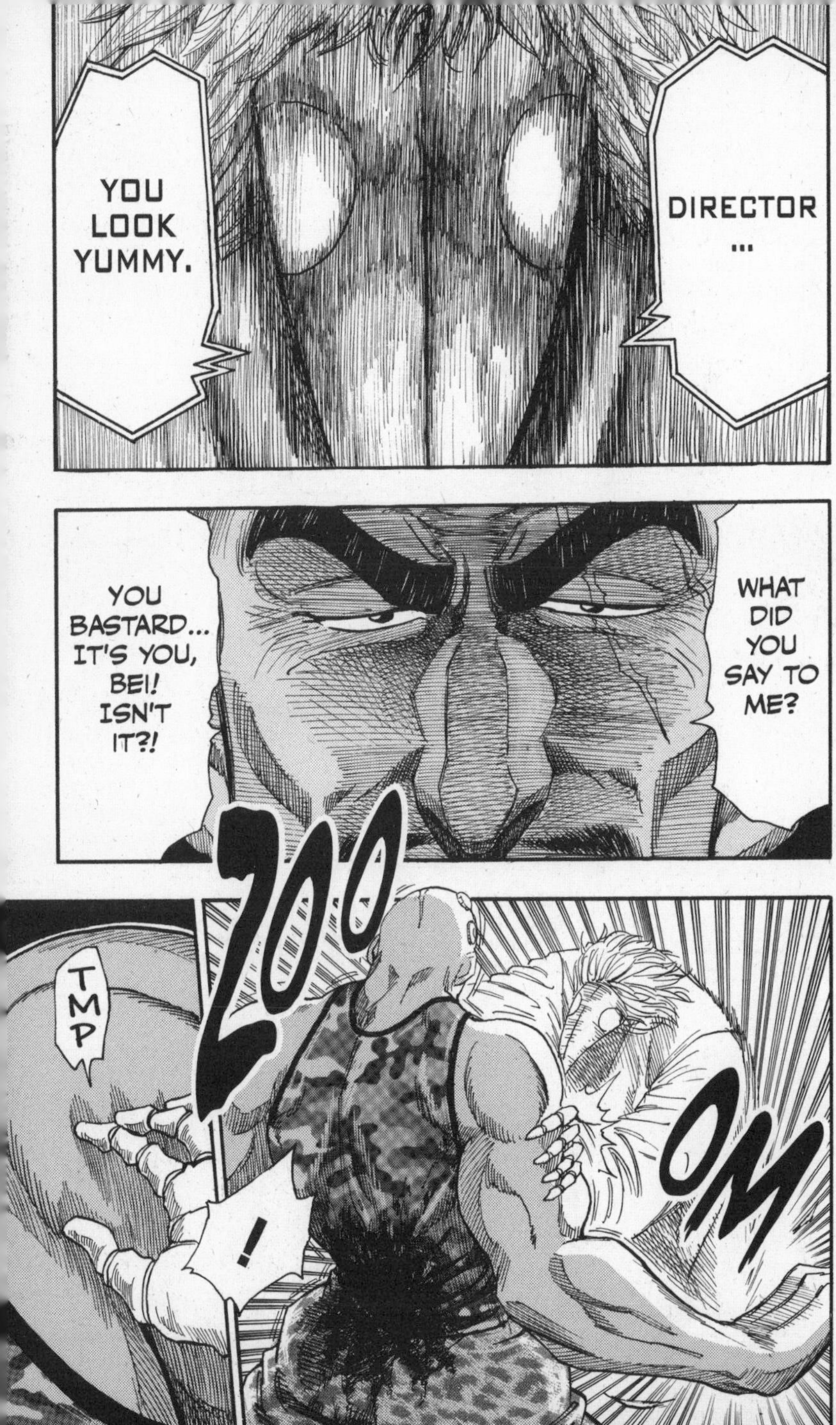
DIRECTOR ...
YOU LOOK YUMMY.
WHAT DID YOU SAY TO ME?
YOU BASTARD... IT'S YOU, BEI! ISN'T IT?!
ZOOOM
TMP
!

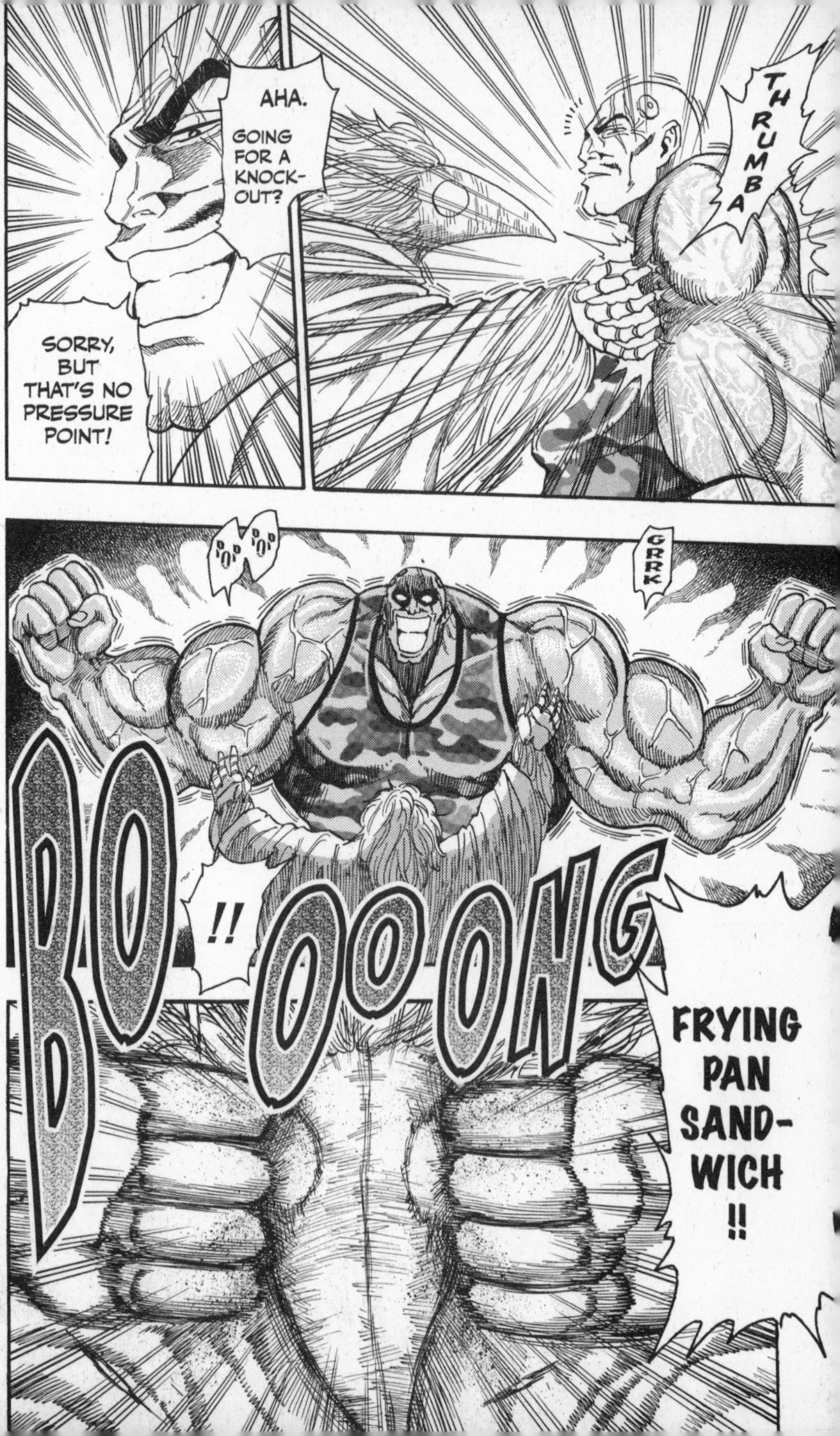
THRUMBA
AHA.
GOING FOR A KNOCK-OUT?
SORRY, BUT THAT'S NO PRESSURE POINT!
GRRK
POP POP
BOOOONG
!!
FRYING PAN SANDWICH !!

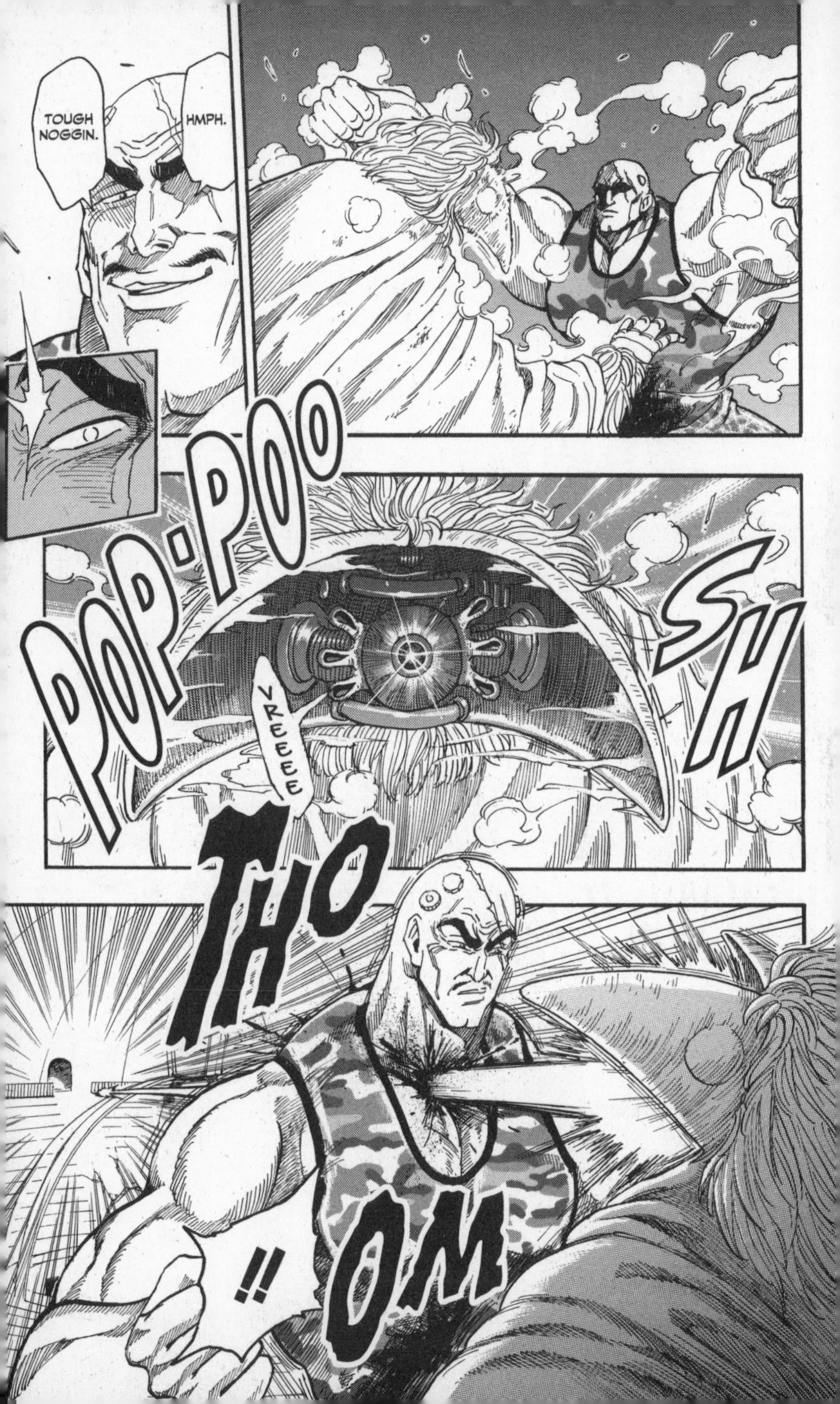
HMPH.
TOUGH NOGGIN.
SH
POP-POO
VREEEEE
THOOM
!!

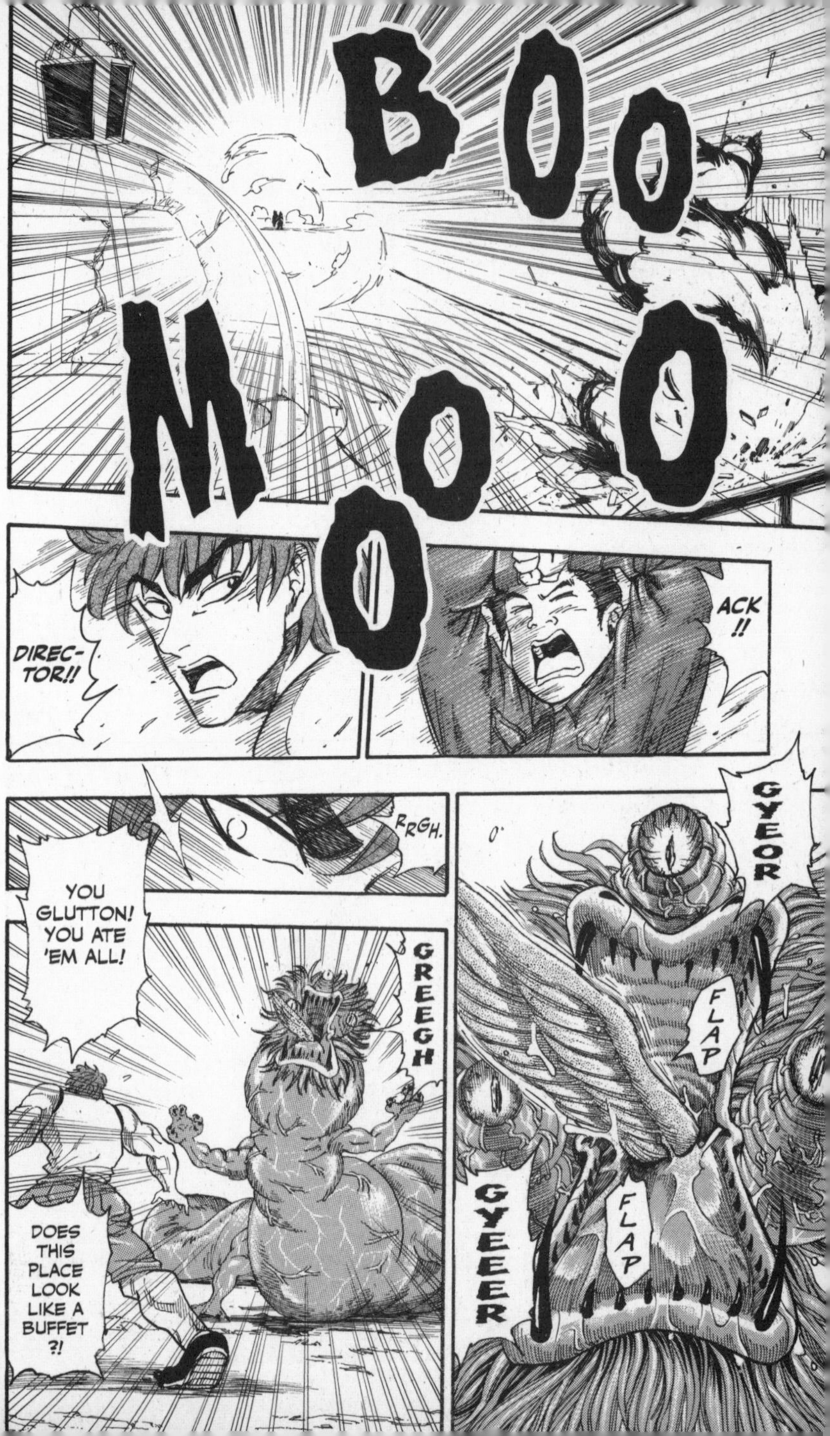
BOOOO
MOOOOO
ACK!!
DIRECTOR!!
GYEOR
FLAP
FLAP
GYEEER
RRGH.
YOU GLUTTON! YOU ATE 'EM ALL!
GREEGH
DOES THIS PLACE LOOK LIKE A BUFFET?!

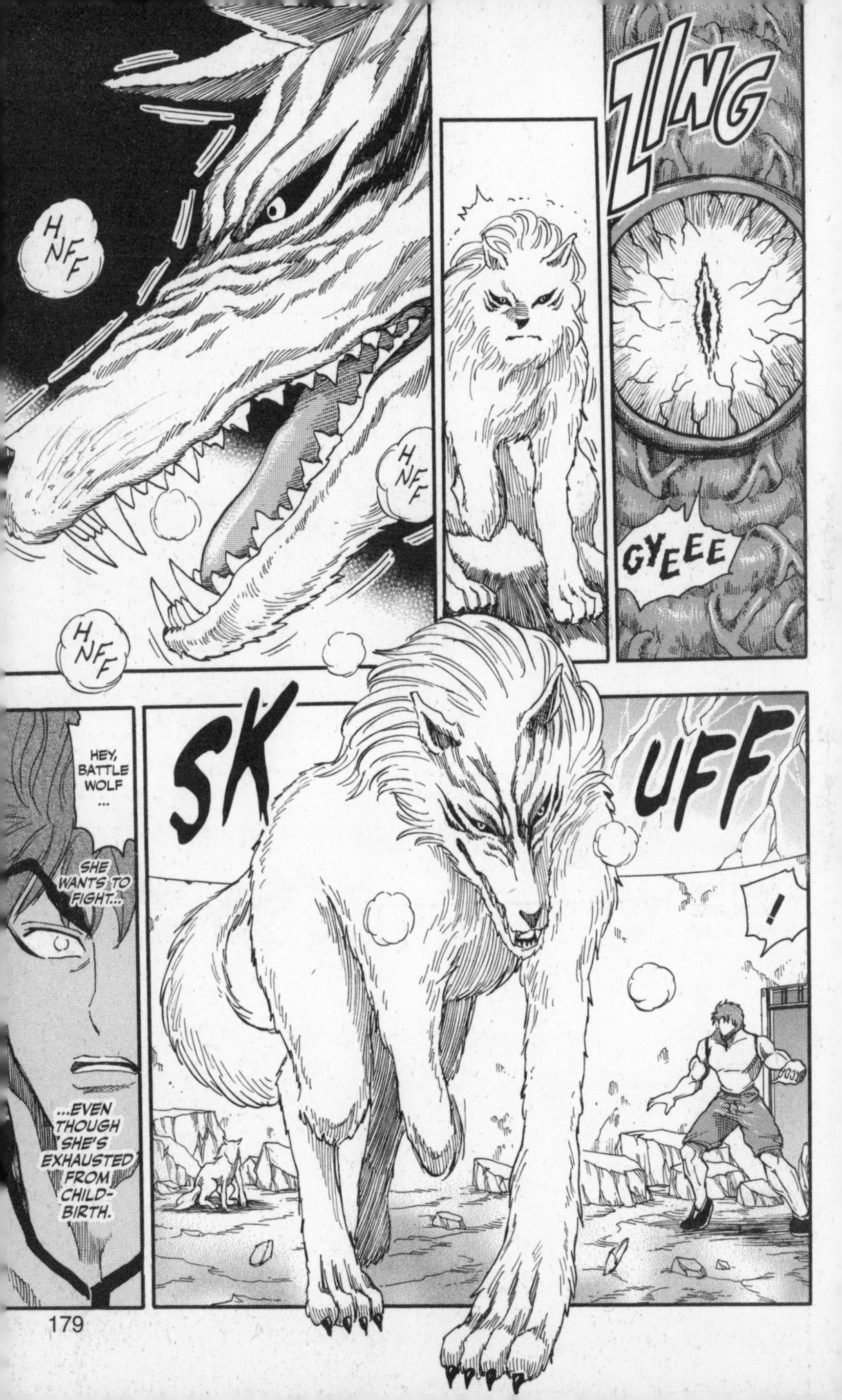
ZING
GYEEE
HNFF
HNFF
HNFF
SK UFF
!
HEY, BATTLE WOLF...
SHE WANTS TO FIGHT...
...EVEN THOUGH SHE'S EXHAUSTED FROM CHILD-BIRTH.

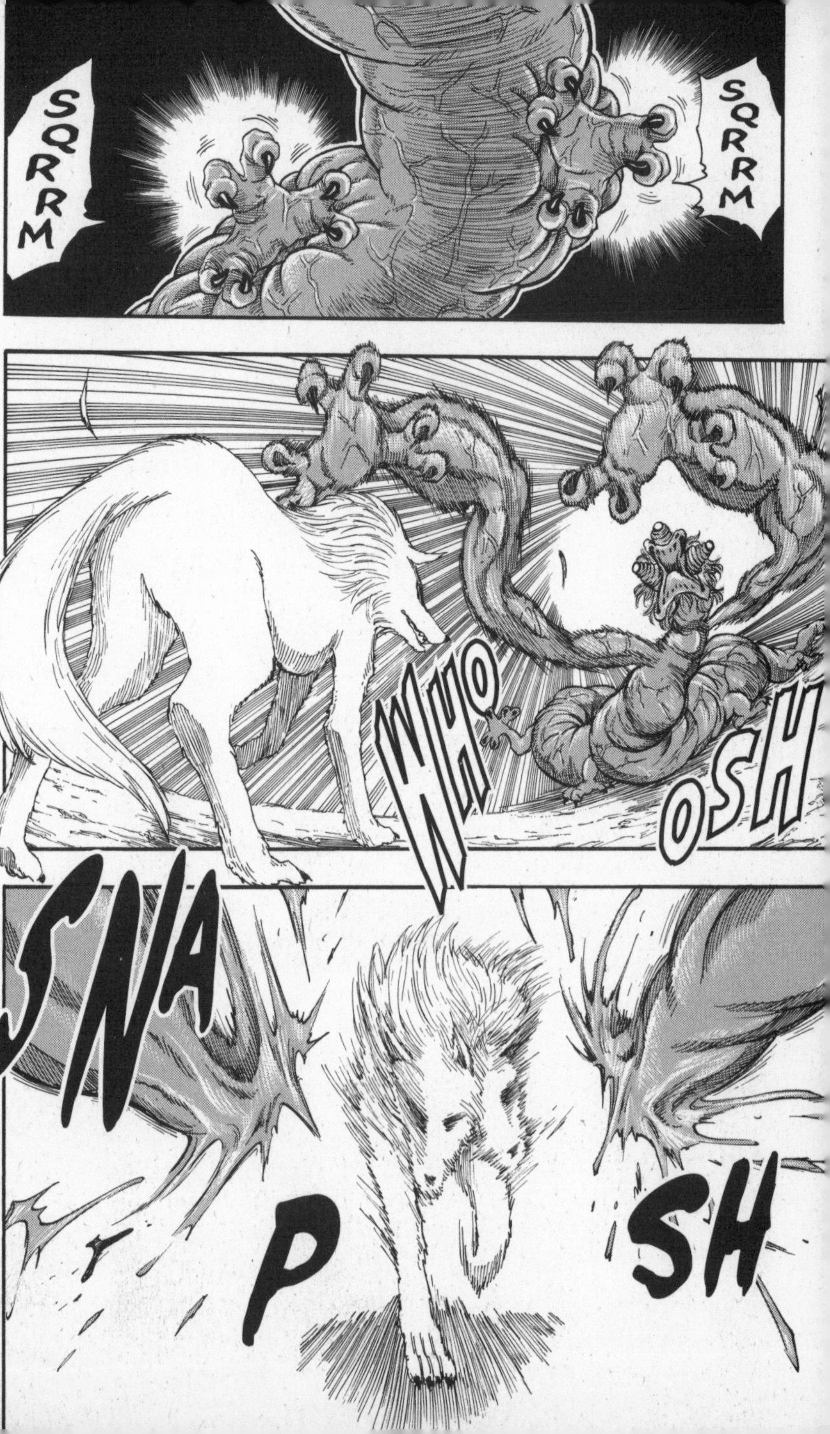
SQRRM
SQRRM
WHO
OSH
SNA
P
SH

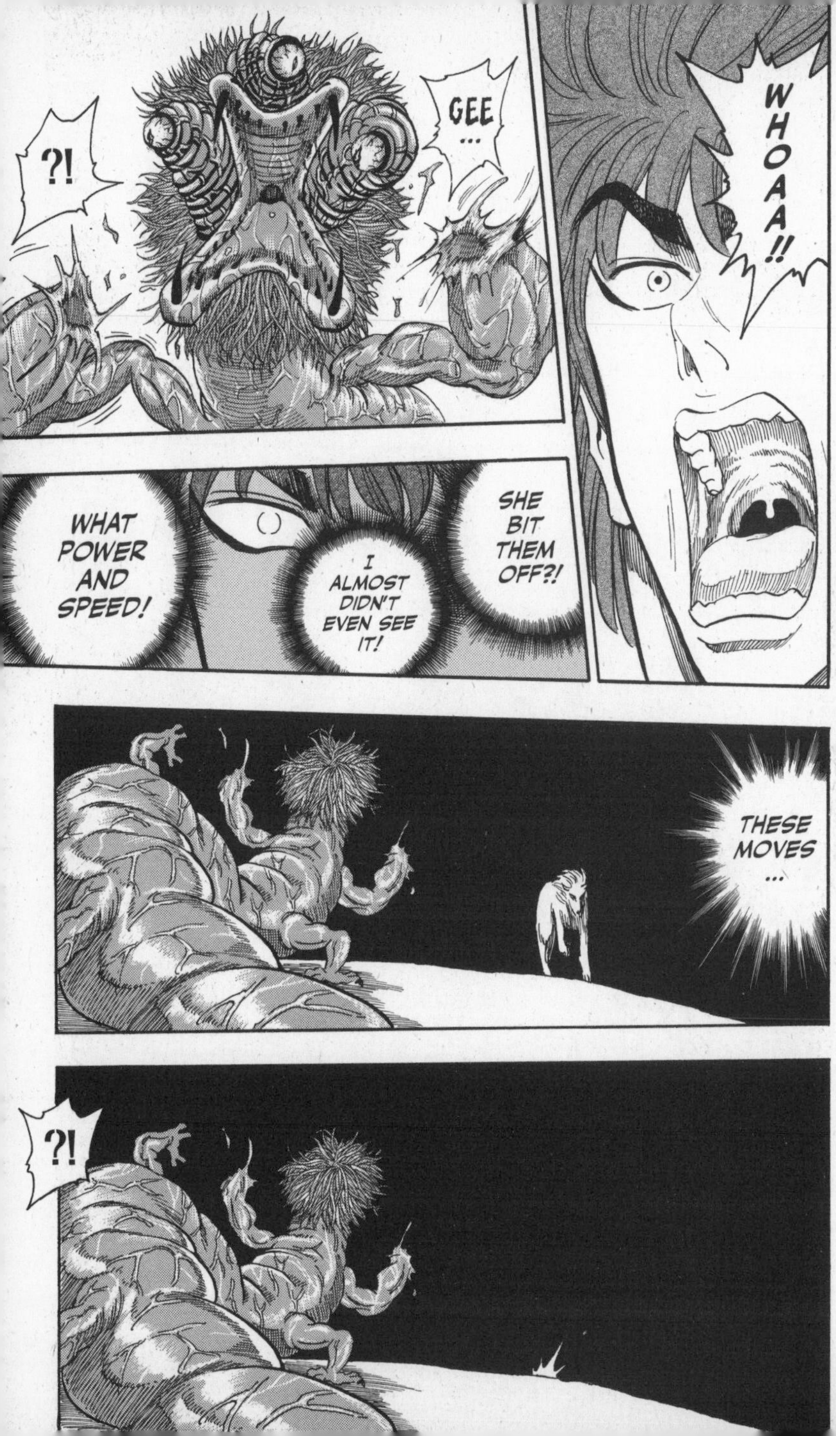
WHOAAA!!
GEE ...
?!
SHE BIT THEM OFF?!
I ALMOST DIDN'T EVEN SEE IT!
WHAT POWER AND SPEED!
THESE MOVES ...
?!

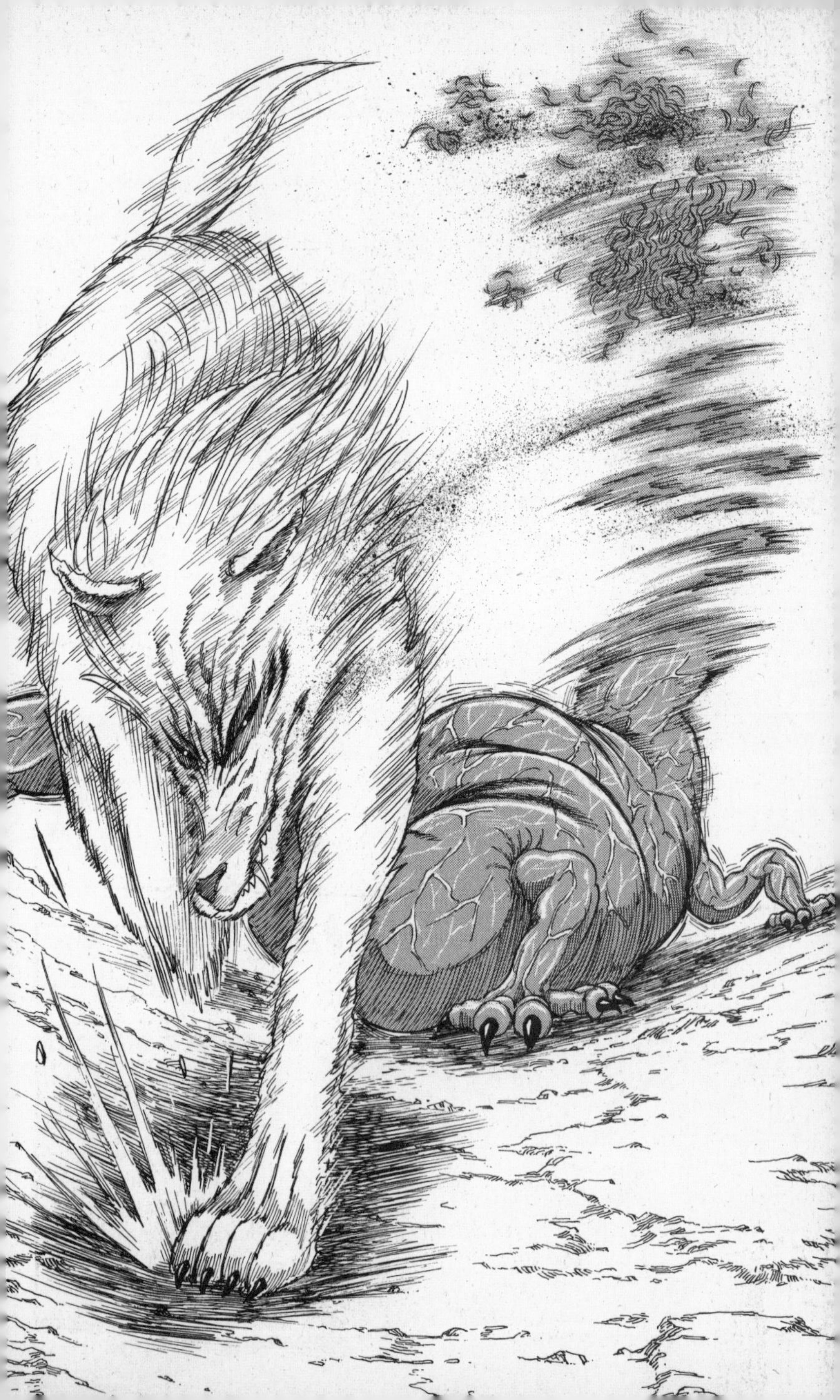

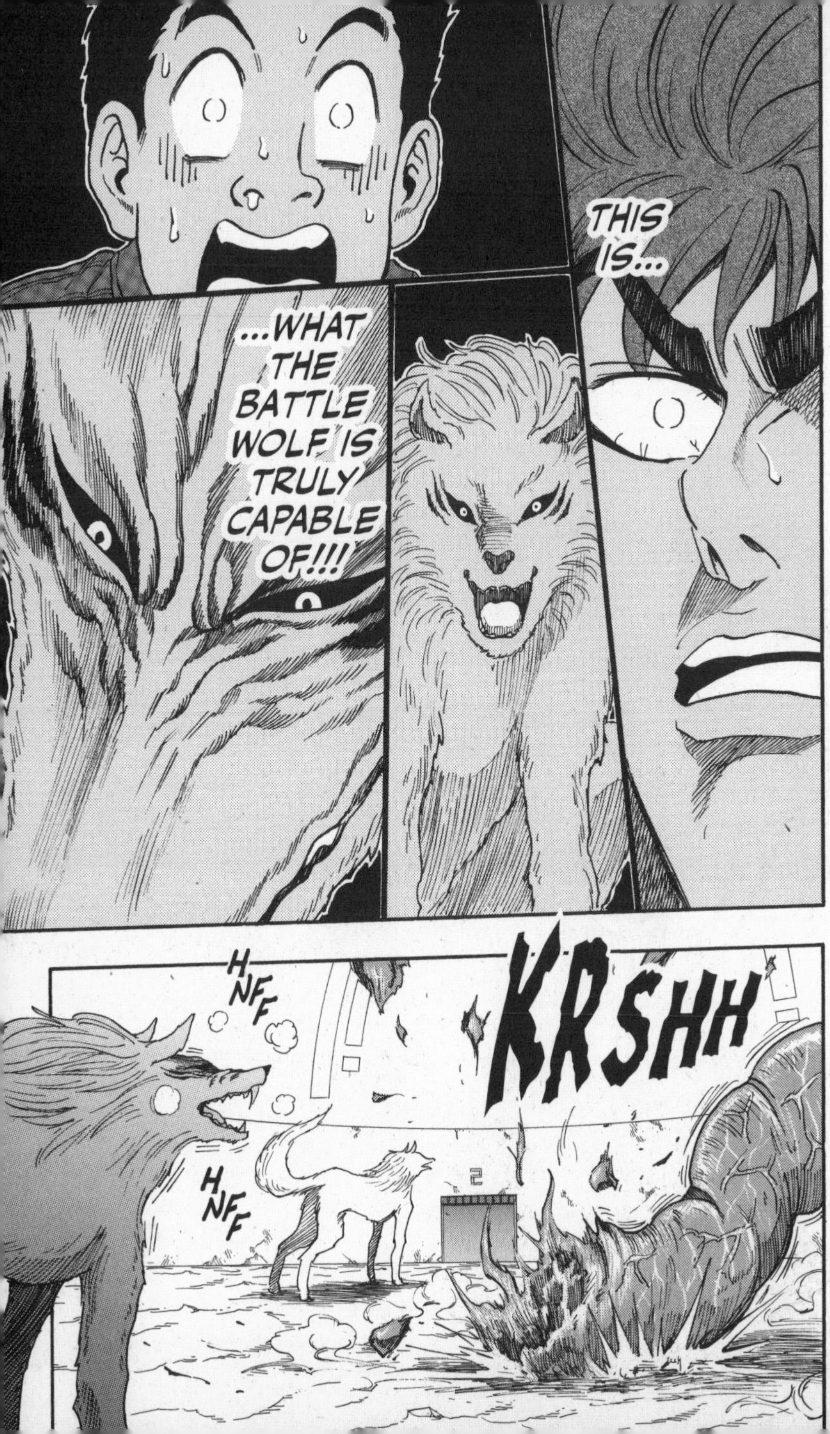
THIS IS...
...WHAT THE BATTLE WOLF IS TRULY CAPABLE OF!!!
KRSHH
HNFF
HNFF

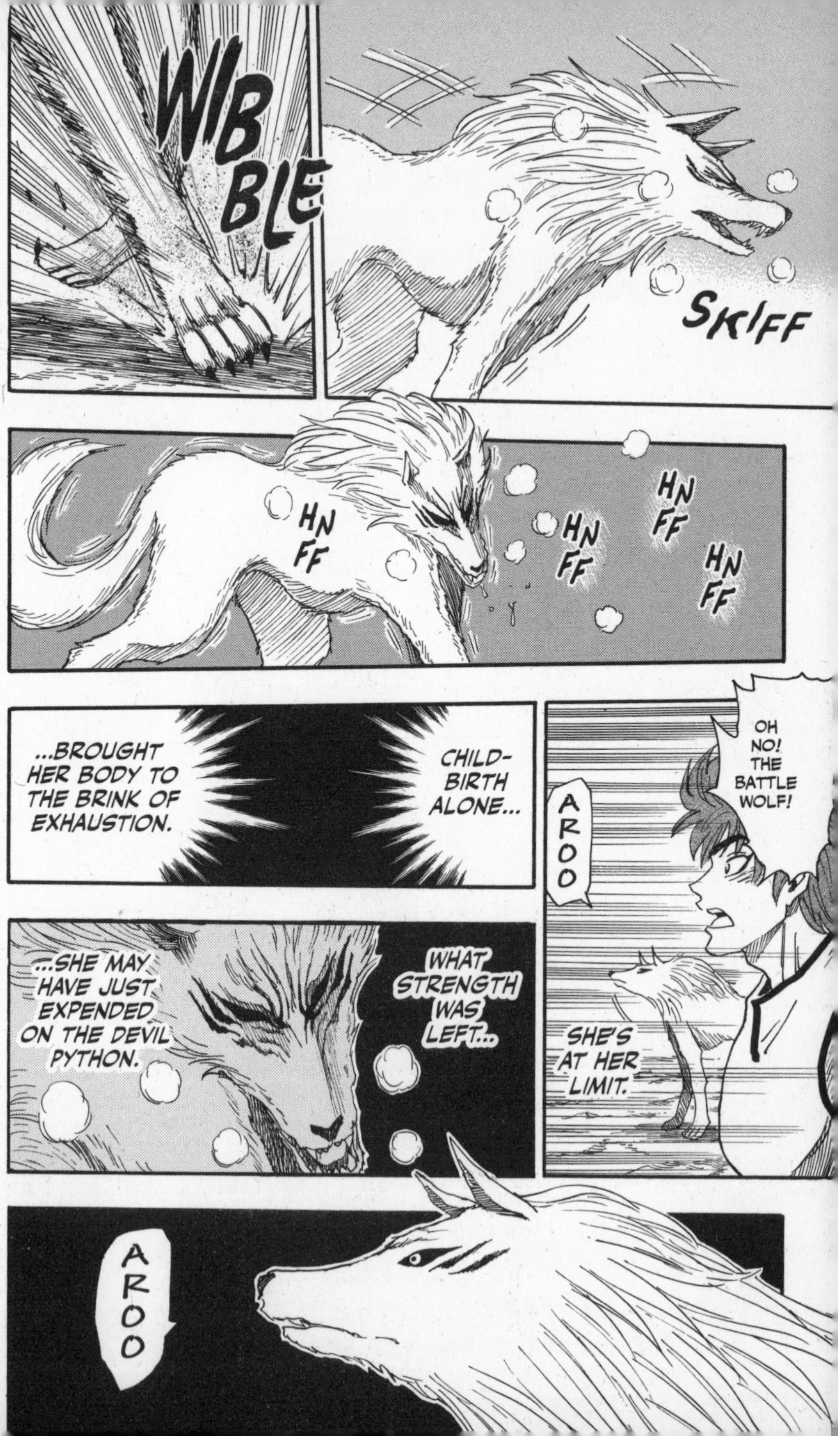
SKIFF
WIBBLE
HNFF
HNFF
HNFF
HNFF
OH NO! THE BATTLE WOLF!
AROO
SHE'S AT HER LIMIT.
CHILD-BIRTH ALONE...
...BROUGHT HER BODY TO THE BRINK OF EXHAUSTION.
WHAT STRENGTH WAS LEFT...
...SHE MAY HAVE JUST EXPENDED ON THE DEVIL PYTHON.
AROO

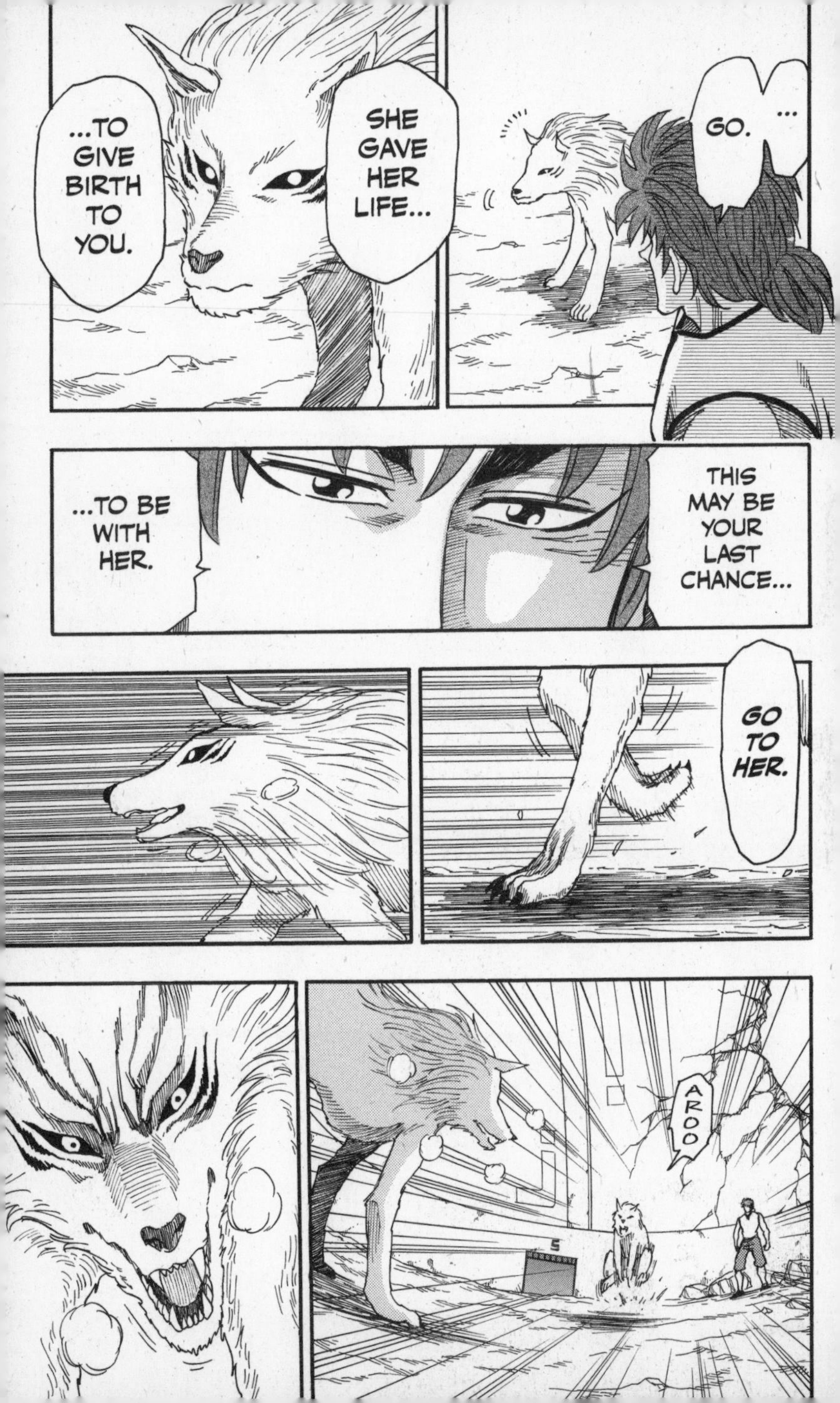
...
GO.
SHE GAVE HER LIFE...
...TO GIVE BIRTH TO YOU.
THIS MAY BE YOUR LAST CHANCE...
...TO BE WITH HER.
GO TO HER.
AROO

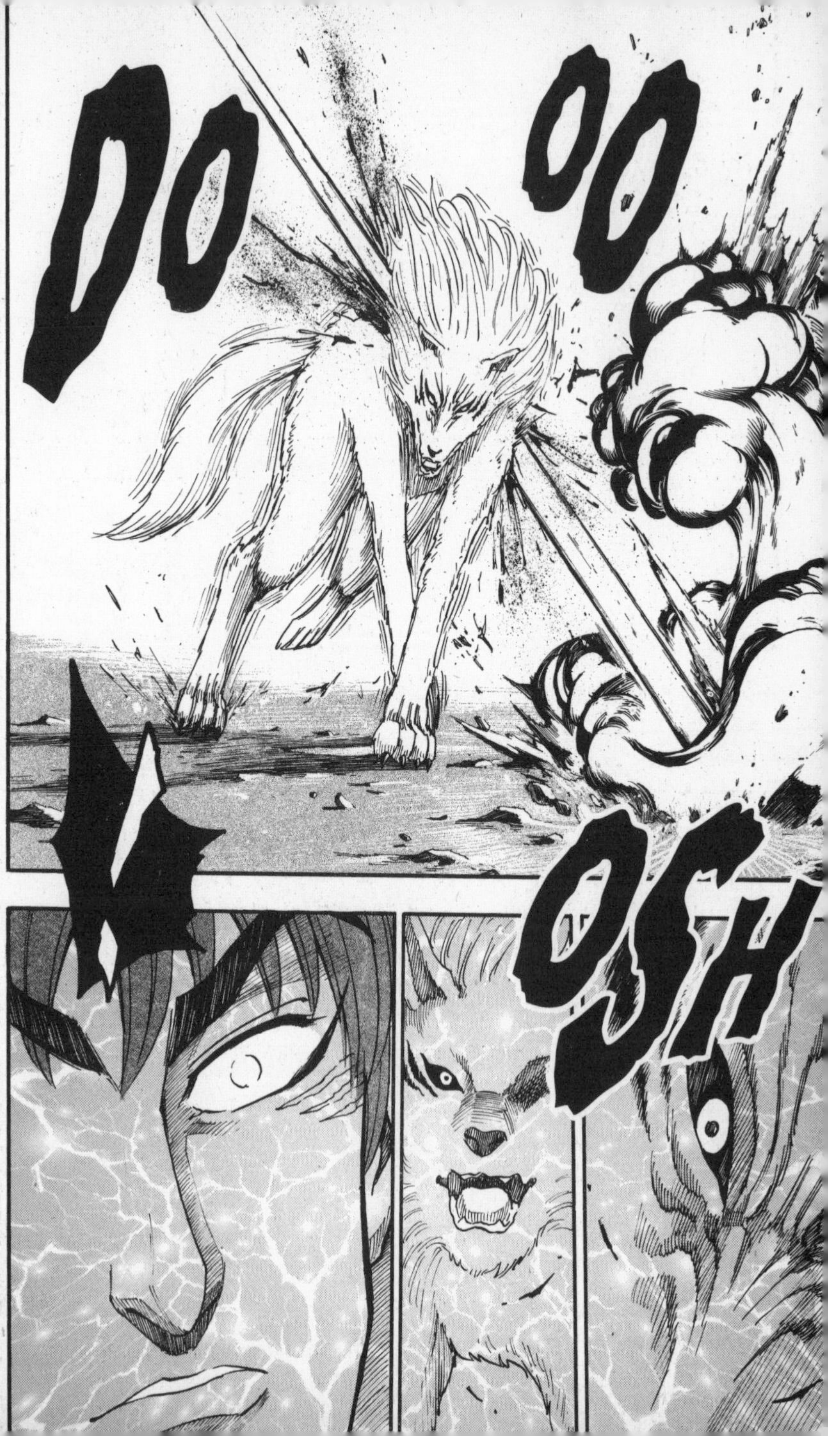
DOOOOSH

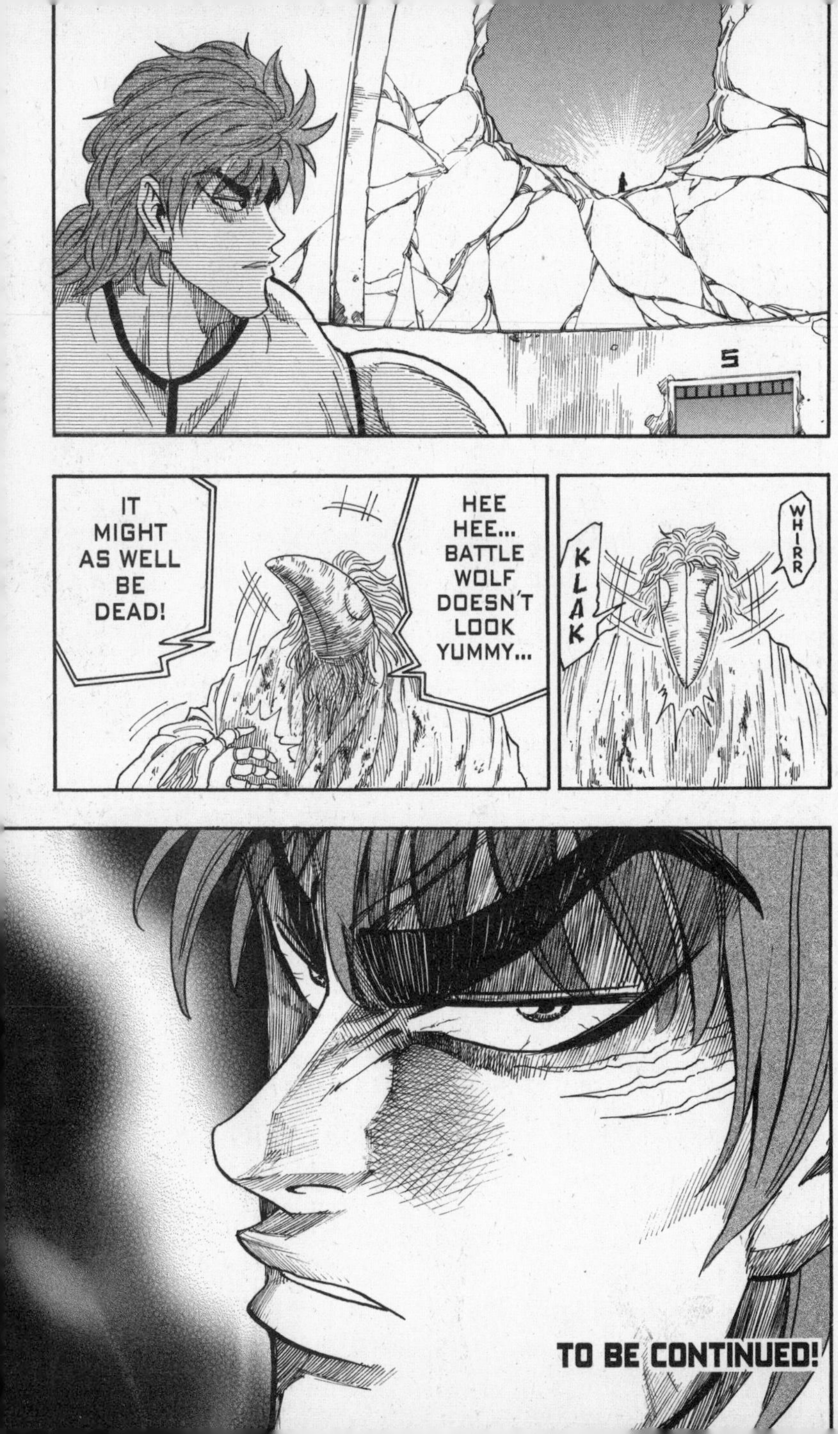
5
WHIRR
KLAK
HEE HEE... BATTLE WOLF DOESN'T LOOK YUMMY...
IT MIGHT AS WELL BE DEAD!
TO BE CONTINUED!

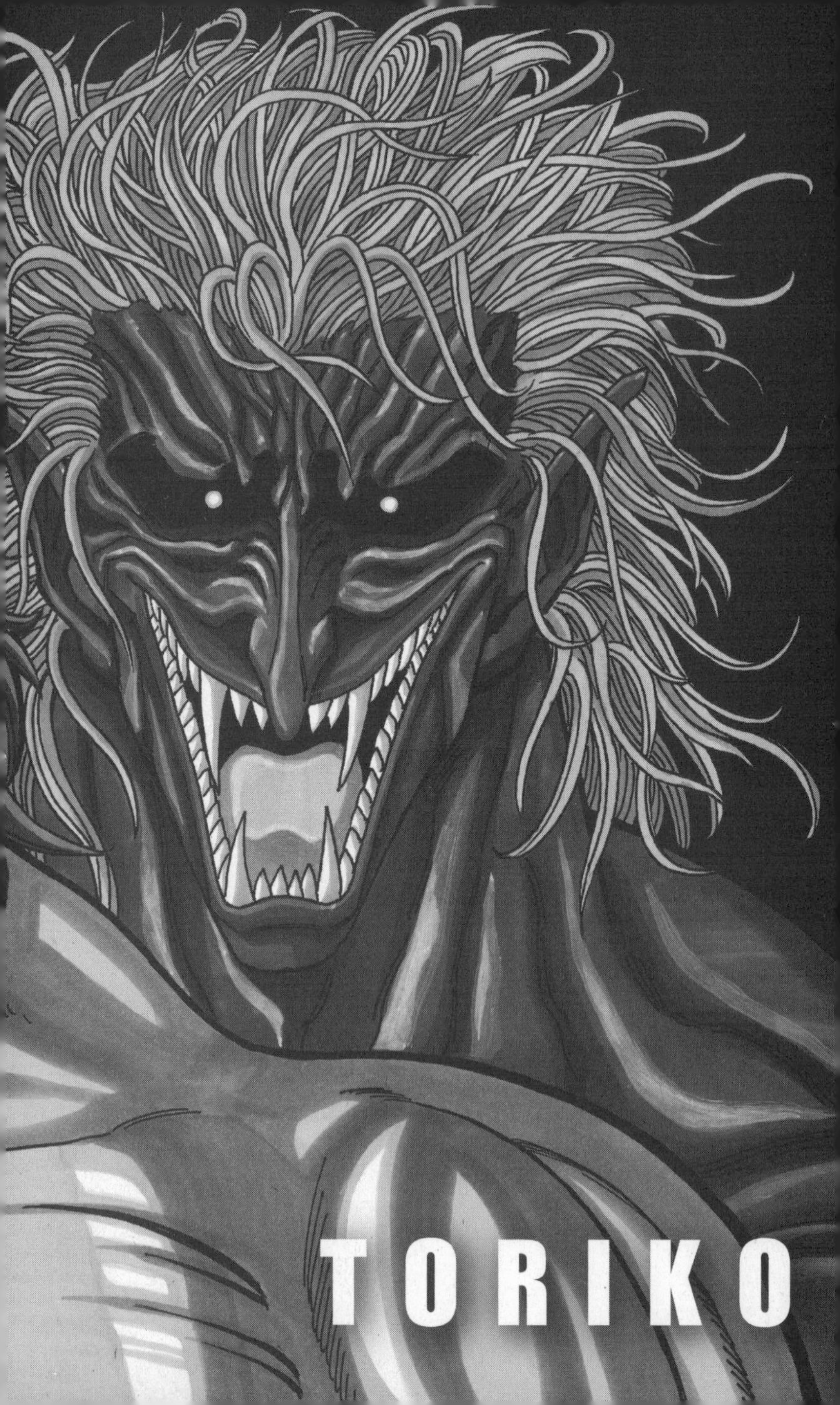
TORIKO

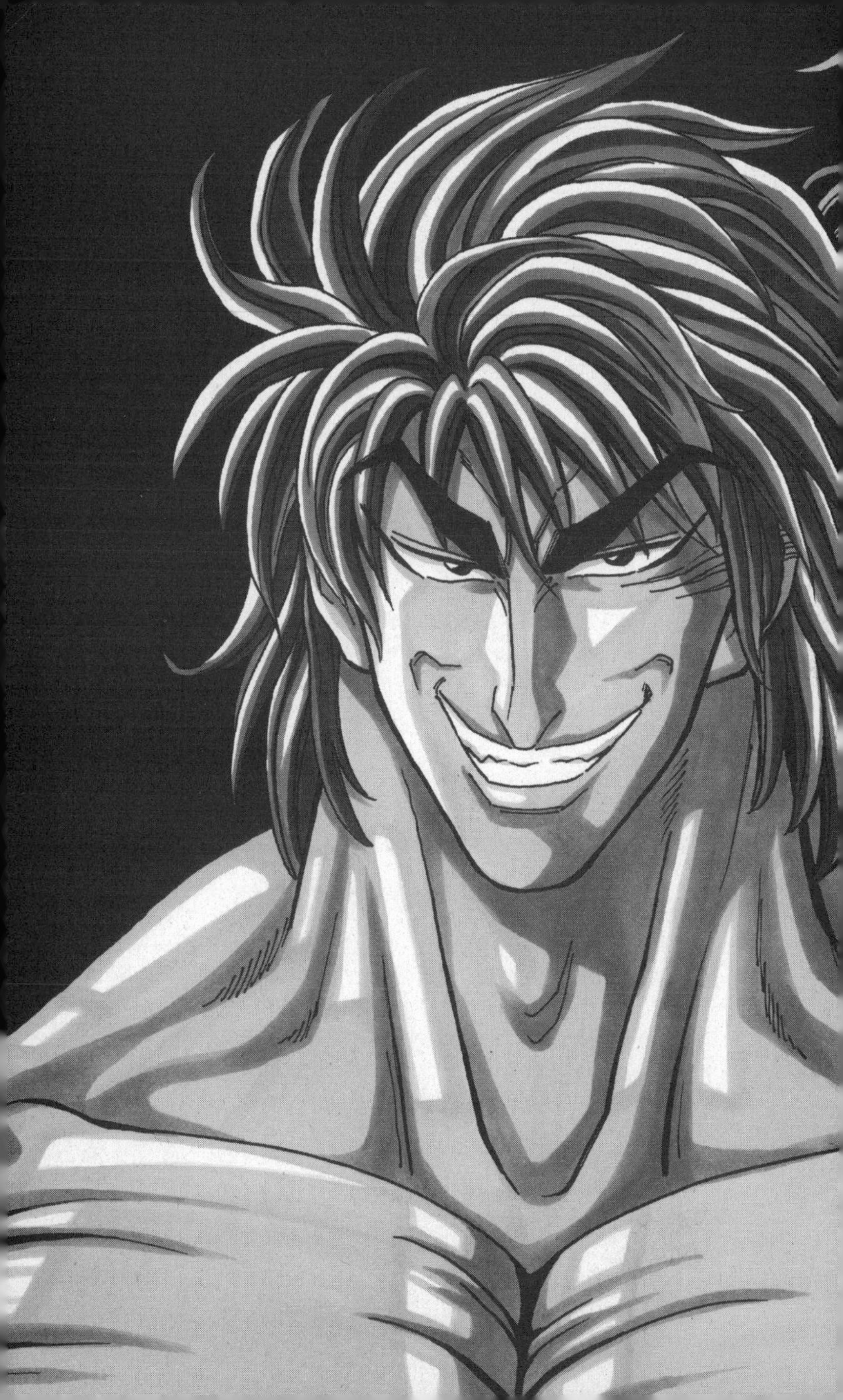

COMING NEXT VOLUME

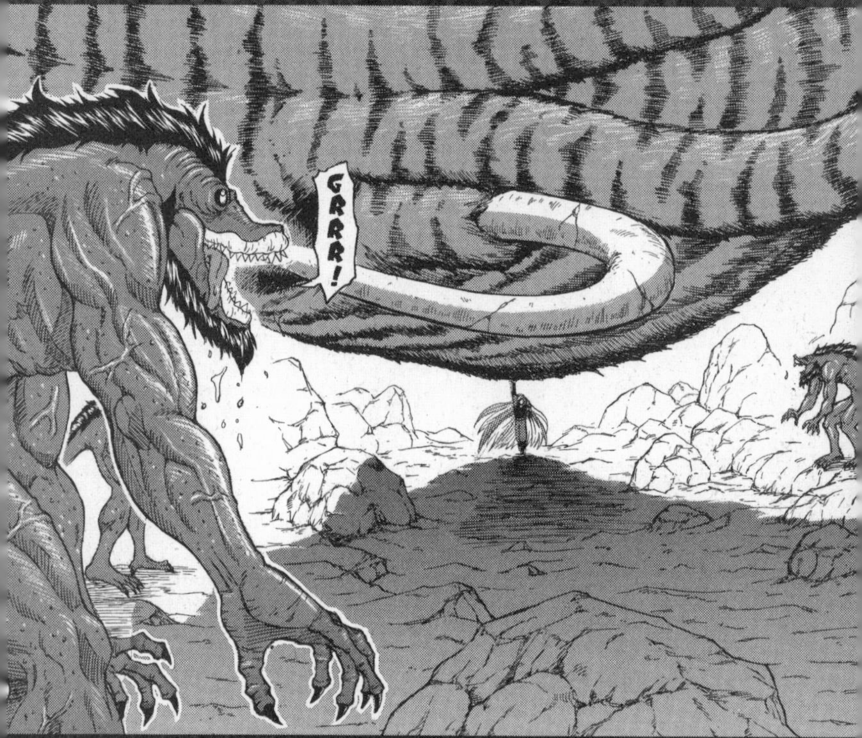
GRRR!

TORIKO'S RAGE

Toriko finally gets his chance against one of the GT Robots sent by the evil Gourmet Corp. But these fighting machines are a lot tougher than they look, and Toriko's going to need every trick in his arsenal to take it down. Meanwhile, one of Toriko's old friends may have already succeeded in capturing the gigantic Regal Mammoth.

AVAILABLE MARCH 2011!